The New Select Committees

The New Select Committees

A study of the 1979 reforms

EDITED BY
GAVIN DREWRY
for the Study of Parliament Group

CLARENDON PRESS · OXFORD
1985

Oxford University Press, Walton Street, Oxford OX2 6DP

London New York Toronto
Delhi Bombay Calcutta Madras Karachi
Kuala Lumpur Singapore Hong Kong Tokyo
Nairobi Dar es Salaam Cape Town
Melbourne Auckland

and associated companies in
Beirut Berlin Ibadan Mexico City Nicosia

Oxford is a trade mark of Oxford University Press

Published in the United States
by Oxford University Press, New York

British Library Cataloguing in Publication Data

The New select committees: a study of the 1979 reforms
1. Great Britain. *Parliament. House of Commons. Committees*
I. Drewry, Gavin   II. Study of Parliament Group
328.41'07657   JN679

ISBN 0-19-822785-X

Library of Congress Cataloging in Publication Data

The New select committees.

Bibliography: p.
Includes index.
1. Great Britain. Parliament. House of Commons—
Committees. 2. Great Britain. Parliament. House of
Commons—Reform. 3. Great Britain—Politics and govern-
ment—1979- . I. Drewry, Gavin. II. Study of Parliament Group.
JN679.N48 1985   328.41'0765   84-23190
ISBN 0-19-822785-X
ISBN 0-19-822784-1 (pbk.)

Set by Butler & Tanner Ltd, Frome and London
Printed in Great Britain at
The University Press, Oxford
by David Stanford, Printer to the University.

Foreword

I accepted the invitation from the editor to write a short foreword to this series of studies with some misgiving. My own attitude—developed over twenty-five years, to what must be the longest-running and most intense campaign for what, superficially, is little more than a minor organizational change in the way that the House of Commons operates, has been equivocal, to say the least. My strong views have been expressed in various Study of Parliamentary Group publications, and elsewhere, but I can use the freedom of a foreword for a few recantations.

When the present range of Select Committees was set up in 1979 I could not help but reflect how rueful would have been the reaction of those stalwart reformers and founder-members of the Study of Parliament Group, Professors Hanson and Wiseman, when their aim was at least achieved, but at the hands of a Conservative government. But perhaps also they would have remarked how much progress had been made since their day. Gone are the respectful hesitations of the Study of Parliament Group of the 1960s, anxious that none of its recommendations should trespass on the sacred territory of ministerial responsibility, nor openly challenge the received difference between the concepts of policy and administration which underpinned it. That this caution produced some considerable contradictions—fudge, to be brutal—in its recommendations was thought to be a small price to pay if some advance could be secured. This initial equivocation, now far less evident, was partly responsible for the lack of any clear rationale for a range of new specialized select committees, a lack of precision of analysis which has persisted. Academic writers, MPs, and reforming ministers have taken refuge in the catch-all formula of 'redressing the balance of power as between the House of Commons and the Executive', when in fact the situation has been more complex, and such a simplistic analysis frequently misleading.

The initial surge of enthusiasm in the 1960s had complex causes, but predominant was the belated recognition by MPs and others of the growth in power of corporate agencies, particularly in the eco-

nomic sphere, together with the increasing practice of policy-making
by government through a process of collaboration with producer
groups, which much diminished the role of Parliament as the importance of primary legislation was reduced and the role of discretionary
action enhanced. These developments were epitomized in the creation
in 1962 of the National Economic Development Council, and perhaps
of more importance in the formation of attitudes towards parliamentary reform were pamphlets such as that produced by a group of
Conservative MPs with industrial connections, published in 1963 by
the Conservative Political Centre under the title *Change or Decay*, urg-
ing a degree of parliamentary collaboration, through institutional reform, with the new processes of economic planning. This view was
reiterated by Andrew Shonfield in his seminal work *Modern Capitalism*,
published in 1965.

The ensuing débâcle of the 'new technocratic state' could perhaps
have been foreseen, given the essential superficiality of the entire
movement, and in such circumstances it is not surprising that in 1968
the Procedure Committee of the House sought to advance on the
reform front by producing a comprehensive and well-argued response
to the smaller problem of control of public expenditure, a limitation
of select committee activity which yet had the solid virtue of deriving
from an established and acknowledged constitutional responsibility of
parliament. Moreover, the acceptance of this new initiative by government was guaranteed, since it was actively, if informally, sought and
sponsored by the Treasury. Just as the Gladstonian Treasury a century before had similarly sought the co-operation of the Commons,
through a Public Accounts Committee, in its attempt to bring spending departments under centralized control, so MPs were to be drawn
systematically into a critical but supportive role in the development
of the 1960s system of public resource planning embodied in annual
Public Expenditure Survey Committee (PESC) exercises. It is ironic
that in the first few years of its existence the Expenditure Committee,
or rather its General Sub-Committee, should have been instrumental
in pinpointing profound weaknesses in the PESC system which
ultimately, as the 1970s wore on, secured its complete demise in most
of its significant aspects.

The Study of Parliament Group attempted in 1976 a retrospective
on the previous ten years of Committee reforms. The tone of this
study, published by PEP under the title *Specialist Committees in the
British Parliament: The Experience of a Decade*, was one of considerable
disillusionment. In the introduction to this I drew attention to the
muddled and often contradictory arguments of the original reformers,
and their lack of political awareness, but also argued—wrongly, in

the event—that there seemed little possibility of an extension of the select committee system to comprehend the more important and politically sensitive areas of government. This occurred in 1979. Similarly I missed the importance—although this was only emerging at the time when the pamphlet was written—of the pioneering and highly significant work on the PESC system which was being done by the new Expenditure Committee. All the authors of the publication failed to discern the contemporary movements in government after the general election of 1974, which were to produce the 1976 Procedure Committee and also the present range of specialized committees.

There can be little doubt, although the 1976 Procedure Committee did not acknowledge it, that its establishment reflected a deep and growing concern amongst many MPs about the effect on the fundamental status of the House of Commons of the so-called 'Social Contract', entered into by the new Labour government with the TUC in 1974. For about two years the House of Commons found that it was being deliberately relegated to the sidelines, and that government—in spheres of public concern extending beyond that of basic economic policy—was being conducted by joint Cabinet/TUC liaison committees. It is not my place here to comment on the meagre return which the government obtained, but to emphasize that the parliamentary response in 1976 of diffused outrage was not triggered—as it had been in the 1960s—by a sense of the growing authority of the executive, but by the undeniable evidence of its weakness in the face of powerful corporate agencies, and of the lengths to which it was prepared to go to placate them. But this remarkable episode also explains the initial and rather surprising enthusiasm of Mrs Thatcher's administration in 1979 as a political move to establish its allegiance to parliamentary government after Labour's apparent rejection of it. That this enthusiasm was not particularly deep-seated was evident in the subsequent fate of Mr St John-Stevas, midwife to the new select committees, whose ministerial career seems to have been curtailed partly because he had brought ministers what subsequently turned out, in their estimation, to be bad news.

But now we have the committees, and this volume is a testament to their functioning over an entire parliament. It raises many questions and gives some answers. I can only offer a few generalized comments, and make a few reservations. The lack of a clear rationale still persists. As David Judge, the editor of a recent set of essays on parliamentary reform, remarked apropos a chapter provided by an active select committee MP and his assistant: 'They seem so engrossed in the practice of parliamentary committee politics that they do not take the time to contemplate exactly what it is that they are doing. Activity becomes a substitute for analysis.' This does not, however, seem to have prevented a much increased enthusiasm amongst back-bench MPs for this type of activity, and as a result the future of the committees seems relatively secure. But it is not surprising that many of them seem unclear as to their motivation. They are attempting to back what is now a debased yet still strong system of parliamentary government and its associated culture, a system which militates strongly against some of the implicit assumptions of select committee organization and practice.

Consider the strength of this system from a number of overlapping viewpoints. From the perspective of the executive, resistance towards co-operation with the committees stems from the desire of the higher ranks of the Civil Service to maintain the underlying concepts of impartiality and anonymity, without which it is vulnerable. This has now been largely worn away, although the guide-lines adopted by the Civil Service Department a few years ago for civil servants called to give evidence in committee hearings, and considered in the final chapter of this book, show clearly what the limits of co-operation are. This constitutional reluctance of the Civil Service is compounded by the attitude of governments anxious not to give the Opposition ammunition by opening up the policy process to informed scrutiny. In an adversary system of two-party politics it could hardly be otherwise. In the Commons, governments with a secure majority have otherwise little to fear from the official Opposition. They generally prefer, and actually stimulate, what has recently been termed the 'mewing and bawling' of much debate on the floor of the House. This predilection is strengthened by the attitude of many back-benchers, who tend— from an overestimation of their rhetorical ability, an ingrained taste for ideological polemics, and probably a lack of ability to do anything more demanding (these categories are not mutually exclusive)— to support the same parliamentary culture. Add the more mundane fact that in any situation when a government is returned with a 'normal' majority upwards of a third of its back-benchers will be rewarded with government office, and the system is complete.

The MPs who man the committees are really trying the impossible: to reform a system and a culture whilst at the same time remaining part of the former and being powerfully affected by the latter. History suggests that this type of system can only be reformed through pressures external to it. In the country at large its political support is visibly crumbling. The Commons is only insulated from these wider movements by the operation of our peculiar electoral arrangements. But the committees are serving to soften up the system from the inside. In such circumstances, it is really rather pointless to dwell on the disparity between their efforts and their achievements in conventional terms, or to try by sophisticated argument to pretend that their influence is greater than it seems. Rather, one should applaud their persistence and determination. In a real sense the committees represent a new House-of-Commons-in-waiting. How long it will have to wait I don't know.

S.A. Walkland
Professor of Political Theory and Institutions,
University of Sheffield

Acknowledgements

This book has a complicated pedigree, a fact that makes the editor's customary task of apportioning credit and acknowledging debt unusually difficult. For the inevitable omissions in what follows I can only apologize.

The work upon which the book is based was carried out by members of a study group set up by the Study of Parliament Group in association with the Royal Institute of Public Administration. Neither of those bodies bears any responsibility for the facts stated and opinions expressed in this book. The same absolution extends to the Nuffield Foundation, which gave us invaluable financial assistance in the form of a Small Grant to cover travel and other expenses.

The study group was established early in 1980 under the convenorship of Michael Lee, who was succeeded as convenor by the present editor in March 1981. The group consisted initially of thirteen 'academics' (two of whom were in fact retired public servants) and nine clerks from both Houses of Parliament. The turnover of members was remarkably small, with only one academic (Roger Williams, who was replaced by Martin Burch) having to withdraw. Two of the original academic members acquired 'alternates' (Donald Shell and Henry Drucker), whose names appear as co-authors of the relevant chapters. St John Bates and Stuart Walkland joined the group at a later stage.

I should like to express sincere thanks to my colleagues on the study group, all of whom were, despite heavy commitments elsewhere, remarkably assiduous in attending group meetings and complying with deadlines. Several members acted in the later stages of the project as members of an editorial sub-committee and greatly facilitated the burdensome task of getting a large and somewhat amorphous collection of material ready for the press in the face of a tight publishing schedule. Although it is invidious to single out individuals in this context, I know that everyone on the study group would wish me to express special thanks to Priscilla Baines, who served for three years as our very efficient secretary and kept us and our voluminous papers in order.

Thanks are also due to Lindy Gill, librarian of the Royal Institute of Public Administration, who compiled the bibliography, to Ruth Harper who assisted with the proofs, and to Iris Walkland who prepared the index.

Behind our large study group was an even larger army of people, without whose generous co-operation this study could not have been undertaken. Much of the material in this book is derived from interviews with committee chairmen, members, clerks, and advisers, as well as with civil servants, pressure group spokesmen, and others. As virtually all such interviews were conducted on a strictly non-attributable basis, our acknowledgement must be in general terms. But I take this opportunity to make clear our great debt of gratitude to all those who gave such assistance. The same applies to the outside speakers—academics, officials, and journalists—who addressed the study group at various times and helped to widen our horizons. None of those at whom these expressions of thanks are directed bears any responsibility for what is contained in this book.

Who then *is* responsible, and for what? Broadly speaking, the editor is answerable for all matters of editorial policy, including the arrangement and balance of the book as a whole, as well as for the contents of the sections to which his name is attached. The other named authors are separately responsible for all that is in their respective chapters.

Bedford College,   Gavin Drewry
May 1984

Contributors

PRISCILLA BAINES is head of the Economic Affairs Section, Research Division, House of Commons Library.

T. ST JOHN N. BATES is senior lecturer in law, University of Edinburgh.

R.L. BORTHWICK is senior lecturer in politics, University of Leicester.

MARTIN BURCH is lecturer in government, University of Manchester.

C.Y. CARSTAIRS is a retired civil servant and former special adviser to the Expenditure Committee.

GAVIN DREWRY is reader in social administration, Bedford College, London.

H.M. DRUCKER is senior lecturer in politics, University of Edinburgh.

GABRIELE GANZ is reader in law, University of Southampton.

PHILIP GIDDINGS is lecturer in politics, University of Reading.

NEVIL JOHNSON is professorial fellow, Nuffield College, Oxford.

J. BARRY JONES is lecturer in politics, University College, Cardiff.

J.G. KELLAS is professor in politics, University of Glasgow.

J.M. LEE is professor of politics, University of Bristol.

GEOFFREY LOCK is head of the Research Division, House of Commons Library.

W.J. REINERS is former director of research policy, Departments of Environment and Transport.

ANN ROBINSON is lecturer in politics, University College, Cardiff.

MICHAEL RUSH is senior lecturer in politics, University of Exeter.

D.R. SHELL is lecturer in politics, University of Bristol.

Contents

III. ASSESSMENT OF THE 1979 REFORMS

Introduction

Gavin Drewry

This book describes and evalutes the operation of the fourteen departmentally-related select committees of the House of Commons from when they were first set up, towards the end of 1979, to the dissolution of Parliament in May 1983. The nature and context of what, according to the then Leader of the House, 'could constitute the most important parliamentary reforms of the century',[1] are outlined in the next chapter. By assembling data relating to a complete Parliament, we have sought to arrive at an informed judgement as to whether the various aims underlying the 1979 reforms have been realized and, more generally, to chronicle an interesting episode of modern parliamentary history.

The task of description has been relatively easy: that of evaluation has inevitably been much harder. Our account does in fact range more widely than might at first sight be apparent. It sets the post-1979 committees in their recent historical context; the committees themselves are considered in relation to the institutional and policy fields in which they have operated; the concluding chapters take note of the re-establishment of the departmentally-related committees after the 1983 general election. We make frequent reference to the Report of the Select Committee on Procedure of 1978 which formed the basis of the following year's select committee reforms,[2] and to the Report of the Liaison Committee in 1982,[3] which was an interim review by 'insiders' of how successful the new committees had been during their first three years of life. The academic contributors to the present volume are, of course, 'outsiders'—a necessary status for this kind of enterprise.

It may be helpful at this point to explain how the work-load was distributed. Academic members of the Study Group were assigned as 'monitors' to each of the departmentally-related committees;[4] the chapters in Part II of the book are products of their work. Another academic member provided an essay (Chapter 2) on the committees of the House of Lords, which display illuminating contrasts to their counterparts in the Commons. Clerks of both Houses served as members of the Group[5] and gave valuable advice, particularly on matters of practice and procedure; two such members, both from the Research Division of the House of Commons Library, have contributed chapters—one (Chapter 1) recounting background to the 1979 reforms and the other (Chapter 18) providing a statistical overview of the committees. The remaining introductory and concluding chapters were written by academic members of the Group.

A study built around the work of so many people, each with his or her own individual assortment of specialist interests and knowledge and a private armoury of critical perspectives, carried out on a part-time basis over several years, in the interstices of other activities, and with several non-author members of the Study Group acting as back-seat drivers, might appear an unpromising basis for coherent analysis. It was, in any case, recognized from the outset that there can be no single 'right way' of examining a select committee, though the Group benefited from previous work in this field, some of it by members of the Group.[6] And it was also quite apparent—and became increasingly so as time went on—that the fourteen departmentally-related committees were, despite superficial appearances to the contrary, highly disparate entities, likely to require a variety of monitoring and analytical strategies. Once this had been realized, any transient temptation to attempt sophisticated across-the-board analysis with a view to identifying behavioural patterns quickly evaporated. And this was just as well, given that our limited resources would have precluded such an exercise.

The research method used to compile this book has been a compromise between centrifugal individualism and co-ordinated team-work. Each committee was carefully monitored in terms of its published output of evidence and reports; official responses to committee reports were also systematically noted. All monitors have in addition, though to a varied extent, observed their committees at work and interviewed those involved—chairmen, members, clerks, specialist advisers, and, in some cases, departmental officials and pressure group spokesmen. The extent of such interviewing, and the precise nature of the questions asked, was left largely to the discretion of each monitor,[7] and did, of course, depend upon the degree of co-operation offered by those who were approached. In at least one case (that of the editor) fewer interviews were conducted than had been intended because of the early dissolution of Parliament.

Monitors approached their source material in different ways, guided partly by their own interests and predilections and partly by an awareness of each committee's idiosyncrasies. At one level, this book can be regarded as a mixed bag of essays on a broadly common theme. But it is much more than that. The exercise was conducted within a framework of guide-lines, discussed and agreed by the Group, to ensure a core of uniform coverage.[8] Each monitor was 'paired' with another to provide an element of interlinkage and cross-checking, and the Group as a whole met regularly to exchange views and discuss particular aspects of the project, often with the benefit of papers from outside contributors. Interim reports on each committee were produced and circulated. It was agreed that each committee chapter would incorporate an annex, in common format, setting out basic factual information about the committees' work—inquiries undertaken, subjects and sizes of reports produced, nature and timing of government responses, volume of oral evidence and written submissions received, and numbers of divisions recorded by each committee. A statistical overview of the committees (see Chapter 18) also helped monitors when preparing final drafts of their chapters to relate their respective committees to the system as a whole.

It will be abundantly clear from this brief description of method that our study lays no claim to being an elaborate exercise in quantitative or behavioural social science. The main data source was the documentary material generated by committee activity, supplemented by observation and informal interviewing. The study is comprehensive within this limited framework, and care has been taken to ensure factual accuracy. The conclusions are based upon impression and informed judgement and may, for that reason, err at times on the side of caution. We are confident, however, that useful insights can be gained and patterns identified through this kind of exercise, and the fruits of our analysis are gathered together in Part III of the book.

THE MONITORS' GUIDE-LINE

Committee monitors worked broadly within a set of agreed guide-lines,[9] which are outlined below. They were based upon the assumption that monitors would be engaged in two, interrelated, tasks. First, they would be compiling a factually accurate 'balance sheet' of what their committees had done, how they had done it, and with what apparent effect. Secondly, they would be accumulating material of a more subjective character (any material derived from interviewing members would fall mainly into this category) about the goals of committees, the perceptions of their members, their internal political 'chemistry', the nature and significance of reports, and so on. The distinction is not sharply maintained in the chapters themselves, but it reflects an important aspect of the underlying rationale of the Group's work and is retained in the following summary of the guidelines.

I. The Balance Sheet

(i) Size and membership of committee; chairmanship; when the committee began work;

(ii) Attendance of members; turnover; remarks on any special features of members' behaviour, status and role;

(iii) Field of activity; priorities; what the committee actually tackled, with summary reports on range of evidence, sources etc.;

(iv) Comments on special features of the inquiry process, e.g. hearings out of London, reliance on technically expert advisers, difficult relations with officials or ministers, extent of reliance on evidence from or talk with 'interested parties', signs of tension between parties on the committee as compared with preference for consensus;

(v) Response of Government and House of Commons to reports; evidence of public or media response to reports.

II. Qualitative Assessment

(i) Is the committee publicity-seeking? Is it internally divided, or a harmonious group seeking unanimity (cf. I (iv), above)? If it appears in more than one of these guises, what factors seem to bear upon this?

(ii) Strength and influence of the chairman; ditto, if applicable, for the senior member of the other party on the committee;

(iii) The kinds of use made of specialist advisers and the considerations that seem to underlie their selection;

(iv) Satisfaction/dissatisfaction with the type and level of staffing;

(v) The ideas that committees (or individual members) have of the rationale or purpose of their work;

(vi) Qualitative assessment of the major reports produced in the light of their nature and intended purpose;

(vii) Use of sub-committees, formal and informal;

(viii) Evidence of links with the parties and their internal structures; any evidence that chairmen or members have any kind of privileged access to ministers.

These guide-lines were a check-list of the kind of things that monitors were expected to look for. Their interpretation varied a good deal in practice. And the solidity of evidence was variable; for example, in assessing media coverage we were not in a position to undertake an exhaustive analysis of the vast area of potentially relevant outlets ourselves and had to rely for the most part on what we were told by those involved. Some aspects—the extent to which committees pursued consensus is a good example—loom far larger in our conclusions than a casual glance at the guide-lines might suggest.

PROBLEMS OF EVALUATION

When description ends and evaluation begins we run inevitably into difficulties of interpretation and measurement. Not that the two activities are strictly separable: our selection of data as 'relevant' for descriptive purposes has inevitably been influenced by our desire to assess the significance and value of the post-1979 select committees. One important aim of this study has been to examine the committees in relation to the bold claims of some of the reformers, notably Mr St John Stevas, that the changes amounted to a significant innovation that would shift the balance of power from the executive towards the legislature (see Chapter 1). More specifically, everyone engaged in this exercise has tried to discover the impact of the committees, both individually and collectively, upon ministers and civil servants, upon Parliament (which is one potentially important channel of influence upon the executive), upon the wider 'policy community', and upon the media and public opinion. Some, necessarily tentative, conclusions about the impact of the departmentally-related committees can be found in Chapter 20.

Even if we confine our evaluation to the question of whether the 1979 reforms were an improvement on what existed before we encounter problems of definition and measurement. We can supply a reasonably confident answer to the purely factual question of whether and in what ways the new committees were *different* from their predecessors, but once we move beyond simple 'before and after' comparisons to consider in absolute or relative terms the success of the committees we quickly find ourselves floundering in deep and muddy waters and grappling with familiar and fundamental questions about the appropriate role of Parliament in the Constitution.

Can we, for example, simply equate high 'impact' upon a government department with 'success'? Surely we must take account of the *quality* of the decisions that result from such impact. We must also consider very carefully the wider constitutional implications of any shift in the centre of gravity of power towards back-bench committees, operating for the most part in a bi-partisan way, off the floor of the House. Parliamentarians themselves are, as we shall see, by no means unanimous in their views on this. In practice it turns out—as might have been predicted from the outset—that these committees, like their predecessors, have by no stretch of the imagination effected a constitutional revolution. But we must not lose sight of the fact that we are dealing in value judgements, in issues which look very different from different standpoints (a minister, a committee chairman, and an academic commentator may legitimately deploy quite different criteria in deciding what constitutes a 'successful' committee), and that the whole subject area does have a constitutional dimension.

It is also the case that the goals of the various committees themselves are far from constant. As will become apparent in Part II, the committees vary in their perceptions of their roles and in their choice of working strategies. And even within a single committee, different exercises may be undertaken for a variety of purposes: large-scale 'royal commission' inquiries into major areas of policy; short, sharp investigations of topical issues; recurrent monitoring of administrative efficiency. The purpose of a report may be to influence a government department, or another public sector agency, or to provide information for MPs to use in a forthcoming parliamentary debate. Clearly these variations in goals, strategies and targets must also be borne in mind when talking about success or impact.

Attempts to measure in any precise way the impact of select committees upon government are bedevilled from the outset by problems of causality. This has been repeatedly pointed out by other investigators of select committees. Nevil Johnson, writing about the former Estimates Committee, observes that it is naïve to suppose 'that one can normally establish a relationship of straightforward cause and effect between what a Committee ... proposes and the continuous adaptation of the work of administrative organisation to the needs of public policy'—committees merely contribute to 'a complex pattern of forces'.[10] He adds, however, that there is no reason to dismiss a committee as ineffective just because we cannot measure what it achieves.

Ann Robinson, in her study of the Expenditure Committee (whose sub-committees were the immediate predecessors of many of the departmentally-related select committees), discusses a number of inter-related problems of measurement.[11] She distinguishes between a committee's short-term impact (instances where a government department quickly accepts specific recommendations) and long-term impact, where a committee's recommendations are taken up later. So far as the latter are concerned, she echoes Nevil Johnson's point about the difficulty of isolating the committee's influence from the many other factors that may contribute to bringing about a change. And, so far as short-term impact is concerned, she points out that acceptance by government may merely be indicative of the fact that a department had been considering the changes in advance of the committee's recommendations and that departmental witnesses 'may even have implanted ideas to that effect in the minds of the committee members'.[12]

Having examined the range of government replies, Ann Robinson concludes that, in terms of immediate response, the Expenditure Committee 'had an extremely limited effect'. But what of less visible effects? K.C. Wheare, among others, has referred to the 'educative' functions of committees engaged in the task of inquiry.[13] Ann Robinson says of a select committee that 'its process of gathering evidence and making recommendations means that it is continually exposing the assumptions of decision makers, the limitations of their information, and the weaknesses of their judgement'.[14] Committees, she suggests, produce in their reports an amalgam of evidence, a lot of it from outside government, which is too radical for immediate departmental acceptance but which 'passes into the general stream of thought on the subject'.[15]

How can we detect the occurrence of this phenomenon, let alone measure it? Civil servants are unlikely to divulge the extent to which their thought processes have been influenced by select committees and would in any case be hard pressed to make an accurate assessment (we are back in the realms of multiple causality, compounded by deliberate or unconscious distortion). So we have to reply on indirect measures—such as the impact of select committees on official workloads, in terms of appearances before the committee (information to which we have access) and of the burden of preparing for such appearances, drafting written evidence, and briefing ministers and senior colleagues (where we have had to rely upon data compiled by the civil service itself for official purposes). Ann Robinson concluded that the establishment of the Expenditure Committee had resulted in 'a substantial increase in the two-way traffic between Parliament and Whitehall'.[16] This is an interesting finding, and one upon which the present study seeks to build: but it still leaves us a long way short of any real measurement of the quantum of influence of committees upon the stream of Whitehall's thought, and still further from an assessment of the benefits of such influence.

Another target of committee activity is Parliament itself. Some inquiries are expressly undertaken in anticipation of parliamentary debate. We have endeavoured to investigate the linkage between select committees and the floor of the House, though here, once again, much of the evidence is invisible and not susceptible to measurement: an MP may make a better speech as a result of reading a report, but we do not know unless he acknowledges his debt, and he himself may not even be aware of such indebtedness. This is another way of approaching the indirect impact of committees upon departments. Although select committees have generally impinged only very intermittently on the business that is transacted on the floor of the House (understandably so given that it is in the whole House that the confidence of the Government and the individual responsibility of ministers is directly engaged), as Nevil Johnson points out, the prospect that *some* committee reports *may* be debated, requiring the minister to defend himself and his department, at least gives some guarantee that departments will take committees seriously.[17]

Various other candidates present themselves as ostensibly plausible criteria for assessing the 'success' of select committees. Many members attach great importance to extensive media coverage; but might it not be the case that a committee that continually hits the headlines is neglecting important but 'unnewsworthy' aspects of its responsibilities? Most committees have striven more or less successfully, to achieve consensus; but might such 'success' sometimes be expensively bought at the price of avoiding divisive but important subjects of inquiry or fudging contentious aspects of a complex problem?

To sum up, this is a wide-ranging and, it is hoped, accurate account of the early history of an important episode in parliamentary reform. It is also an attempt at informed evaluation on the basis of a mixed bag of evidence. As the foregoing caveats make clear, we are not in the business of trying to measure the immeasurable or prove the unprovable. We have laid out evidence upon which informed judgements may be made, and we ourselves have not shrunk from drawing some conclusions of our own.

NOTES

1. HC Debs., 25 June 1979, col. 35.
2. First Report, 1977–78, HC 588.
3. First Report, 1982–83, HC 92. The role of the Liaison Committee, itself a product of the 1979 reforms, is outlined in Chapter 21.
4. Sixteen academics were involved: one withdrew and nominated a replacement. Two monitors acquired alternates, who appear as co-authors of the relevant chapters; one monitor was assigned two committees. Two of the monitors had official rather than academic backgrounds.
5. It was decided, as a matter of policy, that the Group should include none of the clerks responsible for servicing the departmentally-related committees.
6. See, in particular, the works by Nevil Johnson and Ann Robinson, cited below. Also Nevil Johnson, 'Select Committees and Administration' in S.A. Walkland (ed.), *The House of Commons in the Twentieth Century*, Clarendon Press, 1979. The same writer's remarks about the inescapability of 'an impressionistic treatment'

when considering select committees as a whole, also strikes a responsive chord in the context of the present discussion: see Nevil Johnson, 'Select Committees as Tools of Parliamentary Reform: Some Further Reflections', in S.A. Walkland and Michael Ryle (eds.), *The Commons in the 70's*, Fontana, 1977, p. 178.

7. A check-list of interview questions, compiled by Barry Jones, was circulated for the assistance of monitors.
8. See below.
9. Based on part of a paper by Nevil Johnson, dated 29 June 1981.
10. Nevil Johnson, *Parliament and Administration: The Estimates Committee 1945-65*, Allen and Unwin, 1966, pp. 136-7.
11. Ann Robinson, *Parliament and Public Spending*, Heinemann, 1978, ch. 7.
12. Ibid. p. 131.
13. K.C. Wheare, *Government by Committee*, Clarendon Press, 1955, p. 89.
14. Op. cit., p. 140.
15. Ibid., p. 141.
16. Ibid., p. 145.
17. Op. cit., p. 143.

Part I

Committees and Reform

CHAPTER 1

History and rationale of the 1979 reforms
Priscilla Baines

On 25 June 1979, Mr St John-Stevas, as Leader of the House of Commons, moved a motion to set up a new structure of twelve—later fourteen—departmentally-related select committees to replace most of the existing select committees of the House of Commons. He said: 'Today is, I believe, a crucial day in the life of the House of Commons. After years of discussion and debate, we are embarking on a series of changes that could constitute the most important parliamentary reforms of the century.' Mr St John-Stevas's claims for the changes he was introducing were certainly ambitious, but those changes could hardly be described as novel and, as he himself acknowledged, they were evolutionary rather than revolutionary. Select committees were widely used by the nineteenth-century House of Commons, while for much of the twentieth century the idea of a comprehensive select committee system has been associated with campaigns for parliamentary reform. Since the end of the Second World War, and more particularly since the late 1950s, the need for such a system has been a major preoccupation of many of those, both inside and outside Parliament, who have sought means to redress what has been seen as the growing imbalance between the increasing power of the executive on the one hand and the increasing ineffectiveness of Parliament on the other.

Support for select committees gradually gained sufficient ground to lead, during the period described in this chapter (1964-1979), to a series of innovations and adaptations in the system of the House of Commons. Such incremental change is predictable in an institution once described as chronically dissatisfied with its procedures and constantly seeking to adapt them to meet changing demands.[1] That approach could hardly be expected to lead to fundamental procedural innovations, and has not done so. The changes initiated by Mr St

John-Stevas in 1979, far reaching though he claimed they were, were part of a long evolutionary process and need to be considered in that light.

WHY SELECT COMMITTEES?

The case for a system of select committees has traditionally rested on the view that, since the mid-nineteenth century, the increasing strength of the party system has caused the House of Commons to lose control of the executive. The dominance of the governing party imposed through the whips has meant, so it is argued, that the House has lost the capacity effectively to challenge the government of the day on its policies or to act as a check on the actions of ministers and those acting on behalf of ministers in carrying out those policies. The consequences of this loss of effective control have been reinforced by the continuing growth in the scale and extent of government activity, as well as by the increasing complexities of policy-making. Faced with this growth, Members of Parliament have become progressively less well informed and correspondingly less able to exercise their functions and question government activities. The traditional generalist skills of MPs have become inadequate for the exacting tasks of specialist scrutiny. It has been argued that if the House of Commons had the means for its Members to become better informed, as well as the opportunities to open up the decision-making processes of government, hidden behind a façade of individual and collective ministerial responsibility, then Members would be better placed to do their job of holding the executive to account.

Many of those who have considered the problem came to the view that a system of specialized select committees was the best—indeed the only—way to give the House of Commons the investigatory machinery which could restore it and its Members to their proper position. It was unrealistic to try to revert to the conditions which had prevailed in the nineteenth century, while existing machinery, such as debates and question time, was clearly ineffective and incapable of being adapted to meet new needs. Furthermore, select committees might restore to backbenchers a genuine sense of purpose and an effective parliamentary role.

Support for this view goes back to the early part of the twentieth century, but it became increasingly widespread during the late 1950s and early 1960s, when it was strongly advocated by the newly-formed Study of Parliament Group. Parliamentary reform based on an improved select committee system was also closely associated with the more general zeal for institutional reform which marked much of the

1960s. In this context such committees were seen as having the advantage, as a means of strengthening the House of Commons and enhancing the influence of individual Members, that they did not upset the status quo in terms of the power of the government to determine policy, nor did they disturb underlying constitutional assumptions or the political practices that went with them.[2] Critics of committees have argued, on the other hand, that this is precisely why such reforms are cosmetic rather than effective.

The case for what were then termed specialist committees, as it had evolved by the mid-1960s, was stated in the Study of Parliament Group's evidence to the 1964–65 Procedure Committee, which suggested both a theoretical justification and workable role for such committees.

Parliamentary scrutiny of the Executive is fundamental to the whole question of parliamentary reform. For though it is the business of the Government to govern, it is also their business to give a running account of their stewardship to the House of Commons which was elected to support them ... to enable the House to arrive at a correct judgment on the working of administration and on the Government's conduct of affairs, some process of enquiry is needed. Specialist Committees are needed to scrutinise the actions of government in their own fields. The main weakness in Parliament's present methods ... is the limited ability to obtain the background facts and understanding essential for detailed criticism of administration or any informed discussion of policy. Specialist committees, working on lines similar to those of the Estimates Committee or Nationalised Industries Committee ... could go a long way to remedy this.[3]

Fifteen years later, Mr St John-Stevas argued a notably similar case, although with some changes in emphasis, in his speech on 25 June 1979.

The proposals that the Government are placing before the House are intended to redress the balance of power to enable the House of Commons to do more effectively the job it has been elected to do ... The motions on the Order Paper provide the coherent and systematic structure of Select Committees that the Procedure Committee considered and that the Government agree to be a necessary preliminary to the more effective scrutiny of government and the wide involvement that hon Members on both sides of the House have sought for many years ... It will also be an important contribution to greater openness in government, of a kind that is in accord with our parliamentary arrangements and our constitutional tradition.

Mr St John-Stevas's speech reflected the extent of the support which the idea of select committees had attracted by 1979, long after the more general belief in the merits of institutional reform as a panacea had faded. Moreover, although opinions on procedural matters tend to cross party lines in the House of Commons, there was a remarkable breadth of support for an institution more usually associated with adversarial politics.

By contrast, the opponents of select committees have been less united, although not necessarily less consistent in their arguments. There have been criticisms of the reformers of the 1960s for their 'curiously unspecific' arguments,[4] with the suggestion that in practice they offered little more than an act of faith in support of their contentions.[5] There have also been those who, while not opposed to select committees as such, have been sceptical about their ability to live up to the reformers' claims.[6] This scepticism about effectiveness has tended to reinforce the views of the opponents of committees who have advanced two main arguments.

First, such select committees are based on American models which are inherently incompatible with a system where parliament exists to sustain the government in power.[7] It would be wrong in such a system for parliamentary committees to become involved in policy disputes which could ultimately diminish the authority of the executive.[8] This view has often received support from a predictable source, ministers and civil servants, who have claimed that to have select committees constantly examining the work of government departments would impose extra burdens and distract them from their 'real' work. Such committees are, it is claimed, a waste of time and money, spent on parliament's unrealistic and unrealizable aspirations.

The second constitutional argument has been that a system of select committees would distract attention from the proper parliamentary forum, the chamber. This view has had some long-standing champions, most notably Mr Michael Foot and Mr Enoch Powell, despite their otherwise opposing ideological views. Mr Foot argued in the mid-1960s, in a draft paragraph which he tried to insert into the 1964–65 Procedure Committee's report, that the case for select committees was a delusion and that their proliferation was not a cure but part of the disease.[9] More recently, in a debate on 20 February 1979 on the 1977–78 Procedure Committee's report, he restated his belief in the need 'at all costs' to protect the position of the Chamber, since access to the Chamber by an individual Member was the extreme attribute of the House of Commons. If select committees were to rectify the imbalance between the executive and the legislature they would achieve a predominance in Parliament which would be different from anything previously experienced. Committees as proposed in the report would, he felt, not merely drain attention from the Chamber, but with the strength of Parliament being increasingly transferred to such committees, the position of individual Members would also be injured.

Mr Powell voted for the 1976–78 Procedure Committee's proposals for select committees, but he has nevertheless expressed strong views about the potential damage if select committees were allowed to get out of hand. Like Mr Foot, he has argued that:

> ... everything which diminishes true debate on the Floor of the House of Commons strengthens the Executive and weakens Parliament. ... our expertise is as politicians and would-be Ministers facing other politicians and actual Ministers, to strike our finger on places where it hurts, or upon the places where the great clash of politics is going to take place, and fight it out. We can only do that through debate, we can only do that on the Floor of the Chamber.[10]

Another, related, objection to select committees has been that they would create two classes of Member, first-class ones who were on select committees and therefore had access to a great deal of information on individual subjects; and second-class ones who were denied that information. This would not, as the reformers claimed, enrich debates but would mean that debates were dominated by the first-class Members with the second-class ones left behind, ignorant and powerless. Furthermore, the better-informed select committee members would inevitably develop a self-defeating affinity with the executive.[11] In any case, 'information', in the sense used by the advocates of select committees, is regarded by some as irrelevant to the ability of backbenchers to be effective critics in the chamber of government policies and activities.[12]

Most select committee opponents have also pointed to the nature of select committee proceedings as being inimical to the proper function of Parliament. Mr Powell argued in the February 1979 debate that real power in the House of Commons depended on party, while, as Mr Foot suggested on another occasion, 'what we are concerned about is maintaining the conflict of clash of interest'. Select committees, seen as a remedy for the imbalance between parliament and the executive, would reduce the party struggle to technical matters and coalition politics.[13] This view is, not surprisingly, shared by many on the more extreme wings of both the main parties. For them, the bi-partisan, consensus-seeking approach of select committees is incompatible with the party struggle[14]—although that has not invariably meant that such Members have chosen to boycott select committees.

At more mundane levels, select committees have been regarded, possibly somewhat cynically, as an elaborate, expensive and burdensome method of educating Members of Parliament for somewhat questionable ends. They may give back-benchers an occupation and thereby prevent Members from becoming too disillusioned, especially those who fail to become ministers, but that is regarded as a high price to pay for a system which cannot be shown to produce the benefits claimed for it.

Virtually all the views expounded on each side of the argument have provoked vigorous counter-reactions.[15] The way in which select committees have become an established and accepted part of the parliamentary scene is described in the following sections. Such acceptance might be taken to imply that the advocates of select committees have won the argument, and in one sense, of course, they have. That does not, however, mean that the argument is over, only that the ground has shifted and the burden of proof changed. As the later chapters in this book show, the impact of select committees is difficult to measure and it is still by no means clear that they have achieved, or can ever achieve, what the reformers claimed for them. In contrast to Mr St John-Stevas's claims quoted earlier, it is worth quoting Mr Enoch Powell in the February 1979 debate:

I believe it is not factually correct that the balance of power and advantage as between the House and the Government has tilted decisively—certainly not in the past decade or two. The historical truth is that there is a sort of see-saw movement ... I do not believe that there is a historical, continuing and increasing trend towards the increased influence of the Government over the House. I do not imagine, either, that such advantage as is possessed by the Government will be lessened by any procedural Committee or other arrangements that we care to construct. That influence derives from causes which are inaccessible to even the most profound alterations in procedure.

THE 1964-65 PROCEDURE COMMITTEE AND THE CROSSMAN COMMITTEES

The reformist zeal of the early 1960s did not mean that the incoming Labour Government in 1964 had any specific plans for procedural changes in the House of Commons. There was no reference to the subject in the party's election manifesto, although in a speech at Stowmarket in July 1964 the then Leader of the Labour Party, Mr Harold Wilson, had argued a strong case for select committees. There was, however, in both 1964 and 1966 a significant intake of new Members on both sides of the House who were favourably disposed towards reform. The incoming government had only a very small parliamentary majority and was never likely to last its full term, but a Procedure Committee was appointed in December 1964 and produced five reports during the 1964-65 session. Its Fourth Report[16] is often considered one of the foundations on which subsequent development of the select committee system has rested, although its recommendations were limited in scope and only very partially implemented.

In its Report the Committee made its objective clear: 'Your Committee are convinced that a main purpose of Parliamentary reform must be to increase the efficiency of the House of Commons as a debating chamber.' It accepted the need for Members to be better informed, which in turn required a more efficient system of scrutiny of administration, but also played down any intention of elevating 'any Committees of the House to new positions of influence.' This cautious approach is not altogether surprising: the original Committee of sixteen had only three members first elected in 1964, although two more of the new intake were added soon afterwards. The Committee's main recommendations were correspondingly cautious: the Estimates Committee (first set up as long ago as 1911) should be enlarged with wider and more general terms of reference but not ones which would allow it to become involved in politically controversial matters; and it should operate through sub-committees specializing in the various broad spheres of governmental activity. In addition, the Committee should be able to employ specialist assistance, as well as having more staff, and should make use of the power to travel abroad.

The first recommendation received only the most tepid support from the Leader of the House, Mr Herbert Bowden, in a debate on 27 October 1965 on the Procedure Committee's five reports, although he did accept the proposals for more committee staff and that the committees should be allowed, albeit on a limited scale, to travel abroad. The Estimates Committee subsequently tried, as Mr Bowden had suggested, to follow the second recommendation, and in the 1965–66 and 1966–67 sessions appointed seven sub-committees including one steering sub-committee and one on the Supplementary Estimates. The remaining sub-committees were given broad subject areas: technological and scientific affairs; economic affairs; defence and overseas affairs; social affairs; and building and natural resources. These developments were not, however, allowed to become properly established. The creation from 1966–67 of specialist select committees caused problems of overlap, and the membership of the Estimates Committee was run down in the 1967–68 session from forty-three to thirty-six, in order to release members to serve on the specialist committees. The sub-committees abandoned their specialist titles and reverted to 'A', and 'B' and so on. This reduced level of operation continued for the remainder of the 1966–70 Parliament.

While the Estimates Committee came to terms with a diminished role, another path was being followed in the specialist committees set up while Mr Richard Crossman was Leader of the House. The Labour

Party's 1966 election manifesto had referred to the need to improve procedure and the work of committees, and in the debate on the Address on 21 April 1966, the Prime Minister proposed discussions on establishing 'one or two' new committees to concern themselves with administration in the sphere of certain departments. Mr Crossman did not become Leader of the House until August 1966 but, as his *Diaries* reveal, and in contrast to his predecessor, he saw himself very much as a reformer and had distinctly proprietary feelings towards the specialist committees with which his name came to be associated. In a debate on procedure on 14 December 1966 which included motions to set up two 'experimental' new specialist committees—on agriculture and on science and technology—he argued a powerful case for the expansion of the committee system, acknowledging that to be effective such a system had to do more than supervise expenditure and refuting some of the often-voiced fears of the dangers of allowing committees to discuss matters of 'policy'.

Six 'Crossman committees' were set up during the 1966–70 Parliament.[17] They were (with the dates of their creation in brackets): Agriculture (1966), Science and Technology (1966), Education and Science (1967), Race Relations and Immigration (1968), Overseas Aid and Development (1969), Scottish Affairs (1969). There was, in addition, a Select Committee set up in 1967 on the newly-appointed Parliamentary Commissioner for Administration. The genesis of the committees was varied. The Agriculture Committee, for example, was claimed to owe its existence to the willingness of the Minister of Agriculture, Mr Fred Peart, to allow his department to be investigated, although that helped little in the Committee's subsequent conflicts with other government departments. The Race Relations and Immigration Committee was the result of a deal between the two front benches during the passage of the 1967–68 Immigration Bill. The Scottish Affairs Committee was said to be the Government's response to the pressures of Scottish nationalism. The Science and Technology Committee and the Overseas Aid and Development Committee both covered technical subjects otherwise neglected by the House of Commons.

If the genesis of the Crossman Committees was varied, so was their performance. Some, such as the Science and Technology Committee and the Race Relations and Immigration Committee, quickly joined the Nationalised Industries Committee (first set up in the mid-1950s) as established features of the parliamentary scene, while the Nationalised Industries Committee itself developed its role considerably between 1966 and 1970. Others, most notably the Agriculture Committee, were much less successful or had insufficient time in which to establish themselves. Despite Mr Crossman's support, his committees almost all had to endure many vicissitudes, in some cases surprisingly so, given that many precedents—such as sitting in public, calling ministers as witnesses, requesting confidential information from government departments and appointing specialist advisers—had already been set by the Estimates Committee and, more particularly, by the Nationalised Industries Committee. What was unprecedented, however, was the scale of the operation of the new committees and some difficulties were perhaps inevitable, especially once they started to travel abroad, an exercise widely held to have led to the rapid demise of the Agriculture Committee.

The committees did win some notable battles, including some on major matters of principle relating to their work. This had important and lasting consequences for their successors, although by no means all the problems they encountered have entirely disappeared. It nevertheless soon became apparent that some of the victories had been won at a price in terms of loss of support in high places. Government attitudes towards some of the new committees became distinctly and increasingly ambivalent,[18] probably not helped by continuing, and largely irrelevant, arguments about the distinction between 'subject' and 'departmental' committees and about the extent to which committees should be allowed to consider 'policy'. Mr Crossman's own apparent confusion about what he really meant by 'experimental' also contributed to the uncertainties the committees faced. He said on 14 December 1966 that both the two committees to be set up then were experimental, but one—Agriculture—was to be 'departmental' while the other—Science and Technology—was to be a 'subject' committee. Less than a year later, and after the Agriculture Committee had precipitated a major row over a visit to Brussels, it emerged in a debate on 14 November 1967 that, whatever else it might mean, 'experimental' in that context did not mean permanent: Mr Crossman revealed only then that 'our original intention was that a departmental committee should spend one session on each department and then move on'.

Their varied origins and erratic support may at least partly explain the lack of any clear structure in the Crossman committees. The patchwork which emerged has been attributed by one commentator to the government's resorting to expedients in response to political pressures.[19] There was unquestionably a vast increase in select committee activity during the 1966–70 Parliament, but the result of the Crossman initiative was certainly not the creation of a comprehensive system of select committees, especially with the associated rundown of the Estimates Committee.

The Procedure Committee acknowledged the consequences of this unsystematic approach in the 1968-69 report on *Scrutiny of Public Expenditure and Administration*.[20] That report was directed primarily at remedying the weaknesses in the methods by which the House dealt with public expenditure. Even though the Crossman committees had had only a little over two years' working existence when the Procedure Committee reported, that Committee felt able to identify some serious deficiencies. In particular, the specialist committees had not attempted to scrutinize expenditure, while their manner of operation had 'given rise to problems' and their existence had seriously weakened the Estimates Committee. Many of the detailed recommendations were explicitly directed towards achieving a more systematic approach and avoiding the many pitfalls encountered by the Crossman committees.

The Committee's main proposal was very similar to that of its 1964-65 predecessors. An Expenditure Committee should replace the Estimates Committee and operate on a wider and more extensive scale with eight 'functional' sub-committees plus a general sub-committee specifically charged with conducting general reviews of the government's expenditure plans. The functional nature of the sub-committees was intended to allow them not to be restricted either to an individual government department or to a single subject. The whole Committee would be responsible for scrutinizing the government's forward expenditure plans as a basis for informed House of Commons debate. The report also recommended that the Public Accounts and Nationalised Industries Committees should remain, but left open the future of the Crossman committees.

The report was given a guarded welcome by Mr Crossman's successor as Leader of the House, Mr Fred Peart, in a debate on 21 October 1969. Mr Peart acknowledged the report's 'coherent and radical approach' to committees and said it would have to be examined in conjunction with the full-scale review which the Government was conducting of the work of the specialist committees. The remainder of that debate indicated that, whatever the Government's attitude, many back-benchers were already convinved of the merits of the committees. Some also recognized the untidiness of the existing situation. Mr Donald Chapman, who had been chairman of the Procedure Committee, said 'I see no point in beating about the bush over this. Steadily, we will have to absorb the existing specialist committees into the new system.' Only one other speaker made any strong plea for the continuation of Crossman specialist committees; and only one uttered any serious challenge to the whole idea of a committee system. Ma ıy speakers were also attracted by the possibility of scrutinizing expenɟiture, and saw a clear role for committees in doing that—a much more constructive approach than often displayed in the debates of the mid-1960s.

THE EXPENDITURE COMMITTEE 1970-79

The Labour Government's review of the specialist committees was never completed, but the incoming Conservative Government of June 1970 lost little time in publishing a Green Paper on *Select Committees of the House of Commons*,[21] based partly on their predecessors' review and partly on the Procedure Committee's report. Apart from reviewing the developments of the previous four years, the Green Paper made a necessarily hesitant attempt to assess the achievements of the specialist committees, acknowledging that their full potential had not had time to be realized. It was admitted that 'the House had yet to learn how to make the most of its Committees' and that the committees had laboured under difficulties; that many of the committees' contributions were indirect and difficult to quantify; but that they had already acquired expertise and looked at many important issues, as well as opening new channels of communication and doing much to stimulate discussion of current problems.

The Green Paper endorsed the Procedure Committee's approach as providing 'a clean cut and comprehensive solution which would avoid any repetition of the difficulties associated with the setting up and standing down of Specialist Committees'. Reservations were expressed about the size of the proposed Expenditure Committee, accompanied by a suggestion that committees did not necessarily have to be oriented towards expenditure. It was, however, accepted that a rather smaller permanent Expenditure Committee should replace the Estimates Committee and should function alongside the Public Accounts Committee, the Nationalised Industries Committee and some specialist committees, mainly subject ones including Race Relations and Immigration, Science and Technology and Scottish Affairs. There should also be a formal liaison committee, consisting of the chairmen under the chairmanship of the Public Accounts Committee, which would replace the informal one which had functioned from 1966 to 1970.

The proposals would provide for Parliament to scrutinize the long-term projections of public expenditure and would mean that 'The House would have the opportunity of watching the Expenditure and Specialist Committees in operation side by side and at a later stage would be able to decide in the light of practical experience whether to apply more of its Select Committee resources in one direction or the other'. The debate on the Green Paper on 12 November was remarkable for the absence of any expressed opposition to select committees, although there were varying opinions about what such committees could or should achieve. Some long-standing concerns were voiced, particularly whether it was appropriate for select committees to consider 'policy'—then a great worry, especially to some ministers and ex-ministers.

The Expenditure Committee was set up in February 1971 with forty-nine members. Until 1974, the members were appointed each session, with serious consequent disadvantages of lack of continuity and delays in starting inquiries. Only in 1974, and after many representations, were they appointed for a Parliament, with gains of both continuity and greater independence of the whips. The Committee itself acknowledged the benefits of the change in its review of its work during the first four sessions of the 1974–79 Parliament.[22] It was divided from the start into six sub-committees to conduct inquiries: a General Sub-Committee which also acted as a steering committee and regularly reviewed the annual Public Expenditure White Paper, Defence and External Affairs, Environment, Trade and Industry, Education, Arts and Home Office, and Social Services and Employment. This structure was dictated by the size of the whole committee and gave each sub-committee a wide area, usually including the responsibilities of at least two major government departments.[23]

Following the Green Paper's suggestion, some Crossman committees were retained, together with the Public Accounts Committee and the Nationalised Industries Committee, the latter greatly expanding its activities by working through sub-committees. The Science and Technology and Race Relations and Immigration Committees survived and prospered, as did that on the Parliamentary Commissioner for Administration. Overseas Aid and Development, after a prolonged campaign, was revived in 1973, while the Scottish Affairs Committee lasted from 1970 to 1972. Thus the Green Paper's intention of allowing the two types of committee to exist side by side was realized, with a consequent overall increase in select committee activity.

The Government's declared wish as expressed in the Green Paper to avoid the difficulties of the Crossman committees did not mean that the Expenditure Committee immediately established a satisfactory *modus operandi*. Although the Committee consolidated its position in the early 1970s, practical problems emerged fairly rapidly and the Sixth Special Report of 1971–72 on *The Work of the Committee*[24] contained a series of complaints mainly about such matters as the lack of time between the annual publication of the Public Expenditure White Paper and the debate in the House, the inadequate time allowed for debates on Committee reports, and a plea that departmental observations should be issued not more than two months after a report. In a report in 1972–73,[25] when more fundamental doubts about its work emerged, the Committee proposed the setting up of a committee consisting of members of the Public Accounts Committee, the Expenditure Committee and the Procedure Committee to investigate amalgamating the Public Accounts and the Expenditure Committees—a suggestion first made by the Procedure Committee in 1946.[26]

A half-day debate on 15 January 1974 on the Expenditure Committee's role was very much an insiders' occasion but it showed clearly that the Committee had not developed in the way intended by the Procedure Committee. Several speakers commented on how, despite their personal satisfaction with committee work, the Committee lacked cohesion and had reverted to the pattern of the Estimates Committee. There were serious gaps in the sub-committees' coverage, most notably in their failure, other than in the General Sub-Committee, to look at expenditure as such. Some speakers even suggested that it would have been better to proceed entirely through specialist committees.

The Government's reactions to the various complaints were largely dismissive. In response to the 1971–72 report, for example, no promise was made of additional debating time, nor to issue departmental replies within a fixed period.[27] The same points were later discussed with the Leader of the House, Mr James Prior, but the outcome was no more satisfactory.[28] Mr Prior also replied to the January 1974 debate and took up the point about the Committee's lack of cohesion. He supported the need for a 'more pointed' and 'less diffuse' committee system, which would provide stronger, more co-ordinated and more effective scrutiny. He was, however, unwilling to concede any of the numerous practical points made in the debate, except that the Government was 'anxious to help' on staffing and there was a case for setting up committees for a whole parliament. Moreover, despite his purported desire, shared with the 1968–69 Procedure Committee, for a comprehensive system of scrutiny, he made no suggestions to that end. Indeed, his period as Leader of the House saw a proliferation of *ad hoc* select committees on such topics as the civil list, corporation tax and tax credits, plus the Select Committee on European Secondary Legislation which followed United Kingdom entry into the EEC.

Select committees were interrupted by the two general elections of 1974, but the 1974–75 session saw the resumption of a high level of committee activity, with *ad hoc* committees on Cyprus, violence in marriage, and a wealth tax, as well as all the other committees. The decision in 1974 to set up the Expenditure Committee for the whole parliament was followed in the 1976–77 and 1977–78 sessions by reviews by its sub-committees of select expenditure programmes, as well as the production of more substantial reports by the sub-committees.

The uncoordinated nature and scale of committee activity, as well as some continuing operational problems, may have been one factor behind the Government's announcement in the debate on the Address at the start of the 1975–76 session that proposals would be made for a major review of the practice and procedure of Parliament. The proposals were debated on 2 February 1976 and, as one commentator has remarked, the speech by the Leader of the House, Mr Edward Short, evoked considerable scepticism from several Members about the Government's motives, especially Mr Short's emphasis on his concern to speed up legislative procedures and make them more efficient.[29] Mr Short suggested a committee of inquiry which would include some members from outside the House, a suggestion which received so little support in the debate that it was abandoned. He did suggest that there was some scope for the further development of select committees, particularly in the monitoring of expenditure. Opinions in the debate were divided about the need for a radical review. The majority of speakers were in favour but doubts were expressed about the prospects of substantial change and several speakers agreed with Mr Enoch Powell that governments would never allow their own lives to be made more difficult. There was also some repetition of the views expressed two years earlier about the Expenditure Committee's shortcomings, with two speakers describing the existing system as a hotchpotch which urgently needed improvement.

THE PROCEDURE COMMITTEE REPORT AND THE 1979 REFORMS

A select committee was set up on 9 June 1976 'to consider the practice and procedure of the House in relation to public business and to make recommendations for the more effective performance of its functions'. It sat for just over two years, reporting in July 1978.[30] Contrary to Mr Short's expectations in the debate in February 1976, the Committee gave the highest priority to select committees which were discussed in three of its Report's nine chapters. Chapter 5 examined the existing system and recommended a new, permanent committee structure. Chapter 6 discussed the organization of the work of committees, while chapter 7 examined the powers of select committees to send for persons, papers and records.[31]

In view of the claims which have been made about the revolutionary nature of the changes based on the Committee's report, it is as well to examine how the Committee saw its task. It accepted as constitutionally crucial the relationship between the executive and the legislature and noted the widespread concern 'about the present nature of the relationship and the extent to which the balance of advantage was weighed in favour of the government'. It rejected the suggestion that such concern should be answered first by more expeditious passage of the Government's business and then by finding a more worthwhile role for the back-bencher.

We believe that a new balance must be struck, not by changes of a fundamental or revolutionary character in the formal powers of the institutions concerned, but by changes in practice of an evolutionary kind, following naturally from present practices. We have approached our task not in the hope of making the job of Government more comfortable, or the life of the backbencher more bearable, but with the aim of enabling the House as a whole to exercise effective control and stewardship over Ministers and the expanding bureaucracy of the modern state for which they are answerable, and to make the decisions of Parliament and Government more responsive to the wishes of the electorate.

The overwhelming weight of the Committee's evidence favoured the development and rationalization of the committee system of the House, but some Members still had misgivings about the effects of committees on the House.

We are conscious of the dangers involved in attempting to make wholesale changes in procedure and practice without due regard to the effects which new practices, however desirable in themselves, may have on activities which the House now performs very well ... we have therefore taken great care to weigh the advantages of a rational and effective committee system against the need to retain the Chamber as the focus of the political and legislative work of Parliament, and to protect, and if possible, enhance, the opportunities of the individual Member to influence the decisions of the House.

Given this cautious and gradualist approach, it was hardly to be expected that the Committee would make revolutionary recommendations. It identified certain weaknesses in what it saw as the unplanned and unstructured committee system. The House had to some extent facilitated the very large increase in select committee activity since the early 1960s, but 'the development of the system has been piecemeal and has resulted in a decidedly patchy coverage of the activities of government departments and agencies, and of the major areas of public policy and administration ... The unsystematic character of the present committee system has arisen largely because the House has at no point taken a firm decision about the form of specialization to be adopted.' No serious attempt had ever been made to co-ordinate committees' activities.

The Committee argued that any new structure should continue and develop the work of the Expenditure Committee and its sub-committees in examining the expenditure and administration of the civil and public service. It did not, however, suggest that in order to achieve this the committee system should be based on an expansion and rationalization of the Expenditure Committee. Instead, it recommended the abolition of most of the existing committees— Expenditure, Nationalised Industries, Science and Technology, Race Relations and Immigration, Parliamentary Commissioner for Administration and Overseas Development—with the retention of a few— Public Accounts, the two Committees on Statutory Instruments, and European Legislation, and the Joint Committee on Consolidation Bills. There should be a new structure based primarily on the subject areas within the responsibility of government departments or groups of departments.

The Committee's main recommendation was for twelve committees to be appointed under a single, permanent standing order, with about ten members who would be nominated for the duration of a parliament. '... We hope the new committees will concentrate much of their attention on the consideration of Estimates and other expenditure projections.' They were to have wide, 'permissive rather than mandatory' orders of reference and to be charged with the examination of all aspects of expenditure, administration and policy within the responsibilities of the appropriate government departments, as well as any associated nationalized industries or quangos.

The twelve committees were to be Agriculture; Defence; Education; Science and Arts; Energy; Environment; Foreign Affairs; Home Affairs; Industry and Employment; Social Services; Trade and Consumer Affairs; Transport; and Treasury. No specific committees were to cover Scottish, Welsh and Northern Ireland matters but the new committees should cover them for the time being. The new committees should also undertake the work of the various committees to be abolished, with the Home Affairs and Foreign Affairs committees being empowered to set up sub-committees to cover the work of the Race Relations and Overseas Development Committees respectively. The work of the Science and Technology Committee should be covered by the appropriate new committees while, in the case of the nationalized industries, common problems should be considered by a joint sub-committee representing the select committees most directly concerned.

The two chapters of the report devoted to the organization and powers of select committees were an exhaustive examination of the

problems which select committees had encountered since the vicissitudes of the Crossman committees, and contained various recommendations, many of which reflected the lasting concern of Members
about certain aspects of committees' work. Eight Mondays per session
should be devoted to debates on select committee reports; government
departments should respond to reports within two months; more permanent and specialist staff should be provided with specialist advisers
allowed to be appointed as the committees wished; additional accommodation should be provided; and their powers to send for 'persons,
papers and records' should be strengthened. Two important practical
recommendations were that the committees should be nominated on
a motion tabled by the Committee of Selection and not as in the past
by a government whip, although the House should retain the ultimate
right of decision; and that the informal Liaison Committee consisting
of select committee chairmen should be replaced by a select committee, called the Liaison Committee, consisting of one representative
of each permanent committee, with additional members to ensure
that the membership reflected the overall composition of the House.

The two-day debate on the report on 19 and 20 February 1979
revealed how far select committees had become an accepted feature
of parliamentary life. As Mr Kenneth Baker remarked, 'The time of
special pleading is virtually over.' Some speakers had reservations
about the details of the Procedure Committee's proposals, with rear-
guard actions being fought on behalf of the committees scheduled for
abolition, especially the Nationalised Industries Committee. The
overwhelming majority of speakers, many of whom had served on select
committees, accepted the recommendations and showed a surprising
reluctance to view them in the Committee's own cautious terms as
evolutionary rather than revolutionary: there were constant references
in the debate to the fundamental nature of the changes proposed. Mr
Norman St John-Stevas, speaking from the Opposition front bench,
was among a minority in putting the recommendations on select committees into their historical context. He did not, he said, want to
exaggerate the case for reform and emphasized that he saw the report
as radical rather than revolutionary and as suggesting a rationalization based on past experience. He nevertheless committed an incoming Conservative Government to 'positive, constructive and helpful
proposals based on this report.' Mr Michael Foot, as Leader of the
House, spoke twice on the second day of the debate. In his opening
speech, quoted earlier, he argued strongly against any extension of
the committee system but when winding up, he had to acknowledge
that he was swimming against the tide and promised to respond to
the opinions expressed in the debate by instituting all-party discussions.

The Labour Government fell in March 1979 before Mr Foot had an opportunity to put any proposals to the House. That task was left to the newly-elected Conservative Government whose manifesto had included a commitment to implement the Procedure Committee's report. Mr St John-Stevas, as Leader of the House, on 25 June 1979 tabled a motion for a new Standing Order which was agreed to at the end of a debate and which implemented many, although by no means all, of the Procedure Committee's recommendations on select committees. Mr St John-Stevas's enthusiastic approach in the debate and the scale of his claims on behalf of the new committee structure were in distinct contrast to his more muted contribution to the February 1979 debate. Among other speakers there was in several cases a relatively sober and tentative approach, Mr Tony Benn going so far as to say, possibly prophetically, that the very moment of victory was the beginning of another battle, while Mr Edward du Cann, a long-term advocate of select committees, saw the new structure as only a first stage. There was also some predictable scepticism expressed as to the Government's motives in bringing the proposals before the House, a point which Mr St John-Stevas did not seriously attempt to answer.

The new Standing Order (see Appendix) provided for twelve committees 'to examine the expenditure, administration and policy of the principal government departments and associated public bodies.' The committees, which did not entirely follow the structure suggested by the Procedure Committee, were: Agriculture; Defence; Education; Science and Arts; Employment as a separate committee not linked with Industry; Energy; Environment; Foreign Affairs; Home Affairs; Industry and Trade as a combined committee; Social Services; Transport; and Treasury and Civil Service. The Foreign Affairs, Home Affairs, and Treasury and Civil Service Committees were each empowered to set up one sub-committee, while a joint sub-committee drawn from at least two of the Energy, Environment, Industry and Trade, Transport, and Treasury and Civil Service Committees could be set up at any time to consider matters affecting two or more nationalized industries. The committees were given similar powers to those of the Expenditure Committee to send for persons, papers and records, to appoint specialist advisers and 'to adjourn from place to place'. There were to be between nine and eleven members, who were to be nominated for the duration of a parliament and by the Committee of Selection (although the latter arrangement applied only to the new committees and not to all select committees as the Procedure Committee had suggested). The Standing Order also provided for the reappointment of the Select Committee on the Parliamentary Commissioner for Administration, a committee which the Procedure Committee had suggested should be abolished.

The Government's acceptance of the Procedure Committee's general structure did not extend to some of the other recommendations, notably the provision of eight days per session for debates, and more powers to enforce the attendance of ministers as witnesses and the production of papers by government departments. Another gap was the absence from the Standing Order of the Liaison Committee. Some of the gaps were at least partially filled during the debate: Mr St John-Stevas said that the Government would give 'substantially increased priority' to debates on select committee reports and he pledged that all ministers would do everything in their power to co-operate with the new system of committees and make it a success—a promise denounced by several Members as a poor substitute for an enforceable body of procedural rules. He also said that the Government would make available to select committees as much information as possible, including where necessary confidential information on the understanding that committees would treat it in accordance with the conventions governing such matters. The Liaison Committee, however, was not formally appointed until 31 January 1980 when the House approved the necessary motion. The Committee was given powers to consider general matters relating to the work of select committees and to give such advice as might be sought by the House of Commons Commission.

The Procedure Committee had deliberately left open the need for select committees on Scottish and Welsh affairs, pending the outcome of the devolution referendums. Following the collapse of the devolution exercise, a Committee on Welsh Affairs was appointed on 26 June 1979 but there was a delay until the following October before the Scottish Affairs Committee was set up. There was a further delay (accompanied by a good deal of lobbying) until 26 November 1979 when the Committee of Selection finally nominated the members of the new committees. The chairman of that Committee, Mr Philip Holland, had spoken in the debate on 25 June 1979 and had promised wide consultation about membership of select committees. In moving the motion to appoint the members of the new committees, he did not conceal the difficulties and frustrations of the Committee's task, and hence the time it had taken. He emphasized that the final decisions had been the Committee's, not the whips', including their calculation of the entitlement to membership of the minor parties. The committees were all appointed at the end of the debate but, thanks to the time required to elect chairmen, none of them started work until early 1980.

CONCLUSION

By the end of January 1980, the Procedure Committee's main recommendations about select committees had been implemented and the new system had started work. The committees arrived on the parliamentary scene to what might almost be described as a fanfare, accompanied by some ambitious, even extravagant, claims from inside and outside parliament about the significance of their arrival and their probable impact. The other chapters in this book consider the extent to which those claims have subsequently been fulfilled. But on what were the claims based? What changes had been made and what, if anything, lay behind them?

Neither the Procedure Committee nor Mr St John-Stevas was under any illusions about the evolutionary nature of their proposals: both were at pains to emphasize that point. The committees were more permanent in that they were all set up for the duration of a parliament by a single Standing Order which made it more difficult for individual committees to be abolished. The more rational and comprehensive coverage had for the first time at least the potential capacity to cover most major areas of government activity, although one or two gaps remained such as the security services and the law officers' departments. The structure tried to tackle one of the Expenditure Committee's more obvious weaknesses—the failure until the 1976-77 and 1977-78 sessions to treat public expenditure satisfactorily other than at a global level—by weaving the examination of expenditure into the other work of the committees. It also met the obvious desire of many Members that committees should be allowed to be genuinely 'specialist'. As chapter 18 shows, the whole system was on a bigger scale, especially as arrangements were rapidly made to strengthen staffing and provide additional accommodation.

This bigger and more permanent system has been accompanied by detectable changes in attitudes towards select committees. Debates in the House on the committees are usually insiders' occasions and this needs to be borne in mind in assessing the strength of support for the committees among Members. All the same, the two debates in 1979 did reveal the existence of a very wide spectrum of influential back-bench support for the committees, including that of a significant number of Members with ministerial experience. Only one or two Members' views seem to have swung the other way, while the scepticism of some academic observers about select committees seems to have made little impression on the vast majority of back-benchers. The worries expressed about the activities of the Committee of Selection over membership of the new committees were a telling illustration of how

Members felt about them and how anxious many were to serve on them.

What is more significant has been the change in attitudes on the part of governments. As Mr Powell observed in the February 1979 debate, governments may be expected to be ambivalent towards select committees. Indeed, if there is a detectable pattern in the development of the select committee system up to 1979, it is of limited government initiatives, inspired by a variety of motives and often resembling pre-emptive strikes or trade offs to secure net gains for ministers, followed by a more or less rapid loss of enthusiasm. But by 1979 there could be no doubt that the incoming government had accepted that select committees were an integral part of the parliamentary scene and had to be treated accordingly. The release of the official papers may eventually reveal why Mrs Thatcher's first administration decided to implement so rapidly Mr St John-Stevas's commitment given in opposition and repeated in the manifesto. For the present, it is only obvious that he must have persuaded enough of his Cabinet colleagues, including the Prime Minister, of the merits of his case to win their support. He himself subsequently indicated that he had had to seize the opportunity for reform while it lasted: had he tried later he might well not have succeeded.[32]

But Mr St John-Stevas was on strong ground. The committee system was in evident need of rationalization, and the Procedure Committee had produced a well-argued and coherent report with practical, workable proposals for a new system. The report had been acclaimed by the majority of back-benchers on both sides of the House and there could be no doubt about the strength of back-bench views on the subject. Furthermore the proposals were acceptable more or less as they stood without upsetting the constitutional status quo—and it is notable that, *pace* Mr Powell, those proposals which might have disturbed that status quo and therefore made the Government's life more difficult were largely ignored.

As one inside observer has remarked, it is striking that 'in this very serious attempt to make the investigatory committee system more effective the new committees were delegated no greater powers'.[33] They could only examine matters within their terms of reference and report to the House, with no other role, for example in relation to legislation or to approving Estimates. No more time was formally allocated to debates on reports, nor were any undertakings given about the speed with which the government would reply to reports. They were given no more than pledges from the Leader of the House about the attendance of ministerial witnesses and the provision of information, while the Liaison Committee was given no real powers of co-ordination.

Cynics may suggest that this continuing denial of real power was a deliberate and not very subtle attempt to draw the teeth of the new committees and that it was precisely because it was possible to set up the new system without giving the committees such powers that the Government felt able to accept the Procedure Committee's main recommendations. Others may see it as a natural desire to make haste slowly and to allow the new system to prove itself along tried and trusted lines. What does seem probable is that this continuing absence of real powers has in practice been a major reason for the greater acceptance of committees at official levels.

The burden for civil servants of meeting the often exacting demands imposed by select committees, their resistance to innovation, and ingrained dislike of having their work publicly scrutinized, unquestionably lay behind many of the vicissitudes of the Crossman committees. Even without Mr St John-Stevas's pledged in June 1979, it is difficult (but not quite impossible) to imagine such obstacles being put in the way of the new committees. Some civil servants have even admitted to welcoming the existence of select committees, while there has been a slight softening in the tone if not the substance of the guide-lines issued to civil servants appearing before select committees. The Procedure Committee published as an appendix to their report in 1978 the Memorandum of Guidance then in operation. The so-called Osmotherly Rules—the new Memorandum of Guidance issued in 1980—at least recognized the legitimacy of the ambitions of select committees and attached more importance to their reports. The 1983 Reith Lectures by Sir Douglas Wass showed how at least one very senior civil servant's fears about select committees had not been realized[34] and Sir Douglas's reactions were not unique. As Sir Douglas implied, select committees have proved to present no serious threat to the civil service and the civil service has in turn learnt to live with them.

Acceptance by governments that committees have a role—whatever that role may be—is clearly critical to the successful operation of select committees. In the absence of any real powers, they need at least the government's co-operation and goodwill in order to be effective—but the government, even though it may sometimes benefit from them, does not *need* them. Two very perceptive 'outsiders' remarked in 1974 that the government needed only the disciplined tolerance of its back-benchers and certainly not the goodwill of the Expenditure Committee.[35] Theoretically, that remains the position but in practice the government has since had to come to terms with the existence of select committees—and has even sought on occasions to use them for its own ends.

NOTES

1. R.S. Lankester, 'The Remodelled Select Committee System of the House of Commons', *Contemporary Review*, January 1981.
2. Nevil Johnson, ch. 8, 'Select Committees and Administration', in S.A. Walkland (ed.), *The House of Commons in the Twentieth Century*, Clarendon Press, 1979, pp. 462–3; Study of Parliament Group, *Specialist Committees in British Parliament: the experience of a decade*, June 1976, p. 1; and David Judge, *Backbench Specialization in the House of Commons*, Heinemann, 1981, p. 156.
3. Fourth Report from the Procedure Committee, 1964-65, HC 303, pp. 134 and 137.
4. Study of Parliament Group, *Specialist Committees*, p. 3.
5. Nevil Johnson, ch. 11, 'Select Committees as Tools of Parliamentary Reform', in A.H. Hanson and Bernard Crick, *The Commons in Transition*, Fontana, 1970, p. 226.
6. Nevil Johnson has been a notable and consistent exponent of this view. See also Brian Walden's contribution in part 3 of Duncan Crow (ed.), *The State of the Nation: Parliament*, Granada Television, 1973, pp. 161-3; and (somewhat surprisingly) Enoch Powell's speech in the debate on 20 February 1979 on the 1977-78 Procedure Committee Report: cols. 334-40.
7. As Leader of the House, on 13 July 1959, Mr R.A. Butler rejected a Procedure Committee proposal for a Select Committee on Colonial Affairs, arguing that 'it smacks to me far more of Capitol Hill and the Palais Bourbon than of the Parliament in Westminster'. See also Gerald Kaufman's speech on the debate on 25 June 1979 for a very similar view.
8. There is an unexpected statement of this view as held by Michael Stewart in R.H.S. Crossman, *Diaries of a Cabinet Minister*, Hamish Hamilton and Jonathan Cape, 1975-8, vol. ii, p. 308.
9. 1964-65, HC 303, p. xiii.
10. Duncan Crow (ed.) *State of the Nation*, p. 155.
11. John Mendelson, ch. 11 'The Chamber as the Centre of Parliamentary Scrutiny', in Alfred Morris (ed.), *The Growth of Parliamentary Scrutiny by Committee*, Pergamon Press, 1970.
12. Contributions by Enoch Powell (p. 153) and Brian Walden (p. 162) in Duncan Crow (ed.), *State of the Nation*.
13. Ibid., p. 193.
14. David Judge, *Backbench Specialization*, p. 161.
15. See, for example, J.P. Mackintosh's description of the 1960s debates in *Specialist Committees in the House of Commons: Have they failed?*, Waverley Papers (University of Edinburgh), 1970.
16. 1964-65, HC 303.
17. See *inter alia* J.P. Mackintosh, *Specialist Committees in the House of Commons* for a detailed account of the careers of the Crossman Committees; and H.V. Wiseman, ch. 10, 'The New Specialised Committees', in A.H. Hanson and Bernard Crick (eds.), *The Commons in Transition*.
18. Crossman quotes two examples of Harold Wilson's weakening support for select committees—see his *Diaries*, vol. ii, p. 347 and vol. iii, p. 348. See also Ann Robinson, *Parliament and Public Spending: The Expenditure Committee of the House of Commons 1970-76*, Heinemann, 1978, pp. 45-6.
19. Johnson, *House of Commons in the Twentieth Century*, p. 460.
20. First Report, 1968-69, HC 410.

36   *The New Select Committees*

21. Cmnd. 4507, October 1970.
22. Third Report from the Expenditure Committee: *Work of the Expenditure Committee during the first four sessions of the present Parliament*, 1978–79, HC 163.
23. See Ann Robinson, *Parliament and Public Spending*, for a description of the Expenditure Committee during the period 1970–76; the Expenditure Committee's Third Report, session 1978–79; Andrew Kennon, 'Recent Work of the General Sub-Committee of the Expenditure Committee', *Parliamentary Affairs*, vol. xxxiii, no. 2, Spring 1980, and Nevil Johnson ch. 9, 'Select Committees as Tools of Parliamentary Reform: Some Further Reflections', in S.A.Walkland and M.T.Ryle (eds.), *The Commons Today*, Fontana, 1981.
24. 1971–72, HC 476.
25. 1972–73, HC 296.
26. 1945–46, HC 189-I.
27. Cmnd. 5187; January 1973.
28. 1972–73, HC 282.
29. W.A.Proctor (Clerk to the 1976–78 Procedure Committee), 'The House of Commons Select Committee on Procedure, 1976–79', *The Table*, vol. xlvii, 1979.
30. First Report from the Select Committee on Procedure, 1977–78, HC 588.
31. There is a full account of how the Procedure Committee approached its work and a summary of its main conclusions in W.A.Proctor, 'The Select Committee on Procedure'.
32. In a debate on supply procedure on 15 January 1982.
33. R.S. Lankester, 'House of Commons Select Committees related to government departments', *The Table*, vol. xlviii, 1980.
34. Printed in the *Listener*, 8 December 1983.
35. Hugh Heclo and Aaron Wildavsky, *The Private Government of Public Money*, Macmillan, 1974, p. 381.

CHAPTER 2

Select Committees in the House of Lords

T. St J. N. Bates

INTRODUCTION

That a book on departmental select committees in the House of Commons should contain a chapter on the House of Lords may seem
surprising. The Upper House is not elected. Excluding those who
have leave of absence, almost thirty per cent of its members, the
cross-bench peers, are avowedly apolitical. Both in procedure and
style it is markedly different from the Commons. Nevertheless, the
degree of influence of comparable House of Lords' select committees
in the last Parliament suggests that an examination of their work may
contribute to an evaluation of the departmental select committees.

Of the Lords' select committees the three which provide the most
useful comparison are those on Science and Technology, Unemployment, and the European Committees. Unlike the Commons' departmental select committees they were established *ad hoc* and were not
the product of a systematic institutional reform. The Science and
Technology Committee was first appointed in January 1980 'to consider science and technology' as a direct response to the establishment
of the departmental select committees.[1] The Select Committee on
Procedure had reported that 'the House has a great deal of expertise
on science and technology and a select committee on this subject
would fill the gap created by the House of Commons decision not to
reappoint [a Select Committee on Science and Technology]'.[2] The
Committee is a sessional committee which has been re-appointed in
each succeeding parliamentary session. During the 1979–83 Parliament it published nine reports arising from six enquiries.[3]

Following various proposals in 1979, the Select Committee on Unemployment was first appointed in November of that year 'to consider
and make recommendations on long-term remedies for unemployment'.[4] The suggestion that a committee be appointed was initially

greeted with muted enthusiasm by the Government.[5] Some ministers felt that 'it would only create a stick with which to beat the back of the government and others'.[6] It was obviously a subject which would be politically sensitive and also one in which the Commons departmental select committees were likely to take an interest. The Committee published a substantial report in May 1982,[7] and it was not re-appointed thereafter.

The genesis of the Select Committee on the European Communities was quite different. The Committee, and a parallel committee in the Commons, were first appointed in May 1974 to consider and report on European Community legislative and policy proposals.[8] The need for such committees arose from the fact that national parliaments normally have no direct role in the Community decision-making process. They must rely largely on influencing national governments which, in the Council of Ministers, adopt most Community legislation and policy. Of course, once it is adopted, Community legislation either becomes law directly in member states or the states are obliged to implement it domestically. The two Westminster committees were thus a response to a novel parliamentary situation. For the first time a substantial volume of legislation which was effective in the United Kingdom was being adopted by a process in which Parliament had no indispensable constitutional role.

The European Communities Committee, unlike its Commons' counterpart, conducts its inquiries in a manner which is similar to the other committees considered in this book. On the other hand, it should be recognized that, being closely associated with the Community decision-making process, the Committee does have distinctive attributes. In the main, it responds to Community initiatives and is perhaps more reactive than the other select committees considered here. Its function has also attracted procedural advantages. For example, the government has undertaken that, where the Committee recommends that a Commission proposal should be debated in the House, the government will not agree to the proposal in the Council of Ministers until the debate has taken place, save in the most exceptional circumstances.[9] Nevertheless, the Committee provides an interesting example of the development of approach and influence of a select committee over a ten-year period. It is also a productive committee; it published 110 reports during the 1979–83 Parliament.[10]

COMPOSITION AND INFRASTRUCTURE

When compared with the Commons, the composition of Lords Select Committees has a number of distinctive features. The first is their size.

There is no rule as to the maximum number of peers who may be appointed members of select committees of the type examined here. Thus, the Unemployment Committee had twelve, the Science and Technology Committee has fifteen, and the European Communities Committee has twenty-five members.

The members of committees are chosen by the Committee of Selection. A rotation rule applies to sessional committees; their members are required to retire after serving three years but are again eligible for selection after a year. In the case of select committees with essentially apolitical functions, the membership reflects the broad spectrum of party allegiance and the cross-benches, but it is not strictly proportional to the size of these groups in the House. In choosing co-opted members, in particular, there is far more emphasis on expertise and interest than on political allegiance.

These factors have important consequences. First, both the Science and Technology and the European Communities Committees are empowered to appoint sub-committees and their size allows them to use this power in a structured way. The Science and Technology Committee has three sub-committees, two of which conduct inquiries while the third is a general purposes committee which considers future topics of inquiry and follows up past inquiries. The European Communities Committee currently has seven sub-committees corresponding to the main areas of Community activity. Secondly, the process of selection and the power to co-opt tends to result in committees with considerable expertise. Of the initial fifteen members of the Science and Technology Committee, for example, ten could be said to have had practical and senior experience of science-based industry, four had held ministerial office relevant to the Committee's work and three had distinguished careers as academic and research scientists. This pattern was maintained in subsequent sessions and was also reflected amongst the co-opted members. The expertise of the Committee is further enhanced by Standing Order 62 which allows a peer who is not a member of a select committee to attend its meetings, although he is not allowed to vote.

Expertise in the European Communities Committee involves both expertise in Community procedures and also expertise in those subjects in which the Community is most active. Members acquire procedural expertise from serving on the Committee and professional contacts with the Communities and from the staff of the Committee, who have themselves developed considerable knowledge of Community procedure. The level of expertise in areas of Community activity can be illustrated by the membership of the sub-committees in January 1983. For example, the Agriculture, Food and Consumer Affairs

Sub-Committee had fourteen members and co-opted members, of whom eleven were professionally involved in the Sub-Committee's area of competence; the Law Sub-Committee had twelve members and co-opted members, of whom five were Lords of Appeal in Ordinary or retired Lords of Appeal in Ordinary, one was a law professor of nearly twenty years' standing, and three others were barristers or solicitors.

In other respects the composition and infrastructure of the select committees is similar to that of the Commons committees. All three have used specialist advisers on an *ad hoc* basis and the clerks to the committees are assisted by additional clerks who service the sub-committees. However, the European Communities Committee is unusual in that, by convention, its Chairman is also Principal Deputy Chairman of Committees, which is a salaried appointment. The same committee also has a legal adviser and a legal assistant.

CHOICE OF TOPICS OF INQUIRY

The Unemployment Committee was, by virtue of its terms of reference, committed to a politically sensitive inquiry. The other two committees have generally avoided the highly political in choosing topics of inquiry. Nevertheless, as the inquiries usually involve the examination of government or European Commission policy, or concern issues which affect particular sectional interests, they can hardly be described as non-political.

Apart from political sensitivity, other considerations influence the choice of inquiries. Both the Science and Technology and the Unemployment Committees were given wide terms of reference, and to be successful, inquiries must be manageable. The Science and Technology Committee began cautiously with its first two inquiries. One was a modest inquiry into the potential of electric vehicles, taking into account future energy sources, the state of technological development, and available research and development resources. In the words of one member of the Committee: 'We began with a rather discrete area, one we reckoned we could handle and get a report out quickly'.[11] The other was a broader inquiry into the scientific aspects of forestry. However, forestry is a subject which, unlike the Commons, the Lords have had a knowledgeable and sustained interest. The Committee was thus playing to its strengths. Later inquiries of the Committee, although quite broad in scope, were sufficiently delimited to be manageable; the inquiry into the disposal of hazardous waste, for instance, was limited to non-nuclear waste.

The Unemployment Committee, by contrast, found great difficulty in delimiting its inquiry, due in part to political disagreement among its members. Evidence was taken on a wide range of unemployment issues, and the Committee also found particular difficulty with the theoretical aspects of the subject. Two months into the inquiry, the chairman of the Committee remarked: 'What we have really got to work towards is defining what we are really looking at, what are the key things we have to find out about and one of the key problems ... is that we shall get into an awful mess if we go on looking over the whole range of all possible interpretations.'[12]

The European Communities Committee has faced different problems of choice. During the last Parliament the Committee received from the Government over 2,000 Commisssion proposals for consideration. The task of determining which of these proposals merit an inquiry is initially undertaken by the chairman of the Committee, with the assistance of the sub-committee chairmen, the legal adviser and the clerk. Suitable proposals are usually referred to the appropriate sub-committee, although inquiries may be undertaken by sub-committees jointly or by an *ad hoc* sub-committee.

The choice of topics for inquiry is closely related to the Community decision-making process. Annual Commission proposals with important financial implications, such as the budget and farm price proposals, are often the subject of reports. The Commission commonly proposes long-term legislative programmes, such as its environmental action programmes, and these too are natural subjects for inquiries. The Committee also has to be acutely aware of the pace at which a proposal will progress through Community institutions. At the most extreme, it would be of little utility for the Committee to report on a proposal after it has been formally adopted by the Council of Ministers. Again, Commission proposals are often substantially amended during deliberations within the Council of Ministers. Such considerations have led the Committee to an increasing preference for proposals which will have a long gestation period and are of broad Community significance. So, in addition to long-term legislative programmes, the Committee has reported on Community strategic and institutional developments, sometimes including individual legislative proposals within such inquiries. Where an inquiry concerns an individual legislative proposal, it is usually one which has wide implications and is known to be proceeding slowly towards adoption.

Political or public concern and known Whitehall interests in a subject have also been influential considerations for all three committees. It was, in part, public concern which encouraged the Science and Technology Committee to embark on inquiries into the water industry and into the disposal of hazardous waste. Similarly, concern expressed by sectional interests which are likely to be affected by Commission proposals has stimulated inquiries by the European Communities Committee.[13] The European Communities Committee is, of course, assured that Whitehall will be actively interested in specific Commission proposals which are the subject of many of their inquiries. The Science and Technology Committee does not have this assurance, but it has chosen topics of inquiry of public concern which have also been under some degree of consideration in Whitehall. Its inquiry into the scientific aspects of forestry was undertaken in the knowledge of a forthcoming government statement on forestry policy.[14] Its inquiries into science and government, and into engineering research and development, followed White Papers on related aspects of these subjects.[15] On the other hand, a White Paper which was directly on a proposed topic would be a disincentive to undertaking an inquiry.

CONDUCT OF INQUIRIES

As might be expected from the foregoing, the Science and Technology and European Communities Committees' inquiries have been thorough, well-structured, and objective; and they have been conducted in an essentially apolitical manner. However, where the occasion has demanded it, questioning of witnesses has been insistent and incisive. The Science and Technology Committee, for example, put searching questions to Redland Purle Ltd., the firm responsible for a hazardous waste disposal site in Essex, the operation of which had led the Committee to inquire into that subject.[16] The same Committee closely questioned a Minister of State on the extent to which the University Grants Committee had consulted the government and the Forestry Commission before the closure of the only undergraduate course in England which combined study of both forestry and agriculture.[17] Any impression of complacency by civil servants has been dealt with firmly.[18] The Unemployment Committee inquiry, however, may be contrasted with the generality of the inquiries conducted by the other two committees. There was a substantial conflict of opinion on the Committee between those who saw the long-term resolution of unemployment in various forms of qualified reflation and one member who placed reliance on monetarist solutions. Also, for a variety of reasons, some beyond the control of the committee, the inquiry, while thorough, was somewhat unstructured. Although the Committee eventually agreed a report which recommended a two- to three-year programme to reduce unemployment, the evidence taken in the inquiry ranged widely over various aspects of education and unemployment, the means of creating demand for labour and reducing its supply, and the fiscal and social costs of unemployment.

As might be expected in what are generally apolitical inquiries, there have been few problems in obtaining information. Since 1974, the Government has supplied the European Communities Committee with Commission proposals as they are published, and with a departmental explanatory memorandum on each proposal. As the Committee has established itself, early difficulties over obtaining information both on subsequent amendments to proposals and on their progress have largely disappeared. The Science and Technology Committee has also experienced little difficulty in this regard. Where civil servants have felt obliged to avoid individual questions, their reluctance to answer has been well within Cabinet Office guide-lines. Officials of the Department of the Environment, for example, would not express a view on which of those provisions of the Control of Pollution Act 1974, not yet in force, it would be most desirable to bring into force.[19] Neither would they comment on the operation of individual hazardous waste sites, because the Secretary of State has an appellate function in the licensing of such sites.[20]

In addition to their apolitical style, there are other general features of these inquiries which deserve particular mention. All three Committees have tended to be exercised by questions of departmental co-ordination in Whitehall. These are questions which it is less easy to explore in the departmentally-related Commons select committees, and this may be reflected in the emphasis placed on the subject in the Lords. The Unemployment Committee inquiry inevitably involved such considerations. The European Communities Committee inquiries almost invariably involve Commission proposals where the formulation of the government position is a product of departmental co-ordination. However, the Science and Technology Committee also paid close attention to the subject, although it is perhaps less obviously central to its terms of reference. In the electric vehicles inquiry, the Department of Transport was closely questioned on the degree of departmental co-operation in the development of such vehicles. Departmental co-ordination was an important consideration in the inquiry into the scientific aspects of forestry, where the Committee was concerned with the distribution of departmental responsibility for forestry and with the extent of co-operation between the Forestry Commission, Whitehall, and the Research Councils. In the science and government inquiry, the Committee examined the lack of co-ordinated ministerial responsibility for science and technology, other than that which rested with the Prime Minister.

The Science and Technology and European Communities' inquiries are perhaps also distinctive in the range of evidence taken. In addition to departmental and non-departmental evidence from the United Kingdom, both Committees have taken a significant volume of non-domestic evidence. Over the years the European Communities Committee has broadened the range of its evidence and this was quite marked in the course of the last Parliament. In its early years, the non-departmental evidence taken by the Committee largely reflected purely British interests. In the 1974–75 parliamentary session, for example, all the formal non-departmental evidence was of this nature. Although it has always fostered links with the European Parliament, it saw the role of that institution as quite distinct from its own: 'It is likely that for some time to come the primary role of the European Parliament will be to influence the Commission and of national scrutiny committees and parliaments to influence the Council [of Ministers]'.[21] As the Committee has acquired greater familiarity with the Community decision-making process and working relationships have been established with Whitehall and Brussels, its perception of its role has enlarged somewhat and it has certainly broadened the range of the evidence it has taken.

There has, for example, been an increase in formal evidence taken from European Commission officials. Taking the 1981–82 parliamentary session as reasonably representative of the last parliament, Commission officials gave evidence in five of the twenty-one inquiries concerned with long-term proposals or institutional developments. Particularly since direct elections to the European Parliament, the Committee has made a regular practice of taking formal evidence from Members of the European Parliament. Again taking the 1981–82 session, MEPs gave evidence in nine of the twenty-one inquiries and in seven of the nine, oral evidence was given. The evidence has not been limited to United Kingdom MEPs and it is not infrequently taken from the rapporteur on the proposal. Again, the Committee has increased the evidence taken from European interest groups, which include within their membership interest groups from a number of member states and which often have a consultative status with the European Commission. In the inquiry into competition policy practice of the Commission, for instance, evidence was taken not only from the legal profession in England and Scotland and from the CBI, but also from the Consultative Committee of the Bars and Law Societies of the European Community and the Union des Industries de la Communauté Européenne. In addition to such formal evidence, Commission officials meet the Committee or a sub-committee at Westminster for off-the-record discussion of proposals. Members of the Committee and its sub-committees also regularly visit Brussels for

discussions with Commission officials and others in the course of inquiries, and more substantial links have been established with committees of the European Parliament.

This broadening of the range of the evidence has allowed the Committee to evaluate Commisssion proposals from a Community, as well
as a British, perspective. It has also played some part in reducing the
sensitivity of both government departments and the European Commission to giving information to the Committee. Department officials
giving evidence[22] and ministers in debates[23] have become noticeably
more forthcoming about textual changes to proposals in Council of
Ministers' working groups and about the negotiating positions of the
United Kingdom and other member states. The European Commission too has felt able, for example, to agree to the Committee examining its records of national aids to agriculture which previously had
not been publicly available,[24] and to allow the Committee to be the
first to publish an itemized programme of the Commission's proposed
initiatives to regulate noise.[25]

Perhaps because of the international nature of the subject, the Science and Technology Committee demonstrated a similar pattern to
that of the European Communities Committee in taking non-departmental evidence. In three of its inquiries—electric vehicles, science
and government, and engineering research and development—the
Committee examined overseas initiatives and arrangements. In the
engineering inquiry, for example, the Committee's recommendation
that there should be more contacts between higher education and
local industry was based on consideration of a scheme organized by
the Aachen Chamber of Commerce and similar schemes in Japan. In
the same report, after examining the practice of the engineering industry in other countries, the Committee recommended that the
British engineering industry should give more consideration to buying
appropriate technology from abroad as an alternative to developing
it domestically. Similarly, the Committee has demonstrated an awareness of European Community developments and funding opportunities. It examined, for example, the possibilities of Community funding
of research into electric vehicles and it also took evidence from a
senior Commission official on Community engineering research and
development initiatives.

It will be obvious from the range of evidence taken that many of
the inquiries of the three Committees were substantial inquiries. The
Unemployment Committee, for instance, took evidence over twenty
months from sixty-eight witnesses, of whom forty-two gave oral evidence. Owing in part to the political differences within the Committee
it took a further ten months to agree a report. Although there are of

course considerable variations from inquiry to inquiry, the other two Committees have shown a tendency towards increasingly elaborate inquiries. Taking the 1981–82 session, the average inquiry of the European Communities Committee involved oral evidence from six to ten witnesses, and perhaps eight to ten written submissions. Although it remains constrained by the Community timetable in many of its inquiries, the average inquiry in 1981–82 was considerably more substantial than those conducted in the early years of the Committee. Similarly, the final inquiry of the Science and Technology Committee in the last Parliament was also its largest. It involved oral evidence from twenty-seven witnesses and over two hundred written submissions.

Elaborate inquiries take time, and where there is Whitehall interest in the subject, the Science and Technology and Unemployment Committees have found their reports may be overtaken by government initiatives. The Science and Technology Committee's report on engineering research and development, for example, emphasized the need for better public and private finance for innovation. To some extent, government initiatives during this fifteen-month inquiry—for instance, the 'Support for Innovation' programme launched in September 1982—reduced the impact of these recommendations. The Unemployment Committee inquiry provides a more spectacular example. By the time the Committee reported, the Government had already announced a Youth Training Scheme, had adopted a proposal for voluntary registration by the unemployed, and a new Community Enterprise Programme had been introduced.

Such government initiatives can be characterized as a demonstration of the influence exerted by a select committee in embarking on an inquiry. Indeed, a shift in the government's position during an inquiry sometimes occurs as a result of the course which the inquiry is taking. Nevertheless, these government initiatives may distort the focus of an inquiry and reduce the impact of the select committee's report. It may be that, just as the European Communities Committee adapts its work to the Community decision-making process, other select committees will have to become more conscious of the decision-making processes of Whitehall.

DEBATES

One of the important differences between the two Houses is the number of select committee reports which are debated in the House of Lords. The European Communities Committee is, of course, in a privileged procedural position because, as a result of the government undertaking, its reports will normally be debated where it so recommends. Indeed, some of its reports which are presented to the House only for information are also debated. Of the twenty-one reports published in the 1981–82 session, for example, thirteen recommended a debate; all thirteen, plus three others presented for information only, were debated. Although, in assessing the incidence of debates, it must be borne in mind that in the Commons, unlike the Lords, there is the possibility of standing committee debates on Community proposals. The other two select committees did not benefit from such a government undertaking. Nevertheless, all six initial reports of the Science and Technology Committee were debated, as was the report of the Unemployment Committee.

The reports have not only been debated, they have generally been debated promptly. The six initial reports of the Science and Technology Committee were all debated within four months of the order to be printed. In each case, the four month period spanned a parliamentary recess, and in two cases it was a summer recess. The Unemployment Committee report was debated five months after publication, and this period also included a summer recess. Debates on the European Communities Committee reports do not show such a consistent pattern. Given the government undertaking, the timing of the debate is controlled by the date on which the proposal is expected to come before the Council of Ministers for adoption. Taking the 1981–82 reports as an illustration, some were debated within as short a period as three weeks after publication,[26] but most were debated within three or four months. Reports on long-term institutional developments and similar matters, which were less closely tied to the Council of Ministers agenda, were debated after a substantially longer period. The reports on the borrowing and lending capacity of the Communities[27] and on the competition policy practice of the European Commission,[28] for instance, were not debated until fourteen and fifteen months after publication.

The select committee reports are debated either as the subject of an unstarred question or on neutral motions 'to take note' or 'for papers'. The vast majority are debated on 'take note' motions, often moved by the chairman of the committee or sub-committee which undertook the inquiry. Although there are wide variations, debates on the Science and Technology Committee reports usually last between two and four hours, and the average debate on European Communities Committee reports about two hours. A common feature of these debates has been the high percentage of members of the Committee who have participated in them. On average, 50 per cent of the participants in debates on Science and Technology Committee reports were members of the Committee. In debates on the European Communities Committee reports the average was a little higher.

Although they are on neutral motions and a high percentage of the speakers were participants in the inquiries, the debates are of value. One important consideration is that they elicit an early government response to the report. The Government has presented formal responses to the reports of the Science and Technology and Unemployment Committee reports. They are either published as reports of the Committee or as White Papers, or alternatively they are placed in the library of each House. However, except for the Unemployment Committee report, the formal response has been presented some time after the debate. The nature of the work of the European Communities Committee has meant that the Government does not normally produce formal responses to its reports. The Committee, therefore, relies heavily on the debates for a public response from the Government, and for public information on the progress of proposals in the Council of Ministers.

The nature of the government response in the debate depends on various factors, one of the more important being the timing of the debate. The response may be more than a mere holding statement. It is often possible for the government spokesman to indicate quite specific agreement or disagreement with recommendations. In many cases, however, the response is of a more general nature. Where a debate on a major report is brought on quickly there may have been insufficient time for consultation and consideration by the relevant departments. In the case of debates on the European Communities Committee reports, the government response is conditioned by Community considerations. Where a debate is held during, or shortly before, an important phase of negotiations in Brussels, indications of the government position are almost inevitably rather opaque. In other circumstances the Government may declare that it does not feel able to press its own position on a proposal against the wishes of other member states.[29] Where a report concerns a matter largely outside the competence of the Council of Ministers, such as the manner in which the European Commission investigates and enforces Community policy, the government may express a view but also point out that it can take no direct action on the report's recommendations.[30]

The debates also attract publicity, a fact well recognized by pressure groups. They commonly lobby peers prior to a debate for, by comparison with a back-bench MP in the Commons, there is a greater likelihood of a peer being able to participate in a Lord's debate. In debates on Science and Technology Committee reports, for instance, peers have indicated the views of such bodies as the CBI, the Association of County Councils, and the Consortium of Planning Research. Prior to one debate, the National Environment Research Council and the Science and Engineering Research Council submitted a joint paper to peers which contained their immediate reactions to some of the recommendations in the Committee's report.[31]

A debate on a report may well attract more attention than the publication of the report itself. This may be true even within Westminster. The passage of the Forestry Bill through the House of Commons in 1981 provides an example of this. The Science and Technology Committee had published its report on the Scientific Aspects of Forestry some weeks before the second reading of the Bill. Although the report had a bearing on some aspects of the Bill it was only mentioned briefly by two MPs in the second reading debate.[32] However, the report was debated in the Lords during the committee stage of the Bill in the Commons. Once the report had been debated, there were numerous references to the debate, rather than to the report, by MPs in the standing committee. Some references were, of course, tactical but the value of the debate in generating publicity is illustrated by the remarks of Dr Roger Thomas, the Labour MP for Carmarthen: 'In the other place yesterday afternoon their Lordships had an excellent debate on a report ... on the scientific aspects of forestry. I have only had some three-quarters of an hour to read through many pages, indeed five hours of debate, but I should like to congratulate them on the overall standard of excellence of a debate which tends to undermine some of the deeply held wishes of some of us on this side.'[33]

INFLUENCE

At one level, the select committees can record an impressive list of government initiatives which can reasonably be said to be responses to their work. The Science and Technology Committee, for instance, could fairly claim to have played a part in stimulating the Department of Environment to assume responsibility for ensuring the existence of a long-term research strategy for the water industry. It also contributed to more urgent review by the same department of administrative and legislative arrangements for the import, movement, and disposal of hazardous waste. Various institutional developments, such as the establishment of the Forestry Research Co-ordination Committee and the Hazardous Waste Inspectorate, are direct results of its recommendations. By contrast, few of the substantive recommendations in the Unemployment Committee report were accepted by the Government.

Unfortunately, a balance sheet of accepted and rejected recommendations is a poor register of influence. It does not take account of the influence that initiating an inquiry may have on a department. It does not adequately describe the influence of an inquiry where, as in the European Communities, the Government's view is not necessarily determinative. Finally, it may provide no greater evidence of the influence of a committee on a department than of the department on the committee.

However, there is some evidence from Whitehall and Brussels that the reports of the select committees can be influential. In part, the influence stems from the reports being apolitical, well-researched analyses of the issues. A report of this type may provide a fresh approach or a solution or simply reassure a department by confirming its own thinking. An apolitical report is obviously administratively convenient in that it is likely to contain little that is embarrassing to a department. Yet some civil servants see a value in being able to test departmental policy by presenting it in evidence before a well-informed committee in circumstances where the political response will normally be muted. Some European Commission officials take a similar view of giving evidence to the select committees. Clearly, the publication of a well-researched apolitical report can raise political and public awareness of the subject. This is recognized by the committees themselves, by government departments, and by the European Commission. The European Communities Committee, for example, distributes its reports to Commission officials and to MEPs who request them. Some government departments, as a regular practice, distribute the reports to Commission officials and to other member states, irrespective of whether the report has adopted the departmental view. By contrast, reports which deal with sensitive political issues or make recommendations which are inimical to firmly held government policies will inevitably be much less influential. The Unemployment Committee report which recommended a reflationary programme with a gross cost to the Exchquer of £5bn as a long-term solution to unemployment is an obvious example. Another less stark example was the European Communities Committee report on voluntary part-time work,[34] where the Government indicated its opposition both to the Committee's recommendations on a draft directive to extend the rights of part-time workers and to the directive itself.[35]

Within such parameters, the influence of the work of select committees will be enhanced if the subject of the inquiry is one in which there is likely to be a long gestation period before policy is eventually formulated, and particularly where it is a matter which crosses departmental boundaries or is at the periphery of the responsibilities of a

number of departments. The Science and Technology Committee reports on the scientific aspects of forestry and on the disposal of hazardous waste were both influential for these reasons. Similarly, the
European Communities Committee reports on matters such as
harmonization,[36] agricultural trade policy,[37] and the competition
policy practice of the European Commission[38] were also influential.
Their influence in the European Commission can perhaps be
measured by the fact that where such reports diverge from the views
of the Commission they may well provoke a direct or indirect response. Criticism of the use by the Commission of harmonization
provisions in the EEC Treaty by the Committee was promptly
countered by a member of the Commission's legal service in an article
in a British law journal.[39] The conclusion of the Committee on agricultural trade policy 'provoked rather a testy response from the Presi-
dent of the Commission'.[40] Often, however, influence may be less
public and more productive. In the Committee's inquiry into the
practice of the Commission in investigating and enforcing competition
law, formal evidence was taken from a senior Commission official with
direct responsibility for the Commission procedures, and two members
of the Committee, Lord Scarman and Lord Fraser of Tullybelton,
both Lords of Appeal in Ordinary, visited the Commission for discussion. The Commission and the Committee reached similar conclusions
independently, but the Committee inquiry obviously influenced the
Commission's thinking.

In addition to the style and subject of inquiries, the select committees have also enhanced their influence by maintaining a degree of
political momentum, both in the initial inquiry and thereafter. Choosing a topic in which there is current Whitehall interest, and a well-
structured inquiry followed promptly by a debate are all factors which
maintain momentum. Like the departmental select committees, the
Lords select committees apply pressure on dilatory departments to
produce formal responses to their reports. And, like the Commons
committees, they have also published supplementary reports following
an initial inquiry. In the case of the Science and Technology Committee, there were supplementary reports on electric vehicles and on
scientific aspects of forestry, in which specific questions were put to
the relevant departments on the implementation of the Committee's
initial recommendations. So, for example, the Committee has
obtained replies from the Department of Industry on the purchases of
electric vehicles by government departments since its initial report.

In some instances, however, the select committees have been able
to carry this momentum into the legislative process. During the passage of the 1981 Forestry Bill, for instance, Lord Bessborough moved

an amendment which would have implemented one of the recommen-dations of the Science and Technology Committee's report on the scientific aspects of forestry. What was significant was that this amend-ment was the first concerted attempt by the Committee to have one of its recommendations incorporated into legislation. In moving it, Lord Bessborough was able to say that he had 'the support of the whole of Your Lordships' Committee'.[41] There was similar corporate support by the Committee for amendments to the Water Bill in 1983.[42] Such initiatives suggest that there might be utility in the Lords making more extensive use of select committees on legislation, or perhaps adopting the Commons special standing committee pro-cedure.

CONCLUSION

Many of the features of the work of the Lords select committees which have enhanced their influence cannot be replicated in the Commons. Nevertheless, the departmental select committees may note the influ-ence of the well-researched, apolitical inquiry on a long-term issue, although not all Commons committee inquiries could conceivably be of that nature. Their views on the value of formal sub-committees may be reinforced, although they are unlikely to be empowered to co-opt members. They may press for more opportunities to debate their reports, despite the disparity on pressures of time in the two Houses.

There are wider parliamentary considerations too. It is tempting to accept that the scrutiny of government action must be predominantly a function of the elected chamber, and that the Lords must content itself with whatever role the Commons chooses not to assume. Such an approach would not survive reform of the membership of the Lords and it does not resolve other problems. Adequate scrutiny of govern-ment stretches the resources of Westminster, and a minimalist use of the advantages of the Lords may be a mistake. One aspect of a more systematic approach would be to examine whether it is beneficial for Parliament as a whole that the Commons devotes relatively little of its resources to the scrutiny of Community and international affairs as opposed to domestic affairs, whereas in the Lords the balance is, even more markedly, the other way.

NOTES

1. HL Debs., 23 January 1980, col. 441.
2. Second Report, 1979–80, HL 97, p. 1.
3. *Electric Vehicles*, First Report, 1979–80, HL 352; *Scientific Aspects of Forestry*, Second

Report, 1979–80, HL 381–1; *Disposal of Hazardous Waste*, 1980–81, HL 273–1; *Science and Government*, First Report, 1981–82, HL 20–1; *Government Response to Forestry Report*, Second Report, 1981–82, HL 83; *Electric Vehicles (Supplementary Report)*, Third Report, 1981–82, HL 210; *Forestry (Supplementary Report)*, Fourth Report, 1981–82, HL 211; *Water Industry*, First Report, 1982–83, HL 47–1; *Engineering R. & D.*, Second Report, 1982–83, HL 89–1.

4. HL Debs., 21 November 1979, col. 124.
5. HL Debs., 20 June 1979, cols. 1093–4.
6. HL Debs., 16 November 1982, col. 503 (Earl of Gowrie).
7. 1981–82, HL 142.
8. HL Debs., 10 April 1974, cols. 1229–33.
9. HL Debs., 7 November 1974, col. 641; cf. HC Debs., 30 October 1980, cols. 843–844.
10. A complete list of the reports of the Committee will be found in *House of Lords Select Committee on the European Communities: Progress of Scrutiny*, no. D8–iii, 26 July 1983.
11. HL Debs., 11 November 1980, col. 1326 (Lord Shackleton).
12. *Minutes of Evidence*, 1981–82, HL 142–11, Q. 118 (Baroness Seear).
13. e.g. HL Debs., 6 May 1982, col. 1314 (Lord Cledwyn of Penrhos); HL Debs., 14 April 1983, col. 376 (Lord Sherfield).
14. HL Debs., 23 February 1981, col. 895.
15. *Review of the Framework for Government Research and Development*, Cmnd. 5046 (1979); *Review of the Scientific Civil Service*, Cmnd. 8032 (1980); *Engineering Our Future*, Cmnd. 7794 (1980).
16. HL 273–11, QQ. 676–93.
17. *Scientific Aspects of Forestry (Supplementary Report)*, Fourth Report, 1981–82, HL 211, QQ. 28–31.
18. e.g. HL 273–11, QQ. 69–99 and 900.
19. *Ibid.*, Q. 124.
20. *Ibid.*, QQ. 136–7.
21. *Second Special Report*, 1974–75, HL 251, para. 20.
22. e.g. *Second Report of the Select Committee on the European Communities*, 1981–82, HL 29, QQ. 2–57.
23. e.g. HL Debs., 7 December 1982, cols. 165–70.
24. *Seventh Report of the Select Committee on the European Communities*, 1981–82, HL 90, paras, 43–52.
25. *Thirteenth Report of the Select Committee on the European Communities*, 1981–82, HL 175, Annex 11; HL Debs., 21 October 1982, col. 280 (Earl of Cranbrook).
26. e.g. the debate on the *Tenth Report of the Select Committee on the European Communities*, HL Debs., 30 March 1982, cols. 1338–75.
27. *Twenty-first Report of the Select Committee on the European Communities*, 1981–82, HL 226; HL Debs., 14 April 1983, cols. 368–91.
28. *Eighth Report of the Select Committee on the European Communities*, HL 91; HL Debs., 26 April 1982, cols, 737–62.
29. e.g. HL Debs., 18 January 1982, col. 508 (Earl of Avon).
30. HL Debs., 26 April 1982, col. 757 (Lord Advocate).
31. HL Debs., 25 April 1983, col. 761 (Earl of Cranbrook).
32. HC Debs., 26 January 1981, cols. 660 (Mr Bruce Millan) and 666 (Sir Hugh Fraser).
33. Official Report, Standing Committee A, 24 February 1981, col. 120.
34. *Nineteenth Report of the Select Committee on the European Communities*, 1981–82, HL 216.

35. HL Debs., 2 December 1982, cols. 1348-51, 1372-6 (Lord Glenarthur).
36. *Twenty-second Report of the Select Committee on the European Communities*, 1977-78, HL 131.
37. *Second Report of the Select Committee on the European Communities*, 1981-82, HL 29.
38. *Eighth Report of the Select Committee on the European Communities*, 1981-82, HL 91.
39. G. Close, *European Law Review*, Vol. 3, p. 461.
40. HL Debs., 30 June 1982, col. 238 (Lord Greenhill of Harrow).
41. HL Debs., 11 May 1981, col. 423.
42. e.g. HL Debs., 7 February 1983, col. 1015 (Lord Sherfield).

Part II

The New Select Committees

CHAPTER 3

The Agriculture Committee

Philip Giddings

THE FIELD

'Agriculture' seems a relatively self-contained area of policy and administration, and it was for this reason that it was selected for one of the experiments of the 'Crossman era' of specialized committees in the mid-1960s.[1] But appearances, as ever, are deceptive. It is essential to an understanding of the work of the Agriculture Committee to be aware of the underlying complexities. Three features are important. First, it is important to note that the remit of the department is not confined to agriculture, nor does it have a monopoly of agricultural policy-making and administration. It is the Ministry of Agriculture, *Fisheries and Food* (hence MAFF). Although agriculture prodominates, the other two policy fields are not insignificant. In agricultural matters, MAFF shares responsibility with the Welsh and Scottish and N. Ireland Offices. While MAFF takes the leading role, the particular interests of the other departments (especially the Scottish Office) have to be taken into account, for they must (at least) be consulted. This can complicate the policy-making process, and certainly does not shorten it. Where there are differences (e.g. milk marketing and education) critics have the opportunity to compare and contrast. It is also worth noting that the agricultural sector has a substantial number of specialized public agencies[2] with particular spheres of responsibility (marketing boards, regulatory agencies, commissions and councils, and, not least, the Intervention Board for Agricultural Produce) which reflect the multi-faceted nature of state involvement in the industry.

The second, and perhaps dominant, complexity in agricultural policy-making is the EEC, and particularly the CAP. Few aspects of agricultural policy-making do not have a European dimension and for most aspects that dimension has overwhelming importance. This means further links in the decision-making chain, involving the European institutions and other governments. While agriculture is not alone in this respect, it is probably in this sphere of policy-making and administration that the impact of EEC membership is greatest.

A third important feature of this policy field is its place in partisan politics. EEC membership and the CAP have created divisions within the parties as well as between them. Moreover, agriculture is to some extent seen as a 'Conservative subject' in the sense that Conservative members are thought more likely to be interested in it, though that is not to say that there is no Labour interest or expertise in the work of MAFF. However, apart from the CAP, agricultural policy has rarely been a matter of significant inter-party controversy or of wide interest beyond those MPs whose constituencies are directly affected. This ought to make it a subject particularly suitable for bi-partisan, consensus-style select committee work.

THE COMMITTEE: ITS MEMBERS AND STAFF

One crucial feature of the new select committees was that they were established for the duration of a whole parliament, thus encouraging continuity and coherence in their work. The key to continuity lies in membership, and while the Agriculture Committee was fortunate enough to retain the same chairman and senior opposition member through the 1979–83 Parliament, its work in the early sessions was disrupted by changes in membership, particularly those which came in mid-inquiry. By the end of the Parliament, only five of the original nine members remained, a turnover rate of 44 per cent.[3] One-third of the Committee was changed in January 1981 in the middle of the Animal Welfare inquiry, and there was a further change in May 1982 towards the end of that Session's inquiry into Less Favoured Areas (LFAs). The changes arose because of promotions to the front benches. They highlight the vulnerability of the new committee system to this feature of parliamentary life. Clearly, an active committee role, while desired by many back-benchers, is not preferred to the allures of the front bench, or the Whips' Office, even in Opposition. And as it is likely to be the more able and impressive members who are promoted, there is a considerable risk to the quality of the pool left to man the committee system: it may be composed mostly of those without hope of advancement.

The Agriculture Committee's membership had a five to four Conservative majority over Labour, with the former providing the chairman in Sir William Elliott. This meant that the government majority relied on the casting vote of the Chair and was vulnerable to the absence or defection of any of the Conservative members. In the event, absence and defection both proved important on those few occasions when divisions occurred.

Most members, and especially the Conservatives, had some agricultural connections. Four members had served as officers of party back-bench committees on agriculture or horticulture. One Labour member was sponsored by what was then the National Union of Agricultural and Allied Workers. Three members had previously served on other select committees—two (Elliott and Torney, the respective 'party leaders', on the same one, Race Relations and Immigration). One Conservative, Richard Body, had been joint chairman of the 'Get Britain Out' referendum campaign council in 1975 and has published a book[4] attacking the whole basis of post-war agricultural policy, and particularly the CAP. When the Committee began its work, its clerk, John Marnham, was in sight of retirement. His experience in the public service, and the respect and confidence which he commanded, were considerable assets through the initial troubled waters of the European issue. Dr Malcolm Jack took over for the subsequent inquiries and brought to the Committee a largely procedural background, this being his first involvement with select committees.

The Committee used five specialist advisers during its enquiries, out of whom evolved a de facto team of three (Professors Spedding and Britten and Mr Neville Rolfe), although they were appointed individually and for one inquiry at a time. As it happened, those three served for successive inquiries and thus developed a sense of continuity. While it is understandable that a new committee may wish to feel its way with specialist advisers (and vice versa) and to retain the ability to recruit particular individuals for particular topics, it is surely desirable that some degree of tenure should be given for some advisers so that the committee may make the fullest use of their expertise. Both committees and advisers can learn from experience. At least one of this committee's advisers felt at the end of the parliament that he now knew much better how he could help the Committee in its task.

THE COMMITTEE'S WORK

What is the Committee's task? The prologue published with each report states that the Committee is 'to examine the expenditure, administration and policy of the Ministry of Agriculture, Fisheries and Food and associated public bodies and similar matters within the responsibilities of the Secretary of State for Northern Ireland'.[5] But the expression most commonly used, inside and outside Parliament, to describe the Committee's role has been that of 'monitoring' the department. Many see this as part of the wider parliamentary function of scrutiny and control of the Executive. A committee must thus look in two directions at once—to the departments it monitors and to the chamber which receives its evidence and reports. To this end, the Agriculture Committee has followed the traditional style of inquiries on a broad topic on which it has collected evidence, written and oral, and then reported with conclusions and recommendations. Such 'major' inquiries have been conducted one per Session. In addition, the Committee has spent part of July in two Sessions looking at MAFF's estimates.

The topics the Committee have chosen to investigate reflect very clearly its political character and the balance of forces within it. The report titles illustrate this.[6] Each topic is one which deserved investigation. The first and third reflect the divergent political interests of members and, in the third case, a despairing attempt at compromise. In each case the precise area of investigation was more clearly defined as the inquiry progressed and evidence came in. The unwieldy collection of themes for the 1981–82 inquiry became more manageable after an intervention by the Minister in a private session indicated that two aspects (eggs and poultry) had become too delicate in European terms,[7] and one aspect was dealt with as a self-contained part of the report (Horticulture, which was further limited to the implications of the Dutch glasshouse gas subsidies). This enabled the main inquiry to be concentrated on the treatment of less favoured areas. With the exception of that digression into Dutch gas subsidies, the Committee has not opted for the 'short, sharp' topical inquiries which catch the media headlines. Nevertheless, the *Animal Welfare* inquiry did prove to be well timed since it coincided with the revision of some animal welfare codes, and hence became the subject of a debate in the House.[8] With that exception, the Agriculture Committee's inquiries have been of the wide-ranging, general variety which help to form the background for public policy-making rather than seeking to change its direction.

THE COMMITTEE'S METHOD

Thus, following the traditional method, the Committee, having decided on its inquiry topic, has invited written evidence and in most cases supplemented this with oral sessions. The sources of evidence come as no surprise: the Ministry first, followed by associated institutions and the established interest groups, not least the NFUs, and notable individuals. Government departments (the Departments of

Agriculture for Scotland and Northern Ireland, the DES, and the ODA have appeared in addition to MAFF) and their associated public agencies gave all the evidence for the two Estimates inquiries and not far short of half the written (two-fifths of the oral) evidence for the other inquiries.[9] Interest groups gave a further quarter of the written (one-third of the oral) evidence,[10] and of that interest group evidence, 60 per cent (both written and oral) was given by producer or distributor groups. Almost half the written evidence came from producer groups alone.[11] There has thus been no widening of the policy circle as a result of the setting-up of the select committee. Analysis of the evidence also confirms that the more established interest groups are at a significant advantage because of their organizational resources. The relative weakness of consumer groups again stands out. Once again, as in the composition of the Committee and the selection of the topics, agriculture prodominates in the sources of evidence over food and fisheries—though food did feature more strongly in the R & D report.

This traditional method of conducting an inquiry requires no little skill on the part of both MPs and witnesses if it is to achieve the best results. MPs need to know in what direction they wish the inquiry to proceed and how to elicit the necessary information and opinion from witnesses who may be either terse or verbose. The witnesses need to know the areas of the MPs' real interests—the terms of reference are rarely precise enough for this purpose—and how to get their points across in a way which the Committee can readily digest and utilize. The practice of advising witnesses in advance of the likely areas of questions, which sometimes extends to the provision of the list of draft questions prepared for Members, can go some way towards improving the effectiveness of oral evidence-taking. Equally the clerks and specialist advisers can make a good deal out of the written submissions. But ultimately much depends on the taking of the oral evidence and the impression it makes on the minds of Members.

The pattern of questioning from the Agriculture Committee was pretty consistent across all its inquiries, with two or three members taking the leading role after the Chairman's opening. Unlike some chairmen, Sir William Elliott did not seek to dominate the questioning.[12] Some members adopted a particularly inquisitorial style (for example, not surprisingly, Douglas Hogg, a barrister), while others tended to turn their questions into speeches directed as much (metaphorically, anyway) at 'Members opposite' as to the witness whose comments were invited. Inevitably, there was some attempt to lead witnesses into making partisan points (for example, on the CAP), but this was rarely obtrusive and the more experienced witnesses from the departments and interest groups were well aware of the dangers.

So the effectiveness of this method of investigation is debatable. It is clear that some Members and witnesses are better at it than others. There are occasions when Members seem not to have grasped the point on their own (prepared) questions and when they have failed to pursue leading points from witnesses. The desire to share the questioning does not always produce an orderly sequence of thought and discussion. On the other hand, most Members feel at home with this style of investigation and there have been many occasions when important evidence has been elicited by it. And there is no doubt that it is more productive than Question Time or an adjournment debate in extracting information from government departments. Nevertheless, the real test of effectiveness is in the quality of the reports produced and the impact they achieve.

THE COMMITTEE'S REPORTS AND THEIR IMPACT

Of the four major reports produced by the Agriculture Committee, the one on animal welfare has had the most obvious impact to date, though it may well be that the R & D report will prove to have been more significant in the long run. The *Animal Welfare* report[13] reflects a subject which attracts considerable public attention and emotion. It features heavily in MPs' post-bags and 'Minister's correspondence'. It is a highly technical subject which has a high ethical content, providing opportunity for wide and deeply-held differences of opinion. It has also, perhaps because of that, attracted the attention of pressure groups, and groups like Chicken Lib have been more active and visible in the past decade. And as farming techniques have developed, and public sensitivity has increased, it has become more difficult for government to avoid having to take a position on a highly contentious subject. While there is no clear partisan division of opinion, the impression in many quarters that MAFF has too close a relationship with the NFU feeds suspicion that the Ministry is likely to pay too much heed to producers' interests in welfare matters. Such an issue can be very suitable for investigation by a select committee, giving the opportunity for all shades of opinion to be heard and tested against evidence. In spite of nervousness in some quarters about attracting attention from the 'cranky element' of the animal welfare lobby, the Committee's investigation proceeded smoothly, and a weighty and authoritative report was produced.

Here we are at the crux of the problem of assessing impact: the report was timely in that the process of revising welfare codes was under way, as were discussions within the EEC. On these matters the Minister is advised by a carefully constituted Farm Animal Welfare Council which gave evidence to the Committee. Who can say how influential the recommendations of the select committee were in such a complex process—particularly when, on some matters, the committee had shown itself divided, a fact which the Minister was quick to spot?[14] The Government's response made clear that its philosophy 'does not differ significantly'[15] from that of the Committee. Certainly, the Committee's opinions, and the evidence it collected, played a part in forming the context within which ministerial decisions were made, presented, and received—as the debate on the report and revised codes makes clear.[16] Certainly, the Committee's investigation increased the political salience of the welfare issue, and it may have moved it up a notch or two in the Minister's priorities. An extra, and public, forum for debate has been provided. But it is difficult to argue that without the select committee different decisions would have been made, or that parliamentary interest would have been less. What the Committee provided, in its report and in the evidence, is material for continuing parliamentary pressure on the issue if Members wish to pursue it, whether within the Committee or not.

With the dairy policy and Less Favoured Areas reports, it is even more difficult to assess impact and effectiveness. These are essentially European policy questions. In the first report,[17] the Committee's conclusions and recommendations largely endorsed known British Government positions and thus to an extent bolstered its position in Brussels negotiations. It was not surprising therefore that the Minister was able to commend their 'very clear analysis of the problems' and to reaffirm that he was seeking policy changes within the EEC to deal with them.[18] The nearest he came to disagreement was on the Committee's recommendation of a wide-ranging government inquiry into the structure and economics of milk distribution. The Minister pointed out that there had already been several such inquiries, and as two more were in progress (including one by the Director General of Fair Trading), it seemed sensible to await their outcome. Following reports[19] that the DGFT had decided against a Monopolies and Mergers Commission reference, the Chairman wrote to the Minister to enquire what his view now was on the recommendation for an independent inquiry. In his reply, the Minister explained that the Government had concluded that the industry really needed time to adjust to the detailed changes which had been made recently, which changes in themselves 'I hope will go a long way towards meeting the concerns which lay behind the Committee's recommendations'.[20] Accordingly, the Minister felt that it would not be right to initiate an independent inquiry, and hoped that the Committee would agree to leave matters there for the time being. This the Committee agreed to do.[21]

Again, it is possible to see the Committee's inquiry as part of the context within which the Government's decisions were made. But the slight loosening up of the regulation of milk distribution probably owes more to the philosophical stance of Mrs Thatcher's Government than to the Agriculture Committee.

On *Less Favoured Areas* the Committee produced[22] forty-three conclusions and recommendations, mostly in favour of further study, examination, and scrutiny by MAFF of potential detailed policy developments. But there were also several policy items, including the appointment of a Minister of State for Rural Affairs responsible for co-ordinating and integrating a wider-based rural policy. The Committee had concluded that the existing structures were too fragmented and that a new focus was required within the machinery of government—not necessarily attached to MAFF—to 'enable us to exploit to the very full all the resources available to help the integrated development of the LFAs'.[23] The Committee believed that a wider and more comprehensive approach to policy was demanded because, quoting MAFF's evidence, agriculture alone 'cannot provide the whole of necessary economic activity'.[24]

The Government's response[25] to this was lukewarm. While the endorsement of the principles of Government policy was welcome and the Minister undertook that the Committee's specific proposals would be carefully considered, he also pointed out that they implied heavy demands on strictly limited public sector funds and manpower, and would in any case have to be taken in the context of the EEC review of the Structures Directive.[26] And on the Committee's recommendation of a co-ordinating Minister of State, the Government remained of the view that 'the existing arrangements at Ministerial level provide an effective oversight of the problems and needs faced by rural areas', and had no plans to change its arrangements.[27] As the main thrust of the report was the need to view LFAs as integrated wholes rather than develop policy piecemeal, this response was virtually a rejection of the whole report. The Committee were unconvinced and repeated their view in their R & D report the following session.[28]

This kind of interchange—polite taking note but implicit rejection—is much like the responses to the old Estimates Committee's reports and demonstrates that there has been no fundamental change in the underlying realities of the Whitechall–Westminster power relationship. Having said that, it is true that the detailed recommendations which the Government has variously undertaken to re-examine[29] or take account for[30] or keep under surveillance[31] or

simply review, provide ample scope for MPs to follow up—if they
wish to do so. And, as solid gain, one can point to a MAFF leaflet
being prepared specifically for farmers in LFAs in response to the
Agriculture Committee's recommendation.[32]

The remaining parts of the 1981–82 Report proved of less significance. As mentioned above, the intention to investigate the 'grave
plight' of the UK poultry industry was shelved after court action
against the Government's attempts to use a veterinary ban on imports
as a means of support, and the Minister's personal explanation to a
private meeting of the Committee in March 1982 of the delicacy of
the position.[33]

Similarly, on *horticulture* political developments overtook the Committee as concern over Dutch gas subsidies to their glasshouse industry
built up. During the early part of the 1981–82 Session, the Committee
decided to postpone their inquiry 'until some progress had been made
to resolve the Dutch problem at Community level'.[34] However, the
pressure from growers' interests mounted and the Committee decided
to hold some hearings in February 1982 into the state of the industry,
with particular reference to the Dutch problem. Effectively, the Committee endorsed the NFU position that the preferential gas tariff was
an outright national aid incompatible with the basic principles of the
Common Market.[35] The Committee continued to urge MAFF to
'press vigorously' for the EEC Commission to act more speedily on
such national aids. The Government's response[36] showed that those
pressures from the Committee were not unwelcome.

It is too early to judge the impact of the R & D report.[37] No formal
government response had been issued by the end of the Parliament,
though the Ministry witnesses were very defensive when before the
Committee.[38] The report had to be completed very rapidly because
of the calling of the 1983 General Election: the draft passed through
the Committee with only eleven of its eighty-eight paragraphs being
amended, and all by agreement. The report is nevertheless very critical of the 'baroque complexity' of the present R & D system, and
concluded that a major simplification of structure was urgently
needed to enable a national strategy for agricultural R & D to be
evolved.[39] The Committee criticized MAFF for simply failing to
understand the nature of strategy as advocated by almost every witness and even its own advisory board.[40] It also criticized as highly
unsatisfactory the existence of only one MAFF commission concerned
directly with food, for, the Committee argued, food research needed
to be taken seriously and properly funded.[41]

How the Government would respond to this remained to be seen at
the end of the Parliament. The Secretary of State for Education and

Science has already to consider the implications of the Advisory Board for the Research Councils/Agricultural Research Council decision to cut the budget (which, not surprisingly, did not find favour with the Agriculture Committee,[42]) and within the agricultural research community there is considerable support for the line which the Committee endorsed. But Mrs Thatcher's Government is not enthusiastic to create new central authorities, nor are there any signs of more funds becoming available. On the other hand, since the Committee reported, the ministry has acquired a new minister and a new permanent secretary, and enthusiasm for the Rothschild 'contracting principle' seems to be on the wane in Whitehall. The Committee's report advocating change could therefore prove well timed, particularly if the subject is pursued in the new Parliament.

In addition to these major reports, the Committee had two looks at the *Supply Estimates*.[43] These were confined to single sessions of oral evidence taken in July, with the Permanent Secretary and senior MAFF officials ranging over the whole block of estimates, rather than considering any particular vote in depth. Members thus tended to follow their particular fancies, or pursue their own foxes.[44] The main emphasis of the Committee's reports was to seek improvement in the presentation of the Estimates and related material, and to facilitate understanding of links with other decisions, such as the CAP price-fixing and announcements about cash limits.[45] From the point of view of public expenditure control, one obvious difficulty is that subsidies are demand-related. Moreover, the Committee seemed surprised to discover in their first inquiry that different accounting officers were involved. For their second estimates inquiry, the Accounting Officer of the Intervention Board was called, and in their report the Committee gave notice that in future they would also request evidence from the Forestry Commission and the Department of Agriculture for Northern Ireland.[46]

The Committee secured MAFF's agreement to co-operate in an annual examination of the Supply Estimates, though this was frustrated in 1983 by the calling of the General Election and the decision not to re-appoint the departmentally-related select committees until the autumn. Nevertheless, helpful clarification of the complexities of the Estimates, particularly in relation to the Intervention Board, has resulted from the Committee's gentle probings. The Committee has also noted connections between the Estimates and their other inquiries, notably Animal Welfare and R & D.[47]

No one can be under any illusion that such Committee inquiries amount to an in-depth investigation of this block of public expenditure. In particular, it is disappointing that outside evidence has not been taken either on priorities within the agricultural programme or on the value for money obtained.

ASSESSMENT OF THE COMMITTEE

The agricultural horizon is a distant one; patience and persistence are key virtues in the farming industry. Results rarely come quickly or easily. The work of the Agriculture Committee reflects that culture. Its contribution to policy-making has been small—but from little acorns do great oaks grow. The Committee has survived its own internal difficulties and established good relationships with its department. It has provided a respectable number of leads for enterprising back-benchers on either side of the House to pursue in scrutinizing this part of the executive's work. It has provided the departments, interest groups, and others with the opportunity to place on public record their views, explanations, and criticisms of some important aspects of agricultural policy-making. This opening up of an additional and public forum for debate, with the department's policy and administration subject to informed and critical assessment, is perhaps the main achievement of the Committee. But it should be no surprise that it did not radically change the scene either in Parliament or in government. In comparison with the other departmental committees, it was relatively quiet (contrast its predecessor in the 1960s which might have jeopardized the whole committee enterprise), made fewer demands on ministers and departmental officials than most,[48] met less often than any other full committee,[49] but made a lot of visits, ranking third in those going overseas.[50] In sum, it made a useful start but, like a tree, will need a few more seasons' solid growth before it reaches maturity and bears full fruit.

NOTES

1. For an account of these committees see H.V. Wiseman, ch. 10, in *The Commons in Transition*, A.H. Hanson and B. Crick (eds.), Fontana, 1970.
2. See Appendix B for the amount of evidence taken from these agencies.
3. See HC Debs., 29 July 1983, col. 633 (written answer). Agriculture ranks sixth equal out of the 14 committees in turnover.
4. R. Body, *Agriculture: The Triumph and The Shame*, Temple Smith, 1982.
5. Page ii of each report.
6. See Appendix A for details.
7. See para 3 of the Report, HC 41, 1981–82.
8. HC Debs., 19 November 1982, cols. 503–54.
9. See Appendix B.
10. Ibid.
11. See Appendix C for analysis of the sources of evidence.

12. See Appendix D for detailed analysis of questions.
13. HC 406, 1980–81.
14. Cmnd. 8451, paras. 1 and 25.
15. Ibid., para. 26.
16. HC Deb., 19 November 1982, cols. 503–54.
17. HC 687, 1979–80.
18. HC 826, 1979–80, para. iii.
19. *The Times*, 7 March 1981.
20. HC 317, 1980–81.
21. Ibid.
22. HC 41, 1981–82.
23. Ibid., para. 140.
24. Ibid.
25. HC 39, 1982–83.
26. Ibid., para. 2.
27. Ibid., para. 46.
28. HC 38, 1982–83, para. 79.
29. HC 39, 1982–83, e.g. paras. 8 and 18.
30. e.g. ibid., paras. 20 and 36.
31. e.g. ibid., paras. 24 and 26.
32. Ibid., para. 13.
33. HC 41, 1981–82, para. 3.
34. Ibid., para. 4.
35. Ibid., para. 145.
36. HC 39, 1982–83, paras. 47–58.
37. HC 38, 1982–83.
38. Ibid., Evidence, 11 November 1982.
39. Ibid., ch. 5.
40. Ibid., paras. 45 and 82.
41. Ibid., paras. 24 and 49.
42. Ibid., paras. 33 and 34.
43. HC 361, 1980–81; HC 525, 1981–82.
44. HC 361, 1980–81, para. 9.
45. Ibid., para. 8; HC 525, 1981–82, para. 3.
46. HC 361, 1980–81, para. 5; HC 525, 1981–82, para. 3.
47. HC 525, 1981–82, paras. 6 and 7.
48. HC Deb., 29 July 1983, cols. 637–43 (written answer).
49. Ibid., cols., 645–6 (written answer).
50. Ibid., cols., 634–6 (written answer).

Annex 3.1 Agriculture Committee

Report	Date of first oral evidence (no. of evidence sessions)	Date of publication of report	Date and form of govt. reply	Length of report (pages)	No. of oral qq./no. of written submissions	No. of divisions
Session 1979–80						
Economic, Social and Health Implications for the United Kingdom of the Common Agricultural Policy on Milk and Dairy Products (HC 687)	31.1.80 (14)	24.7.80	14.11.80 (HC 826, 1979/80) and 24.7.81 (HC 317, 1980/81)	36	1242/64	6
Session 1980/81						
1st Animal Welfare in Poultry, Pig and Veal Calf Production (HC 406)	6.11.80 (15)	23.7.81	5.11.81 (HC 474) and 17.12.81 (Cmnd. 8451)	53	1233/36	10
2nd Supply Estimates (HC 361)	11.6.81 (1)	20.7.81	5.11.81 (HC 475)	6	72/5	—
Session 1981/82						
1st Financial Policy of the EEC, of Member States and, as appropriate, of other countries, in relation to Agriculture, with particular reference to Poultry, Horticulture, Eggs and Less Favoured Areas (HC 41)	19.11.81 (13)	27.7.82	25.11.82 (HC 39)	53	1083/64	3
2nd Supply Estimates (HC 525)	15.7.82 (1)	15.11.82	Appendix to HC 525	4	75/10	—
Session 1982/83						
1st Organization and Financing of Agricultural Research and Development (HC 38)	11.11.82 (14)	20.6.83	21.3.84 HC Debs., C. 501 WA	46	660/41	—

Annex 3.2 *Analysis of Sources of Evidence to Agriculture Committee*

Source	Pages of oral evidence (written)				Total	Share %
	Dairy Policy	Animal Welfare	LFAs etc.	R & D		
Govt. Depts.	24 (47)	81 (35)	44 (58)	45 (34)	194 (174)	26 (19)
Govt. Agencies	20 (29)	18 (52)	57 (45)	52 (53)	147 (179)	20 (19)
Professional Assocs.	6 (16)	25 (30)	—	26 (25)	57 (71)	8 (8)
Lobbies	65 (134)	89 (92)	39 (78)	11 (21)	204 (325)	28 (35)
Others, incl. individuals	34 (21)	23 (30)	17 (44)	58 (83)	132 (178)	18 (19)
Total	149 (247)	236(239)	157 (225)	192 (216)	734 (927)	100 (100)

Note:
All the evidence to the two Supply Estimates inquiries came from MAFF or the Intervention Board.
Sources:
Minutes of Evidence to Agriculture Committee Reports,
HC 687 (1979/80); HC 406 (1980/81); HC 41 (1981/82); HC 38 (1982/83).

Annex 3.3 *Analysis of Lobby Evidence*

Group	Pages of oral evidence (written)				
	Dairy policy	Animal welfare	LFAs/ Hortic.	R & D	Total
Producers	12 (30)	45 (52)	31 (47)	9 (12)	97 (141)
Distributors	20 (52)	—	—	2 (9)	22 (61)
Consumers	18 (23)	3 (10)	—	—	21 (33)
Unions	15 (29)	—	8 (31)	—	23 (60)
Cause Groups	—	41 (30)	—	—	41 (30)
All Groups	65 (134)	89 (92)	39 (78)	58 (83)	204 (325)

Annex 3.4 *Analysis of Questions*

Number of questions (%)

Member	Dairy policy	Animal welfare	Supply estimates	LFAs/etc.	Supply estimates	R & D	Total
Elliott	200 (16)	210 (17)	5 (7)	130 (12)	5 (7)	124 (19)	674 (15)
Torney	136 (11)	87 (7)	12 (16)	43 (4)	3 (4)	67 (10)	348 (8)
Spence	209 (17)	135 (11)	—	114 (11)	10 (14)	145 (22)	613 (14)
Body	58 (5)	112 (9)	18 (24)	91 (8)	13 (18)	38 (6)	330 (8)
Maynard	41 (3)	139 (11)	9 (12)	52 (5)	7 (10)	59 (9)	309 (7)
Hogg	193 (15)	235 (19)	—	284 (26)	22 (31)	N/M	734 (17)
Stott	57 (5)	12 (1)*	N/M	N/M	N/M	N/M	69 (2)
Hughes	272 (22)	46 (4)*	N/M	N/M	N/M	N/M	318 (7)
Goodlad	76 (6)	21 (2)*	N/M	N/M	N/M	N/M	97 (2)
Myles	N/M	90 (7)*	17 (23)	198 (18)	—	107 (16)	412 (9)
Newens	N/M	122 (10)*	14 (18)	150 (14)	8 (11)	75 (11)	369 (8)
Cohen	N/M	24 (2)*	N/M	21 (2)	4 (5)	26 (4)	75 (2)
Temple-Morris	N/M	N/M	N/M	N/M	N/M	19 (3)	19 (1)
Total	1,242	1,233	75	1,083	72	660	4,365

Notes:
* Member of Committee for only part of the inquiry.
N/M Not a member of the Committee for this inquiry.

CHAPTER 4

The Defence Committee

R. L. Borthwick

Although formally established, like the other new committees, towards the end of November 1979, the Defence Committee was heir to a slightly longer tradition. It was the direct successor to the Defence and External Affairs Sub-Committee of the Expenditure Committee which operated from 1971 to 1979. Three members of the new committee had served on the earlier committee, as had the clerk and two of the specialist advisers. Perhaps more important was the existence of an established liaison system between the Ministry of Defence (MOD) and a Commons committee. This system continued unchanged after 1979. For those MPs who served on both committees there was a natural tendency to think of them as one continuous entity. One must be careful not to exaggerate the extent of continuity: when the Defence Committee began work in January 1980, eight of its eleven members had had no such experience.

Of these eleven members, six were Conservative and five Labour, with a Conservative chairman under the agreement between the two major parties. Among those who had been members of the predecessor Sub-Committee, was Dr Gilbert, who had been Minister of State at the Ministry of Defence from 1976 to 1979. Of the other members, four had been serving officers. Mr (later Sir) Patrick Wall, for example, had been an officer in the Marines; in addition to his strong naval links, he had been Vice-Chairman of the Conservative Defence Committee from 1965 to 1977. Mr Cartwright, who began as a Labour member of the Committee, was Chairman of the Parliamentary Labour Party Defence Group from 1979 to 1981. The first chairman of the Committee, Sir John Langford-Holt, had been a war-time naval officer but otherwise had no particular background in defence. Having been an MP since 1945, however, he was the most senior member of the Committee. None of the founding members was a newcomer to the Commons, though Mr McKay had been elected only in 1978, and Mr George and Mr Mates in 1974.

Of the original members of the Committee, seven were to remain on it throughout the Parliament. Turnover was thus confined to four places which were occupied in all by ten people in the course of the Parliament. The official figure for turnover (36 per cent),[1] therefore, is somewhat misleading since it is based simply on the number of original members still on the Committee at the end of the Parliament. Such a figure obviously cannot reflect the replacement of replacements. The Committee was fortunate in retaining the loyalty of a solid core of members. Some of the changes were caused by political promotion: Mr McKay became an Opposition Whip and Mr Onslow a Minister following the Falklands resignations. Calculations of the membership changes in party terms are complicated by the establishment of the Social Democratic Party (SDP) in March 1981. At that time one of the original members of the SDP (Mr Cartwright) was a member of the Committee. The replacement for Mr McKay, Mr Dunn, who joined the Committee in March 1981, subsequently moved over to the SDP; so that there were for a time two SDP members of the Committee. Mr Cartwright was replaced by a Labour MP but Mr Dunn's replacement was another SDP MP, suggesting that by that stage the SDP had established a claim to a place on the Committee.

In contrast to its relatively stable membership, the Committee had three chairmen in the course of the 1979–83 Parliament. The first chairman stepped down on completion of the Committee's major inquiry into Strategic Nuclear Weapons in May 1981, though he continued to serve as a member of the Committee until the end of the Parliament when he retired from the House. His successor as chairman, Mr Onslow, had a relatively brief tenure; his elevation to ministerial office ended his occupation of the post after only eleven months. The third chairman, Sir Timothy Kitson, took the Committee to the end of the Parliament. He too retired from Parliament at the dissolution.

Any measurement of attendance at Defence Committee meetings is bound to be misleading, because the Committee in its early days made some use of informal sub-committees. This followed the rejection, very early in the Committee's life, of a request to be allowed to appoint a formal sub-committee.[2] The published figures[3] suggest a level of attendance (75 per cent) which is about average for committees as a whole. Of three inquiries which were begun in June 1980, two (on the D Notice System and on RAF Pilot Training) were, in effect, conducted by sub-committees. Even so there were probably some strains on members and staff in trying to run three inquiries simultaneously.

The use of informal sub-committees has certain disadvantages. For example the Chairman of the Committee is unable to attend meetings of the sub-committee without being obliged to take the chair; members of the Committee inevitably appear less assiduous in their attendance; there is no possibility of a formal sub-committee report; and the presence of members of the Committee who have not participated in the inquiry at the final drawing up of the report stage may cause some awkwardness. This last problem was evident in the D Notice inquiry chaired by Dr Gilbert. Some members of the Committee felt aggrieved that members who had not attended for the evidence-taking sessions were able to help force through a report that differed in some respects from the views of some of those who had. On the other hand, it is quite clear that constitutionally nothing improper occurred. In the other instance where use was made of the device, the inquiry into RAF Pilot Training chaired by Mr Conlan, no such divergence emerged.

THE WORK OF THE COMMITTEE

In the first session of its life, the Committee completed three inquiries and began work on two others; in view of the fact that it hardly got going until January 1980, this was a very diligent start. The Committee's first inquiry, into Ammunition storage sites for British forces in Germany, was chosen partly in order for members to get to know each other. As part of the inquiry, the Committee visited Germany; this not only helped the process of developing committee cohesion but also set the pattern for what was to be an extensive programme of travelling. In their report, the Committee made a number of suggestions on the need to improve NATO-wide agreement in this area and for better storage and speedier handling facilities for ammunition.

The Committee then moved on to an examination of Defence Estimates in the shape of the 1980 Defence White Paper. This was an extremely rushed inquiry: evidence was taken at four sessions over three successive days in mid-April, with the Committee meeting seven times in nine days in order to have material available for the Commons debate on the White Paper. The Committee expressed the hope that in future more time would be allowed to it between the publication of the White Paper and the debate. Such hopes were not to be realized: in 1981 their report had again to be produced very hurriedly, while in 1982 the Falklands crisis meant that the whole timetable was disrupted and the Committee took evidence from the Secretary of

State without producing a report. Despite these difficulties the Committee has taken seriously its task of attempting some scrutiny of expenditure proposals. In addition, in the aftermath of the Falklands, it examined the Winter Supplementary Estimates at the start of the 1982–83 session.

After its first excursion into a White Paper examination, the Committee embarked almost simultaneously on three inquiries. Two, as we have seen, were sub-committee efforts; the third was a major investigation into strategic nuclear weapons policy. Of these only that into the D Notice system was completed within that session. This report, though it endorsed the idea behind such a system, made some critical observations about its operation. The inquiry into RAF Pilot Training took a considerable time: the report was not published until April 1981. In general it was not especially critical, except on points of detail.

The strategic nuclear weapons inquiry was perhaps the most important of those undertaken by the Committee during the 1979–83 Parliament. Certainly it was the most contentious and the longest lasting (the report was published exactly a year to the day after the first evidence was taken). The concern with the perceived need for a replacement for the Polaris system made the topic almost inescapable for the Committee. Nevertheless, the Government would probably have preferred it not to have been tackled and may well have hoped that the inquiry would have been even more limited than it was.

The inquiry began with a row about the terms of reference: attempts were made to exclude any consideration of alternatives other than Trident as replacements for Polaris and to exclude considerations of cost. Although not successful, they probably set the tone for the investigation. It was the only inquiry undertaken by the Committee where real political rancour showed through. Further efforts to limit the Committee had partial success. In July 1980, after the Government had announced their choice of Trident, a second attempt was made to prevent consideration of alternative forms of replacement. The move was successful to the extent that a compromise proposed by Dr Gilbert—that the topic be relegated to consideration in a 'working group of the Committee'—was accepted on a division, though even this compromise was opposed by two Conservative members of the Committee. In March 1981 after the choice of Trident as the replacement for Polaris had been approved by the House of Commons, an attempt was made in the Committee to require the final report to be confined to the implementation of that choice. Again the attempt was not wholly successful: this time a compromise from one of the Conservative members of the Committee resulted in the Committee's curiously having the first paragraph of the Chairman's draft report agreed before it finished taking oral evidence. The impact of this paragraph was less restrictive than the first proposal, though it steered the report in the direction of implementation of the Trident decision.

Undoubtedly time worked against the Committee on this inquiry: hardly had it begun to take evidence than the Government announced their decision to buy Trident, and Parliamentary approval of that came before the Committee had finished their work. To meet that situation it was obliged to issue a special report drawing the House's attention to the evidence so far published. The Committee might have hoped that a debate on the adoption of Trident could have been delayed until it had finally reported. As with the White Paper debates, the activities of the Defence Committee seem to have weighed rather lightly with the whips in arranging the House's business.

In its eventual report, the Committee was fundamentally divided. Three Labour members produced their own draft report (at 110 paragraphs, longer than the report that was eventually adopted), which was highly critical of the decision to adopt Trident. This was duly voted down, and the Committee accepted a report which endorsed the basic decision and confined its criticism to such matters as cost. The Committee returned to the subject in the following session with a special report, after its questioning of the Secretary of State about the decision to opt for the larger version of Trident.

In the 1980-81 session, the Committee published evidence on two topics without any accompanying reports. They undertook also a study of a very precise topic: the Sting Ray lightweight torpedo. This was an important report in its way, because it represented an endorsement of the development of a British lightweight torpedo as against purchasing its American rival.

In the 1981-82 session, the life of the Committee was dominated by two things: first, a major investigation into MOD organization and procurement and, secondly, by the sudden eruption of the Falklands crisis (though in terms of Committee inquiries, the latter features in the 1982-83 session). The Committee began the session with an investigation into problems concerning Allied forces in Germany, in the course of which it had a meeting with the Bundestag Defence Committee, one of a number of contacts which the Committee had with its equivalents in other countries. The procurement inquiry, while not the most exciting of the Committee's inquiries, was important because of the volume of defence expenditure and relations with industry. It was also one that was especially favoured by the second chairman of the Committee. The subject had been pursued by the predecessor Expenditure Sub-Committee; as the Committee pointed out in its report '[proposed] reforms have been generally welcomed but ultimately not always implemented. We are determined that on this occasion the opportunity to bring in proposed changes should not be lost.'[4] To that end, the Committee gathered a great deal of evidence on an enormous topic.

From April 1982 the life of the Defence Committee came under the shadow of the Falklands issue. In 1982–83 the Committee, having been elbowed out of a more major investigation of the topic by the appointment of the Franks Committee, undertook two major inquiries into particular aspects of the affair. The first, into the handling of press and public information during the conflict, inevitably attracted massive interest from the media, both for its evidence-taking sessions and for its report. This, to the disappointment of some, broadly endorsed MOD policy but made some suggestions for improvements, particularly in the co-ordination of the presentation of information. The other aspect of the Falklands tackled by the Committee was the future defence of the islands. Work on this was completed after the dissolution of Parliament was announced in May 1983. The Committee's report dealt with a number of important matters, such as the siting of a new airfield and the appropriate levels of forces on the islands. Earlier, following a visit there, the Committee had reported on British forces in Hong Kong.

The calling of the General Election brought fewer problems for Defence than for some other Committees. The investigation into positive vetting had to be left merely with the publication of the evidence and without a report. The Committee's final publication was a report surveying their previous recommendations and the Government's responses to them. It included a session of evidence on how far action had been taken (at this, the Committee was outnumbered by the witnesses, eleven to five, though four of the latter were silent throughout).

THE OPERATION OF THE COMMITTEE

One of the most striking characteristics of the Defence Committee is the low level of political partisanship revealed in its proceedings. In only two of its inquiries were differences of opinion pressed to a vote (on D notices and strategic nuclear weapons) and even these cases did not seriously upset the generally good working relations. The disagreements over the Trident inquiry were undoubtedly the most serious which the Committee produced (exceptionally, for this inquiry Conservative members held occasional caucus meetings); but even here at least some Labour members of the Committee adopted a fairly matter-of-fact approach. Knowing in advance that their viewpoint would not prevail, they were content to make their case by way of a draft report and, having seen it voted down, to allow the work of the Committee to continue.

In all, there were just seven instances of a vote being taken in the Committee. Two of these occurred in the D notice inquiry; in each case the Committee split along party lines four to four and the chairman resolved matters by voting with his party colleagues. The other five divisions came at various stages of the strategic nuclear weapons inquiry. Three were at the outset of the inquiry, in the argument over terms of reference; two were settled four to three in favour of the Labour members, while on the attempt to exclude considerations of cost from the inquiry, one Conservative member found himself alone on the issue and was defeated by four to one. The draft Labour report was supported by its three sponsors and Mr Cartwright, who by that time had joined the SDP, but five Conservatives were enough to defeat them. One subsequent proposed amendment by Mr Cartwright was pressed to a division in which he was defeated five to one by the same group of Conservative members.

There are several factors which explain the generally good working relationships on the Committee. They obviously derived partly from the personalities of the members of the Committee and their views on defence. It is significant that the range of opinions on defence matters among Labour members of the Committee was much less than among Labour MPs as a whole. Although there is no direct evidence that Labour MPs of a different viewpoint were kept off the Committee their presence would obviously have presented real problems for the working of the Committee. Perhaps more than any other of the committees, Defence depends on confidentiality: the Committee has access to some highly classified information. Such access would not be forthcoming if there were doubts about the reliability of its members.

A second factor in the successful chemistry of the Committee was the style of chairmanship. Although the three Chairmen were very different in many ways, each had a strong sense of the need to establish a consensual atmosphere, in which, especially on procedural matters, due heed would be paid to the views of opposition members. In part this derived from a recognition of the knowledge and exerience of some of the opposition members of the Committee—especially the senior Labour member, Dr Gilbert, who was established, in effect, as the Deputy Chairman of the Committee at its first formal session in December 1979. He was the most knowledgeable member of the Committee about defence matters and, having been a minister in the MOD, was able to speak with an authority which no other member of the Committee quite achieved (and to deal on occasion more fiercely with witnesses than any of his fellows). Another element in the relationship was that, although the chairmanship of the Committee belonged to the Conservatives, there was a recognition that their choice had to be acceptable also to the Labour members of the Committee. This is clearly an important element in maintaining good working relations among members of a committee.

A third part of the explanation has to do with the nature of the subject of the Committee's responsibilities and of the particular inquiries which it undertook. Given the centrality of defence to the most fundamental questions about the nature and existence of the state, there is a tendency for disagreements to be fewer in this area—at least among those who share a broad conception of the national interest. An additional factor is that to some extent policy is determined outside the immediate defence field, for example by the Foreign and Commonwealth Office, and thus defence issues may often amount to matters of implementation. At any rate it is clear that the Committee did not feel it worth tackling some of the more visible issues in the field. For example, it steered clear of the question of the siting of Cruise missiles and did not seek confrontation with CND. It is possible that the experience of the Trident inquiry left the Committee anxious to avoid a repeat performance. For whatever reason, the Committee preferred to concentrate on problems where there was less chance of members being drawn into ideological squabbles. In the end the Committee did what its members wanted it to do, and here again there were elements of a procedural consensus. Ideas for inquiries were freely discussed among the members and there was no sense of an imposed agenda.

The desire to proceed by general agreement extended also to the use of specialist advisers. Such appointments were matters for agreement among the Committee as a whole. The Committee did not employ a large number, preferring instead to use a small number on a more regular basis. For quite some time the Committee used only four advisers, of whom three had service backgrounds and the fourth was an academic. Two of these had served the Expenditure Sub-Committee. In the final year or so of the Parliament, the Committee used another five advisers as the breadth of its inquiries widened; one of these, Mr Pincher, moved into the group of 'regular' advisers. The Committee was concerned to use its advisers efficiently: material produced by them (suggestions for lines of questioning, for example) was channelled through the clerk; nothing went directly to the Committee.

To that extent there was no danger in the case of Defence that advisers would take over the Committee. In addition to these specialist advisers, the Committee had the services of an audit officer on secondment from the Exchequer and Audit Department. Initially the Committee sought the appointment of two such officers; in the end they had to be content with one. The Defence Committee was unique in having the services of such an individual, and he played an important part in providing background analysis for the Committee. Inevitably a great deal of the evidence taken by the Committee came from official sources: the Committee did not place great faith in evidence from outside such circles. Although one member was anxious to gather more academic opinion, the Committee as a whole was sceptical about its value.

In the course of its investigations and as part of its general education the Committee travelled extensively. Among the places it visited were Germany, the United States, Hong Kong, Japan, and the Falklands. Early in its life the Committee ran up against a cost problem. Wishing to visit the United States in the course of its strategic nuclear weapons investigation, the Committee was informed that such a visit would be possible for only half its members (travelling first class). Arguing that it made no sense to send half the Committee when all were involved in this major inquiry, the Committee made representations through the Liaison Committee to the House of Commons Commission with the result that the whole Committee was able to go at tourist class rates involving no greater cost. In addition to overseas travel the Committee made a considerable number of visits at home to military bases, dockyards, shipyards, and research establishments.

The Committee does not seem to have gone out of its way to attract media attention; indeed, the fact that it met a good deal in closed session made such attention more difficult. Members seemed to be satisfied with the coverage they did receive. Sometimes this was considerable, especially (and not surprisingly) in the cases of the two inquiries which bore directly on the media (D notices and Falklands information). In addition to the general media coverage, the Committee attracted considerable attention in the specialist press.

AIMS AND ACHIEVEMENTS

Like other select committees the Defence Committee had a number of different aims. The most clearly articulated was 'to elicit facts in order to help the House make an informed judgment on governmental decisions'.[5] Certainly that was the prevailing view among the chairmen. However, the Committee had other aims as well: in part it sought to influence opinion and action within the MOD either by focussing on particular issues which compelled a response or by the force of its conclusions, which in turn demanded a reasoned reply from the Ministry. Inevitably, the Committee was concerned a good deal with matters of administration: for example, seeking more effective training in various fields and better value for taxpayers' money. As we have seen, there was a tendency to steer clear of some areas of broader policy. One member, Mr George, argued publicly for a more vigorous approach, suggesting that the Committee should '... go for the red meat of policy and expenditure rather than the limp lettuce of administration'.[6]

The MOD responded to the Committee's recommendations in what was, by the prevailing standards, a reasonable length of time. According to the published figures,[7] the average time for a reply for Defence was ninety days, which is rather less than the average for all the new committees of 102 days. Although this was rather longer than the aim of a reply within two months, the mechanics of printing may account for as much as a month's delay. The majority of replies came in the form of command papers, but a few appeared as committee special reports, which actually allows slightly more time for the Department to produce its reply.

It would of course be misleading to try to measure the impact of the Defence Committee by the number of its recommendations accepted by the Government. Clear cut acceptance is rarely to be found in the government observations on committee reports. Equally, it should be said, outright rejection is also not frequent. More often the tone is one of pointing out problems or of arguing that the recommendation is already in operation. Even when the changes made coincide with a committee recommendation, it is difficult to isolate the impact of a committee report from other factors that may have played a part. Therefore it is difficult to measure the impact of a select committee with any degree of precision.

One can certainly point to cases where the Defence Committee appears to have had influence. As the Chairman pointed out in his report to the Liaison Committee, in some instances (the examples quoted are ammunition storage sites, RAF pilot training, and the Sting Ray lightweight torpedo) where 'forward decisions needed to be made by the Government to enhance or maintain defence capabilities',[8] the Government acted on some of its recommendations. It may well be of course that the department would deny that the Committee's work made any real difference to what eventually happened. Even where an inquiry apparently had less success, it may have spurred others into action. This was arguably the case with the D notice investigation, where the official D Notice Committee was obliged to react to the work of the Select Committee and to make some changes, although these fell far short of the Defence Committee's recommendations. Even in this case, the department and related bodies had to present evidence to the Committee and if some of that evidence did not look well, then no doubt that fact in itself had some bearing on opinion in Whitehall.

Clearly the Committee were more likely to be influential if they found topics where final decisions have not been taken (as with Sting Ray). By contrast, where options were closed (as with Trident), the Committee had less chance of having a direct influence, though even here the Committee succeeded in raising doubts about the financial impact on the rest of the defence budget of the decision to buy Trident. In some cases it might not even be necessary to produce a report in order for a committee to exert influence. At the time of writing it is not clear whether the reconstituted Defence Committee will return to the topic of positive vetting, but the Committee has already had some impact on the subject simply by virtue of the evidence it has published.

Given the declared aims of the Committee, perhaps its main achievement has been simply to improve the level of information about defence matters available to the House as a whole. Although more difficult to pinpoint or document, it is plausible to argue that the Committee had an impact in other less direct ways. For example, the existence of the Committee as an active critical forum was a factor which civil servants and others presumably had to bear in mind: they might be called upon to justify their decisions before it and they might receive some rough treatment in so doing. In addition, the Committee could compel civil servants and ministers to focus on certain topics simply by calling for evidence on them. The Committee undoubtedly helped to secure more openness in government; more things were made matters of public record than was formerly the case.

Here we are up against a special problem for the Defence Committee. As we have already seen, the Committee had access to classified information and had to take some of its evidence in closed session. This means that not only was some of its evidence not published but that the Committee might wish to say things that could not be included in its published reports. The conflict of interest here between Parliament and the executive is inherent and unavoidable. The problems raised by the use of sidelining (that is, non-publication at the request of those giving the evidence) were brought out into the open in the Committee's very first inquiry. The report on ammunition storage sites contained an appendix which raised the issues involved and acknowledged—in classic understatement—that there was a row on the matter: 'We have not found it an easy task to reach an agreement with the Ministry of Defence on those passages to be excised or redrafted.'[9] In a sense the problem is insuperable; inevitably, there will be disagreement about where any boundary should be drawn. As the Committee pointed out, they would continue to watch the mater very carefully. In this particular case, the solution adopted was to send an unexpurgated version of the Report to the Secretary of State with the expectation 'that those parts to which the Ministry cannot respond in public will receive an appropriate reply through the established means of communicating classified material to us'.[10] On some subsequent reports similar deletions were necessary, but acceptable compromises appear to have been reached.

That is one aspect of the different interests of Committee and departments. Problems may also arise over access to papers and persons. On the former, the only serious problem was in the autumn of 1980 over access to a number of documents relating to defence spending which were leaked to the Press Association. After failing to obtain copies from the MOD, the Committee made do with photocopies from the Press Association. Access to persons seems not to have presented any great difficulties. The Committee may not always have obtained the witnesses it sought but this may have been due to the tendency to seek witnesses at a slightly higher level in the hierarchy than is strictly necessary.

From the department's point of view, the Committee's demands are the necessary price of accountable government. The burden on certain people's time was undoubtedly considerable: over the Parliament, 310 officials made a total of 397 appearances before the Committee. These figures are far in excess of those for any other of the new committees. To the burden of work which preparations for and appearances before the Defence Committee represented, were added the demands of other committees, notably the Public Accounts Committee, some of whose inquiries were squarely in the defence field. It may be that the dangers of overlapping inquiries will increase in future. Or course, not all the demands are necessarily regarded as a burden by the department. It could be argued that on the Falklands information inquiry, for example, the MOD was able to put over its views to a more impartial jury than any other available and that it emerged from the inquiry better than might have been predicted.

It is clear that relations between the Committee and the department have been generally harmonious. This reflects a usually good relationship between the chairmen of the Committee and the Secretaries of State, and also the fact that the liaison machinery has worked smoothly (helped no doubt by the liaison officer's travelling with the Committee on visits at home and abroad if defence personnel were to be interviewed).

CONCLUSION

The Defence Committee in its first four years produced solid and workmanlike reports on a variety of topics, some of which undoubtedly had an impact. Its members were, with very few exceptions, conscientious and had a considerable pride in the work of the Committee. Certainly the Committee was a success if one measures this by the desire (especially among Conservative MPs) to belong to it. The Committee was a serious-minded and hard-working body which emerged from the Parliament with a reputation as one of the more successful products of the 1979 reforms.

NOTES

1. HC Debs., 29 July 1983, col. 633 (written answer).
2. First Special Report from the Defence Committee, 1979–80, HC 455.
3. HC Debs., 29 July 1983, col. 633 (written answer).
4. Second Report from the Defence Committee, 1981–82, HC 22–I, p. vii.
5. Defence Committee, 1980–81, HC 362, q.1 (Mr Onslow).
6. *The Times*, 7 September 1981.
7. HC Debs., 29 July 1983, col. 633 (written answer).
8. First Report from the Liaison Committee, 1982–83, HC 92, p. 42.
9. First Report from the Defence Committee, 1979–80, HC 556, Appendix (p. xx).
10. Loc. cit.
11. HC Debs., 29 July 1983, col. 638 (written answer).

Annex 4.1 *Defence Committee*

Report	Date of first oral evidence/(no. of evidence sessions)	Date of publication of report	Date and form of govt. reply	Length of report (pages)	No. of oral qq./no. of written submissions	No. of divisions
Session 1979–80						
1st *Ammunition Storage Sites for British Forces Germany* (HC 556)	23.1.80 (4)	5.6.80	20.8.80 (WP Cmnd. 8021)	13	377/6	—
2nd *Statement on the Defence Estimates 1980* (HC 571; 555-i-iv)	15.4.80 (4)	3.6.80	13.11.80 (Committee Special Report (2nd) HC 816)	12	437/–	—
3rd *The D Notice System* (HC 773; 640-i-v)	11.6.80 (5)	28.10.80	7.1.81 (WP Cmnd. 8129)	10	746/33	2
Session 1980–81						
1st *RAF Pilot Training* (HC 53; 649-i-iii)	12.6.80 (5)	2.4.81	11.6.81 (WP Cmnd. 8265)	17	546/9	—
2nd *Statement on the Defence Estimates 1981* (HC 302)	28.4.81 (3)	15.5.81	14.8.81 (Committee Special Report (2nd) HC 461)	8	388/–	—
3rd *Sting Ray Lightweight Torpedo* (HC 218)	10.3.81 (2)	23.6.81	16.11.81 (Committee Special Report (3rd) HC 473)	5	278/2	—
4th *Strategic Nuclear Weapons Policy* (HC 36)	25.6.80 (14)	25.6.81	9.10.81* (Letter to Chairman, Open Government Document, and oral evidence to Committee, 17.3.82)	18	1696/23	5

Annex 4.1 *Defence Committee*

Report	Date of first oral evidence (no. of evidence sessions)	Date of publication of report	Date and form of govt. reply	Length of report (pages).	No. of oral qq./no. of written submissions	No. of divisions
Session 1981–82						
1st *Allied Forces in Germany* (HC 93)	8.12.81 (1)	18.3.82	9.6.82 (WP Cmnd. 8571)	10	176/–	—
2nd *Ministry of Defence Organisation and Procurement* (2 vols.) (HC 22-I-II)	11.11.81 (14)	22.7.82	6.10.82 (WP Cmnd. 8678)	49	1699/51	—
Session 1982–83						
1st *The Handling of Press and Public Information during the Falklands Conflict* (2 vols.) (HC 17-I-II)	21.7.82 (12)	16.12.82 (Evidence 22.12.82)	3.3.83 (WP Cmnd. 8820)	58	1911/55	—
2nd *British Forces Hong Kong* (HC 176)	1.2.83 (1)	14.4.83	20.7.83 (WP Cmnd. 8894)	7	73/1	—
3rd *The Future Defence of the Falkland Islands* (HC 154)	19.1.83 (12)	14.6.83	25.10.83 (WP Cmnd. 9070)	51	1600/6	—
4th *Previous Recommendations of the Committee* (HC 55)	16.11.82 (1)	14.6.83	Not yet received	3†	167/6	—

Notes:
* Date of letter from Secretary of State to Chairman of Committee.
† Plus an Annex of 26 pages of recommendations with parallel observations.

Other proceedings

Special Reports not noted above

1979–80   (1st) *Sub-Committees* (HC 455), published 5.3.80, 1 page.

1980–81   (1st) *Strategic Nuclear Weapons Policy* (HC 130), published 12.2.81, 1 page.

1981–82   (1st) *Strategic Nuclear Weapons Policy* (HC 266), published 11.5.82, contains evidence taken 17.3.82, 1 page, evidence of 134qq and 2 written submissions.

1982–83   (1st) *Positive Vetting Procedures in HM Services and the Ministry of Defence* (HC 242), published 14.6.83, contains evidence taken on 4 occasions beginning on 2.3.83, the Report of 1 page is in effect the publication of evidence without a considered report. Evidence 746qq and 3 written submissions.

Publication of evidence without any report

1980–81   *Defence Cuts and Defence Estimates* (HC 223), published 1.7.81, contains evidence taken on 2 occasions beginning on 11.3.81, 235qq and 3 written submissions.

1980–81   *Royal Dockyards and the Dockyard Study* (HC 362), published 8.9.81, contains evidence taken on 5 occasions beginning on 11.6.81, 619qq and 2 written submissions together with a third item listing a further 7 not published but placed in the Commons Library.

1981–82   *Statement on the Defence Estimates 1982* (HC 428), published 2.8.82, contains evidence taken 23.6.82, 128qq and 1 written submission.

1982–83   *Winter Supplementary Estimates 1982–83* (HC 89), published 17.2.83, contains evidence taken on 2.12.82, 214qq and 1 written submission.

Miscellaneous

1979–80   Minutes of Proceedings volume (HC 842).

CHAPTER 5

The Education, Science and Arts Committee[1]

Michael Rush

The lineage of the Education, Science and Arts Committee can be traced back through the Education, Arts and Home Office Sub-Committee of the former Expenditure Committee to two of the old 'Crossman committees'—the Select Committee on Education and Science, and the much longer-lived Science and Technology Committee. The former Education, Arts and Home Office Sub-Committee had an enormously wide remit, and the decision in 1979 to plump for departmental committees appeared to solve this problem; but it did not take into account the disparate responsibilities of some departments. The Department of Education and Science (DES) does not provide the most telling of examples, but the new committee was certainly faced with four distinct areas of policy to monitor: education, science, the arts, and library policies, which also involved fifty-three 'associated public bodies' in 1980.[2] In 1979, in fact, a separate Office of Arts and Libraries was created, headed by a Minister for the Arts, a post held by Norman St John-Stevas in conjunction with his more important roles as Chancellor of the Duchy of Lancaster and Leader of the House of Commons. When St John-Stevas was dismissed from the Cabinet in 1981, however, the Office of Arts and Libraries was made part of the DES and St John-Stevas's successor as Minister for the Arts, Paul Channon, was appointed a Minister of State in the DES.

The Education Committee therefore had to decide how best to divide its attention between these areas,[3] bearing in mind that it was one of the committees with only nine members and did not have the power to appoint a sub-committee.

MEMBERSHIP AND CHAIRMANSHIP

The Education Committee had nine members: five Conservative, three Labour and one Plaid Cymru. It was the only departmental committee on which the Welsh Nationalists were represented. Turnover on the Committee was very small: eight of the members appointed in 1979 were still members at the dissolution in May 1983—a turnover of 11.1 per cent; indeed, no change took place at all until early in the 1981–82 session, when Stan Thorne (Lab.) was replaced by Martin Flannery (Lab.).

Of the original nine members, two had been elected in 1966 or earlier, two in 1970, two in February 1974, and three entered Parliament in the election of 1979. Martin Flannery was first elected in February 1974. All ten Members who served on the Committee could claim some relevant experience. No less than six came from the teaching profession, and they included a former headmaster, Martin Flannery, and two former deputy headmasters, Patrick Cormack and Harry Greenway (Cons.). Several others had been members of local education committees and a number had served on back-bench party committees or subject groups. Patrick Cormack (Cons.) was chairman of the Conservative back-bench Arts and Heritage Committee and of an all-party group, whilst Martin Flannery was chairman of the Labour Education and Science Subject Group. Two members had served on earlier relevant select committees—John Osborn (Cons.) on the Science and Technology Committee and Christopher Price (Lab.) on the former Education and Science Committee. Price had also been editor of *New Education* in 1967–68 and then education correspondent for the *New Statesman* from 1968 to 1974. He had also been Parliamentary private secetary (PPS) to the Secretary of State for Education and Science in 1966–67 and 1975–76. Dafydd Thomas had been the Plaid Cymru spokesman on social, educational, and cultural policy since 1975. The majority of members stated that they had actively sought membership of the Committee.

It had been agreed through the usual channels that the Education Committee would be chaired by a Labour Member, and the whips' nominee was Christopher Price. This was accepted by the Committee. In terms of experience alone, Price was an obvious choice.

SUBJECTS OF INQUIRY

Very early in its life, the Education Committee decided that, in the absence of the formal power to appoint a sub-committee, the only effective way to cope with its varied remit was to make use of *de facto* sub-committees. This undoubtedly enabled the Committee to cover a wide variety of topics in its inquiries. By the end of the 1979-80 session a fairly consistent pattern had emerged, although this pattern became somewhat more elaborate in succeeding sessions. First, the Committee as a whole conducted a major inquiry in each of three of the four sessions: in 1979-80 the topic was the funding and organization of courses in higher education; in 1980-81 it was the secondary school curriculum and examinations for 14-16 year-olds; and in 1982-83 it was education and training for 16-19 year-olds. Second, at least one inquiry in each session was dealt with by a *de facto* sub-committee: for example, information storage and retrieval in the British Library service in 1979-80, a major inquiry into the public and private funding of the arts in 1980-81 and 1981-82, and further and higher education in Northern Ireland, and public records in 1982-83. Third, the Committee investigated topical matters at short notice: for example, the future of the Promenade Concerts in 1979-80, the future of *The Times* supplements in 1980-81, and the future of the Theatre Museum in 1981-82, while university funding was the subject of investigation in all four sessions. Fourth, every year the Committee held regular 'scrutiny' sessions, starting with a single session in 1979-80, increasing it to two from 1980-81 (though the dissolution of Parliament prevented a second session being held in 1982-83). These sessions were attended by the Secretary of State, DES officials and Her Majesty's Inspectors (HMIs), and in the last two sessions junior ministers also appeared with the Secretary of State before the Committee. A separate arts scrutiny session attended by the Minister for the Arts was introduced in 1982-83. Finally, from 1980-81 the Committee also instituted an annual examination of public expenditure on education and other matters within its remit.

In addition, in the course of several inquiries the Committee took up specific problems that came to its attention, such as the new British Library building, overseas students' fees, the retention of works of art in Britain, and the research base in biotechnology.

The subjects of inquiry emerged from generally amicable discussions within the Committee. In the early stages of its operation the Committee asked Mark Carlisle, then Secretary of State for Education, and Norman St John-Stevas, then Minister for the Arts, what matters concerned them as ministers, and took their replies into account in deciding what to investigate. In other cases, the force of events played an important role, and it was hardly surprising that the topic of university funding should receive attention every year—twice in one particular year, in fact. The various interests of members of the Committee were also important: some were primarily interested in education, some in the arts, others in science; but several members remarked upon the prominent part played by Christopher Price, as chairman, saying that he frequently gave a strong lead. In general, the Education Committee managed to cover a wide range of topics, without losing sight of education as its main focus.

STAFFING

Until the 1982–83 session, the Education Committee had only one full-time clerk, but from that session on there were two clerks, one of whom dealt with mainly education matters and the other with arts matters. In addition, the Committee had a temporary committee assistant and two secretarial staff. Members of the Committee were evenly divided on whether this was adequate, one observing that it was adequate at this stage in the development of the select committee system; he clearly envisaged more help being required in the future. This view was reinforced by the chairman in his report to the Liaison Committee.[4]

The Committee made extensive use of its power to appoint specialist advisers, appointing a total of twenty-one individuals over the four parliamentary sessions. After making a number of appointments in 1979–80 for particular inquiries, two advisers on financial matters were appointed for the duration of the 1980–81 session. Towards the end of that session, these two and a further two were appointed for the duration of the Parliament. A fifth adviser for the duration of the Parliament was appointed in November 1982. These five advisers covered the greater part of the Committee's remit: two advised on further and higher education (one of these had originally been appointed to advise on financial matters), one on school education, one on expenditure and local government matters, and one on arts matters. They came from a variety of professional educational backgrounds: registrar of the University of Warwick, deputy director of the Polytechnic of the South Bank, former director of the Schools Council Industry Project, research fellow at the North-East London Polytechnic, and lecturer in history at the University of Sussex. One of the advisers appointed for the duration of the Parliament partly filled the gap left by the appointment of one rather than two clerks until the 1982–83 session.

Of those appointed for specific inquiries, four were appointed for more than one inquiry and, counting these individuals more than once where appropriate, twenty-five advisers were appointed for eleven inquiries. Members of the Committee were united in the view that the provision and availability of specialist advisers was adequate. The advisers played some part in advising on the choice of witnesses, but, according to the chairman, this was not a very important role. Of much greater importance and value was their advice in preparing for committee hearings and in offering assistance in pursuing a particular line of questioning *during* sittings.

THE COMMITTEE AT WORK

The Education Committee's regular day of meeting was Wednesday, but it frequently met more than once a week. Apart from the shortened 1982–83 session, the Committee met for approximately the same number of sittings in each session: forty-five in 1979–80, forty-four in 1980–81, fifty-one in 1981–82, and twenty-six in 1982–83. With the exception of the 1979–80 session, a majority of the Committee's sittings in each session were evidence-taking rather than deliberative. The balance varied noticeably from one session to another, however, with a considerably higher proportion of evidence-taking sittings in the 1980–81 and 1982–83 sessions. The larger number of deliberative sessions in the 1979–80 and 1981–82 sessions is mainly attributable to a combination of the larger number of reports presented and divisions within the Committee over some of those reports.

The Committee made considerable use of its power to travel, both within the United Kingdom and abroad. However, with the use of *de facto* sub-committees the Committee members adopted a self-denying ordinance in that they did not go on visits related to inquiries in which they were not involved. Although the Committee did not hold a large number of formal evidence-taking sittings in other parts of the country—fourteen such sittings were held—it paid informal visits to different parts of the United Kingdom on more than twenty occasions. In fact, no evidence-taking sittings were held outside Westminster until the 1981–82 session, when sittings were held in Stirling and Birmingham on university funding, in Edinburgh on the funding of the arts, and in Belfast on further and higher education in Northern Ireland. In 1982–83, sittings were held in Middlesborough, Winchester and Richmond-upon-Thames on the education and training of sixteen- to nineteen-year-olds.

One unusual use of the power to travel, which required the specific permission of the House of Commons Commission, was the holding of a weekend meeting at Cumberland Lodge, Windsor, to discuss the evidence the Committee had received in its inquiry into higher education prior to the presentation of the chairman's draft report. The House of Commons Commission subsequently refused to grant permission for further deliberative sessions to be held outside the precincts of the Palace of Westminster, a decision deplored by the Chairman.[5] On a later occasion, however, the Committee paid an informal visit to the arts centre at the University of Warwick and used the occasion to discuss its report on the arts.

For a committee whose remit was entirely domestic, the Education Committee travelled extensively abroad. Five overseas visits were made. In two cases they were used to gather information on more than one subject of inquiry. In May 1980 the Committee visited Brussels and Luxembourg as part of its inquiry into information technology; in June 1980 the Committee went to Washington DC, Albany, and New York for its information technology and higher education inquiries; in March 1981 it visited Denmark, Bonn, and Rome in connection with the secondary school curriculum and funding of the arts inquiries; in May and June 1981 it visited Washington and New York for a second time, and Houston to gather information on arts funding; and in March 1983 the Committee went to France in connection with its sixteen- to nineteen-year-olds inquiry and a possible follow-up to the arts inquiry of the previous year.

The mean attendance of Committee members over the four parliamentary sessions was 71.4 per cent, including the chairman, and 69.2 per cent, excluding the chairman. However, attendance was highest in the 1979–80 session, when the mean figure was 79.3 per cent, and tended to decline in subsequent sessions, falling to 63.3 per cent in 1982–83.[6] In the 1979–80 session, attendance by Conservative and Labour members was virtually identical; but in the following session, Conservative attendance was markedly higher, even if the Labour chairman is included (73.6 per cent against 56.8 per cent, including the chairman). In the last two sessions of the Parliament, however, this position was reversed and Labour attendance, regardless of whether the chairman was included, was much higher (89.9 per cent Labour, *excluding* the chairman against 68.1 per cent Conservative in 1981–82 and 75.0 per cent Labour, *excluding* the chairman against 56.9 per cent). However, Conservative attendance in the 1982–83 session was affected by the absence through illness for several months of Patrick Cormack, one of the Committee's most active members. Similarly, there is no doubt that Labour attendance in the 1980–81 session was much affected by the increasing conflict felt by Stan Thorne (Lab.) between his committee work and other demands on his parliamentary time—a conflict which eventually led to his resignation from the Committee at the beginning of the 1981–82 session. In 1979–80 Thorne had been one of the Committee's most regular attenders. Conversely, the Labour figures in 1981–82 and 1982–83 reflected the assiduous attendance of Martin Flannery, who became a very active member of the Committee.

Attendance in general was significantly affected by the Committee's use of *de facto* sub-committees and by the interests of particular members of the Committee. The use of such sub-committees was quite open, as witnessed by a comment by the chairman in opening a sitting:

... nearly all sessions of this [funding of the] arts inquiry have been chaired by my colleague Mr Patrick Cormack of the unofficial Sub-Committee (we are not allowed to have Sub-Committees), but I felt it was such an important session that I had to keep abreast with what is happening and if I was here I should take the chair, but you may find that Mr Cormack asks rather more questions than I do.[7]

The use of sub-committees was similarly acknowledged by the chairman in his report to the Liaison Committee.[8] The use of sub-committees and the different interests of members tended to affect the attendance of Conservative more than Labour members, no doubt largely because with five members the Conservatives could afford to be more flexible, whereas Labour, apart from the chairman, had only two rather than the normal three members. Thus amongst the Conservatives, Patrick Cormack and Tim Brinton showed a particular interest in arts matters and John Osborn and David Madel in scientific matters. The Labour side was not entirely unaffected and, as illustrated above, Christopher Price was quite happy to allow *de facto* sub-committees to be chaired by other members of the Committee—a role fulfilled at various times by Patrick Cormack, John Osborn, and David Madel, while John McWilliam (Lab.) also showed a particular interest in scientific matters.

The lowest attendance record was that of Dafydd Thomas (PC), but it should be borne in mind that, as one of only two Plaid Members, the demands on his time were considerable and, though selective in his attendance, Thomas was an active member of the Committee in the questioning of witnesses and the discussion of reports.

On average, members of the Committee estimated that they spent thirteen hours a week, including Committee meetings, during the parliamentary session. However, the range of estimates was considerable: one member said it was between four and six hours, another as many as thirty in some weeks. This too was affected by the use of sub-committees: whilst leading the arts funding inquiry, Patrick Cormack spent an estimated twenty hours per week on the Committee's work. The chairman estimated that he spent on average thirty hours per week, and in some weeks as much of 40 per cent of his time on the Committee's work.

Although levels of participation as measured by the questioning of witnesses varied between members of the Committee, with the important exception of the chairman, it was not the case that a small group of members dominated questioning (see Table 1). Clearly, even excluding sittings at which he was chairman, Patrick Cormack was a very active member of the Committee. Similarly, Harry Greenway in three of the four sessions and Martin Flannery in the two sessions when he was a member of the Committee, were also very active. Two other committee members, Tim Brinton and Dafydd Thomas, were particularly active in the 1980–81 session. In general, the levels of participation were noticeably consistent over the four sessions and this

Table 5.1 *The Questioning of Witnesses*[1] *in Evidence-Taking Sections of the Education, Science and Arts Committee, 1979–83*

Member	Session and percentage of questions asked			
	1979–80	1980–81	1981–82	1982–83
Christopher Price (Lab.) (Chairman)	39.6[2]	38.2[4]	44.2[8]	50.9[10]
Tim Brinton (Con.)	5.2	13.8	6.1	5.4
Patrick Cormack (Con.)	15.2	9.3[5]	13.1[9]	6.7[11]
Martin Flannery (Lab.)	Nm	Nm	8.1	11.7
Harry Greenway (Cons.)	9.9	12.1	6.0	10.4
David Madel (Cons.)	7.4	6.5[6]	6.4	6.9
John McWilliam (Lab.)	7.5	3.8	6.6	1.4
John Osborn (Cons.)	5.5[3]	4.9[7]	4.8	3.2
Dafydd Thomas (PC)	6.0	9.7	4.7	3.3
Stan Thorne (Lab.)	3.7	1.6	Nm	Nm
Totals	100.0	99.9	100.0	99.9

Nm: not a member of the Committee.

Notes:

[1] The figures shown in the table *exclude* incidental remarks made by the chairman (and other members of the Committee), such as those welcoming witnesses or minor clarifications of questions asked or asides which have no bearing on the evidence being heard. However, they *include* substantive statements made by members of the Committee during the hearing of evidence.

[2] Including three sittings when Osborn was chairman. It should be noted that Price did not attend sittings when another member of the Committee was in the chair.

[3] Excluding three sittings when he was chairman.

[4] Including nine sittings when Cormack was chairman, one sitting when Madel was chairman, and one sitting when Osborn was chairman.

[5] Excluding nine sittings when he was chairman.

[6] Excluding one sitting when he was chairman.

[7] Excluding one sitting when he was chairman.

[8] Including three sittings when Cormack was chairman.

[9] Excluding three sittings when he was chairman.

[10] Including one sitting when Cormack was chairman.

[11] Excluding one sitting when he was chairman.

may also reflect the use of sub-committees, which, with fewer members present, allowed greater participation by those attending.

In the first two sessions, the level of participation by Conservative members was above the expected norm as measured by the proportion of Conservative members on the Committee (71.6 and 75.6 per cent against a norm of 62.5 per cent). Conversely, Labour participation, excluding the chairman, was well below average, especially in the second of the two sessions (18.4 and 8.6 per cent against a norm of 25.0 per cent). In the other two sessions, however, Conservative participation was only a little above the norm, and Labour participation almost exactly corresponded to it. In three of the four sessions, Dafydd Thomas's participation was below the expected norm, but, as with attendance, the additional demands made upon minority party Members have to be borne in mind.

Ministers were questioned by the Committee on twenty-four occasions, at nine of which questioning by Labour members (excluding the Chairman) was above the norm, and at twelve of which questioning by Labour and Plaid members combined was above the norm. Similarly, oral evidence was given by civil servants on nine occasions, with Labour questioning above the norm four times, but in no case did the combined opposition questioning exceed the norm.

Oral evidence was presented to the Committee by nearly 700 individuals, most of whom represented government departments or other organizations. Apart from appearances with ministers, officials from no less than eleven Whitehall departments and one Northern Ireland department gave evidence to the Education Committee between 1979 and 1983. Obviously, civil servants from the DES made the largest number of appearances—eighteen in all—and HMIs appeared before the Committee on ten occasions. Civil servants from the Office of Arts and Libraries gave evidence three times, and other departments which gave evidence were the Department of Industry, the Home Office, the Treasury, the Department of Energy, the Department of Employment, the Lord Chancellor's Department, the Department of Health and Social Security, the Inland Revenue, and the Foreign and Commonwealth Office. Evidence was also heard from the Cabinet Office and the Central Policy Review Staff.

Inevitably, the Secretary of State for Education and Science appeared before the Committee more frequently than any other minister, with thirteen appearances. In addition, Ministers of State at the DES appeared twice and Parliamentary Under Secretaries nine times, while the Minister for the Arts made three appearances. Ministers from the Treasury, the Department of Industry (including the Secretary of State), and the Northern Ireland Office (again including the Secretary of State) also gave evidence.

Professional bodies, including a number of quangos, and pressure groups were the most common presenters of evidence by outside organizations, and the range and variety of such bodies was considerable. Professional bodies and quangos included the Committee of Vice-Chancellors and Principals (CVCP), the University Grants Committee (UGC), the Arts Council, the Standing Conference on Museums and Galleries, the Secondary Heads Association, the Association of Teachers of Mathematics, the Equal Opportunities Commission, the Schools Council, the Commission for Racial Equality, the Biochemical Society, representatives of the BBC, ITV, the British Museum, and the National and Tate Galleries—to name but a few. Pressure groups included Heritage in Danger, the National Secular Society, the British Humanist Association, the National Confederation of Parent-Teacher Associations, and the Campaign for the Advancement of State Education. Evidence was also presented by the TUC, twelve trade unions, several local authority associations, and a number of individual local authorities—over 130 organizations in all.

This oral evidence was, in most cases, supplemented by written evidence, and many other organizations and individuals submitted memoranda, but did not give oral evidence. Altogether the Committee received more than 750 memoranda.

Unusually, at one sitting the Education Committee heard evidence in private. Normally, of course, all evidence-taking sessions of the Committee were open to the public, but in hearing evidence from the CVCP and the UGC on university funding on 23 July 1981 the Committee decided to exclude the public. The evidence, however, was subsequently published in full.

Clearly the Committee ranged very widely in receiving evidence and, although this is in part a reflection of its remit, it is due far more to the wide range of topics it chose to investigate and to its desire to encourage as many groups and individuals as possible to submit evidence. However, the Committee did have difficulty on two occasions in securing the information it sought. The first of these concerned a refusal by ministers at the DES, including the Secretary of State, to provide the Committee with information about consultations within the Government that had led to the decision to increase overseas students' fees. Indeed, the Committee felt sufficiently strongly about the matter to issue a special report to the House drawing its attention to the problem.[9] The second occasion was when Miss S.J. Browne, the Senior Chief Inspector of Schools, backed by the Secretary of State, refused to identify LEAs named in an internal report prepared by her. In both cases the Committee eventually secured the information it required, but not until after it had overcome a good deal of ministerial resistance. Moreover, in giving evidence to the Committee on 11 November 1981, the Secretary of State, Sir Keith Joseph, made it clear that communications between the minister and his advisers 'should, in my view, remain private', and that in this context advisers included not only civil servants, but the chairman of the UGC.[10]

The Education Committee published nineteen substantive reports during the 1979–83 Parliament and, had the final session been completed, two more reports would have been published. Of these nineteen reports, three—those on the funding and organization of higher education, on the secondary school curriculum, and on the funding of the arts—were major reports and, had it been completed, the report on education and training for sixteen- to nineteen-year-olds would also have been a major report. In addition, the Committee undertook a number of subsidiary inquiries, usually conducted by *de facto* sub-committees, and these accounted for a further three reports. The remaining thirteen reports fell into two categories—interim reports arising out of other inquiries and reports on matters of topical interest or concern, although some of the interim reports also related to matters of immediate concern. Seven interim reports were spawned by other inquiries. The funding of higher education, for example, produced a report on overseas students' fees, while a report on the proposed merger between the New University of Ulster and the Ulster Polytechnic arose out of the inquiry into further and higher education in Northern Ireland, but no less than three interim reports were presented in the course of the inquiry into the funding of the arts, one on the retention of works of art in the United Kingdom, one on the impact on the arts of VAT and one on the preservation of archive film. Equally important numerically were reports on topical issues, such as expenditure cuts in higher education, the construction of a new British Library building, the future of the Promenade Concerts, and the protection of the research base in biotechnology. In addition, on two occasions the Committee issued reports without taking specific evidence: one on the International Centre for the Preservation and Restoration of Cultural Property in Rome and the other on school meals.

The Committee's specialist advisers tended to play an important role in the drafting of reports, but their role and that of the clerks and the chairman varied from one inquiry to another. In some cases the role of the clerks was greater than others, and the chairman often played an important part in informal drafting sessions, along with individual members of the Committee involved in the particular inquiry.

There were, however, a number of inquiries conducted by the Committee which did not result in reports. Apart from the two inquiries terminated by the dissolution, this was quite deliberate. They included annual scrutiny meetings at which the Secretary of State and other ministers and their officials answered questions on a wide variety of matters, and the annual expenditure session which started in 1980–81. However, the Committee also used similar sessions to gather evidence on topics such as science policy and university funding as a means of providing information for public discussion, without producing a report.

Table 5.2 *Divisions on draft reports of the Education, Science and Arts Committee, 1979–83*

Session	Party divisions		Cross-party divisions		Total		Number of reports
	n	%	n	%	n	%	
1979–80	38	97.4	1	2.6	39	100.0	2
1980–81	—	—	—	—	—	—	—
1981–82	21	44.7	26	55.3	47	100.0	3
1982–83	28	100.0	—	—	28	100.0	1
Totals	87	76.7	27	23.7	114	100.0	6

It would be misleading to say that party conflicts over the Committee's reports were unimportant, but the extent of party conflict needs to be put in perspective. Although three-quarters of the divisions on draft reports were on straight party lines,[11] these divisions occurred on only six of the Committee's nineteen reports. Furthermore, two-thirds of the divisions were on two reports and 92 per cent on just three—the funding and organization of higher education, the secondary school curriculum, and prison education. Out of a total of 1,358 paragraphs, 323 were amended without a division, compared to nine amended on a division, and a further forty-eight amendments and twenty new paragraphs rejected on a division. Of the forty-five divisions on the secondary school curriculum report, more than half were cross-party rather than straight party divisions. As one member of the Committee put it: party divisions were 'relatively unimportant'.

In fact, members of the Committee were evenly divided on whether party conflicts on the Committee were important in its operation, ranging from 'not important' (Conservative) and 'not very important' (Labour), through 'substantial, but compromises were reached' (Conservative), to 'very important' (Labour). Another Conservative said:

'We worked well together but agreed to keep off the most controversial subjects' and one of his Labour colleagues remarked that the chairman 'sought to minimize conflicts'. The available evidence would suggest that party conflicts played an important role over particular issues, but were far from being a constant feature of the Committee's operation. The questioning of ministers by Labour members of the Committee, including the Chairman, was occasionally brusque, but Conservative members could be just as sharp with ministers and party differences were often unapparent.

THE IMPACT OF THE COMMITTEE

The difficulties of measuring the impact of select committees on government policy are well known. An analysis of the Government's responses to the Education Committee's recommendations shows that, although fewer than a third were accepted, only a similar proportion were rejected, leaving the largest proportion in the somewhat uncertain status of being kept under review. While this latter category may

Table 5.3 *Government responses to recommendations made in reports from the Education, Science and Arts Committee, 1979–83*

Response	n	%
Accepted	48	26.5
Keep under review	84	46.4
Rejected	49	27.1
Totals	181	100.0

Note:
At the time of writing two reports were awaiting a Government response.

in some cases be a euphemism for rejection, in many others it was an appropriate response from the Government, if only because it was precisely what the Committee itself recommended. In any case, education is a service, much of which is provided, not by the DES, but by semi-autonomous agencies. Clearly such recommendations and responses need subsequent monitoring, and this is an area which the Education Committee had hardly begun to develop. The Committee did examine the question of university funding in each of the four sessions, but this owed more to the continued importance (albeit to a narrow audience) of the subject than to any systematic monitoring or following-up process. Of course, it can be argued that the following up of committee recommendations is a task which should grow in importance as the new select committees enter the second Parliament of their life, but it was a process which could have been profitably developed towards the end of their first Parliament.

Tracing the fate of recommendations is no doubt the most important measure of the impact of the Committee, but it should be remembered that some of its recommendations were not directed at the Government but at other bodies, such as local authorities, quangos, and, indeed, private or non-governmental organizations. In fact, some of the Education Committee's reports had nothing to do with the Government at all: for example, in its inquiries into the future of the Proms and of *The Times* Supplements, the Committee simply felt that it could contribute to the solution of the problems involved by taking evidence in public.

It can also be argued that the Education Committee played a role in the wider policy process by making information publicly available through its hearing of oral evidence and the publication of much written evidence, evidence which, in many cases, would not otherwise have been available or would be more difficult to obtain. Furthermore, the interest shown in the Committee by professional organizations and pressure groups was considerable, and the Committee provided them with an additional means of making their views known. The specialist media also took an interest in the Committee's activities and reports, and the Committee chairman in particular worked hard to cultivate media interest in the Committee's work.

What specific impact, however, can the Committee claim to have had? Establishing causal links is a hazardous process, but Christopher Price did make four specific claims:

... our British Library report was immediately followed by a government decision to build it, our higher education report led to the establishment of a National Advisory Board in the public sector, our 'Proms' report restored the concerts to the Albert Hall and our ICCROM[12] report re-established the British subscription to that organization.[13]

Other members of the Committee were evenly divided on whether the Committee had had a significant impact on the Government. Both they and the chairman were more concerned with claiming that the Committee had played a part in opening up the policy process, if only to a limited extent. Ministers, it was claimed, had been better prepared in giving evidence than had been the case in earlier Parliaments. The Committee had, most of them thought, a significant impact outside Parliament, but mainly with those interested in or concerned about the issues the Committee had investigated. The Committee had established a foundation on which to build. Whether these were the inevitable views of optimists, time alone will tell.

CONCLUSION

The Education Committee was one of the most active of the select committees. A major reason for this was its practice of using *de facto* sub-committees, a practice which also enabled the Committee to cover a wide range of topics and to react flexibly to issues as they arose without unduly increasing the burden on its members. It did not entirely avoid controversial matters and with them the attendant risks of party conflict, but party conflict was allowed to take its course, and there was a significant degree of cross-party sympathy and co-operation. The role of Christopher Price as chairman was extremely important: it was clearly his main parliamentary task, and he brought to it a strong interest in education and a determination that, if at all possible, the Committee would succeed. Members of the Committee were united in seeing the Committee as a major means of monitoring government policy, and of keeping Parliament and the public informed about government policy and actions, but they were divided about the extent to which the Committee should become more deeply and systematically involved in the development of policy. One member, a Conservative, wanted to see the select committees replace standing committees in dealing with legislation, not merely at the committee stage but with the introduction of pre-legislative hearings on all Bills. In fact, Christopher Price did chair the evidence-taking sessions of the Special Standing Committee on the Education (Special Provisions) Bill in 1981, but only one other member of the Education Committee, Harry Greenway (Cons.) was also a member of the Special Standing Committee. There were also divided views on whether the Committee should be seen as a channel for pressure or interest groups. One thing was clear, however: most thought the Education Committee a success and wished to see it continue its work in the new Parliament.

NOTES

1. A useful interim study of the Committee can be found in Nigel Nixon, *The Reformed Select Committee Structure, with particular reference to the workings of the Education, Science and Arts Committee and the part played by specialist advisers*, Institute of Education, University of London, June 1982.
2. *1982–83 Liaison Committee Report*, p. 50.
3. In fact, one of the Committee's subjects of inquiry, Prison Education, is the responsibility of the Home Office and not the DES.
4. *1982–83 Liaison Committee Report*, p. 49.
5. *Ibid.*, p. 48.
6. The median figures are very similar, with an overall median of 69.0 per cent and a range from 80.0 per cent in 1979–80 to 65.4 per cent in 1982–83.

7. *Education, Science and Arts Committee, Minutes of Evidence*, HC 106, 1980–81, 13 May 1981, q. 764.
8. *1982–83 Liaison Committee Report*, p. 47.
9. *Education, Science and Arts Committee, First Special Report: The Provision of Information by Government Departments to Select Committees*, HC 606, 1979–80.
10. *Education, Science and Arts Committee, Minutes of Evidence*, HC 24, 1981–82, 11 November 1981, qq. 2–5.
11. Dafydd Thomas (PC) normally voted with the Labour members of the Committee in such divisions.
12. International Centre for the Preservation and Restoration of Cultural Property, Rome.
13. *1982–83 Liaison Committee Report*, p. 48.

Annex 5.1 *Education, Science and Arts Committee*

Report	Date of first oral evidence/(no. of evidence sessions)	Date of publication of report	Date and form of govt. reply	Length of report (pages)	No. of oral qq./no. of published written submissions[g]	No. of divisions
Session 1979–80						
1st *Overseas students' fees* (HC 552 & 663)	16.1.80(8)	April 1980	Cmnd. 8011, Aug. 1980	29	816/15	7
2nd *The British Library Building* (HC 607)	6.2.80(3)	June 1980	Cmnd. 8237, Apr. 1981	2	Under 4th report	0
3rd *Future of the Promenade Concerts* (HC 722)	17.7.80(1)	August 1980	Not applicable	5	69/–	0
4th *Information storage and retrieval* (HC 767)	6.2.80(4)	October 1980	Cmnd. 8237, Apr. 1981	21	262/29[ab]	0
5th *Funding and organization of courses in higher education* (HC 787)	16.1.80(6)	October 1980	Cmnd. 8139, Jan. 1981	55	487/79[a]	32
1st *Special Report: the provision of information to select committees* (HC 606)	—	January 1980	Cmnd. 7912, Jul. 1980	2	—	0
Session 1980–81						
1st *The future of* The Times *Supplements* (HC 152)	11.2.81(1)	April 1981	Not applicable	8	72/2	0

Report						
2nd International Centre for the Preservation and Restoration of Cultural Property: Rome (HC 274)	No oral evidence	April 1981	Letter 26.11.81	4	—	0
3rd The retention of works of art in Britain and their acquisition by public bodies (HC 106 and 275)[c]	19.1.81(2)	May 1981	Cmnd. 8538, Apr. 1982	9	208/7	0
Session 1981–82						
1st Expenditure cuts in higher education: the effects on the 'Robbins' principle and on the universities (HC 82)	No oral evidence	December 1981	Letter 1.2.82	6	—	1
2nd The secondary school curriculum and examinations: with special reference to 14–16 year olds (HC 116)	21.1.81(17)	February 1982	Cmnd. 8551, May 1982 & Cmnd. 8648, Sep. 1982	111	1,654/76(49)	45
3rd VAT and the arts[c] (HC 239)	4.3.81(8)	March 1982	Letter 29.6.82	4	See 8th Report, 1981–82	0

Annex 5.1 *Education, Science and Arts Committee* (cont.)

Report	Date of first oral evidence/(no. of evidence sessions)	Date of publication of report	Date and form of govt. reply	Length of report (pages)	No. of oral qq./no. of published written submissions[g]	No. of divisions
4th *The nitrate problem at the National Film Archive* (HC 240)	18.2.81(1)	March 1982	Letter 23.7.82	5	See 8th Report, 1981–82	0
5th *The future of the Theatre Museum* (HC 472)	14.7.82(1)	August 1982	Letter 11.8.82	9	107/2	0
6th *Interim report on the protection of the research base in biotechnology* (HC 289)	24.3.82(7)	July 1982	1st Spec. Report. (HC 208, 1982–83.) Feb. 1983	40	470/30[a]	0
7th *School meals* (HC 480)	19.7.82[d]	September 1982	Cmnd. 8740, Nov. 1982	10	11/4	1
8th *Public and private funding of the arts: main report* (HC 49)	19.1.81(9)	October 1982	Cmnd. 9127, Jan. 1984	129	2,049/125(83)[e]	0
9th *Further and higher education in Northern Ireland: interim report* (HC 557)	25.10.82(4)	November 1982	See 2nd Report 1982–83	4	See 2nd Report, 1982–83	0
Session 1982–83 1st *Prison education* (HC 45)	15.11.82(4)	April 1982	Cmnd. 9126, Jan. 1984	50	428/53(11)	28

		June 1983	4.7.84 Cmnd. 9278	68		o
2nd *Further and higher education in Northern Ireland: main report* (HC 180)	2.2.83(1)	—	—	68	524/39^f	0
Incomplete inquiries, 1982–83 *Public records* (HC 81)	29.11.82(5)	—	—	—	503/41	—
The education and training of 16–19 year olds	20.12.82(5.5)	—	—	—	762/29	—
Other proceedings *1979–80* Scrutiny session (HC 786)	23.7.80(1)	—	—	—	118/2	—
1980–81 Public expenditure on education (HC 87)	17.12.80(1)	—	—	—	117/9	—
Scrutiny session I (HC 120)	28.1.81(1)	—	—	—	102/6	—
Scrutiny session II (HC 411)	6.7.81(1)	—	—	—	114/4	—
University funding (HC 449)	23.7.81(1)	—	—	—	155/4	—
Science policy (HC 254)	25.3.81(1)	—	—	—	96/2	—

Annex 5.1 *Education, Science and Arts Committee (cont.)*

Report	Date of first oral evidence/(no. of evidence sessions)	Date of publication of report	Date and form of govt. reply	Length of report (pages)	No. of oral qq-/no. of published written submissions[g]	No. of divisions
1981–82						
University funding and the Government's reply to the 5th Report of 1979–80 (HC 24)	11.11.81(1)	—	—	—	138/5	—
Science policy (HC 58)	25.11.81(2)	—	—	—	180/3	—
Information technology (HC 107)	14.12.81(1)	—	—	—	83/-	—
Scrutiny session I (HC 328)	19.4.82(1)	—	—	—	110/4	—
Scrutiny session II (HC 480)	19.7.82(1)	—	—	—	169/12	—
Public expenditure on education (HC 190)	10.2.82(2)	—	—	—	311/9(14)	—
University funding (HC 274)	29.3.82(3)	—	—	—	368/16[a]	—

1982-83

Public expenditure on education (HC 116)	13.12.82(1)	—	—	142/8	—
Scrutiny session (HC 194)	9.2.83(1)	—	—	160/5	—
Arts scrutiny session (HC 158)	19.1.83(1)	—	—	110/2	—
The funding of higher education (HC 293)	28.3.83(1)	—	—	129/19	—

Notes:

a   Plus an unspecified number of written submissions not published.
b   Including evidence on the British Library Building (2nd Report).
c   Interim report on the public and private funding of the arts.
d   Evidence heard during the 2nd Scrutiny Sessions, 19 July 1982 (HC 480).
e   Including evidence on VAT and the arts (2nd Report) and the nitrate problem at the National Film Archive (4th Report).
f   Including evidence heard in the 1981–82 session.
g   The numbers of unpublished submissions, where known, are given in brackets.

CHAPTER 6

The Employment Committee 1979-83
Nevil Johnson

REMIT AND MEMBERSHIP

Ostensibly the Select Committee on Employment has a very wide remit: it is concerned with all aspects of employment in the British economy. But in the four years after November 1979 when the Committee was set up, it was not so much employment and its attendant problems which claimed a major part of the Committee's attention as unemployment and all its effects. Unemployment as an economic, social, and political problem provided the context within which the Committee pursued its inquiries and sought to establish some definition of its purposes and principal interests. Yet though a rising level of unemployment might have been expected to broaden still further what appeared already to be a wide remit, in practice it is questionable whether this happened. As will be indicated later in rather more detail, what looked like very far-reaching terms of reference were interpreted in a strictly practical way, with the main emphasis on the work of the Department of Employment itself and of the agencies dependent on it. Consequently, the Committee did not generally tackle broader issues of economic policy which may have a bearing on unemployment. Instead it tended to work outwards from the responsibilities, policies and initiatives of those parts of government which it was asked to oversee.

The Employment Committee had a membership of nine and no power to appoint sub-committees. Of the nine members initially appointed, five were Conservative and four Labour. All but one were back-benchers who had not held ministerial office; several on the Conservative side had business interests and management experience, and on the Labour side there were some close links with the trade unions. By the end of the 1979-83 Parliament there had been six departures, four on the Labour side and two on the Conservative.

This meant that only one of the original Labour members remained (Mr Jim Craigen, who became the Committee's second chairman at the end of 1982), whilst on the Conservative side there was substantially more continuity with three founding members remaining. An important change in December 1982 was the resignation from the chairmanship of Mr John Golding (Lab.) who had held that position since the Committee started. His successor, Mr Jim Craigen, had also sat on the Committee from the beginning, but his tenure of the chairmanship turned out to be too short to provide any clear indication of a change of style and method. It was, therefore, Mr Golding's tenure of the chairmanship which contributed decisively to the manner in which the Committee developed. He had previously been a junior minister in the Department of Employment, had strong trade union connections, and during the last Parliament was a member of the National Executive Committee of the Labour Party. He thus brought to the chairmanship familiarity with the field covered by the Committee as well as wide-ranging political experience.

As chairman, Mr Golding recognized from the start that it was going to be difficult to hold the Committee together and do useful work if its members were constantly caught up in the party political controversy so easily generated by many of the issues within its remit, most notably unemployment and the Government's trade union legislation. His response to this challenge was two-pronged. First, he consistently stressed the improvement of accountability as the main objective of the Committee (and indeed of select committees generally), a view which he reiterated in his contribution to the Liaison Committee's 1982-83 report on the *Select Committee System*. As he wrote there: 'The new system has improved the accountability of Department of Employment Ministers to Parliament ... In the Select Committee ... we can question Ministers in depth for sessions of an hour-and-a-half or so on any aspect of their responsibility, and this puts more pressure on them'.[1] By taking this view of the role of the Committee, he was firmly within a well-established parliamentary tradition which appealed to both Labour and Conservative Members. Furthermore, he was proposing a role which was realistic and for the most part acceptable to the ministers and officials being called to account. Secondly, he did not encourage the Committee to pronounce at length on complex and usually contentious policy issues, because in his view this was bound to exacerbate differences.[2] Instead he steered the Committee towards topics on which they could reach agreed conclusions and in particular preferred to see the process of inquiry itself as the main instrument for asserting accountability. It is for this reason that many of the reports issued by the Committee are slender documents, sometimes being little more than short comments on the inquiry itself. For, when the topic was inherently controversial, it was precisely this kind of report that could secure all-party support in the Committee. As a consequence of this approach, deliberative proceedings were characterized by a total absence of amendments pressed to a division. Admittedly a price had to be paid for this stress on enforcing the accountability of Ministers and officials at the expense of Committee pronouncements on substantive issues of policy: sometimes differences of opinion within the Committee had to be acknowledged openly in the shape of remarks to the effect that some members thought one thing, others another. Inevitably reporting in this style runs the risk of having little direct impact on a department. But this kind of outcome may still be justified if it has been preceded by a serious dialogue between the Committee and representatives of the executive.

SCOPE OF THE COMMITTEE'S INQUIRIES

Before examining more fully the style and character of the Employment Committee, it is desirable to outline what it actually did in the first four years of its life. Initially it got off to a rather slow start and did not find it easy to determine topics for inquiry. However, during its first session (1979-80) it did point the way to what were to become continuing themes. Apart from familiarizing members with the organizations within their remit through a general survey of the work of the Department of Employment Group, the Committee decided to examine the Manpower Services Commission's Corporate Plan for 1980-84 and began work on the legal immunities of trade unions and other related matters. The examination of the MSC's Corporate Plan became a regular annual feature of the Committee's inquiries and undoubtedly helped to build up a close working relationship between senior officials of the MSC and the Committee. At the beginning, the MSC was reluctant to provide the Committee with a copy of its Corporate Plan before this had been submitted to and approved by the Secretary of State. But the MSC and the Minister soon bowed to pressure exerted by the chairman of the Committee and agreed to furnish the Corporate Plan in draft form, a step which not only made it easier for the Committee to come to grips with these matters, but also enabled it to do so earlier in the annual cycle of corporate planning.

In examining successive Corporate Plans the Committee was engaged chiefly in a form of monitoring: its concern was not to challenge the whole basis of MSC policy but to find out what was being done, what was planned, and how resources were being distributed. Naturally, in the course of such monitoring Committee members did not fail to press those aspects of MSC's programmes nearest to their own concerns, and the Committee was throughout keenly interested in both the scale and the effectiveness of MSC's various schemes for the relief of unemployment and the provision of industrial training for the young unemployed. Whilst the Committee showed interest in the distribution of MSC expenditure, it would be an exaggeration to suggest that it invested a lot of effort in detailed financial scrutiny: the magnitude of the unemployment problem was such as always to suggest that MSC needed more rather than less resources.

The topic of trade union law was prompted by government proposals in 1980 for new measures to regulate such matters as the closed shop and picketing. In the first session the Committee did no more than report comments on the draft codes of practice on picketing and on the closed shop, and it continued its work into the 1980-81 session when it then reported[3] on the Green Paper on trade union immunities, but in terms of what the minority thought and what the majority concluded. In so doing it recognized that there were strong divisions of opinion within the Committee and that no agreed substantive recommendations were possible. Conservative members supported the Government's proposals to restrict certain immunities hitherto enjoyed by trade unions, and some indeed were critical of Mr Prior (then Secretary of State for Employment) for proceeding too cautiously. On the other side the Labour members gave full support to the trade unions and were anxious to use the evidence-taking sessions as opportunities for underlining what they regarded as the shortcomings and objectionable features of the Government's proposals.

The Committee did not again report on trade union law, but it continued to come back to the subject whenever further action was contemplated or taken by the Government. Its approach then was usually to take evidence and simply to leave that on the public record. A good example of such a reaction occurred in early 1983 after Mr Tebbit, who had succeeded Mr Prior as Secretary of State for Employment in 1981, had published a Green Paper on further measures to regulate the affairs of trade unions. The Committee asked him to give evidence within the framework of hearings on the work of the Department of Employment group, which he did on two occasions. Apart from demonstrating the Committee's continuing concern with industrial relations legislation, such hearings also highlighted the Committee's awareness of the publicity it could gain by responding quickly to ministerial initiatives, though it has to be noted that Mr Tebbit too was by no means unaware of the benefits he also could gain by engaging in a dialogue with the Committee. For a minister as shrewd and self-confident as Mr Tebbit, the exaction of parliamentary accountability was a price well worth paying for the opportunities it offered him to present his case.

Apart from the two continuing interests just referred to, the Committee was anxious to identify topics and problems in the employment field which it could examine in some depth. This was not always a straightforward matter, chiefly on account of inernal party political division of opinion, and on more than one occasion the Committee began to look at a subject only to find that it did not seem worth pursuing or was likely to provoke serious argument. The Committee reported on *Homeworking* in 1982[4] after a slow start, and during the final session of the 1979–83 Parliament it was working on two aspects of industrial safety (asbestos and scaffolding) and had begun to look at the effects of government plans for privatization on employment levels. It did manage to report in 1982 on *The Working of the Health and Safety Commission and Executive: Achievements since the Robens Report*,[5] though again the published evidence far outweighed the slender and benign report which accompanied it.

The difficulties experienced by the Committee in identifying suitable subjects for sustained inquiry reflected both its own preferences and the very real difficulty of finding such topics in the area of activity for which it was responsible. There was undoubtedly some reluctance to indulge in the royal commission type of inquiry, since to do so is time-consuming and would necessarily have diminished the Committee's scope for asserting the day-to-day accountability of the agencies concerned with employment problems and conditions. But it must also be recognized that in relation to employment, the labour market, the provision of jobs and training, the maintenance of proper working conditions, and so on, the position is always changing. Behind the particular organizations which the Committee was entitled to examine lies a complex network of activities, chiefly of private persons and organizations, related in all kinds of ways to the provision of employment and exposed all the time to the pressures of economic forces. Against this background it is understandable that the Committee should have laid most stress on discerning occasions when it was practicable for it to intervene, and often this meant reacting to some action taken or contemplated by one of the organizations under its wing. Thus it picked up in 1981 the MSC's review of the quota scheme for the employment of disabled people and reported on this;[6] in the same session it reported on a new training initiative directed to youth unemployment;[7] and also in the same session there was a report on the draft code of practice about to be issued by the Commission for Racial Equality.[8] The latter inquiry was something of a success since the Committee did persuade the Commission and the Minister to promise changes which would take account of the special needs of small firms and remove anxieties about the retention of information on the ethnic origins of employees. Moreover, the Committee's work brought to light the peculiar fact that the Minister had no power to amend draft regulations and codes of practice put to him by the CRE; the Government later agreed to take powers to remove this limitation.[9]

Looking at the record of four years of activity it must be acknowledged that the published output of the Committee was modest in scale and scope. Eleven reports came out, none of which exceeded six pages in length. On the other hand, several of these short reports did focus clearly and directly on specific questions and to these the Government had to respond. Eleven special reports appeared conveying the observations of the Secretary of State and of the organizations examined by the Committee. In addition, supporting evidence appeared, though this too was never voluminous. The report and evidence issued in July 1982 on the Health & Safety Commission and Executive, for example, ran to barely 140 pages in total, comprising nine memoranda, eight appendices and the record of four public hearings at which seventeen witnesses were present (only two of whom actually came from the Health & Safety Commission and Executive). So even in respect of the demand for evidence the Committee was relatively parsimonious. In addition, the Committee pubished evidence on matters on which it did not actually report, for example in 1982 on proposed industrial relations legislation, the abolition of industrial training boards, and employment creation.

PRINCIPAL THEMES IN THE COMMITTEE'S WORK

In so far as it is possible to ascribe some pattern to the Committee's inquiries, four themes can perhaps be detected, two of which run together and complement each other. There was first a persistent concern with the organizations in the Department of Employment's field, notably with the Manpower Services Commission which is the largest, employing about 24,000 people. This meant that the Committee called a lot of witnesses from the Department of Employment, from the MSC, the Health & Safety Commission, and from other official organizations concerned in various ways with employment conditions. Contact was probably closest with the MSC and a large amount of material relating to that body's methods, policies, and spending was published, including its annual Corporate Plans. This, then, can best be designated continuing administrative oversight. And in the case of the Employment Committee the emphasis was much more on how policies were being carried out than on detailed financial scrutiny. Expenditure was looked at, especially as set out in the Corporate Plans of the MSC. But this too was done chiefly in order to provide a basis for looking at activities rather than for the sake of checking narrowly on financial considerations and practices. In other words, the Committee had no desire to concentrate on the examination of estimates and expenditure: its main interest was in activities rather than money.

Secondly, there was the theme of problem analysis and problem-solving, that is to say the attempt to identify subjects of general importance which might usefully be opened up and investigated in some depth. On the whole, this was a muted theme for reasons already alluded to. The Committee found only a few topics of this kind which were sufficiently uncontroversial to allow its members to look at them thoroughly. A topic such as trade union immunities, which in principle might have been regarded as appropriate for sustained examination, was on political grounds quite unsuitable for this kind of treatment, both on account of divisions within the Committee and because the Government was constantly developing its own initiatives, and doing so with a firm intent to legislate.

Thirdly, there was a concern to respond to current problems and decisions, to make an effort both to call upon the Government to explain and defend its proposals and to insert the Committee's thinking into whatever considerations were moving the Government. Several examples of such action by the Committee have already been mentioned, each illustrating in different ways the manner in which the Committee tried to keep abreast of events and to respond both critically and constructively to action proposed. Sometimes such attempts to react to new developments took place within the framework of the Committee's investigation of its major agencies as, for example, its comments on the Youth Opportunities Programme in 1981 when it was examining more broadly the work of the MSC. Most of the attention paid to labour law and trade union immunities fell under this heading too: the Committee sought to respond as quickly as possible to avowed intentions on the part of the Government.

Finally, there was in a minor key the theme of review of legislation. It would not be correct to attribute to the Employment Committee a sustained policy of seeking to examine either existing law or legislative proposals likely to be put before Parliament. But it did happen that in responding to current developments and in trying to detect prospective policy changes, the Committee was several times drawn into a consideration either of legislative plans or of draft changes in regulations and administrative codes. Thus in trying to enhance the accountability of the public bodies within its ambit, the Committee at the same time indulged in a modest amount of pre-legislative scrutiny. It probably created at least the shadow of an expectation that it might in future be consulted about proposals likely to lead to legislation or the exercise of delegated powers.

METHODS OF OPERATION

Having considered the kind of inquiries conducted by the Committee, we can now return to the manner in which it carried out its task. Attendance at meetings in the first two years of the Committee's life was reasonably good (averaging about 70 per cent), though it later became rather more irregular on the part of some members. All the Committee members present at meetings usually took part in the questioning of witnesses, but the chairman maintained a firm grip on proceedings, showing himself capable of calling to order both members and witnesses who were creating difficulties for the Committee. There is some evidence that the main lines of questioning were usually agreed beforehand between the chairman and the senior Conservative member, Mr John Gorst, and indeed this way of preparing for evidence-taking sessions was referred to in Mr Golding's submission to the Liaison Committee.[10] The inability to set up a sub-committee did not turn out to be a serious handicap. In any event, when the Committee took up a subject of close interest to only a few of its members (homeworking), it proved possible to make progress through what was in effect a sub-committee of those members keen on the topic, though technically it operated as the full Committee.

Relations between Committee members and witnesses were generally friendly and co-operative, though in July 1982 there was some reluctance on the part of a civil service witness to answer questions which appeared to go beyond the limits laid down in the Memorandum of Guidance to officials on how to handle requests from select committees. The appearance of trade unionists was not always a success and the Committee had a stormy time with Mr Scargill from the National Union of Mineworkers in 1980. It is also possible to detect certain traces of impatience in the Committee's exchanges with representatives of the Commission for Racial Equality. But for the most part, the Committee had no difficulties in securing the evidence—written and oral—that it required, its relations with the MSC were good, and, despite sharp differences of opinion on matters of policy on the part of the minority party in the Committee, it was able to establish amicable relations with successive Ministers.

The Committee did not confine its attentions to witnesses based in London, whether officials or the representatives of important pressure groups and organized interests. It took evidence from numerous private individuals and travelled quite widely. In its first year the study of the work of the Department of Employment Group took some Committee members to Thurso, Newcastle upon Tyne, Liverpool, and Plymouth. In 1981 a visit was paid to Northern Ireland and in 1982 there were trips to Birmingham and Glasgow. When holding public sessions out of London, the Committee inevitably heard very large and varied groups of witnesses: such occasions tended to become just as much opportunities for the Committee to encourage participation as means of collecting evidence on specific questions. Nor did the Committee restrict its travel to Britain. It was assiduous in travelling overseas, to Canada, West Germany, Norway, Sweden, the USA, and Japan, for example. The justification for such visits was essentially in terms of informing members by enabling them to find out how problems familiar at home (for example, job creation programmes, legally enforceable employment agreements) were handled in other countries. It is, of course, impossible to make any assessment of the value of such foreign visits: clearly they usually relate only loosely to a particular topic of inquiry, but may despite that have very beneficial effects in terms of widening members' perspectives on issues before them at home.

The conventional wisdom of recent years has suggested the importance for select committees of securing effective specialist advice, additional to that which can be gained from witnesses and organizations submitting written and oral evidence. The specialist adviser has also been seen as a necessary supplement to the House of Commons clerks who service committees. Yet despite all this, it has remained difficult in practice to decide what kind of specialist advice is most needed by a particular committee, what kind of adviser will work most effectively with both a committee and its regular staff, and how much specialist support it is reasonable to engage. The Employment Committee came up against these difficulties and met them by proceeding rather cautiously in the use of advisers. During the 1979–83 Parliament, it engaged nine specialist advisers at different times, having at the end of that Parliament three still working for it. The Committee (and especially its chairman) showed a strong preference for securing on a strictly part-time basis the help of advisers with practical experience of particular problems or sectors of organization with which the Committee was concerned. Thus, for example, one adviser was closely involved with the work of the Health & Safety Executive, another in the training activities of MSC. There was little interest in turning to advisers whose experience was solely in the academic world, but there was for a while some attempt to engage a small number of advisers whose political sympathies coincided with those of the two parties represented on the Committee. This arrangement proved unsatisfactory and did not last long.

As far as the actual use of advisers goes, the Committee did not in fact make heavy demands on their time. In the first couple of years they were called upon fairly regularly to prepare papers, advise on lines of inquiry and comment on draft conclusions. But later on, the part they played tended to diminish and the Committee relied chiefly on its clerk for support in the conduct of inquiries. There is no doubt that the Committee's policy of reporting briefly and avoiding long, complex and possibly controversial surveys of particular problems made it easier for it to stick to the customary reliance on its House of Commons staff. There was simply little room for a substantial contribution at the report stage from temporary specialist advisers. Nor does it appear that members of the Committee were dissatisfied with the level and type of specialist advice engaged: most of them did not dissent from the chairman's pragmatic view that the problems in the Committee's field should be within the grasp of any competent member without the need for elaborate theoretical instruction. What was required was an experienced resource on which the Committee could draw to throw light on some of the technically abstruse problems encountered in its inquiries, and to highlight practical issues in the operation of particular organizations or the provision of services which the outside observer might miss.

It will already be apparent that the preparation and drafting of reports was very much a matter for the chairman and the clerk. However, this certainly did not mean that the chairman prepared a report and then simply presented it to the Committee for discussion, amendment, and approval. Mr Golding had a keen sense of what was practicable and attainable and, therefore, preferred to proceed by securing the broad agreement of Mr John Gorst, leader of the Conservative group on the Committee, to a draft before the matter was formally dealt with in a deliberative session. Indeed, what this approach meant was that the chairman and the *de facto* vice-chairman accepted the desirability of close consultation and co-operation at all stages: choice of topics, conduct of inquiries, and preparation of reports. The difficulty of reaching any agreement on controversial questions such as trade union immunities or the general principles of the Government's policies bearing on levels of employment pointed to the wisdom of this approach. But, of course, it did have the effect of encouraging the production of reports which were sometimes little more than brief notices to the effect that an inquiry had taken place. Not surprisingly in these circumstances deliberative sessions were brief and generally amicable; division on amendments did not occur, and there was hardly any sharp controversy, since the grounds for such argument had usually been excluded beforehand.

IMPACT AND INFLUENCE

It follows from the character of the Committee's reports that there is little evidence of its work having a marked impact either on the Department of Employment and its dependencies, or on the House of Commons. None of its reports was debated, though some of its members played an active part in debates on employment matters, trade union legislation, and youth training. Additionally, there were signs that the Committee's work increased the amount of information drawn on by Members of Parliament on such matters as the various MSC programmes directed to the relief of unemployment. But overall it is necessary to be cautious in drawing any conclusions about the scale and importance of the Committee's contribution to the work of the House of Commons in debate and legislative scrutiny. Turning to the impact on the executive, it is clear that the Committee established itself as an interlocutor, though this did not mean that it sought, still less gained, a major influence on the decisions taken by the Government and its agencies. It did not see itself as being in the business of proposing alternative policies and, as its first chairman observed, 'I do not consider that we can be a realistic source of coherent alternative policies'.[11] By pursuing the theme of accountability and seeing its role chiefly in terms of requiring ministers and officials to explain what they were doing, the Committee succeeded in establishing itself as an accepted point for the exchange of information and arguments between the administration and Parliament. In developing this approach to its task, it shrewdly judged what was tolerable to the executive, even of some benefit and value to ministers, and yet at the same time conducive to effective working relationships within the Committee.

This interpretation of the Committee's role owed most to the lead given by its first chairman who appreciated well enough the force of the traditional assumptions about the proper relationships between select committees and the executive, and was concerned to put the Committee on to a viable basis which would leave room for its future development. Significantly, the Conservative members tended to share

this view of the Committee's role: as active back-benchers they preferred an approach which allowed them to exert some pressure on
ministers, but without straining their loyalty to the Government they
were elected to support.

The ministers with whom the Employment Committee had to deal
showed sympathy for the way in which it interpreted its task. There
was no unwillingness to appear before the Committee; indeed it heard
the Secretary of State on thirteen occasions, and there were fourteen
appearances by other ministers. Only rarely did officials show reluctance to respond to questions put by the Committee, and when this
happened, as in July 1982, the chairman of the Committee expressly
stated his view of the Committee's rights in correspondence with the
Minister. The official responses to Committee reports were usually
within the target of two months laid down for reacting to select committee findings, but there were exceptions to this. For example, the
Committee's report on the draft Code of Practice issued by the Commission for Racial Equality did not elicit observations for almost
eleven months, a delay attributable largely to the need for consultations between the Department and the Commission on what were
sensitive and difficult issues. (Moreover, the Committee decided
eventually to interrogate the Minister on this delay, receiving from
him a fairly full account of the reasons.) Whilst the character and
scope of many of the Committee's reports made it easy for the Department to reply benevolently on the lines of 'noted with interest', it
is also worth remarking that when the Committee picked up important issues in current policy and presented a reasoned criticism of the
action proposed, the Department and its associated agencies were
usually willing to make a serious effort to accommodate the Committee's suggestions. One or two examples of this kind have already
been mentioned and to these can be added the one quoted by the
chairman in his contribution to the Liaison Committee's report. This
latter was the response of the Secretary of State to the report, *Youth
Unemployment and Training: the New Training Initiative*.[12] Here the
Secretary of State explicitly confirmed that in considering benefit
arrangements, his decision owed much to the views expressed by
the Committee. However, it is also worth noting that he gave no
assurance that he would not later revert to his original intention of
removing from sixteen-year-olds who refused offers under the Youth
Training Scheme their statutory entitlement to supplementary benefit.
This matter was reserved for subsequent review.

The development of the Employment Committee was, therefore,
characterized by the establishment of a generally co-operative relationship with the Secretary of State and the senior officials of the

various organizations within the Employment Group. However, this relationship depended very much on the personalities involved in it: there happened to be a chairman, a leader of the majority party group on the Committee, and successive Secretaries of State who accepted the value of such a relationship and were ready to work with each other on that basis. As a result it was not unusual for the chairman along with the leader of the Conservative group to have a couple of meetings per session with the Secretary of State to discuss ideas for the forward programme of the Committee. Such contacts underline the importance of trust and fair dealing within select committees: a chairman can seek to establish good relations with a minister, but not entirely on his own account. To be successful he needs to carry the opposing party with him, all the more so if he and his party are in the minority.

Yet there is no inherent reason why the type of relationships outlined should endure: different personalities, different attitudes within the Committee, a shift in the balance between parties, a change of minister, moments of irritation in Committee hearings, these and many other contingent circumstances can alter the style that a Committee has acquired. Even as the last Parliament drew to a close, there were signs of such contingent effects. The Committee failed to produce any further reports in its final session, in part perhaps because a new chairman did not have quite the same sure touch as his predecessor in ensuring before a conclusion was reached that his colleagues in the majority party would go along with his proposals. Precisely because they are small, intimate groups, select committees cannot escape the profound effects of the personal dispositions of their members and, in particular, of the two or three who by virtue of office or reputation are expected to give a lead. For this reason alone generalizations about select committees are always hazardous; the starting-point in analysis must always be the individuality of members and the subtle chemistry of personal relationships within a procedural framework which necessarily requires some neutralization of partisan passion.

A CRITICAL ROLE LIMITED BY THE NEED TO FIND POINTS OF AGREEMENT

What has just been said points to a conclusion. In the study of select committees much atention has been paid to the relevance of what is called the 'consensus model' as opposed to some adversarial or eristic model of behaviour. Yet whilst consensus is conventionally regarded as a desirable state of affairs, it is also widely recognized that the pursuit of consensus can lead to passivity, deference, quiescence, even to collusion. Consequently, in discussion of the potentialities of select committees as means of strengthening parliamentary control of the executive, it has sometimes been argued that select committees should beware of too overt a search for consensus: as watch-dogs they should be capable of biting, and they are hardly likely to do this unless they are agreed (after argument) on a target worth attacking. Nevertheless, it remains hard for select committees to mount a serious attack on the executive, since to do so presupposes that there is a majority opinion within the committee prepared to oppose strongly the policy or procedures of the Government. Such an outcome is inherently unlikely, the more so now that select committees are explicitly empowered to scrutinize policy as well as administration and expenditure. It follows that whatever effectiveness select committees may hope to achieve in respect of being listened to by the executive must depend heavily on their success in achieving within their own ranks an adequate degree of consensus. Occasionally this may be manifested in a genuine cross-party agreement on recommendations highly critical of the Government. But a more usual state of affairs is for committees to agree on rather second-order issues, to see faults in *how* something is being done rather than in *what* is being done. In other words, that degree of consensus which is needed if a committee is to hold together and to appear to the executive as a plausible group of critics can be secured only by a tacit agreement within the committee to exclude as objects of recommendation those matters on which party commitment is the decisive influence.

The record of the Employment Committee in the last Parliament neatly illustrates this view of the constraints under which select committees have to operate. For reasons which have been considered, it accommodated itself realistically to the limits under which it had to operate in deciding how to interpret its remit. Sharp differences of opinion within the Committee were not suppressed, but found expression in the activity of interrogating witnesses rather than in any attempt to fashion a unanimous Committee view on some of the contentious issues it examined. Where agreement on substantive recommendations could be found without too much difficulty, the opportunity was taken. But it was in the extension of the procedures for enforcing executive accountability in a public dialogue that the Committee saw its principal achievement during the first four years of its existence.

NOTES

1. Liaison Committee Report 1982–83, HC 92, p. 55.
2. In the Liaison Committee Report, op. cit., p. 56, Mr Golding wrote: 'It must also be recognised that on major policy issues the Commitee are unlikely to reach an agreed view between Conservative and Labour members. We have therefore sought those policy items where Members of different parties can agree. ... Recognising the existence of party divisions we try to minimise their effect on our work.'
3. Employment Committee, 2nd Report 1980–81, HC 282.
4. Employment Committee, 1st Report 1981–82, HC 39.
5. Employment Committee, 6th Report 1981–82, HC 400.
6. Employment Committee, 2nd Report 1981–82, HC 27.
7. Employment Committee, 4th Report 1981–82, HC 221.
8. Employment Committee, 5th Report 1981–82, HC 273.
9. The ministerial response to the 5th Report, 1981–82, HC 273, was given in the form of a letter sent to the Committee and reported in the 2nd Special Report 1982–83, HC 319.
10. Liaison Committee Report, p. 55.
11. Liaison Committee Report, p. 56.
12. Employment Committee, 4th Report 1981–82, *op. cit.*, 5th Special Report 1981–82, HC 425.

Annex 6.1 *Select Committee on Employment 1979–83*

Report	Date of first oral evidence (no. of evidence sessions)	Date of report	Date of govt. reply	Length of report (pages)	No. of oral qq./no. of written submissions	Divisions
Session 1979–80 1st *MSC's Corporate Plan 1980–84* (HC 444)	13.2.80(5)	30.7.80	1st SR, HC 817, 29.10.80	6	305/7	Nil
2nd *Legal Immunities of Trade Unions and other Related Matters: Draft Code of Practice on Picketing and the Closed Shop* (HC 822)	20.2.80(9)	3.11.80	2nd SR, HC 848, 13.11.80	6	671/10	Nil
Session 1980–81 1st *MSC's Corporate Plan 1981–85* (HC 101)	14.1.81(1)	28.1.81	1st SR, HC 296, 15.4.81	5	53/1*	Nil
2nd *Legal Immunities of Trade Unions and other Related Matters: the Green Paper on Trade Union Immunities* (HC 282)	8.4.81(6)	17.7.81	1st SR, 1981–82, HC 85, 2.12.81	5	983/26	Nil
3rd *Work of the Department of Employment Group: The Employment Service Division of the MSC & Private Employment Agencies* (HC 51)	3.12.80(9)	21.7.81	2nd SR, 1981–82, HC 220, 24.2.82	2	520/9**	Nil

Annex 6.1 *Select Committee on Employment 1979–83 (cont.)*

Report	Date of first oral evidence (no. of evidence sessions)	Date of report	Date of govt. reply	Length of report (pages)	No. of oral qq./no. of written submissions	Divisions
Session 1981–82 1st *Homeworking* (HC 39)	24.3.81 (7)	18.11.81	3rd SR, HC 311, 31.3.82	5	508/18	Nil
2nd *MSC's Review of the Quota Scheme for the Employment of Disabled People* (HC 27)	11.11.81 (3)	16.12.81	6th SR, HC 556, 25.10.82	6	192/27	Nil
3rd *MSC's Corporate Plan 1982–86* (HC 195)	10.2.82 (1)	17.2.82	4th SR, HC 332, 21.4.82	2	49/1***	Nil
4th *Youth Unemployment & Training: New Training Initiative* (HC 221)	24.2.82 (4)	19.5.82	5th SR, HC 425, 23.6.82	4	253/26	Nil
5th *Commission for Racial Equality: Draft Code of Practice* (HC 273)	17.3.82 (3)	26.5.82	2nd SR, 1982–83, HC 319, 13.4.83	5	173/8	Nil
6th *The Working of the Health & Safety Commission & Executive: Achievements since the Robens Report* (HC 400)	9.6.82 (6)	14.7.82	1st SR, 1982–83, HC 36, 10.11.82	6	304/17	Nil

Notes:

* Appendix consisting of MSC's Corporate Plan 1981–85.

** No oral evidence is appended to the report, but in fact hearings were held on employment creation and published separately as Minutes of Evidence.

*** Appendix answering an oral question.

CHAPTER 7

The Energy Committee
Martin Burch

The Energy Committee worked conscientiously and quietly on a carefully selected range of issues. In terms of its output, number of meetings, and overall workload it ranks slightly better than the average for all fourteen departmental select committees. Although at first sight it might appear to be an unexceptional committee, it did, nevertheless, develop a particular approach to business and it produced some useful and informed reports. Its work is examined in the pages that follow. The chapter begins with a factual profile of the Committee's membership, staffing, and activities. Thereafter, consideration is given to the Committee's internal operation and its links with the wider world of energy policy-making.

COMMITTEE PROFILE

During the 1979–83 Parliament, the Energy Committee's brief was to examine the operations of the Department of Energy (D.En.) and associated public bodies, including similar matters relating to Northern Ireland. This covered the major nationalized energy supply industries (coal, electricity, and gas), the United Kingdom Atomic Energy Authority, and the British National Oil Corporation. The eleven-man Committee was chaired by Mr Ian Lloyd and was originally split into six Conservative and five Labour members, though one of the latter (Mr Ednyfed Hudson Davies) later joined the SDP.[1] There was a relatively high continuity in membership, and with a turnover of 36 per cent the Committee ranked fifth lowest amongst all fourteen select committees.[2] By June 1983, seven of the original members remained, though there had been five changes amongst the other four members.[3]

Committee attendance for the whole Parliament was the lowest of all the select committees at 64 per cent.[4] The relatively poor attendance figures in part reflect a change in the operation of the Committee which, following its first report, tended to divide into two unofficial, informal sub-committees. These operated within the existing standing orders so that, in the agreed absence of the Chairman, an acting chairman (Mr Palmer) took over while Mr Lloyd chaired a separate sub-committee enquiry. All members were free to attend any meeting of either sub-committee, though in practice (with the exception of Mr Rost) most tended to specialize. This arrangement meant that in effect there were three energy committees: the full committee and the two unofficial sub-committees. The result was an increase in Committee output and a more effective use of members' time.

There was some disparity amongst members in terms of the effort and commitment they put in to committee work. While calculating the time spent on committee work (especially preparatory and background work) raises difficulties, the average commitment per week by each member varied from a maximum of twenty hours to a minimum of about four hours. Seniority also played a part, for some members— Mr Lloyd, Mr Palmer, Mr Rost, Mr Leadbitter, and Mr Wainwright—brought with them a long experience of select committee work through previous memberships of the earlier committees on Science and Technology and Nationalised Industries. Taking into account time spent on committee work and breadth of experience (the two are not wholly complementary), it is possible to speak about an 'inner core' of five or six members.

The Committee was served by a clerk, an assistant clerk, and one secretary. The clerk, apart from overall responsibility for the administrative side of the Committee's work, generally concentrated his activities on Mr Lloyd's sub-committee, while the assistant clerk was primarily concerned with the operation of Mr Palmer's group. The Committee engaged a total of ten advisers, and these included businessmen, university academics, and energy consultants. Four of these—Professor W Murgatroyd, Professor G Manners, Mr J Chesshire and Mr J Surrey—served on more than one inquiry and the latter two were either singly or jointly involved in most of the Committee's major inquiries, and thus might be best regarded as permanent rather than temporary part-time advisers.[5]

The Committee produced fifteen reports and, at the time of the dissolution of Parliament in May 1983, one major inquiry awaited completion (see annex). Seven of these reports account for more than 95 per cent of the pages of report published by the Committee, and they fall into two categories. First, those covering long-term inquiries dealing with a subject in depth: these include investigations into government policy on the new nuclear programme, North Sea oil depletion policy, energy conservation in buildings, combined heat and power, and (not completed) the Department of Energy's strategy for research, development, and demonstration.[6] Secondly, reports of short, sharp inquiries, often on a topic of current interest involving the examination of a limited range of witnesses and evidence. Into this category can be placed reports on industrial energy pricing, the Department of Energy's estimates, and pit closures.[7] A further five reports are either concerned with procedural matters or appended to evidence without containing any substantive comments,[8] while the remaining three mainly contain government replies to earlier reports.[9] The Committee also, especially towards the end of the Parliament, undertook a number of follow-up investigations into the subjects of its earlier reports, as in the case of the tax aspects of North Sea oil depletion, energy conservation in buildings, and developments concerning the pressurised water reactor (PWR).[10]

Long-term inquiries account for about 74 per cent of the Committee's published reports and recommendations. The first full year was taken up with the investigation into the Government's nuclear power programme. It alone accounts for 30 per cent of the pages of report produced, major witnesses heard, and evidence sessions undertaken by the Committee.[11] The Committee came out strongly against the idea of the Government's giving *carte blanche* support to a series of nuclear stations stretching far into the future and which might cost in excess of £15,000m in 1980 prices. This was meant to avoid the trap, revealed in the first and second nuclear programmes, of embarking on programmes which could not subsequently be stopped or amended in the light of future circumstances. Consequently, the Committee recommended that the Central Electricity Generating Board (CEGB) should judge the economic case for each successive nuclear power station on its merits rather than commit themselves to a comprehensive programme. The Committee questioned some of the assumptions underlying the CEGB's forecasting of future electricity demand, and expressed concern about the safety aspects of PWRs. In addition the Department was criticized for having no clear idea of whether investing in a nuclear plant might be as cost-effective as spending a similar sum to promote energy conservation. On this point, the Committee recommended that in future the Department should assess the economic costs and benefits of energy conservation with the same rigour as that required for the appraisal of a new generating plant.

In the case of North Sea oil depletion policy, the Committee found no grounds for government intervention to restrict the rate of exploration and oil production with the information then available, but they urged the Government to continue its close monitoring, and accepted the need for reserve powers to reduce depletion, should that become desirable in the future. The Committee also considered that development of North Sea oilfields was in danger of being discouraged as a result of licensing procedures and tax regulations, and recommendations were made about reforms in these areas.

The last two reports of major long-term inquiries published by the Committee returned to the theme of energy conservation. In its report on conservation in buildings the Committee concluded that, by using existing technology, effective energy conservation measures could produce savings in the order of 30 per cent of present energy consumption, and that one major obstacle to the achievement of these savings was the fragmentation of responsibility amongst government bodies and the lack of political will at the heart of government. Criticizing the Government's lack of commitment to conservation, the Committee proceeded to advocate more government expenditure, and the more effective co-ordination of energy conservation either by a single government department or by a separate institution. In their report on combined heat and power (CHP), the Committee recommended 'that steps be taken to put in hand appropriate Lead City schemes for district heating/CHP'.[12]

Short inquiries account for about 21 per cent of the Committee's published reports and recommendations. The inquiry into industrial energy pricing policy was carried out in response to the CBI's and other organizations' concern about the alleged heavy burden of energy costs upon industry. It took place over a six-month period, involved four principal sets of witnesses, and resulted in thirty-eight published memoranda. The Committee found that about 5 per cent of industrial consumers were suffering substantially higher energy costs than those being charged to their counterparts abroad, and recommended a long-term change in the basis of energy pricing.

The consideration of the Department of Energy's Estimates for 1981–82 involved an interview with the Permanent Secretary and the examination of seven memoranda in addition to the estimates. The Committee concluded that there was a lack of strategy in the Department's pattern of expenditure, and especially drew attention to the 'imbalance between the scale of resources devoted to energy supply and the much smaller commitments to reducing demand'.[13] The Committee also questioned the economic case underlying the Government's decision of February 1981, following the threat of industrial disruption, to provide additional funds to enable the National Coal Board (NCB) to keep open a number of economically marginal pits.

The question of pit closures was raised once again in the Committee's last short inquiry which investigated the allegations made by the National Union of Mineworkers (NUM) that the NCB had compiled a secret 'hit-list' of pits for closure. The inquiry lasted six weeks from initiation to publication and drew on evidence from the NUM, the NCB, and the Department, which was gathered in three hearings and from eighteen memoranda. The Committee found no evidence of a 'hit-list', drew attention to the sizeable coal stocks held by the NCB and the cost of these to public funds, urged the Board to cut its marginal capacity and surplus stocks and thus reduce the production costs of coal, and called on the Department to avoid further subsidies to uneconomic pits.

In pursuit of its investigations the Committee held 150 meetings, which ranks it fourth amongst the fourteen new select committees. Fifty-five per cent of these meetings were evidence sessions which, with one exception, were held in public, and the remaining 45 per cent were private deliberative sessions. Four evidence sessions were held outside Westminster, and the one private session concerned the construction of PWR reactors for the Royal Navy's nuclear submarines.[14]

INTERNAL OPERATION

The internal operation of the Energy Committee can be examined in terms of the relationships and working patterns which developed amongst Committee personnel, and the characteristic mode of operation which the Committee exhibited. The Chairman set the tone by taking a relatively detached and neutral approach to Committee business. He operated as the leader of a team, and did not attempt to dominate his colleagues. His approach was essentially democratic. He frequently consulted the senior Labour member, Mr Palmer, on matters of Committee organization, and he allowed members to express and register their views on the selection of topics, witnesses, and the amendment of draft reports. His central concern was to produce agreed reports which all members of the Committee could support. This was achieved with the single exception of the inquiry and report into possible pit closures, which was opposed and voted against by one Labour (NUM-sponsored) member. Mr Lloyd also extensively delegated to the clerks most administrative tasks and, unlike the chairmen of some other select committees, avoided involvement in the organizational business of the Committee.

The Committee's approach was essentially non-partisan, and this was a clear attraction to most members. There were, however, some differences of opinion between them as to the proper function of the Committee. The Chairman emphasized its role in establishing facts, informing the House, and contributing to long-term thinking. Others stressed its monitoring responsibilities in relation both to current developments in the energy field generally and to the work of the Department in particular. One member saw the Committee as a further channel of representation, serving as a 'post-box' for outside interests either with a genuine complaint about Departmental actions or a sense that their arguments had failed to register or been ignored in the process of energy policy-making. A number implied that the Committee had an important role in highlighting, questioning, and possibly counteracting, the policy assumptions and biases (especially towards energy supply) prevalent in the Department of Energy's approach.

Variations in views on the purpose of the Committee led to some unhappiness about its operation. While the majority were content, a number felt the Committee should have engaged in more short, sharp inquiries, and more follow-up investigations. Newer members and especially those who had no experience of earlier select committees felt that large-scale inquiries of the 'Royal Commission' type tended to be too wide-ranging, long-term, and limited in their impact. Others were concerned to establish the Committee's knowledge base, on the grounds that follow-up inquiries needed something sound and substantial to follow up. Indeed, following the nuclear power inquiry, a decision was made to avoid over-long investigations, and from there on the Committee undertook follow-up and shorter inquiries with increasing frequency.

The effective operation of the Committee depended very much upon the work of the clerks and advisers. It was they, subject to the overall approval of the Committee, who drew up the initial list of witnesses, and determined the phasing of evidence and the timetabling of the proceedings. The advisers had an important part to play in briefing members for evidence sessions by providing, in conjunction with the clerks, background information and lists of possible questions and topics to cover. On occasion, they and the clerks liaised with witnesses independently of the Committee, though with its general approval, in order to clear up matters of fact or detail, usually in relation to statistical matters, or to prepare the ground for evidence sessions. When it came to writing up the reports, the clerks, with the assistance of advisers, produced the initial outlines of proposals (heads of report papers) and, subject to the views of the Committee on the heads of report paper, undertook the preparation of the Chairman's draft report.[15] All these activities point to a very substantial role being played by clerks and advisers. There were, however, limitations upon their influence, and these to some extent ensured that the Chairman and members remained paramount.

The first limit was one of staff numbers, time, and resources. As already noted, there were only two clerks serving the Committee and one secretary. Moreover, the advisers, being part-time, had other employments and commitments to fulfil. Additionally, the more permanent advisers and the clerks developed through their experience close knowledge of the Committee's interests and concerns. This helped them to tailor their advice and assistance in line with members' requirements. The most important limit, however, was provided through the Committee's vetting of inquiry timetables, heads of report papers, and draft reports. These were discussed by the Committee and thoroughly read by the Chairman (and where relevant, the acting Chairman), as well as being carefully scrutinized by other members of the Committee. So it may be said that the clerks and advisers, while they played a substantial part in the Committee's activities, were limited in their influence both by the extent to which they were operating in line with members' own wishes and by the extent to which the Chairman and members kept fully on top of the material submitted to them.

Certain other features of the organization of Committee business are worth noting. In the first place, there was a fairly systematic approach to topic selection. Following the establishment of the Committee, members drew up a list of about two dozen potential topics, including nuclear power development, energy conservation, North Sea oil and gas, coal, energy research and development, and government relations with the management of nationalized energy industries. This initial listing provided a framework for subsequent choice, though some topics, notably industrial energy pricing and pit closures, arose independently as issues of current political debate. Occasionally, the choice of topic was a matter of some argument, as in the case of pit closures, but in every instance an agreed view emerged and votes were never taken. Secondly, the Committee went to some trouble to see that its members were well prepared for evidence sessions. As already mentioned, the clerks, with the assistance of the advisers, provided members with a list of twenty to thirty possible questions and a broader briefing. Members would usually study these, and always spent about fifteen minutes prior to interviewing a witness determining the line of questioning to be pursued.

Another noticeable feature of the Energy Committee's approach was the way in which informal deliberative meetings were used as a way of reaching some consensus about a draft report, before moving into more formal deliberative sessions when amendments could be proposed and, if necessary, voted upon. The aim of these informal meetings was to heighten the likelihood of producing a report which had been agreed. According to some members, by the time draft reports reached the formal deliberative stage, 99 per cent of the report was already decided. However, there were exceptions, most notably in the inquiries on nuclear power, energy pricing policy, and pit closures.

The picture that emerges of the internal operation of the Committee is of a relatively settled organization in which clerks, advisers, Chairman, and members developed a balanced and consensual style of operation. It was a committee of equals, though an important part was played by an inner core of active and/or senior members. As already indicated, the Committee took great pains to reach agreement and to pursue a non-partisan approach. When differences arose, they were *not* on the basis of party. For example, of the thirteen divisions recorded in the Committee's reports, only one (on pit closures) can be clearly defined as being along party lines. Moreover, members often supported reports that might be seen as going against certain aspects of their own parties' philosophies, as in the case of the support by Labour members for the proposal to relax North Sea oil taxation, and the acceptance by Conservative members of the need to establish a more interventionist approach to energy conservation and efficiency. The emphasis upon a consensual style appeard to arise spontaneously within the Committee, and became a kind of unconscious, unarticulated convention governing the Committee's deliberations.

THE EXTERNAL ENVIRONMENT

An interesting aspect of all the new departmental committees was the way in which they initiated and gradually developed their links with other agencies in their respective policy areas. A select committee largely depends on others for information, opinion, and assistance, and connections which become too close and familiar may effectively undermine its ability to speak out boldly and impartially. The danger of becoming a spokesman for a particular interest or a mouthpiece for the Department is always present. As will be shown, the Energy Committee managed to maintain a clear degree of independence from its Department as well as from party and pressure group influences, although, at the informal level, as a matter of mutual convenience, the links with the Department of Energy were developed during the 1979 to 1983 period.

The main formal link between the Committee and the D.En. was provided through the Department's liaison officers. Day-to-day responsibility was exercized by a principal, assisted by a higher executive officer, under the oversight of an assistant secretary. On the ministerial side, a junior minister was specifically responsible for liaison: initially Mr David Mellor, later Mr John Moore, and subsequently Mr Giles Shaw. The liaison officers acted as a contact point between the Committee and the relevant section of the Department. They ensured that witnesses were available and briefed, that requested memoranda were prepared, and in general co-ordinated the Department's response to the Committee's requests. When the Committee was sitting and its investigations involved the Department, about 20 to 30 per cent of the two main liaison officers' time was usually taken up with Committee work. The D.En. was generally co-operative. It never turned down the Committee's requests for interviews, though it did refuse to provide certain documents in evidence, and some officials appearing as witnesses were restrained when it came to answering questions on certain aspects of policy formulation. Overall, the priority given to Committee requests by the Department was high, and was said to be second only to that given to policy submissions to ministers and equivalent to the attention paid to parliamentary questions.

In addition to these formal links a number of less formal connections developed. These included, most obviously, the contacts between ministers and Committee MPs, especially with those who were government back-benchers. These were supplemented by connections on the official side of the Department. Initially, when Mr David Howell was Secretary of State, members of the Committee, plus the clerks and advisers, visited the Department on at least two occasions in order to meet officials over lunch. These were intended as opportunities for the two groups to get to know each other, though with fifteen either side of the table they proved to be rather unworkable and became like Committee sessions with members quizzing officials. A more successful point of contact was developed through a series of smaller, less formal meetings between departmental officials, other prospective witnesses, and clerks and advisers. Authority to carry out these sessions was delegated by the Committee. There were about seven in total, and they usually took place in the clerks' offices. They began after the nuclear power inquiry, but most took place in the autumn of 1982 in preparation for the investigation into energy research, development, and demonstration. Two of these involved the Department's former Chief Scientist—Sir Herman Bondi and his successor, Dr Challis—and one involved personnel from the International Energy Agency at which officials from the Department were present. These preliminary explorations committed neither side to particular points of view, but they helped in identifying both the relevant issues and hence the choice of witnesses who could assist the inquiry. They also had benefits for the Department in that they provided some indication, and some forewarning, of the Committee's likely line of inquiry.

A further informal link existed between the clerks and the liaison officers. The clerks would usually contact the liaison officer twenty-four hours or so in advance of a session involving a witness from the Department. The purpose of such communication was to inform the liaison officers of the areas which were likely to be covered in the session and even, in some instances, to provide some indication of the questions that might possibly come up. This procedure proved useful. It helped to ensure that witnesses were properly and adequately briefed and that the Committee got an informed response from them.

In general the Committee maintained a friendly but distant relationship with the Department. The contacts between the two organizations tended to become progressively less formal, though the frequency of contact depended on the nature of the inquiry being undertaken and the Department's involvement in it. Energy research and development, for example, was almost wholly concerned with the Department's policies and procedures, while the inquiry into industrial energy pricing involved the Department far less. This informal relationship was of mutual benefit. The Committee and its advisers acquired information and inside knowledge, while the Department benefited from gaining some inkling of what the Committee's future actions might be.

This distant but relatively amicable relationship became strained towards the end of the Parliament over the issue of energy conservation. One problem was an internal, departmental 'Rayner' review of the Government's administrative machinery for, and expenditure on, energy conservation. This initially remained unpublished, but it was known to advocate the bringing together from all departments of government responsibilities for energy conservation into a special unit within the Department—a proposal very much in keeping with the Committee's own recommendations. A copy of the 'Rayner' review was sent to the Committee by the Secretary of State, Mr Lawson,[16] and consequently members prepared to interview Dr Finer, the senior official responsible for its production. The review was subsequently published in time for the relevant session.[17] The Committee had also received two other departmental documents which attempted to evaluate the relative costs of energy conservation *vis-à-vis* those of energy supply. These had arisen through the public inquiry into the proposed erection of a nuclear reactor at Sizewell. One was authorized for publication, and the other was an internal policy advisory document which was not intended for publication and had come into the hands of the Committee unofficially.[18] Dr Finer and the witness on the authorized energy conservation document, Mr Price, came before the Committee at the same hearing. Both were restricted in what they could say by a ruling from the Secretary of State which involved a tight interpretation of the 'Osmotherley' rules governing the appearance of civil servants before select committees. Mr Price was not able, for instance, to discuss the contents of the officially unpublished paper, nor could either he or Dr Finer make any comments about inter- and intra-departmental disagreements or opinions on the 'Rayner' review or conservation more generally. Faced with this apparent lack of co-operation, the Committee determined to take the matter up with Mr Lawson. In the event, the June 1983 general election intervened and the meeting did not take place.

In addition to contacts with the Department, the Committee was subject to a measure of lobbying by organized interests. Many were involved in the provision of evidence, and these ranged from large companies such as the British oil majors and Rolls Royce Ltd., to overtly recognizable pressure groups such as the NUM, Friends of the Earth, and the Confederation of British Industry. In total, about 35 per cent of the major witnesses appearing before the Committee represented organized, non-governmental interests.

An element of lobbying also played a part in the choice of topics for inquiry, especially in the case of North Sea oil depletion and industrial energy pricing. Suggestions for possible investigation were often put to members, the chairman and the clerks. Particular pressure tended to come from those groups and individuals who felt excluded from the established channels of communication with the D.En. such as those, for instance, who were pressing the case for renewable sources of energy. In some cases, particular companies approached the Committee, as did the consumer councils of the various nationalized energy supply industries. In sum, a good deal of lobbying tended to come from individual enthusiasts or relatively small-scale groupings, rather than the larger, established, and incorporated pressure groups.

The influence of parliamentary parties on the operation of the Committee was, compared with the role of the D.En. and organized interests, relatively unimportant. The whips had a part in the nomination of Committee members, though beyond that formal influence by party organizations played little part. Some of the members were officers of the relevant back-bench party committees (notably Mr Palmer on the Labour side, and Mr Morris and Mr Speller among the Conservatives) but this reflected their interest in energy questions rather than any desire (or attempt) deliberately to bring party concerns into Energy Committee work.

The Committee also developed contacts with various international bodies such as the EEC and the International Energy Agency as well as some of its counterpart committees in overseas legislatures, most notably those in Canada and the USA. It might be claimed that during its first four years, the Energy Committee established itself and carried out the essential groundwork for its gradual acceptance as a central part of the network of energy institutions in the UK.

CONCLUSION

Five principal features of the Energy Committee deserve emphasis: (a) its non-partisan, consensus seeking approach; (b) its neutral, non-interventionist and relatively non-manipulative chairmanship; (c) its dependence on administrative and certain more or less permanent advisory staff to ensure its effective day-to-day operation; (d) its development of a detached and increasingly informal relationship with the D.En; and (e) its gradual emergence as an integral part of the world of energy politics.

Two other aspects of the Committee's operation are also worth noting. As already seen, the Committe showed clear signs of learning from experience and of building on its previous work. Moreover, in its reports and recommendations the Committee acted as it were as a foil to the policy predispositions prevalent within the D.En. In particular, the Committee tended to favour certain viewpoints on energy questions, especially the promotion of energy conservation and a more even-handed approach to the development of alternative energy sources. These were in direct contrast to the Department's leanings towards energy supply and the interests of large scale, nationalized energy supply industries. Arguably the pin-pointing and publicizing of this departmental bias was one of the most useful and important functions that the Energy Committee fulfilled.

The impact of the Committee, however, requires to be assessed more extensively. Evidence of an overt and direct effect upon policy-making is difficult to come by. Four of the Committee's reports elicited specific responses during the Parliament, though most of these tended to be rather bland and negative.[19] The report on nuclear power was the subject of a full day's debate in the House on a motion for the adjournment,[20] but no other reports were the subject of specific debates nor were any referred to on the Order Paper. During oral questions to the Energy Department, the Committee was specifically referred to on twelve occasions in the 1981-82 session and eleven occasions in 1982-83. In addition there were three items of government policy on which the Committee could reasonably claim some immediate impact: the decision to avoid a firm ordering programme for PWRs, the 1983 Budget changes in North Sea oil taxation, and the approach to energy loss in public buildings which led to the creation in October 1983 of a new Energy Efficiency Office. Apart from these instances, there are no other obvious examples of the Committee's having an immediate effect on government actions.

The matter of impact, however, cannot simply be reduced to observable and direct influences on government behaviour. Committee influence is also likely to be long-term and indirect. Certainly the Energy Committee was taken seriously by the D.En., as is illustrated by the priority given to its requests. If the Committee did not serve to change the broad thrust of policy within the Department, it at least helped to concentrate the minds of ministers and officials on certain apparently neglected areas of energy policy-making, and to expose and publicize issues and information which in previous times might have remained hidden.

Further claims about the indirect impact of the Committee can be made, though they are difficult to substantiate. Some evidence can be found of a tendency within the D.En. and other Departments to anticipate and pre-empt the Committee's conclusions. This appeared to happen in the cases of combined heat and power and energy conservation in buildings. In the latter case, the Department of the Environment actually announced new building regulations at the outset of their cross-examination by the Committee. In addition, the Committee may have had a longer term influence on departmental activities by providing evidence that could be used by one section in the D.En. against another or by the Department itself against another department in some matter of inter-departmental dispute. The latter tendency was partly revealed in the case of the 'Rayner' review, while the Committee's work on North Sea oil taxation undoubtedly assisted the D.En. in persuading the Treasury to carry through reforms in the complex structure of North Sea oil taxation in its 1983 budget. The Committee might also justifiably claim to have contributed to shaping and informing the climate of opinion surrounding energy questions. Its work on nuclear power helped to publicize the uncertainties surrounding the economic case for the Sizewell PWR,[21] and its findings on pit closures highlighted the problems of uneconomic pits and the mounting cost of support for the coal industry. More generally, the Committee's interest in conservation may have contributed to the shift in emphasis in the energy debate away from questions of energy supply to those of energy demand.

In sum, though the Committee had some direct impact, its major contribution was in bringing issues to the fore, helping to establish the context and pattern of debate, and indirectly influencing the climate and pace of government decision taking. Moreover, the Committee's reports and published evidence have placed on the public record informed, thorough, and authoritative statements on a number of key energy questions. It was not a spectacular beginning, but it was a sound one which offered a firm foundation for the future.

NOTES

1. The following, with party affiliations in brackets, were nominated as members of the Committee on 26 November 1979: Michael Ancram (Cons.), David Crouch (Cons.), Ednyfed Hudson Davies (Lab.), Michael Latham (Cons.), Ted Leadbitter (Lab.), Mark Lennox-Boyd (Cons.), Ian Lloyd (Cons.), Arthur Palmer (Lab.), Peter Rost (Cons.), David Stoddart (Lab.), Edwin Wainwright (Lab.).
2. HC Debs., 29 July 1983, col 633 (written answer).
3. David Crouch was repaced by John Watson (Cons.) on 14 December 1979; Mark Lennox-Boyd was replaced by Robert McCrindle (Cons.) on 23 January 1981; John Watson was replaced by Tony Speller (Cons.) on 11 June 1982; Michael Latham was replaced by Michael Morris (Cons.) on 12 November 1982; David Stoddart was repaced by John Spellar (Lab.) on 21 January 1983.
4. HC Debs., 29 July 1983, col. 633 (written answer).
5. Each served on four major inquiries.
6. First Report from the Select Committee on Energy, *The Government's Statement on the New Nuclear Power Programme*, 1980-81, HC 114-I; Third Report from the Select Committee on Energy, *North Sea Oil Depletion Policy*, 1981-82, HC 337; Fifth Report from the Select Committee on Energy, *Energy Conservation in Buildings*, 1981-82, HC 401-I; Third Report from the Energy Committee, *Combined Heat and Power*, 1982-83, HC 314-1.
7. Second Report from the Select Committee on Energy, *Industrial Energy Pricing Policy*, 1980-81, HC 422-I; Second Report from the Select Committee on Energy, *Department of Energy's Estimates for 1981-82*, 1981-82, HC 231; Second Report from the Energy Committee, *Pit Closures*, 1982-83, HC 135
8. First Special Report from the Energy Committee, *Sub-Committees*, 1979-80, HC 585; Second Special Report from the Energy Committee, *Isle of Grain Power Station*, 1979-80, HC 770; Third Report from the Select Committee on Energy, *The Gas Industry in Northern Ireland*, 1980-81, HC 463; First Report from the Select Committee on Energy, *The Disposal of the British Gas Corporation's Interest in the Wytch Farm Oil-Field*, 1981-82, HC 138; First Special Report from the Select Committee on Energy, *Energy Research, Development and Demonstration in the UK*, 1982-83, HC 373.
9. First Special Report from the Select Committee on Energy, *Government Observation on the Second Report of The Committee, Session 1980-81 (Industrial Energy Pricing Policy)*, 1981-82, HC 169; Fourth Report from the Select Committee on Energy, *Government Observations on the Second Report of the Committee, Session 1981-82 (The Department*

of Energy's Estimates for 1981–82), 1981–82, HC 366, First Report from the Energy Committee, *North Sea Oil Depletion Policy: The Government's Observations on the Committee's Third Report of Session 1981–82*, 1982–83, HC 134.

10. First Report, 1982–83, HC 134; Minutes of Evidence, Dr E G Finer *et al.*, 1982–83, HC 310; Minutes of Evidence, Sir Walter Marshall, 1982–83, HC 91.

11. These percentages are calculated from figures which exclude the evidence taken in relation to the inquiry into energy research, development, and demonstration.

12. Third Report, 1982–83, HC 314-I, p. 41.

13. Second Report, 1981–82, HC 231, p. xviii, para. 33.

14. Edited minutes were published, Minutes of Evidence, *Rolls Royce and Associates*, 1979–80, HC 397-vii, pp. 234 ff.

15. The pattern of influence within the Committee is examined in Martin Burch, 'Inside the Energy Committee', in Dilys Hill (ed.), *Parliamentary Select Committees in Action: A Symposium*, Strathclyde Papers in Government and Politics, No. 24, University of Strathclyde, 1984, pp. 170–96.

16. This was received by the Committee on 9 February 1983, Minutes of Evidence, Dr Challis, 1982–83, HC 108-viii, q. 578.

17. Published on 30 March 1983, Minutes of Evidence, Dr Finer *et al.*, 1982–83, HC 310, q. 1.

18. For some background to this see Rod Chapman, 'Complacency stars in "save it" sideshow', the *Guardian*, 18 April 1983.

19. In addition to ref. 9 above, see also, *Nuclear Power*, Cmd. 8317. The Government's reply to the conservation report was published on 31 October 1983 to coincide with the official launch of the new Energy Efficiency Office.

20. HC Debs., 1 February 1982, cols. 21–102.

21. HC Debs., 16 November 1981, col. 114, and 20 January 1982, cols. 284–90.

Annex 7.1 *Energy Committee*

Report	Date of first oral evidence (no. of evidence sessions)	Date of publication of report	Date and form of govt. reply	Length of report (pages)	No. of oral qq./no. of published submissions	No. of divisions
Session 1979–80						
1st Special Report Sub-Committees (HC 585)	— (0)	30.4.80	—	1	0/0	0
2nd Special Report Isle of Grain Power Station[a] (HC 770)	23.6.80 (5)	31.7.80	—	1	413/15	0
Session 1980–81						
1st Report The Government's Statement on the New Nuclear Power Programme (HC 114)	30.1.80 (20)	13.2.81	July 1981 White Paper: Nuclear Power Cmnd. 8317	77	1908/104	8
2nd Report Industrial Energy Pricing Policy (HC 422)	11.12.80 (4)	15.7.81	22.12.81 Written reply published by Committee on 5.2.82 (HC 169)	15	235/38	3
3rd Report The Gas Industry in Northern Ireland (HC 463)	— (0)	30.7.81	—	2	0/9	0
Session 1981–82						
1st Report The Disposal of the British Gas Corporation's Interest in the Wytch Farm Oil-Field (HC 138)	— (0)	5.2.82	—	1	0/3	0

Report		Date				
1st Special Report Government Observations on the 2nd Report of the Committee, Session 1980–81 (Industrial Energy Pricing) (HC 169)	— (o)	5.2.82	—	—	0/1	o
2nd Report The Department of Energy's Estimates for 1981–82 (HC 231)	21.7.81 (1)	9.3.82	11.3.82 Written reply published by Committee on 11.5.82 (HC 366)	23	82/7	o
3rd Report North Sea Oil Depletion Policy (HC 337)	6.5.81 (11)	7.5.82	July 1982 Written reply published by Committee on 21.12.82 (HC 134)	43	833/27	o
4th Report Government Observations on the Second Report of the Committee Session 1981–82 (The Department of Energy's Estimates for 1981–82) (HC 366)	— (o)	11.5.82	—	1	0/5	o
5th Report Energy Conservation in Buildings (HC 401)	8.6.81 (7)	10.6.82	2.11.83 Typescript (unpublished)	33	666/69	o
Session 1982–83 1st Report North Sea Oil Depletion Policy: The Government's Observations on the Committee's Third Report of Session 1981–82 (HC 134)	— (o)	21.12.82	—	4	0/1	o

Annex 7.1 *Energy Committee* (*cont.*)

Report	Date of first oral evidence (no. of evidence sessions)	Date of publication of report	Date and form of govt. reply	Length of report (pages)	No. of oral qq./no. of published submissions	No. of divisions
2nd *Report* *Pit Closures* (HC 135)	25.11.82 (3)	21.12.82	Letter to Chairman	18	223/18	2
3rd *Report* *Combined Heat and Power* (HC 314)	24.11.81 (12)	18.4.83	8.5.84 As appendix to 1983–84 (HC 416)	41	1077/58	—
1st *Special Report* *Energy Research, Development and Demonstration in the UK* (HC 373)[b]	8.12.82 (14)	11.5.83	—	1 Awaiting full report plus memoranda	966 No memoranda published by end 1983 session	0

Notes:

a Evidence and Report on the Isle of Grain was integrated into the Nuclear Power Report, HC 114, 1980–81.
b Short, interim report on progress—full report not finalized prior to dissolution of Parliament.

CHAPTER 8

The Environment Committee

W. J. Reiners

When it was set up in November 1979 to examine 'the expenditure, administration and policy of the Department of the Environment and associated public bodies and similar matters within the responsibilities of the Secretary of State for Northern Ireland', the new committee was not lacking in scope. The Department (D.o.E.) was then one of the major spending departments, accounting for 12 per cent of government expenditure in 1979–80. Housing and local government—the principal responsibilities of the Department—are the concern of all Members, many of whom have recent experience in local government and maintain close contact with these issues in their constituencies. Labour members in particular have traditionally attached great weight to public sector housing and have defended it vigorously in the House.

Planning, the D.o.E.'s other main responsibility, tends to lie dormant politically between infrequent forays into questions of land ownership and development rights, but it is a source of continuous pressure from landed and commercial interests and of corresponding resistance from conservation groups. It was the central interest in the 1974–79 Parliament of the Committee's predecessor, the Expenditure Committee's Sub-Committee on the Environment, which made lengthy enquiries into planning procedures and the redevelopment of London Docklands. Other departmental responsibilities include pollution control (water, noise, clean air, radioactive wastes), water supply, sewage and waste disposal, and the countryside. These attract a good deal of public interest but little parliamentary attention. The Department is responsible in government for sport and recreation, ancient monuments and historic buildings, and for the management of the Government's building estate through the Property Services Agency. It is the 'sponsor' department for the construction industry, and thus its point of contact and spokesman in government. It has responsibilities for building regulations and building research.

A distinctive feature of the Department's work is its relationship with local government, which requires close contact with many individual authorities in England, mainly through regional offices. There is close liaison with the Scottish Office which has parallel functions, and with the Welsh Office which is the point of contact with Welsh authorities, although it shares a legislative framework with the D.o.E.

MEMBERSHIP AND SUPPORT

The Committee met for the first time on 26 November 1979 with eleven members, six Conservative and five Labour, none of whom had served on the Expenditure Sub-Committee. Two members were discharged within the first month, and indeed throughout the life of the Committee continuity of membership was disrupted, mainly by promotions. Only three members served throughout (Miscampbell, Squire, Winnick) giving a turnover rate of 73 per cent (not 66 per cent as given by the Leader of the House).[1] Of the twenty-three members who served at some time, five stayed for less than one year, ten for between one and two years, four between two and three years, and four for more than three years. The average period of service was nineteen months, or twenty-three months excluding the two initial discharges.

Initially the membership for both parties included both new and experienced Members. Three of the initial Conservative members were new to Parliament and, if replaced, were succeeded by their like. Select committees may offer a convenient way of 'blooding' new Members, and the whips may consider them to be more amenable to party discipline. It is notable that Conservative gaps were filled without a break in continuity, while intervals of two to three months occurred on the Labour side, suggesting difficulty in filling vacancies.

The first chairman elected from the Labour members was Bruce Douglas-Mann, a London solicitor with a long-term involvement in housing through local government and membership of Shelter Board. An avowed enthusiast for the new committees, he spoke in their support at a meeting of the Royal Institute of Public Administration in March 1980, expressing the hope that the committees would escape from the political strait-jacket and find new areas of agreement on issues and policies. He expected to be supported in this aim by the senior Conservative member, Nicholas Scott, with whom he shared a deep interest and common approach to problems of housing. When Douglas-Mann joined the SDP, he became unacceptable as chairman to his Labour colleagues on the Committee (although Tom Bradley retained the Transport Committee chairmanship in like circumstances), and he was discharged from the Committee on 5 February 1982.

After one meeting chaired by Brian Mawhinney in the interregnum, the Chair was taken by Reg Freeson, a late appointment to the Committee (13 April 1981). He had served as Minister of Housing and Construction in the previous government, and was thus fully conversant with the issues, and knew both the staff involved in the D.o.E. and the information available to them. He was closely involved in the major review of housing policy published as a Green Paper in 1977,[2] and with the formulation of policy on inner cities. A journalist by profession, with experience of local government in Brent and Willesden, he came under heavy pressure in his constituency from a move to replace him as a candidate in the 1983 election by Ken Livingstone. Thus Ray Freeson, like Douglas-Mann, did not command support across the whole range of the Labour Party.

When Nicholas Scott was appointed junior Minister in Northern Ireland in November 1981, the lead on the Conservative side was taken by Brian Mawhinney, a new Member with a background of research into radiation physics and little evident interest in consensus politics. His questioning of witnesses was particularly searching, suggestive of the disdain of the physical scientist for evidence which cannot be validated by repeated experiment. On his promotion to Treasury Parliamentary Private Secretary in June 1982, he was succeeded in the leading role by Robin Squire, another new member of an independent turn of mind and a constructive, if relatively passive, approach to the Committee and its work.

The attendance of members ranged from a minimum of 43 per cent of possible meetings to a maximum of 97 per cent for Nicholas Scott. The average attendance was 65 per cent for all members, 63 per cent for Conservatives and 68 per cent for Labour members. If the Chairman is omitted, the latter figure is reduced to 62 per cent, very close to the Conservative figure. The high attendance rate achieved by Scott, who missed only two meetings in two sessions, was exceeded for the sessions 1980-81 and 1981-82 by David Winnick, who missed only one meeting in that period. Winnick was also distinguished by his outspoken and uncompromising opposition to the new committee system from the outset. He was one of the twelve members who voted against the motion for their establishment in June 1979,[3] and continued to express his opposition through committee press conferences, letters to the papers, and on radio. He was generally active in the Chamber, as were most of those resistant to consensus politics.

The central figure in the secretariat supporting the Committee was the clerk, in this case a retired member of the diplomatic service rather than the more usual career clerk. The heavy work load imposed by the broad programme of enquiry initiated by the Committee was relieved by the appointment of a temporary assistant, one of only five appointed to the new committees, and by the employment of specialist advisers.

The nine specialist advisers employed at various times by the Committee were mainly academics working in housing research, for whom the post provides insights into the process of government, but they included an accountant and a retired civil servant. They were employed for specific enquiries, but occasionally worked on two in parallel. They were selected by the Committee from a list submitted by the clerk to provide a balance of knowledge and skills with some reference to political orientation. Specialist advisers, who need to work to tight timetables within briefs set formally by the Committee but in practice by the chairman and clerk, assist in planning the form of the inquiries, drawing up questionnaires, analysing the responses, and drafting technical sections of the report and appendices. The overlapping of the roles of clerk and specialist adviser clearly offers scope for conflict, which was generally avoided by flexibility on both sides, but on one exceptional occasion was sufficiently vigorous to attract attention in the Press.[4]

The Committee relied heavily on its specialist advisers to make good the dearth of information from the Department, and it was fortunate in securing relevant skills and expertise in a relatively narrow field. Some advisers had experience of particular value, having worked in the D.o.E. in the preparation of the 1977 Green Paper on housing policy. The post of specialist adviser is attractive to many academics working in areas of social policy since it offers an insider's view of government, but it calls for policy analysis rather than research and the ability to work closely to a brief and timetable. Recruitment of these fairly rare capacities at a time of academic expansion might present difficulties which would be eased by the employment of a nucleus of specialist staff with some security of tenure.

THE COMMITTEE IN ACTION

The role of chairman makes heavy demands on time and energy. Bruce Douglas-Mann estimated that when it was in full spate the Committee absorbed some twenty hours per week of his time, including four to five hours in session, four hours with the clerk and specialist advisers, and nine hours' reading and paperwork. The load on individual members was much less. Often they attended for only part of a session, and some appeared to read their papers while witnesses were being examined. Progress thus depends critically on the drive and assiduity of the chairman, and much of the Committee's early impetus was reduced by Douglas-Mann's ill health in the early months of 1981.

Excluding press conferences, the Committee met in 116 sessions, of which forty-seven included examination of witnesses and sixty-nine were deliberative. At first, the Committee met twice per week, holding thirty-seven meetings in the 1979–80 session. In 1980–81, only twenty-four meetings were held, in two of which witnesses were examined. With Reg Freeson's appointment the impetus was restored, the Committee began to meet twice weekly again, and thirty meetings had been held in 1982–83 before the dissolution of Parliament.

Inquiries were initiated by the issue of a press notice inviting the submission of evidence, with specialist invitations to those considered to have experience or knowledge of particular relevance. In the local government finance inquiry, the request for evidence was limited to selected organizations in order to avoid duplication of the departmental consultation on the Green Paper. In general, invitations were sent to the D.o.E., local authorities or their associations, commercial and professional organizations, pressure groups, and academics. There were more than 600 written submissions for the eight completed inquiries, 90 per cent of which related to the four inquiries on specific issues. The substantial cost of preparing these must often have been disproportionate to the use made of them. In the West Midlands Region inquiry, of the 214 organizations invited 116 responded with submissions which were deposited in the House of Commons Library and sent to the D.o.E. without publication.

Witnesses were called for examination in all but the West Midlands Region inquiry. In total, forty-nine groups or individuals were examined with a further twenty-seven for the uncompleted parts of the urban renewal inquiry. The clerk provided a brief to guide the questioning of witnesses, but this seems to have influenced some members less than their own experience and constituency interests, especially when examining local authority witnesses representing an area in or near their constituency. Bruce Douglas-Mann worked hard in the chair to bring all members, particularly the Conservatives, into the questioning, so that normally four or five members participated more or less equally while he asked typically 20–25 per cent of the questions from the chair. When Reg Freeson assumed the chair he dominated the questioning, asking more than half the questions in each inquiry. Of the members, only Winnick throughout, and Dobson and Scott while members, were consistently active in questioning. Conservative members tended to be inactive, and in the inquiry into *Urban Renewal (Merseyside Initiative)*, they asked in all only 12 per cent of the questions.

Attendance reached a peak when all members were present to examine Michael Heseltine for the first time on D.o.E. expenditure plans. Nine members took an active part, Conservatives asking 35 per cent of the questions. By contrast, when Heseltine appeared again before the Committee in its second inquiry into D.o.E. expenditure plans, Conservative members together asked only five of the 108 questions.

The opposition spokesman for the Environment was initially Roy Hattersley, followed in 1980 by Gerald Kaufman, significantly a resolute opponent of the new select committee system. He was one of the twelve who voted against their establishment in the June 1979 debate, when he expressed the fear that committee members 'would get very great power and disproportionate attention in debate'.[5] For much of the Parliament Gerald Kaufman and Michael Heseltine competed in adversarial abrasiveness, suggesting the continuation of a personal confrontation begun in the Oxford Union thirty years earlier. The character of the debate on housing issues in this period consequently offered little scope for the carefully reasoned arguments of a select committtee, for the existence of which the relevant members of both front benches showed little enthusiasm.

When the Secretary of State first appeared before the Committee on 24 April 1980, he responded to questions on the implications of D.o.E. expenditure plans for housing policies by saying that they represented the Government's estimate of what the country could afford on housing; and that, given the discretion allowed to individual local authorities, central government was unable to say what the effect of the reductions in total expenditure would be. Predictions of the level and composition of public expenditure had always been in error, in his view, and the Committee's estimate of the likely outcome would be as good as his. On the housing need, he 'did not think it useful to publish any such material'.[6]

The frustration induced in the Committee members by these replies can be gauged by Brian Mawhinney's question, 'Is the Secretary of State seriously telling the Committee ... that he is going to reduce the expenditure on housing by 50 per cent and that he has given no serious thought to the consequences that are likely to follow from that reduction'.[7] The Committee also found it scarcely credible that the Secretary of State should have used the crude housing surplus as an indicator of housing need in his discussions with the Treasury. The report, which complained about the lack of information available on major issues of policy, was agreed without amendment, the eight amendments proposed by Winnick to stiffen the criticism of the Government being rejected by the Conservative majority.

The cohesion induced by Michael Heseltine's evidence did not survive the *Council House Sales* inquiry which dealt with the controversial right to buy given to local authority (and housing association) tenants by the 1980 Housing Act. Consideration of the report extended over three meetings in which there were 126 divisions—or two for each three paragraphs of the report. Although he attended only two of the interview sessions, Brian Mawhinney took the lead in proposing amendments, many of which suggested close agreement with D.o.E. policy. Several of those accepted were echoed with approval in the Department's reply.[8] Only 57 of the 126 recorded divisions were decided strictly on party lines. The adoption of the report was agreed by a majority of five to four in which for the first time Dobson, Mawhinney, Thornton, and Winnick voted together against Freeson, Johnson-Smith, Miscampbell, Scott, and Squire. At the press conference, Bruce Douglas-Mann maintained that, although the majority for acceptance seemed slight, the voting went against party lines and showed that the Committee could focus and express a balanced critique even on controversial issues. The conference was dominated, however, by members distinguishing their individual position. A personal statement issued as a press notice by Nicholas Scott explained that his support for the report did not conflict with his acceptance of Conservative policy on the 'right to buy' and, while falling short of a Galilean recantation, suggested some recent sight of the instruments— it would seem that the report caused displeasure at the highest levels in government.

The later reports under Reg Freeson's chairmanship did not cause significant dissension within the Committee. There were thirteen divisions on the *Private Rented Housing Sector* report but only one significantly affected the report by omitting one paragraph. Nine amendments were proposed by David Winnick and were defeated on party lines. There were nine divisions on the report on *Local Government Financing* but none on the reports on *Urban Renewal (Merseyside Initiative)* and on the *Winter Supplementary Estimates*, both of which were concluded hurriedly at the end of the Parliament.

The withholding of information from the Committee seriously impaired the effectiveness of its critique of government policies. It contrasted with the assurances given to the House at different times by Norman St John-Stevas and Francis Pym[9] that the Government would make available to the committees as much information as possible and that every minister would do all in his power to co-operate with them. Michael Heseltine is a strong advocate of open government, as exemplified by his publication of Management Information Systems for Ministers (MINIS). Examined on MINIS by the Treasury and Civil Service Sub-Committee he said 'I am in favour of providing Parliament, wherever there is no overriding political or policy restraint, with as much information as possible'.[10] The reservations or restraints, of course, are capable of wide differences of interpretation. The material withheld from the Committee did not involve a refusal to give access to any specific paper. That would have presented a clearer issue to bring before the House, with which the capacity to enforce committees' powers to send for persons and papers rests, rather than with the individual committees. Members of the Environment Committee do not appear to have pursued the issue further in the House and did not participate in the debate on 16 January 1981 when restraints on the provision of information to select committees were discussed.

ACHIEVEMENTS AND INFLUENCE

The Committee was appointed to 'examine the expenditure, administration and policy' of the D.o.E. and its achievements may best be considered under those headings.

Administration

The Committee's sole inquiry into the Department's administration examined the performance of its West Midlands Regional Office. The inquiry[11] was suggested by the three D.o.E. Permanent Secretaries when they met the Committee informally at the outset to discuss its programme, and it was conducted with thoroughness. The report, based on some 116 replies to a questionnaire, revealed general satisfaction with the service given by the regional office, although questions were raised about the degree of delegation from D.o.E. headquarters and the overlap of functions with the Housing Corporation. The latter issue was already under scrutiny by the Public Accounts Committee which is well equipped to maintain the necessary long-term pressure on the D.o.E. Permanent Secretary. Such a clean sheet was inevitably something of an anticlimax, and the Committee made no further inquiry into D.o.E. administration. Such inquiries demand a closer knowledge of a department than committee members can normally achieve, although for the D.o.E. the publication of MINIS may provide a point of entry in the future.

Expenditure

The first two inquiries[12] into departmental expenditure plans and their implications for housing policies had the advantage that the issues were clearly defined and the evidence confined mainly to the D.o.E. and its ministers. The unanimous reports made forceful attacks on the Secretary of State's handling of housing policy, in particular his failure, in deciding the level of the cuts imposed, to take adequate account of their consequences, for which the Committee gave its own estimates. Little use was made of this material to attack the Government in the Commons, but in the Lords Baroness Birk used material from the first report in the second reading debate on the Housing Bill 1980.[13]

The third expenditure inquiry[14] dealt with the D.o.E. winter supplementary estimates 1982–83 and reported first on a guarantee for the London Zoological Society which involved issues of financial management rather than policy. The section on housing complained again about the lack of information, but went on to question the consequences of short-term changes in the housing programme through moratoria and spending sprees. The cost penalties of departmental improvisation need more careful examination than was possible in the time available but the topic has been identified for later investigation.

Policy

The council house sales inquiry[15] was intended initially to run in parallel with that on the private rented housing sector, but went ahead on its own when the latter was postponed. It started too late to influence the second reading of the 1980 Housing Bill in the Commons on 15 January 1980.

The evidence from the examination of witnesses was published between April and July 1980 and was available to the Lords for their debates on the Bill, in the course of which amendments were passed relaxing the right to buy provision for houses built for the elderly and houses in designated rural areas[16]. The Government was embarrassed further when, in reply to a supplementary question from Gerald Kaufman, John Stanley stated the Government's intention to reject the amendments before the Lords had completed their hearings.[17] After a show of resentment, the Lords suspended their sitting.

The Committee's evidence may well have influenced the Lords to make the amendment on rural areas, but Baroness Birk found more support for her case on housing for the elderly in the publications of the D.o.E.[18] Bruce Douglas-Mann wrote to Michael Heseltine drawing his attention to the Committee's evidence before the Commons debate on the Lords' amendments, but their acceptance by the Government must be considered to follow more directly from John Stanley's premature reply. Nevertheless, the Committee can reasonably claim some part in freeing 300,000 houses from the right to buy provision.

The report was published a year after the passage of the relevant legislation. The national press gave more attention to the dissension in the Committee over its approval than to its findings, but the latter were picked up in professional and technical journals. It drew attention to the likely impact of the right to buy on public sector housing, correcting an error in the Department's calculations of the loss of relets presented to Parliament at the time of the Commons debates. It considered the effect on the stock if only the more attractive houses were sold and the impact on housing for special groups for which the Lords' amendments gave only a partial relaxation. The report reinforced criticism in evidence to the Committee by the Comptroller and Auditor-General of the Department's financial appraisal,[19] although the effect is appreciable only in the longer term. It made a careful examination of the consequences of the policy for individuals who may overstretch their resources by purchase, but did not set this in the context of the number of satisfied buyers. The report concluded with strong recommendations for research and monitoring on a list of topics.

The report evidently did not convert the Government to its way of thinking, since it went ahead to extend the right to buy to charitable organizations in its Housing and Building Control Bill, which was delayed by the Lords and lost in the dissolution. When the Bill was introduced in the new Parliament, little or no use was made of the Committee's reports in the debate.[20]

Private rented housing may be considered a Conservative interest, balancing the Labour interest in council house sales. It is a complex subject, with little firm information, and much prejudice and vested interest, the ground of old skirmishes over municipalization, security of tenure, and rent control, but treated recently by both parties as peripheral to their preoccupation with owner-occupation and council housing. The inquiry was limited in scope and, after the initial delay was pushed quickly to a report[21] which drew attention to the continued decline of the sector and the increasing difficulty faced by the mobile and poorer households which rely on it. After reviewing the problems of both landlord and tenant in terms of return on investment, security of tenure, harassment, and the growth of lettings outside the Rent Acts, the report called for government action including additional monitoring of the effect of legislation.

The report satisfied neither landlord nor tenant groups, but it had a good press and stimulated some lively correspondence there. The Department's reply followed the conventional form of restating the Department's own policies, but expressed the intention of following up the recommendations on harassment and of considering the establishment of a Housing Court. Although the report thus had little immediate effect it may help to stimulate action in the next Parliament.

Local government finance has been the subject of many lengthy inquiries and little government action over the years, and the decision of the Conservative members to make this inquiry against the wishes of the Labour members could be seen as aiming to provide an excuse for further inactivity. D.o.E. officials said[22] that they had received 1130 submissions in response to their Green Paper, and the Committee's inquiry was sensibly confined to a few selected witnesses. It had the advantage for them over departmental consultation that their evidence was published and assessed on its merits. The report[23] ruled out the abolition of domestic rating, which had been part of the Government's 1979 Manifesto commitment, as well as a local sales tax and a poll tax. It argued for less direct control by central government over local government expenditure, and asked for detailed consideration of a local income tax. The public impact of the report was not great but the response was generally favourable. The Government's reply, made in the next Parliament in its White Paper on Rating,[24] accepted many of the findings of the report. Reg Freeson suggested in his report to the Liaison Committee[25] that the Committee's report influenced the Government to reconsider its Manifesto commitment, but the inherent difficulty of those proposals may offer a more plausible explanation.

The final policy inquiry into urban renewal was considered in three parts, of which only the one dealing with the Merseyside initiative had been completed by the dissolution. The published evidence[26] illustrates both the problems of securing collective action by local agencies and the influence an active Secretary of State can exert if he concentrates his attention on one locality. The report found it premature to assess the success of the scheme and suggested that the Department should publish its own asssessment. While recognizing the advantages of a 'Minister for Merseyside', it accepted that they could not be generalized and that there were potential confusions of responsibilities. For the remaining parts of the inquiry, dealing with 'inner city policies, partnerships and programmes etc.' and 'the role of the private sector', interviews with twenty-seven bodies had been completed, sixteen of which had been published.[27] Although the published report has had some impact, the discontinuity inherent in the select committee system at a dissolution puts at risk full exploitation of the contributions of witnesses, members, and staff. In its final Special Report,[28] the Committee expressly invited its successor to carry on the inquiry.

ASSESSMENT AND CONCLUSION

Judged by the criterion of its achievements in the House of Commons, the Environment Committee must be considered one of the less successful of the new committees. Although it presented coherent, well-argued reports on a number of contentious issues, they were often badly timed and too complex to make much impact in the House. The Committee was unfortunate that within its membership and amongst the relevant front-bench spokesmen there were some resolute opponents of the new committee system. And the early impetus of the Committee was disrupted by the ill-health and subsequent resignation of its first Chairman. The achievements of the Committee, however, need to be considered in a wider context than the House of Commons. Its consensus policies might carry little weight in the Commons, but the House of Lords has recently had a significant influence on housing legislation and its members have shown themselves to be more receptive to the Committee's reports. The Committee has a role in providing information for the public, especially through the professional and technical press, as well as to Parliament, and there are manifest advantages in a form of consultation which allows the publication of evidence over the traditional method.

The Government's withholding of information seriously prejudiced the Committee's ability to examine housing policy. In a dispersed and diverse subject like housing, *ad hoc* surveys confined to organizations able to compile relevant information are no substitute for systematic monitoring and research. The Department could reasonably comment on the *Council House Sales* report that the Committee had taken no account of those who benefited from sales. This restraint on information which is potentially damaging to governmental policies raises wider issues concerning the organization of monitoring and research. Developments following reports by Trend[29] and Rothschild[30] have increasingly concentrated on the financial and managerial control of research, other than basic research, in central government departments. In his later report on the Social Science Research Council,[31] Lord Rothschild revised his view of the scope of the customer-contractor principle when he wrote, 'It would be too much to expect Ministers to show enthusiasm for research designed to show that their policies were misconceived. But it seems obvious that in many cases the public interest will be served by such research being undertaken.' The need to secure an independent base for policy-oriented research raises a wider issue affecting the machinery of Government as a whole and may lie outside the scope of the select committees. It might perhaps be recognized as a suitable subject for inquiry by the House of Lords.

The Committee's effectiveness could be improved in the shorter term by a stronger secretariat. While resource restraints may prevent even a scaled-down version of the Congressional system, greater continuity of employment for specialist advisers, chosen for their ability in policy analysis rather than expertise in a narrow field of research, would permit the setting-up of a standing office able to build up a background of information, sources and contacts. This would relieve the currently excessive load on the chairman and would speed up the response to the Committee's needs.

The experience of the Environment Committee offers little support to the view of the Speaker, expressed in a radio interview with Norman St John Stevas on 3 November 1981, that the select committees gave Members more power than at any time since the seventeenth century. Given the existing disposition of powers, the committees are unlikely to pose any serious threat to the Government's 'elective dictatorship'[32]—and any such threat would probably ensure their demise. But at a time of increased polarization in the House of Commons, and in spite of some initial dissension the Environment Committee demonstrated to a wider public the possibility of bi-partisan policies with which more radical programmes could be compared.

NOTES

1. HC Debs., 29 July 1983, col. 633 (written answer).
2. *Housing Policy: A Consultative Document*, Cmnd. 6851.
3. HC Debs., 25 June 1979, cols. 249–50.
4. The *Guardian*, 15 July 1981.
5. HC Debs., 25 June 1979, cols. 172–8.
6. 1979–80, HC 578-i.
7. Ibid., q. 4.
8. Cmnd. 8377: see particularly paras. 9 and 11, referring to paras. 56, 62, and 65 of 1980–81, HC 366-I.
9. HC Debs., 25 June 1979, cols. 45–6; 16 January 1981, cols. 1305–14.
10. 1981–82, HC 360-iv, q. 577.
11. First Report, 1980–81, HC 60.
12. First Report, 1979–80, HC 714; Third Report, 1980–81, HC 383.
13. HL Debs., 30 July 190, cols. 1018–19.
14. Third Report, 1982–83, HC 170.
15. 1979–80, HC 535, i–ix.

16. HL Debs., 21 July 1980: amendment on housing for the elderly agreed by 109–74.
17. HC Debs., 30 July 1980, col. 1489.
18. HL Debs., 21 July 1980, col. 12: *Housing for Old People*, D.o.E.
19. Second Report, 1980–81, HC 366–III, pp. 1–9.
20. HC Debs., 5 July 1983.
21. First Report, 1981–82, HC 40.
22. 1981–82, HC 217–iv, q. 568.
23. Second Report, 1981–82, HC 217.
24. Cmnd. 9008.
25. 1982–83, HC 92, Liaison Committee Report, p. 72.
26. Third Report, 1982–83, HC 18; Minutes of Evidence, 1982–83, HC 103.
27. 1982–83, HC 103; 1982–83, HC 325.
28. 1982–83, HC 406.
29. Report of the Committee of Enquiry into the *Organization of Civil Science*, Cmnd. 2171, 1964.
30. *A Framework for Government Research and Development*, Cmnd. 4814.
31. Cmnd. 8554, para. 3.12.
32. Lord Hailsham, *The Dilemma of Democracy*, Collins, 1978.

Annex 8.1 *Environment Committee*

Report	Date of first oral evidence (no. of evidence sessions)	Date of publication of report	Date and form of govt. reply	Length of report (pages)	No. of oral qq./no. of written submissions	No. of divisions
Session 1979–80 1st Report *Inquiry into the implications of the Govt.'s Expenditure Plans 1980–1 to 1983–4 for the Housing Policies of the D.o.E.* (HC 714)	24.4.80 (1)	26.8.80	15.12.80 Cmnd. 8105	13	67/1	8
Session 1980–81 1st Report *The D.o.E. and the West Midlands Region* (HC 60)	— (0)	18.12.80	—	2	0/116	0
2nd Report *Council House Sales* (HC 366)	1.4.80 (10)	14.7.81	8.10.81 Cmnd. 8377	61	1019/144	126
3rd Report *D.o.E.'s Housing Policies: Inquiry into Govt.'s Exp. Plans 1981–2 to 1983–4 and the updating of the Com.'s 1st Report for the Session 1979/80* (HC 383)	23.6.81 (2)	28.8.81	27.11.81 Cmnd. 8435	9 —	108/13	5
Session 1981–82 1st Report *The Private Rented Housing Sector* (HC 40)	1.12.81 (6)	8.9.82	18.11.82 Memo pub. HC 54 Session 1982–83	36	584/166	13

Report	Date of first oral evidence (no. of evidence sessions)	Date of publication of report	Date and form of govt. reply	Length of report (pages)	No. of oral qq./no. of written submissions	No. of divisions
2nd Report Inquiry into the Methods of Financing Local Govt. in the context of the Govt.'s Green Paper Cmnd. 8449 (HC 217)	2.3.82 (8)	9.9.82	2.8.83 Reference in Cmnd. 9008 (White Paper on Rates)	31	877/29	7
Session 1982–83 1st Special Report Memo. from the D.o.E. in response to the 1st Report from the En. Com. (Session 81–82) (HC 54)	— (o)	6.12.82	n/a	1	0/1	0
1st Report The Private Rented Housing Sector—A Report on the Memo. from the D.o.E. in response to the Com.'s 1st Report, Session 1981–82 (HC 201)		3.3.83	—	5	—	—
2nd Report D.o.E.'s Winter Supplementary Estimates 1982–83 Relating to the Zoological Soc. and Housing Matters (HC 170)	3.2.83 (1)	3.6.83	—	5	77/1	0
3rd Report The Problems of the Management of Urban Renewal (Appraisal of the Recent Initiative on Merseyside) (HC 18)	9.11.82 (5)	29.6.83	—	34	556/161	0
2nd Special Report Proposals for Future of the Enquiry (into Urban Renewal) (HC 406)	—	27.5.83	—	1	—	0

Other Proceedings and Publications
Evidence from incomplete enquiries was published as follows:
1. Inner cities, policies, partnerships, programmes etc.: HC 103 (i–x) 1982–83.
2. The role of the private sector: HC 325 (i–iii) 1982–83.

Annex 8.2 *Environment Committee Membership Succession*

Period	Member (constituency)	Attendance %	Background
26.11.79– 14.12.79.	Donald Anderson (Lab) Swansea East	—	74–79 PPS, LG, NUR
1.2.80– 15.2.83.	John Sever Birmingham (Ladywood)	60	74–79 PPS, APEX, (later Op Sp Ov Dev)
15.2.83–	Alec Woodall	77	74–79 PPS, LG, NUM
26.11.79– 14.12.79.	Donald Atkinson (Con) Bournemouth East	—	LG, YC, CD
14.12.79– 19.6.81.	Geoffrey Johnson-Smith East Grinstead	79	71–74 JM CSD, Defence, ex VC Cons Party, 1922 Com,
19.6.81– 4.12.81.	Robert Dunn Dartford	43	New MP (Con Gain), LG later JM Education
4.12.81–	Teddy Taylor Southend	43	70–74 Scottish Office
26.11.79– 24.5.82.	Frank Dobson (Lab) Holborn & St Pancras	49	New MP, LG (later Op Sp Education)
24.5.82–[1]	John Forrester Stoke (North)	51	LG, NUT
26.11.79– 5.2.82.	Bruce Douglas-Mann (Lab) Mitcahm & Morden	93	Solicitor, LG, Shelter Board, Cmn Soc Lab Lawyers
24.5.82–[1]	Geoffrey Lofthouse Pontefract & Castleford	64	LG, APEX
26.11.79– 23.1.81.	Jim Marshall (Lab) Leicester (South)	43	74–79 G Whip, LG (later Op Sp Home Affairs)
14.3.81–	Reg Freeson Brent East	89	74–79 Min H&C, LG, Journalist
26.11.79– 11.6.82.	Brian Mawhinney (Con) Peterborough	63	New MP (Con Gain) Scientist, MRC
11.6.82–[3]	John Heddle Litchfield & Tamworth	46	New MP (Con Gain), LG Surveyor, Con Com on Env.
26.11.79–	Norman Miscampbell (Cons.) Blackpool (North)	67	LG Barrister, Cons. Legal Com. (Sec.)
26.11.79– 13.11.81.	Nicholas Scott (Cons.) Chelsea	97	70–74 JM Employment LG, 1922 Com.
13.11.81–[2]	Fergus Montgomery Altringcham & Sale	87	70–74 PPS, LG, YC

Annex 8.2 *Environment Committee Membership Succession (cont.)*

Period	Member (constituency)	Attendance %	Background
26.11.79–	Robin Squire (Cons.) Hornchurch	72	New MP (Cons. Gain) LG, YC, Accountant
26.11.79– 13.11.82.	Malcolm Thornton (Cons.) Liverpool (Garston)	44	New MP (Cons. Gain) LG (Chmn AMA) River Pilot
13.11.81–(2) 11.6.82.	James Pawsey Rugby	67	New MP (Cons. Gain) LG, CD
11.6.82–(3)	Richard Alexander Newark	52	New MP (Cons. Gain) LG, Solicitor
26.11.79–	David Winnick (Lab.) Walsall North	90	LG, APEX

Notes:
JM: Junior Minister; LG: Local Government; YC: Young Conservatives.
CD: Company Director.
(1),(2),(3) Appointments made on the same day and succession unclear.

Annex 8.3 *Programme and Progress*

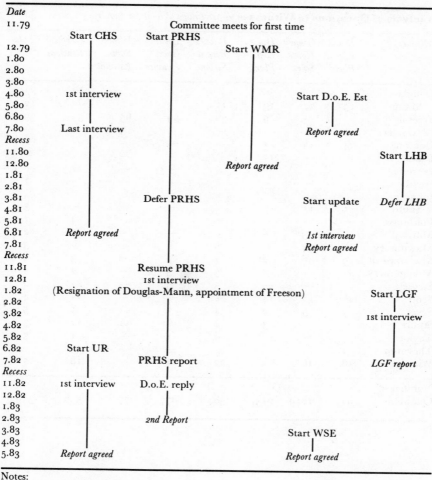

Date				
11.79		Committee meets for first time		
	Start CHS	Start PRHS		
12.79			Start WMR	
1.80				
2.80				
3.80				
4.80	1st interview			Start D.o.E. Est
5.80				
6.80				
7.80	Last interview			*Report agreed*
Recess				
11.80				Start LHB
12.80			*Report agreed*	
1.81				
2.81				
3.81		Defer PRHS	Start update	*Defer LHB*
4.81				
5.81				
6.81	*Report agreed*		*1st interview*	
7.81			*Report agreed*	
Recess				
11.81		Resume PRHS		
12.81		1st interview		
1.82	(Resignation of Douglas-Mann, appointment of Freeson)			Start LGF
2.82				
3.82				1st interview
4.82				
5.82				
6.82	Start UR			
7.82		PRHS report		*LGF report*
Recess				
11.82	1st interview	D.o.E. reply		
12.82				
1.83				
2.83		*2nd Report*		
3.83			Start WSE	
4.83				
5.83	*Report agreed*		*Report agreed*	

Notes:

CHS—   Council House Sales
PRHS—   Private Rented Housing Sector
WMR—   West Midlands Region
D.o.E. Est.—   D.o.E. Expenditure plans
LGF—   Local Government Financing
UR—   Urban Renewal
WSE—   Winter Supplementary Estimates
LHB—   Listing of Historic Buildings

Annex 8.4

Analysis of Questions to Witnesses *as percentage of total for Inquiry*

Member	D.o.E. Exp. Plans	Council House Sales	D.o.E. Exp. Plans	Private Rented Sector	Local Govt. Finance	Winter Supp. Estimates	Urban Renewal	Total
Douglas-Mann	19	27	19	11				12
Freeson	—	—	9	36	59	65	57	33
Alexander	—	—	—	—	—	3	1	—
Dobson	24	13	24	—	—	—	—	6
Dunn	—	—	11	—	—	—	—	—
Forrester	—	—	—	—	—	—	2	—
Heddle	—	—	—	—	—	—	3	1
Johnson-Smith	1	11	—	—	—	—	—	3
Lofthouse	—	—	—	—	1	1	4	1
Marshall	—	5	—	—	—	—	—	2
Mawhinney	12	4	—	6	2	—	—	3
Miscampbell	5	6	2	1	3	8	3	4
Montgomery	—	—	—	3	5	—	2	2
Pawsey	—	—	—	5	3	—	—	2
Scott	16	11	14	—	—	—	—	4
Sever	3	5	2	4	3	11	7	5
Squire	—	1	3	4	6	11	2	3
Taylor	—	—	—	8	4	—	1	3
Thornton	1	1	—	—	—	—	—	—
Winnick	18	16	25	22	14	—	18	17
Number of Questions	67	1019	213	584	877	77	556	3393

CHAPTER 9

The Foreign Affairs Committee

C. Y. Carstairs

The Foreign Affairs Committee (FAC) was set up on 25 June 1979 'to examine the expenditure, administration and policy of the Foreign and Commonwealth Office and of associated public bodies'.[1] Membership was fixed at eleven and the quorum at three and, unless otherwise ordered by the House, would continue for the rest of the Parliament. The Foreign Affairs Committee (FAC) like others was empowered to send for persons, papers, and records, to sit during adjournments of the House, and to appoint specialist advisers. The FAC was empowered, but not required, to appoint one sub-committee. Its original membership was:

Miss Betty Boothroyd (Lab.)
Mr Christopher Brocklebank-
  Fowler (Cons., later SDP)
Mr Eric Deakins (Lab.)
Mr (now Sir) Anthony Grant
  (Cons.)
Mr Eldon Griffiths (Cons.)

Mr Frank Hooley (Lab.)
Mr (now Sir) Anthony Kershaw
  (Cons.)
Mr Kevin McNamara (Lab.)
Mr (now Sir) Peter Mills (Cons.)
Sir Anthony Royle (Cons.)
Mr Nigel Spearing (Cons.)

Mr Kershaw was elected chairman, and he, with Mr Griffiths, Mr Hooley, and Mr Spearing, continued in membership throughout the 1979–83 Parliament. 'Newcomers' during the Parliament were Messrs Dennis Canavan (Lab.), George Foulkes (Lab.), Ivan Lawrence (Cons.), Jim Lester (Cons.), Cyril Townsend (Cons.), Michael Welsh (Lab.), and Bowen Wells (Cons.).

When the Committee was reappointed in November 1983, it included as many as six of those who had served in the preceding Parliament, among them being the chairman, Sir Anthony Kershaw.

In all, nineteen Members served on the FAC. Of those who left, practically all did so on appointments to 'shadow' or government posts or party office of one kind or another, so that the turnover rate (about 73 per cent) is not an indication of disenchantment with the work of the Committee.

ORGANIZATION

In their 1977-78 report, the Procedure Committee, although they advised against the continuance of the Select Committee on Overseas Development, recommended 'that overseas development should become a responsibility of the new Committee on Foreign Affairs, but that the Committee should be empowered to appoint a sub-committee on overseas development either permanently or whenever the Committee think necessary'.[2] The debate of 25 June 1979, like that of 19 and 20 February 1979 on the Procedure Committee Report,[3] revealed a good deal of support for the continuance of specific provision for work on overseas development. In the event, the FAC did appoint such a sub-committee, and it continued throughout the Parliament. The initial membership was ten (that is, the whole membership less the Chairman), but as time passed there was some falling away, so that for the Committee's Fourth Report for 1982-83 it stood at four from Labour and three Conservative. The original chairman of the Sub-Committee was Mr McNamara (Lab.), followed in February 1982 by Mr Hooley (also Lab.).

Apart from the Sub-Committee, the FAC itself was not without precedent. The function of examining the work of the Foreign and Commonwealth Office (FCO) was inherited from the Defence and External Affairs Sub-Committee of the Expenditure Committee. One of the original members of the FAC, Sir Anthony Kershaw, has been a member of that Sub-Committee; and Messrs Brocklebank-Fowler, Hooley, McNamara, and Spearing had all served on the Select Committee on Overseas Development. While some would certainly have preferred overseas development to have continued to be the remit of an independent select committee, the combination corresponds to the government decision to bring the Ministry of Overseas Development under the overall responsibility of the Secretary of State for Foreign and Commonwealth Affairs. The setting up of the Sub-Committee also reflected the fact that the Overseas Development Administration(ODA) retained considerable operational independence under its own Minister. Since the four Members inherited from the Overseas Development Committee were all very assiduous, it is not surprising that the Sub-Committee inherited much of the style of its predecessor and tended to be something of a lobby for overseas development. The Sub-Committee was an active one. Of the twenty-one reports completed by the FAC during the 1979–83 Parliament, nine were based on evidence taken by the Sub-Committee.

COVERAGE

Short titles of the FAC's reports are given in the Annex. These fall broadly into four categories: first, scrutiny of the organization and working of the departments and other public bodies with which the FAC was concerned (six reports);[4] secondly, Estimates (three reports);[5] thirdly, topics arising mainly though not wholly in the Sub-Committee, in respect of present or recent British overseas dependencies (four reports);[6] and, fourthly, (eight reports), what might be called targets of opportunity—topics of current or prospective political importance likely to call for action by the House and on which a preliminary elucidation by the Committee of the facts and issues might be of value.[7]

In terms of reports, the fourth category (targets of opportunity) and the first (organizational) received the heaviest emphasis. This is broadly in accordance with the weight of questioning, which showed a general average of 347 questions per inquiry. Eleven of the eighteen inquiries at which oral evidence was taken involved fewer than 400 questions each.

EVIDENCE

The range of written and oral evidence varied widely according to subject. Inquiries concentrating on the organization and methods of work of a department or agency might involve only official witnesses, and perhaps not many of these. By contrast, the Afghanistan inquiry[8] involved nineteen witnesses or groups of witnesses, some appearing several times, and that on the Caribbean and Central America[9] involved fifteen. The Committee took pains to make it known that they would be willing to consider unsolicited written submissions, and in respect of some inquiries these were fairly numerous; for example, the inquiry into overseas students' fees[10] (forty-three submissions). The inquiry into the role of Parliament in relation to the British North America Acts[11] attracted, in addition to the documents which the Committee printed, no fewer than 188 unsolicited memoranda, letters, telegrams, etc., of which 177 came from Canada.

Apart from this undoubtedly exceptional instance, and also to some extent the inquiry into the ODA Scientific and Special Units,[12] the FAC was not the target of anything like such a barrage of unsolicited representations as were some of the committees dealing with home affairs, where there are often alert, vigilant, well-funded, and sophisticated lobbies and pressure-groups. There are interest groups concerned with overseas matters, notably aid, but as they are not often 'self-interest' groups they tend not to be so powerful, well-organized, and well-financed as those dealing with major domestic matters.

This notwithstanding, the papers received by the FAC—whether solicited or not—were for the most part full and substantial, notably the departmental ones. There was perhaps something of a no-win situation here. Departments felt it on the whole best to be comprehensive, so that as many oral questions as possible might be dealt with by reference to material already in members' possession. Some members, on the other hand, felt that there might at times be a tendency to blind them with science, although departments equally felt on occasion that members' questioning showed that they had hardly looked at the material which had been furnished to them with considerable effort and sometimes at short notice. This problem may have arisen in part from inquiries being initiated with only a general idea of their objectives, so that departmental and other witnesses might start with little clear idea of what was expected.

TRAVEL

As might be expected, the FAC and the Sub-Committee found it necessary to travel abroad in connection with several of their inquiries. Their travel expenses over the first three sessions, at about £90,000, were the largest of those of all the departmentally-related committees. Visits were paid to Kenya, Malawi, Bangkok, and Amman;[13] to Bahrain, Oman, Thailand, and Jordan;[14] to Zimbabwe;[15] to Gibraltar and Madrid;[16] to Paris, Malawi, Tanzania, and Kenya;[17] to Mexico, Costa Rica, Nicaragua, El Salvador, Jamaica, Venezuela, Grenada, Trinidad, and Barbados.[18] The parties on this last inquiry also collected evidence on the Commonwealth Development Corporation.[19] The Committee also visited the United Nations in New York and the Falklands in connection with their report on a policy for the Falkland Islands,[20] which in the event was not completed. This last visit was perhaps unique in that something like one in fifty of the entire population of the islands attended public hearings of the Committee, which also visited more than half of the settlements in the territory.

USE OF SPECIALIST ADVISERS

The Committee made free use of its power to appoint specialist advisers. In all, some thirty individuals were appointed at one time or another. Advisers were usually engaged *ad hoc* for individual inquiries and sometimes more than one adviser served on a single inquiry. In choosing them, apart from relying on personal knowledge or other sources of advice (for example, the FCO), the FAC regularly consulted Mr David Watt, the Director of the Royal Institute of International Affairs (Chatham House). He also advised on specific inquiries, as did other members of the staff of Chatham House. Whereas some advisers served more than once, the FAC deliberately cast its net fairly wide, in the belief that work for the Committee could be of advantage to the advisers themselves, and so to the academic community at large, as well as to the Committee. While most were drawn from the academic world, the FAC also took on advisers from accountancy, management consultancy, authorship, pressure groups, a retired FCO official, and a retired army officer. In all, the FAC made appreciably more use of specialist advisers than the other new committees (see Chapter 18, Table 7).

Advisers played no part in the choice of subjects for inquiries. In general, they were appointed after topics had been chosen and with particular reference to them. The adviser or advisers concerned with particular inquiries were almost invariably identified in reports: and memoranda by advisers were at times published among papers annexed to reports.

Although there is no provision for this in standing orders, reports were to a considerable extent drafted by advisers. This procedure contrasts with the more usual practice whereby drafts are prepared under the chairman's direction and on his behalf by the clerk to the committee, in consultation with advisers. This relatively novel practice raises certain problems—ones by no means peculiar to the FAC, though this Committee's exceptionally extensive use of specialist advisers makes it appropriate to discuss them here.

The use made of advisers was not specifically due to the 1979 changes, though the tone of the Procedure Committee Report and of the Commons debates of 19 and 20 February and 25 June 1979 may have served as an encouragement. The powers of committees in this respect were exactly the same as those of their predecessors, the only difference being that the FAC in particular made much more use of them. There was also an important difference in the *way* in which specialist advisers were used, not only (to quote the orders of reference) '... to supply information which is not readily available or to elucidate matters of complexity ...' but, more often than not, actually to draft the reports themselves. This was not a function foreshadowed or envisaged either in the Procedure Committee Report or in the debates of February or June 1979.

Accepting that, to begin with at any rate, this change may have been due at least in part to pressure of work on the permanent staff of the House, it is a question whether this was an advance. Bearing in mind that the purpose of select committees is fundamentally to elucidate matters actually or potentially calling for decisions by the House (that is to say political decisions), it is appropriate that the results of inquiries should be expressed in terms bearing as clearly, directly, and briefly as possible on those decisions. To do this is not necessarily within the experience or skill of specialist advisers, and there is a consequent possibility that reports may simply add to the volume of technicalities and complexities which it is part of the object of the exercise to cut through. The skill and experience here are those of the permanent staff of the House, working of course as necessary in collaboration with the specialist advisers.

There is also the cognate view of the then Clerk of the House, Sir Richard Barlas, in his evidence to the Procedure Committee,[21] that 'The value of Select Committee reports is that they are reports of elected Members of Parliament to elected Members of Parliament. It is doubtful if their value would be enhanced if they became reports of specialists which had received the formal endorsement of a Committee.' He was not alone in the view, though the Procedure Committee seemed to disagree,[22] and it is clear that there would be a long way to go before there were any parallel at Westminster with the horrors described in respect of the Congress of the United States by Malbin and Scully.[23] There, for example, it seems that Senators are outnumbered by committee staff to the extent of 70 to 1, and are correspondingly overwhelmed by paper and out of control of the doings of many committees. But the tendency may have to be watched. In the USA, the post-war developments described by Malbin and Scully were certainly unintended.

CONTACTS WITH MINISTERS AND OFFICIALS

Apart from the novel and extensive use of advisers, the methods of work of the FAC appear to have been substantially unchanged from previous practice, except for the practice of having hearings of the Secretary of State for Foreign and Commonwealth Affairs and other ministers unconnected with specific inquiries and not resulting in reports (although these hearings were reported to the House in the normal way and the transcripts published). These hearings, when Lord Carrington was Secretary of State, enabled Members of the House of Commons to have discussions with the Secretary of State for which they would not otherwise have had the opportunity; but his practice did not arise from the 1979 changes. Such hearings were valuable to the Committee both for general background and to help it plan its inquiries.

Both the FAC and the Sub-Committee routinely saw a great deal of the ministers and officials of the FCO and the ODA in connection with specific inquiries. The burden which the calls of the Committee put on ministers and departments was substantial, particularly for the FCO, but was nevertheless borne with good grace. The FCO is after all not in the business of gratuitously making enemies, whether in Westminster or anywhere else. From the departmental point of view, willingness to meet the Committee's requests—even when the reason for them might not seem immediately obvious—would be regarded as bread upon the waters, to be repaid by general goodwill and understanding of the department's problems and approach.

Relations with the FCO and ODA seem in general to have been straightforward without being 'cosy'. The FAC and the Sub-Committee seem to have been confident and sure of themselves: and the departments for their part seem to have taken the view that candour was in the best interests of all concerned. Apart from other considerations, the departments appear to have come to regard the presentation of evidence—written or oral—to the FAC as a useful means of putting departmental ideas into circulation in a less formal way than would be called for in statements and debates in the House itself.

However, in some respects full consentaneity had not been achieved by the end of the 1979–83 Parliament; perhaps it never can be, given the inherent difference of view between Whitehall and Westminster. In the FCO there seems to have been a feeling that at times the FAC did not fully realize that external affairs are not an area in which the government can command results (as it can in some areas of domestic policy), and that the national interest might not always be best served by too public an airing of all material considerations. Members of the Committee sometimes felt that the FCO might at times be bolder in showing its hand and not take refuge so often behind considerations of discretion and tact. On one or two occasions, there were departmental rejoinders to reports which might be regarded as sharp, e.g. those on the Turks and Caicos Island hotel development,[24] and airport development on Providenciales (Turks and Caicos Islands),[25] and that on the ODA's scientific and special units.[26] Nevertheless, both sides appeared to understand and respect—if not completely to share—the other's point of view, and there appeared to be no problem that would not yield to experience and goodwill, particularly if these were evinced from the top.

RELATIONSHIPS BETWEEN PARTIES

No useful generalization is possible about the relations between the parties on the FAC. Whether the Committee divided on party lines seems to have depended in the main on the party–political content of the subject under inquiry. On the whole, where there are strong party lines on subjects, inquiries seem unlikely to lead to any very useful result and the interrogation of witnesses seems to constitute at times less a search for information than a desire to impart it. Thus one must recognize the possibility that certain categories of subject may not be appropriate for the select committee technique.

As may be seen from the Annex to this chapter (and Table 9, Chapter 18), the FAC resorted to divisions on draft reports more than most. On the reports which they completed the FAC divided ninety-four times, but the figures varied markedly from report to report. On some there were no formal divisions at all, whereas the Olympic Games and the Caribbean and Central America reports evoked sixteen and forty-five respectively. These were however outclassed by the discussions on a partial draft of a report on the Falkland Islands,[27] which evoked no less than ninety-four divisions, as many as those on all the completed reports put together.

Thus the FAC was not among those committees which accommodated differences among members by stating that on a particular point some thought this and others that. The reader of an FAC report was left in no doubt about the view of the majority of the Committee, be it only a majority of one.

It could be wrong to conclude from this that the proceedings of the FAC were marked by unusual bad feeling or endemic hard party lines. The free resort to divisions seems to have been at least in part due to a concern for style and phraseology. Interestingly, of the Falklands divisions thirty-seven were on straight party lines, and thirty-seven involved Conservative and twenty-three Labour cross-voting. As the totals indicate, in some divisions both parties were divided. The cross-voting was often by a single member, but by no means always the same member or from the same party.

It is not easy to judge the effect of the number of divisions on the impact of a report. Outside Westminster, there is no evidence that it had any effect at all. Within Parliament, much depends on the facts of particular cases. To some extent the fact that a draft has been much divided on may diminish the value and impact of the eventual report (especially if it simply reflects a party division). On the other hand it may be taken as evidence of hard and energetic thought. The primary readership, i.e. Members of the House, is best placed to assess this.

ASSESSMENT

To what extent does the experience of the FAC bear out the large claims by Mr St John Stevas that the new committees constituted 'the most important parliamentary reform of this century'?

It is not easy to evaluate impact on government. The best compliment is of course a speedy and acknowledged acceptance of a committee's recommendations. But response is seldom so clear cut. In the annex are set out the dates of publication of reports and of the departmental replies. The intervals between these vary a good deal, from a few weeks to several months, usually two to three months. The length of response varies also, from one page to twenty-four, many falling between four and ten pages. A difficulty perhaps peculiar to the FAC is, as indicated earlier, that the FCO deals in the main in matters only partly within the control of the government. It is therefore seldom appropriate (in the realm of policy rather than administration at any rate) to recommend clear-cut actions which may be seen to be taken or not taken. While the position with the ODA is slightly different, the difference is one of degree rather than kind. Much of the ODA's activity also depends as much on what beneficiary governments want and on local conditions as on what the government is able and willing to do.

Taking together Parliament and departments, it is doubtful whether reports under the first of the four categories described earlier had very much impact. The inquiry into the organization of the FCO,[28] while no doubt useful to the Committee by way of initial orientation, does not appear to have attracted attention in the House. For the FCO itself it came at a time when the new administration was making certain changes, and the exercise of explaining matters to the FAC may have influenced the FCO in that process.

The inquiry into the ODA development divisions[29] was more in the main line of select committee inquiries, in that the study of organizational provision in this case to some extent raised questions of policy. Here again there was no repercussion in Parliament, and the Committee did not find itself at odds with the department. This was broadly true also of the study of the Commonwealth Development Corporation.[30] That on the ODA scientific and special units[31] did not evoke whole-hearted agreement from the department; but neither this nor the exchanges on Wilton Park[32] had any repercussions in Parliament, although the Committee's report on the latter was mentioned in a House of Lords debate on 16 March 1983.

The second category, namely the study of Estimates, constituted a conscientious attempt to carry out a task explicitly laid on the FAC in its orders of reference, namely 'to examine the expenditure ... of the Foreign and Commonwealth Office and of associated public bodies'.[33] It cannot be said that the results were of much moment or impact, the upshot largely being recommendations on such matters as the handling of the Government Hospitality Fund and the departmental responsibility for the Passport Office. The reason for this state of affairs probably lies not in any lack of zeal on the part of the FAC but in the form and nature of the Estimates as they come before the House. This is a matter which has received, and will no doubt continue to receive, attention by the Select Committee on Procedure (Finance) and others, and is unaffected by the 1979 changes.

Thirdly, the FAC, largely through the work of the Sub-Committee, undertook a number of inquiries regarding overseas territories for which Britain still has responsibility or has only recently relinquished it. Of these, that into the British role in Zimbabwe[34] was probably the most effective, taking place as it did at a time when policy was still in the formative stage. The influence of the inquiry was directly on the FCO and did not occasion debate in the House. The two reports on the Turks and Caicos Islands[35] were fairly sharply critical of the ODA's handling of the matter of hotel and airport development on the island of Providenciales; but whether they affected action is not clear—claims are made both ways.

IMPACT ON PARLIAMENT

The overt response of the House of Commons, as measured by mentions on the floor of the House, can range from none at all, through 'take note' debates, to use in debates on motions to which reports may be pertinent. Several of the Committee's reports fall into the first category, but this does not necessarily imply that they were to no purpose. Some, notably those on Estimates and those concerning departmental organization, really constituted dialogues with the departments concerned and their impact is not to be judged by the amount or nature of mention of them in debates. As to 'take note' debates, it is difficult to quarrel with the judgement of Mr D.A.M. Pring, then Clerk of Committees, in evidence to the Procedure Committee: '... I think debates on committee reports in the House are frequently very sad occasions. Generally it is members of the committee who come along and talk to each other on the floor of the House and the amount of other Members who are prepared to challenge them, or to take further the arguments they produce is very limited indeed.'[36] Yet many Members regard debates on the floor of the House as the due of select committee reports. Mr Kenneth Baker's comment in the debate on 25 June 1979 is typical: 'If these reports are to be effective, the circle must be completed, and they must come back and be debated on the Floor of the House so that what goes on upstairs is given the wider publicity that only debates in this House can give.'[37] By this standard the reports of the FAC certainly failed to be accorded their full due.

It was the reports of current or prospective parliamentary relevance which, as might be expected, aroused most interest in the House. That on the 1980 Moscow Olympic Games,[38] though not itself the subject of a debate, obtained attention in Parliament, and that on the Soviet invasion of Afghanistan[39] did not pass unremarked, nor did those on the Mexico Summit[40] and on Gibraltar.[41] However, by far the greatest impact was made by the Committee's work on the 'patriation' of the Canadian Constitution and the role of Parliament in relation to the British North American Acts.[42] The context was the Canadian initiative to remove the power to amend the Canadian constitution from Westminster to Canada and so end the anomaly which had persisted since the Statute of Westminster of 1931. The reasons for this are illuminating. The problem was one which could not be evaded but which was both unfamiliar in Westminster and potentially embarrassing in its implications for relations with Canada. Secondly, there was enough time for the FAC to go into the matter in depth. The Committee picked it up in the autumn of 1980, when Canadian policy was still being formed, whereas the Bill in its final shape did not come before Parliament until February 1982. In the interval the FAC was able to produce three reports. Paradoxically, the greatest impact of the FAC'S work, and in particular of the first of the three reports,[43] was probably in Canada itself and may have played a significant part in bringing about the result that the Bill which eventually came before Parliament did so in a form different from, and less objectionable to much Canadian opinion than, the measure adumbrated in 1980. The reports were not themselves debated as the subjects of motions but the relevant debates in both Houses[44] abound in references to them as important contributions to the elucidation of the problems raised by the Bill. These circumstances owe nothing in principle to the 1979 changes. The action taken by the FAC could equally have been taken by the Defence and External Affairs Sub-Committee of the Expenditure Committee, had it still existed.

The report on the Caribbean and Central America[45] by contrast did not have anything like the impact of the series on the Canadian constitution. The reasons seemed to be, first, that the inquiry appeared to lack a clear central purpose and focus. It was in effect two inquiries, one on the Caribbean and one on Central America, regions which have vastly different problems and widely different traditions and histories. Also, the FAC was deeply divided, there being forty-five divisions on the draft report, a figure only exceeded in the FAC (though then substantially) on consideration of a partial draft report on the Falkland Islands.[46] Practically the only concrete recommendation to come out of it was that a British mission should be reopened in Managua. Here as in other cases the moral seems to be that, given subjects of actual or potential political moment, impact is likely to be proportional to the clarity of the task which the Committee has set itself. This may, however, involve an effort of preliminary planning to which committees may not always be prepared, or able, to devote the necessary time.

IMPACT: MEDIA AND PUBLIC OPINION

It is not so long—a dozen years or so—since no general effort was made to make public the forthcoming activities of select committees other than to post a notice each Thursday outside the St Stephen's entrance to the Palace of Westminster setting out next week's programme, though efforts were made at times by staffs to acquaint interested journalists and others with the programmes of particular inquiries. But since that time the media have been kept regularly informed, week by week, and the FAC for one have taken pains to try to arrange public hearings and press conferences on reports at times thought to be convenient to the media. The result was somewhat uneven. Television news at times featured select committee affairs, and *The Times* and the *Guardian* in particular followed the FAC fairly systematically. Apart from this, however, coverage has been patchy. Apart from the straight reporting of proceedings on the floor of the House, parliamentary coverage continues to concentrate on the strictly political scene, personalities, the struggle for power, and the news behind the news. Select committee proceedings are seldom newsworthy in this sense, and in general it may be said that only if the work of a select committee develops a 'floor of the House' dimension does it attract the serious attention of parliamentary specialists in the media.

This is not to say that the proceedings of the FAC, for example, are not of interest to media specialists on particular subjects, and it is here that there has on the whole been the most consistent and serious impact. Nor are departments idle. It is generally in their interest that what they have to say—on paper or orally—be noticed. But there still remains much to be done to ensure that select committees receive the notice which their members feel is their due, and committee staffs are continually acquiring experience and skill in bringing this about.

The media cannot, however, realistically be expected to rate the importance of select committees more highly than does the House itself. Fine words notwithstanding, there is continuing evidence in debates that there are elements in the House (not only on the back benches) by no means anxious that select committees should get more of the limelight which they feel belongs to the floor of the House. Were the attitude of the House to show a significant change in this respect, that of the media might be expected to follow suit. Here, the remedy seems to lie in the hands of select committees themselves. So far as the FAC is concerned, the experience of 1979 to 1983 seems to show that the work of the Committee has aroused attention and respect in direct proportion to the extent that it has borne upon the problems that engage the attention of the House, for example, the 1980 Olympic Games, the Soviet invasion of Afghanistan, and above all the patriation of the Canadian constitution, notwithstanding the fact that none of these reports was itself the subject of a motion.

Nevertheless, in terms of committees' impact on public opinion and the media, there had been steady improvement over recent years. This may have been due in some measure to the indication of the value set by the House itself on the select committee system in the 1979 debates; this apart, media attention to the work of the FAC appears in the main to have been proportional to its actual or potential parliamentary relevance.

CONCLUSION

In sum, for the Foreign Affairs Committee the 1979 changes were followed by an enhancement of effort, a probably useful combination of overseas development with other aspects of external affairs, and an increase in the use of specialist advisers. These developments did not constitute a change in kind but rather in degree, and could in theory have taken place without the 1979 reorganization. The experience of one Parliament, however, is hardly enough to permit of more than a tentative judgement. Much will probably depend on whether, against recent precedent, the new arrangements are allowed to continue and settle down for more than a decade or so.

NOTES

1. HC debs., 25 June 1979.
2. First Report of the Select Committee on Procedure, 1977–78, HC 588-i, para. 5.43.
3. HC Debs., 19 and 20 February 1979, *passim*.
4. Second Report of 1979–80, *FCO Organization*, HC 511; Fourth Report of 1979–80, *Development Divisions*, HC 718, i and ii; Fourth Report of 1981–82, *Commonwealth Development Corporation*, HC 71; First and Third Reports of 1982–83, *Wilton Park*, HC 117 and 250; Fourth Report of 1982–83, *ODA Scientific and Special Units*, HC 295.
5. Fourth Report of 1980–81, *Supply Estimates 1981–82* (Class II, Votes 1, 2, 3, 5 and 6), HC 343, i and ii; Second Report of 1981–82, *Supply Estimates 1982–83 (Class II, Votes 10 and 11)*, HC 330; Third Report of 1981–82, *Supply Estimates 1982–83 (Class II, Votes 1–6)*; *Spring Supplementary Estimates 1981–82 (Class II, Vote 6)*, HC 406.
6. Third Report of 1979–80, *Overseas Students' Fees: Aid and Development Implications*, HC 553; Third report of 1980–81, *Turks and Caicos Islands: Hotel Development*, HC 26, i and ii; Second Report of 1982–83, *Turks and Caicos Islands: Airport Development on Providenciales*, HC 112; Sixth Report of 1981–82, *Zimbabwe: the Role of British Aid in the Development of Zimbabwe*, HC 117.
7. First Report of 1979–80, *Olympic Games 1980*, HC 490; Fifth Report of 1979–80, *Afghanistan: the Soviet Invasion and its Consequences for British Policy*, HC 745; First Report of 1980–81, *British North America Acts: the Role of Parliament*, HC 42, i and ii; Second Report of 1980–81, *Supplementary Report on the British North America Acts: the Role of Parliament*, HC 295; First Report of 1981–82, *Third Report on the British North America Acts: the Role of Parliament*, HC 128; Fifth Report of 1981–82, *The Mexico Summit: the British Government's role in the Light of the Brandt Commission's Report*, HC 211, i and ii; Seventh Report of 1980–81, *Gibraltar: the Situation of Gibraltar and United Kingdom Relations with Spain*, HC 116; Fifth Report of 1981–82, *Caribbean and Central America*, HC 47.
8. Fifth Report of 1979–80, *Afghanistan: the Soviet Invasion and its Consequences for British Policy*, HC 745.
9. Fifth Report of 1981–82, *Caribbean and Central America*, HC 47.
10. Third Report of 1979–80, *Overseas Students' Fees: Aid and Development Implications*, HC 553.
11. First Report of 1980–81, *British North America Acts: the Role of Parliament*, HC 42, i and ii; Second Report of 1980–81, *Supplementary Report on the British North America Acts: the Role of Parliament*, HC 295; First Report of 1981–82, *Third Report on the British North America Acts: the Role of Parliament*, HC 128.
12. Fourth Report of 1982–83, *ODA Scientific and Special Units*, HC 295.
13. Fourth Report of 1979–80, *Development Divisions*, HC 718, i and ii.
14. Fifth Report of 1979–80, *Afghanistan: the Soviet Invasion and its Consequences for British Policy*, HC 745.
15. Sixth Report of 1981–82, *Zimbabwe: the Role of British Aid in the Development of Zimbabwe*, HC 117.
16. Seventh Report of 1980–81, *Gibraltar: the Situation of Gibraltar and United Kingdom Relations with Spain*, HC 116.
17. Third Report of 1981–82, *Supply Estimates 1982–83 (Class II, Votes 1–6)*; *Spring Supplementary Estimates 1981–82 (Class II, Vote 6)*, HC 406.
18. Fifth Report of 1981–82, *Caribbean and Central America*, HC 47.

19. Fourth Report of 1981–82, *Commonwealth Development Corporation*, HC 71.
20. Minutes and Proceedings of the Foreign Affairs Committee, 1982–83, HC 830.
21. 1977–78 Procedure Committee Report, vol. ii, p. 122.
22. 1977–78 Procedure Committee Report, vol. i, para. 6.39.
23. Michael J. Malbin, 'Our Unelected Representatives: I Congressional Committee Staffs: Who's in Charge Here?'; Andrew Scully, 'Our Unelected Representatives: II Reflections of a Senate Aide', *The Public Interest*, no. 47, Spring 1977, pp. 16–48.
24. Cmnd. 8386, October 1981.
25. Cmnd. 8979, July 1983.
26. Cmnd. 9003, July 1983.
27. Minutes and Proceedings of the Foreign Affairs Committee, 1982–83, HC 830.
28. Second Report of 1979–80, *FCO Organization*, HC 511.
29. Fourth Report of 1979–80, *Development Divisions*, HC 718, i and ii.
30. Fourth Report of 1981–82, *Commonwealth Development Corporation*, HC 71.
31. Fourth Report of 1982–83, *ODA Scientific and Special Units*, HC 295.
32. First and Third Reports of 1982–83, *Wilton Park*, HC 117 and 250.
33. Standing Order no. 99.
34. Sixth Report of 1981–82, *Zimbabwe: the Role of British Aid in the Development of Zimbabwe*.
35. Third Report of 1980–81, *Turks and Caicos Islands: Hotel Development*, HC 26, i and ii; Second Report of 1982–83, *Turks and Caicos Islands: Airport Development on Providenciales*, HC 112.
36. 1977–78 Procedure Committee Report, q. 443.
37. HC Debs., 25 June 1979, col. 116.
38. First Report of 1979–80, *Olympic Games 1980*, HC 490.
39. Fifth Report of 1979–80, *Afghanistan: the Soviet Invasion and its Consequences for British Policy*, HC 745.
40. Fifth Report of 1981–82, *The Mexico Summit: the British Government's Role in the light of the Brandt Commission's Report*, HC 211, i and ii.
41. Seventh Report of 1980–81, *Gibraltar: the Situation of Gibraltar and United Kingdom Relations with Spain*, HC 116.
42. First Report of 1980–81, *British North America Acts: the Role of Parliament*, HC 42, i and ii; Second Report of 1980–81, *Supplementary Report on the British North America Acts: the Role of Parliament*, HC 295; First Report of 1981–82, *Third Report on the British North America Acts: the Role of Parliament*, HC 128.
43. First Report of 1980–81, *British North America Acts: the Role of Parliament*, HC 42, i and ii.
44. HC Debs., 17 and 25 February, and 3 and 8 March 1982; HL Debs., 18, 23, and 25 March 1982.
45. Fifth Report of 1981–82, *Caribbean and Central America*, HC 47.
46. Minutes and Proceedings of the Foreign Affairs Committee, 1982–83, HC 830.

Annex 9.1 *Foreign Affairs Committee*

Report (*denotes inquiry by sub-c'tee)	Date of first oral evidence (no. of evidence sessions)	Date of publication of report	Date and form of govt. reply	Length of report (pages)	No. of oral qq./no. of published submissions	No. of divisions
Session 1979–80						
1st Olympic Games 1980—HC 49	20.2.80 (3)	26.5.80	14.7.80 HC 697	15	229/10	16
2nd FCO Organization—HC 511	16.1.80 (4)	25.5.80	14.7.80	2	226/26	—
3rd Overseas Students' Fees, HC 553*	5.2.80 (5)		7.8.80 Cmd. 8010	17	476/43	7
4th ODA Development Divisions— HC 718*	15.4.80 (7)	16.9.80	20.1.81 Cmnd. 8130	29	400/54	3
5th Afghanistan—HC 475	20.2.80 (11)	11.9.80	22.10.80 Cmnd. 8068	29	949/25	4
Session 1980–81						
1st British North America Acts— HC 42	12.11.80 (3)	30.1.81	11.12.81 Cmnd. 8450	82	221/23	4
2nd ditto (supplement)	none	24.4.81	,, October '81	18	none	—
3rd Turks and Caicos Islands: Hotel Development—HC 26*	25.11.10 (3)	22.7.81	October '81 Cmnd. 8386	19	292/16	3
4th Estimates—HC 343	3.6.81 (2)	22.7.81	September '81 Cmnd. 8366	14	179/16	4

5th *Mexico Summit*—HC 211*	5.8.80 (6)	23.7.81	23.9.81 Cmnd. 8369	20	466/34	2
6th *Zimbabwe: British Role*—HC 117*	27.1.81 (4)	30.9.81	1.12.81 Cmnd. 8438	45	213/34	—
7th *Gibraltar*—HC 166	18.2.81 (5)	28.8.81	May '82 HC 374	55	285/31	—
Session 1981–82						
1st *British North America Acts (Third Report)*—HC 42	none	18.1.82	—	12	—/1	—
2nd *Supply Estimates (Overseas Aid)*—HC 330*	20.4.82 (5)	22.7.82	November '82 Cmnd. 8734	18	294/16	—
3rd *Spring Supplementaries*—HC 406	14.6.82 (2)	29.7.82	20.10.82 Cmnd. 8682	18	149/21	4
4th *Commonwealth Development Corporation*—HC 71*	1.12.81 (4)	7.17.82	April '83 Cmnd. 8857	42	418/26	2
5th *Caribbean and Central America*—HC 47	23.11.81 (14)	16.12.82	March '83 Cmnd. 8819	63	993/48	45
Session 1982–83						
1st *Wilton Park*—HC 117	25.10.82 (1)	19.1.83	see 3rd Report	2	104/6	—
2nd *Turks & Caicos (Airport)*—HC 112*	9.12.82 (1)	March '83	13.7.83 Cmnd. 8979	9	155/5	—
3rd *Wilton Park (Supplement)*—HC 250	none	April '83	in 3rd Report	1	—/2	—
4th *ODA Special and Scientific Units*—HC 295*	26.10.82 (10)	16.6.83	July '83 Cmnd. 9003	32	896/28	—

CHAPTER 10

The Home Affairs Committee

Gavin Drewry

As M. Jourdain might have been startled to discover, all that is not foreign affairs is home affairs; and all that is not home affairs is foreign affairs. The Home Office began life in 1782 as the by-product of a regorganization of the functions of the Secretaries of State, most of whose preoccupations in those days lay in overseas matters.[1] Subsequent expansion of the number of central departments has left the Home Office as the 'residuary legatee'[2] of miscellaneous domestic policy functions, many of which attract a great deal of parliamentary and media attention. Home Secretaries have often to contend with 'tropical storms that blow up with speed and violence out of a blue sky, dominate the political landscape for a short time, and then disappear as suddenly as they arrived'.[3] Officials, it has been suggested, have had 'a slightly defensive expectation that whenever the Home Office attracted attention it would also attract public blame'[4]—an attitude which can hardly promote self-confidence when appearing before a select committee.[5]

The wide-ranging scope and high political salience of the principal department concerned with 'home affairs' has a crucial bearing upon the nature of the select committee with which this chapter is concerned. At its first public evidence-session—an exploratory meeting on 10 December 1979 with the Home Secretary and senior officials—the Committee's chairman confessed that he and his colleagues had been gazing at the long list of subjects covered by the Home Office 'with some degree of trepidation'.[6] And the field of home affairs extends further into the territories of other departments—many of which have inherited tasks that once belonged to the Home Office. It should be borne in mind at the outset that this committee, even more than most of its fellows, cannot be regarded strictly as a 'departmental' committee, and this is true, *a fortiori*, of its sub-committee on race relations and immigration.

THE FORMAL REMIT OF THE COMMITTEE

The motions approved by the Commons on 25 June 1979 established a Home Affairs Committee with a maximum membership of eleven. It was one of only three of the new committees to be allowed a sub-committee, and this facility was used to set up a Sub-Committee on Race Relations and Immigration, a successor to the Committee on Race Relations and Immigration, established in 1968, which perished in the 1979 upheavals. The 1976–78 Procedure Committee had sympathized with the concern expressed by the then chairman of the Race Relations Committee, Fred Willey,[7] that its disappearance would leave a gap in parliamentary scrutiny, but it concluded 'that the Home Affairs Committee will be the appropriate committee to review policies in relation to the operation of the Race Relations Act and the admission of Commonwealth citizens and foreign nationals for settlement ... since the Home Office is the "lead" department with responsibility for co-ordinating government policy in those areas'.[8] It recommended that the HAC be empowered to refer detailed consideration of such matters to a sub-committee.

The Procedure Committee envisaged the terms of reference of the HAC as including the Lord Chancellor's Department and the Law Officers' Department.[9] However, the Leader of the House spoke of the potential threat to judicial independence that might arise 'if a select committee were to investigate such matters as the appointment and conduct of the judiciary and its part in legal administration, or matters such as confidential communications between the judiciary and the Lord Chancellor and the responsibility of the Law Officers with regard to prosecutions and civil proceedings'.[10] Several members retorted that matters like the administration of the courts and prosecution policy, not to mention legal aid, are perfectly legitimate subjects for parliamentary scrutiny and have little to do with 'judicial independence'; and that this is true, *a fortiori*, of such matters as public records, for which the Lord Chancellor is also responsible.[11] But an amendment to add the LCD and the LOD to the Committee's terms of reference was defeated.

CHAIRMANSHIP AND MEMBERSHIP

The HAC was constituted with six Conservative and five Labour members. At its first meeting, on 3 December 1979, a Conservative,

Jill Knight, was absent, and there was a tied vote on the motion that Sir Graham Page, a Conservative ex-minister, be called to the chair.[12] A counter-motion to give the chairmanship to a Labour ex-minister, Alex Lyon, also gave rise to a tie, five votes each way. Sir Graham was then moved into the chair—the outcome that had been pre-arranged through the 'usual channels'—though for that meeting only. This meant, however, that discounting the new chairman's casting vote, Labour members had a fortuitous majority at this session, and the Committee proceeded to nominate its sub-Committee, to comprise three Labour members and two Conservatives—not at all what the whips had intended. The Sub-Committee later appointed Alex Lyon as its chairman, and he presided over its first inquiry.

It may be noted that the government's theoretical majority of one on this small, usually bi-partisan, committee could never be guaranteed, particularly as the chairman was a Conservative. Fourteen out of the sixty-three divisions in the HAC were tied and (apart from the two instances just cited, where the chair was vacant) had to be resolved by the chairman's casting vote; and in eleven other cases, at least one Conservative voted with the Opposition. A comparable situation existed on the Sub-Committee, which had (following the replacement of Alex Lyon, see below) a Conservative chairman and only four other members. Division figures for the Sub-Committee must be interpreted even more cautiously than those for the Committee itself, given that dissentients often chose to keep their powder dry until a report came before the main committee; there were twenty-seven divisions in all, nine of which were resolved on the chairman's casting vote, and eighteen (including some of the nine just mentioned) involved cross-party voting—John Hunt (Cons.) in alliance with either Jo Richardson (Lab.) or Alex Lyon (Lab.).

After being outmanœuvred over the composition of the Sub-Committee, the whips quickly closed in to restore order. Sir Graham Page was duly confirmed as chairman. A Labour member, Arthur Davidson, was discharged from the Sub-Committee and replaced by a newly elected Conservative, John Wheeler, who was then elected chairman of the Sub-Committee.[13]

Though new to Parliament, John Wheeler had relevant experience, having been an assistant prison governor and a member of the Home Office standing committee on crime prevention. He was a compromise choice as chairman; of the other two Conservatives on the Sub-Committee, John Hunt was considered too uncomfortably left-wing by others in his party, while the right-winger, George Gardiner, was unacceptable both to Labour members and to John Hunt.

The chairmanship of the main Committee changed hands in midterm. Sir Graham Page, a solicitor, had held land and housing port-folios under Edward Heath. First elected to the House in 1953, he had recently served as chairman of the Joint and Select Committees on Statutory Instruments, and had been a member of the Committee on European Legislation. He came to the HAC with a reputation as a hard-liner on law and order but with no overt experience of home affairs (an attribute which at least two of the eight HAC members interviewed considered an advantage, in that he had no obvious axes to grind). In October 1981 he died. His successor, Sir John Eden, had had a similar career; he had entered the House in 1954, gained the reputation of being rather a hard-liner, held various middle-ranking non-Home Office posts under Mr Heath, and been Chairman of the Select Committee on European Legislation and a member of the Trade and Industry Sub-Committee of the Expenditure Committee. Chairmanship of a prestigious select committee thus provided respect-able employment for two senior, middle-weight, party loyalists cast adrift by the changing currents of Conservative politics.

Much speculation preceded Sir John's appointment. Another ex-minister, Mark Carlisle, was apparently considered as a possible con-tender for the chairmanship, but his dismissal from the Cabinet was at that point still uncomfortably recent. Another strongly tipped can-didate was Janet Fookes, erstwhile chairman of the Expenditure Com-mittee's Education, Arts and Home Office Sub-Committee, part of whose remit had passed to the HAC. Members of the Committee were not formally consulted about the chairmanship (though it appears that members did in effect veto some of those rumoured to be conten-ders). In the end Labour members were left with a feeling that a chairman had been foisted on them and there was a token division against Sir John's appointment.[14] Sir John remained in the post for the rest of the Parliament, but retired at the 1983 general election.

Given the breadth of 'home affairs', it is not hard to find aspects of the backgrounds of most MPs that might be considered relevant to the work of the HAC. Some members of the Committee were lawyers; John Blackburn had been a policeman; William Waldegrave was a juvenile court magistrate; Alex Lyon was once Minister of State at the Home Office (dismissed in 1976 for his robust views about immi-gration policy). Another ex-minister was Richard Luce, who joined the HAC in November 1982, soon after resigning, with the Foreign Secretary, over the Falkland Islands episode. Several members, espe-cially on the Labour side, were associated with relevant interest groups: Robert Kilroy-Silk had been active in penal reform groups such as the Howard League and the National Association for the Care and Resettlement of Offenders; Jo Richardson had been on the Executive Council of the National Council for Civil Liberties; Alf Dubs was chairman of Westminster Community Relations Council.

Members of the HAC were active members, in some cases officers, of party and all-party back-bench committees: for example, Robert Kilroy-Silk and John Wheeler served during the 1979–83 Parliament as chairman and vice-chairman respectively of the all-party Penal Affairs Group; John Hunt was joint secretary of the Parliamentary Human Rights Group; Alex Lyon chaired the PLP Home Affairs Group. Members interviewed could think of few concrete instances of cross-fertilization between their activity on back-bench committees and their work on the HAC.

The HAC had no continuity of membership with its predecessor, the Education, Arts and Home Office Sub-Committee of the Expenditure Committee. Robert Kilroy-Silk and Jill Knight had both served on the Race Relations Committee, but neither joined the new Sub-Committee. Several members (including both chairmen of the HAC) had had select committee experience: Edmund Marshall had been chairman of the Trade and Industry Sub-Committee of the Expenditure Committee.

It has been argued that the relatively permanent position of the post-1979 committees would give a sense of security, and encourage them to build up a cumulative body of wisdom and expertise. However, the development of a cumulative, corporate memory depends to some degree upon continuity of membership. The HAC had a relatively moderate turnover of members and it is interesting to compare its membership near the beginning of its life with the situation at the 1983 dissolution (see Table 10.1).

More than half (55 per cent) of the original membership of this prestigious committee melted away and few remained in the next

Table 10.1. Membership of the Home Affairs Committee

January 1980	left Committee	May 1983
Sir Graham Page (Cons.)	1.10.81 (died)	replaced by Sir John Eden (Cons.)
Arthur Davidson (Lab.)	30.1.81†	replaced by Alf Dubs (Lab.)*
George Gardiner (Cons.)*	19.11.82	replaced by Richard Luce (Cons.)
William Waldegrave (Cons.)	13.11.81†	replaced by John Blackburn (Cons.)*
Philip Whitehead (Lab.)	23.1.81	replaced by Edmund Marshall (Lab.)
Jo Richardson (Lab.)*	26.11.82	replaced by Ken Weetch (Lab.)
John Hunt (Cons.)*	n/a	John Hunt (Cons.)*
Robert Kilroy-Silk (Lab.)	n/a	Robert Kilroy-Silk (Lab.)
Jill Knight (Cons.)	n/a	Jill Knight (Cons.)
Alex Lyon (Lab.)*	n/a	Alex Lyon (Lab.)*
John Wheeler (Cons.)*	n/a	John Wheeler (Cons.)*

Note: *denotes member of the Sub-Committee. †Left on promotion to front-bench posts.

Parliament. One of the survivors, Alex Lyon, lost his seat in the 1983 election. Of the rest, Edmund Marshall failed to get re-selected by his constituency party and Sir John Eden did not stand.

SUBJECTS OF INQUIRY

The annex to this chapter lists the 20 reports published by the HAC during the 1979–83 Parliament, twelve of them based upon inquiries by the Sub-Committee. At the dissolution, the Committee had just begun an inquiry into dangerous drugs, and the Sub-Committee had launched an inquiry into the problems confronting the Chinese community in Britain.

One report, 'Sus' no. 2 (1979–80), was not based upon specific evidence. Conversely, two 'reports', Racial Attacks and Revised Immigration Rules (both 1981–82), placed evidence on the public record without making recommendations. The first elicited police reactions to a Home Office report on racial attacks. The second recorded ministerial evidence on proposed revisions to the Immigration Rules: the exercise was intended to inform MPs in advance of a debate on the Rules, but played no obvious part in the Government's subsequent defeat in a division, resulting from maladroit handling of a right-wing back-bench revolt.[15] The intention behind this inquiry was similar to that which had motivated the Sub-Committee's earlier examination of the Immigration Rules in the light of the European Convention on Human Rights; but that exercise—undertaken by the Sub-Committee during Alex Lyon's brief reign as chairman—had been a more elaborate, and much more abrasive affair. The 1980–81 inquiry into Numbers and Legal Status of future British Overseas Citizens was also intended mainly to lay evidence before the House, though the report did in this case summarize that evidence; the ostensibly technical nature of the exercise was inevitably infected by the controversy surrounding the British Nationality Bill, then in standing committee. The Sub-Committee took evidence from Foreign Office officials and from academic experts in international law.

Four recorded evidence-gathering exercises are listed in the annex as 'other proceedings' (the distinction between these and evidence-only 'reports' is highly arbitrary). The first, already mentioned, comprised two exploratory sessions, first with the Home Secretary, and then with the Permanent Secretary and no fewer than nine of his senior colleagues: 'I understand that today you wish to range over the whole of the Home Office's activities, and that is why so many officials have come to this session'.[16] The second such item, cryptically captioned 'Immigration Topics', consisted of evidence given to the Sub-

Committee by Home Office junior minister, Timothy Raison, and officials, and by DHSS officials, including Sir Henry Yellowlees, the Department's Chief Medical Officer: it covered various aspects of policy and procedure for detecting illegal immigration, including much publicized allegations about the oppressive employment of medical procedures, such as the use of X-rays to determine age. The third group of sessions took ministerial evidence about progress towards implementing the Committee's recommendations, a year earlier, in the massive Racial Disadvantage report. The Sub-Committee heard not only Timothy Raison and William Whitelaw but also Sir Keith Joseph, Secretary of State for Education and Science, and two junior ministers—Tony Newton (DHSS) and Sir George Young (D.o.E.)—whose responsibilities had recently been extended (perhaps partly in response to the Sub-Committee's call for better government co-ordination in this area) to include explicit reference to race relations aspects of departmental activities. A point was clearly scored when a question directed at Mr Newton resulted in his learning, from one of his officials, about an aspect of his duties of which he had hitherto been unaware.[17] Finally, in October, 1982, the HAC met members of the Home Office Working Party on Prosecution Arrangements, apparently so that the latter could hear the views of the Committee, as well as vice versa.

Most of the work of the HAC and the Sub-Committee generated reports of varying length. In 1979–80 the main Committee examined, and effectively scotched, claims by a Labour MP, Michael Meacher, about an allegedly sinister pattern of deaths in police custody. When he gave evidence, Mr Meacher was treated as severely by Labour members of the Committee as by the Conservatives:[18] the Committee took care to avoid any appearance of adjudicating in particular cases.[19] Bi-partisan harmony was much less in evidence in the Public Order inquiry, which touched upon the right to hold political demonstrations, and the desirability of restricting demonstrations on the highway in support of industrial disputes (an issue that had caused much controversy in the Grunwick case in 1977). The Committee divided on party lines; Labour members tried to modify the report (there was nearly an upset at first when alternative paragraphs drafted by Alex Lyon were approved by a 5 to 4 Labour majority, a Conservative member being absent).[20] The majority report achieved the feat of displeasing both the National Front (which had given written evidence and whose representative noisily intervened at the press conference to launch the report) and the National Council for Civil Liberties (which had given both written and oral evidence). A decision to exclude the National Front from giving oral evidence had meant excluding the Liberal Party as well, to the latter's understandable annoyance.

In the 1980–81 session, the inquiry into vagrancy offences generated twelve divisions, far more than any other report. Robert Kilroy-Silk led a group of Labour colleagues in support of the view of the Campaign for the Homeless and Rootless (CHAR) that the offences of sleeping rough and begging should be abolished; but Alex Lyon, convinced by police evidence to the contrary, voted with the Conservatives (and was joined in some divisions by Edmund Marshall). The main inquiry of the session related to the Prison Service—following to some extent, from an Expenditure Committee Report several years previously[21] but, more immediately, from the May Report on the UK Prison Service, published in October 1979.[22] Here there was something of a false start when it soon became clear that organizational problems were secondary to the issue of how to relieve gross overcrowding in prisons, and that this entailed looking at penal policy and sentencing policy. The Lord Chancellor contributed the final item of oral evidence.[23]

The Police Complaints inquiry, the HAC's main venture in 1981–82, was undertaken in the light of the Scarman Report's recommendation[24] in favour of an independent complaints procedure, and following a private talk with Lord Scarman a few days after his report was published. In the end, the majority of the Committee recommended a new system of regional complaints offices (Home Office evidence had favoured centralized machinery): Alf Dubs preferred a police ombudsman system, and was supported on this and other proposed amendments by Robert Kilroy-Silk, but opposed by his Labour colleague, Edmund Marshall. The Miscarriages of Justice inquiry was prompted by well-researched media stories about allegedly wrongful convictions, and the Committee was strongly influenced in its conclusions by disquieting evidence that it received from the legal reform group, Justice.

The 1982–83 session was dominated by the inquiry into the Representation of the People Acts. The Committee divided on party lines over a recommendation that the franchise be extended to British citizens living abroad and on a proposal to give postal votes to holiday-makers. Cross-voting brought a tied vote on an amendment to lower the proposed threshold for forfeiture of candidates' deposits (the Committee unanimously favoured the deposit being raised from £150 to £1,000) from 7.5 per cent to 5 per cent, and the issue was resolved by the chairman's casting vote, in favour of the higher threshold.[25] The Liberal Party, not represented on the HAC (though it did give evidence), expressed annoyance that the inquiry had not looked at the issue of proportional representation, and disputed some of its conclusions, particularly those concerning the electoral deposit.

The Sub-Committee attached some priority to the task of assembling evidence on complex and controversial matters, and laying such material before the House and the informed public. Its two reports on 'sus' in 1979-80, will be considered later. Much of its attention was given to the massive inquiry, from May 1980 to August 1981, into Racial Disadvantage. It gave rise to twenty sessions of oral evidence, including day-long visits to Bristol, Liverpool, Manchester, and Leicester, and the Committee received 108 written submissions. The Committee largely made up the terms of reference of the inquiry as it went along. The exercise took place against the backcloth of racial disturbances in Bristol and Brixton; and further disorders in the late summer of 1981, notably in Toxteth and Southall, occurred after the final session of evidence but before the report was completed. The Sub-Committee commissioned a report on business activities among West Indians in Britain from the SSRC Research Unit on Ethnic Relations at Aston University; and this was one of the few occasions where use was made of a specialist adviser—David Smith of the Policy Studies Institute, author of a major study published by Political and Economic Planning of racial disadvantage. The Committee's report contained 57 recommendations, directed at several central departments (note also the follow-up sessions with ministers, a year later) and at other public and private bodies, and was accompanied by two large volumes of evidence and a separate volume of appendices. Remarkably, this report prompted only six divisions in the main Committee; George Gardiner and Jill Knight forced divisions in respect of recommendations concerning ethnic monitoring in employment, and for that reason also voted against approval of the report as a whole.

Two subsequent inquiries stemmed directly from the Racial Disadvantage exercise. The Sub-Committee investigated the Commission for Racial Equality (CRE), not having been 'greatly impressed by the quality of evidence' submitted by the Commission in the course of the earlier inquiry.[26] It concluded that the CRE was characterized by 'incoherence' and spent disproportionate effort pursuing ambitious and vague promotional projects in the field of race relations, funding undeserving projects, while not effectively pursuing its investigative functions. The Commission's chairman angrily rejected the report as 'destructive, ill-considered and unjustified',[27] and there was resentment about what was felt to be a patronizing attitude on the part of the Committee. In the result, the Government sided with the CRE[28] (though some subsequent organizational changes may be attributable to the Report), and the backwash from the Commission's indignation was thought by some to have damaged at least temporarily the Committee's credibility in the eyes of the ethnic communities.

The Ethnic and Racial Questions inquiry in 1982-83 also followed up in much greater depth an issue touched upon in the Racial Disadvantage Report which had regretted a government decision not to include any question on ethnic or racial origin in the 1981 census. It was regarded as a particularly important and successful exercise by the Sub-Committee, having attracted a good deal of unsolicited evidence, generated a lot of media interest, and given rise to lively 'open meetings' in Birmingham and elsewhere.

The work of the Sub-Committee (and to a lesser extent that of the main Committee) ran for a while in parallel with the inquiry undertaken by Lord Scarman into the Brixton disorders. The Scarman Report[29] cited repeatedly the Racial Disadvantage report, which it called 'a masterly review' deserving of 'a positive response from Government'.[30] This endorsement, in the context of a vivid illustration of the social tensions that can stem from racial disadvantage, made the Committee's recommendations that much harder to ignore, and the Scarman Report was cited in the Government's reply to the Committee's report.[31]

The Sub-Committee examined the Government's declared policy of imposing charges on overseas visitors seeking to use the National Health Service, though the exercise was to a large extent overtaken by a ministerial policy statement before the inquiry was completed.[32] Immigration from the Indian Subcontinent took the Sub-Committee on a visit to Bangladesh and India to examine the procedures for processing applications for special vouchers in the Subcontinent, particularly those where family relationships of applicants to their sponsors were in dispute. An open meeting held in Jamnagar, Gujurat, to which people in the voucher queue were invited, produced an attendance of about 200. An investigation of the implications of the Government's revised policy in respect of fees for naturalization and registration of citizenship, disclosed that a large profit had been made due to miscalculation of the impact of the British Nationality Act: a ministerial letter defending the profit was later described by the Sub-Committee's chairman as 'a pathetic, miserable little document'.[33]

How were subjects of inquiry chosen from the vast range of possibilities available? Topics generally emerged through an amicable process of elimination, with members being drawn towards the topical, and wary of the long-drawn-out and technical. The 'tropical storms' that characterize Home Office affairs thrust certain items onto the agenda—e.g. Mr Meacher's allegations about deaths in police custody and a BBC Panorama programme about miscarriages of justice. The much larger Prisons inquiry perhaps belongs in the 'tropical storms' category, given the background of a Prison Officers' industrial dispute, though it was also a follow-up to the recent May Report. Several inquiries, particularly those in the evidence-gathering category, were responses to impending or recent changes of public policy (for example, the Immigration Rules inquiries, Nationality Fees) and/or the publication of a consultative document (NHS Charges, Public Order): the Police Complaints inquiry followed upon recommendations in the Scarman Report. Some of the later inquiries by the Sub-Committee (CRE, Ethnic and Racial Questions) were sequels to the Racial Disadvantage exercise: indeed, members of the Sub-Committee justified the decision to hold the latter inquiry—on the face of it a diffuse and time-consuming exercise—as providing an overview of many important issues within the Sub-Committee's remit, and an important reservoir of inspiration for subsequent, more specific, investigations. The main Committee seldom sought overtly to influence or question the Sub-Committee's choices of subject, though Jill Knight and William Waldegrave did vote against giving it leave to hold the Overseas Citizens inquiry.[34]

Individual members often suggested topics. The Representation of the People Acts inquiry was inspired by Edmund Marshall, though ironically he was unable to take much part in it because of his involvement in the Labour Party's abortive litigation against the Boundary Commissions' reports. In this instance, some Conservative members may have seen in the inquiry an attractive possibility (which failed to materialize) that something might be done to restrict the Irish vote, which overwhelmingly favours the Labour Party: indeed, for this very reason, at least one of Dr Marshall's Labour colleagues regretted that the issue had been raised at all, though the inquiry was not in fact conducted on partisan lines.

Obviously a committee operating in such a wide and diffuse policy field will turn down promising subjects of inquiry, for various reasons. In one case the suggestion of holding an inquiry into religious cults was considered seriously, but dropped after a feasibility study. Data protection was mooted as a possible candidate at one point, as were prison medical services, the Gaming Board, various aspects of broadcasting, and matters to do with the status of the Channel Islands and the Isle of Man.

THE COMMITTEE AT WORK

Most of the work of the HAC and its Sub-Committee relied upon oral questioning augmented by written submissions. This requires a good deal of homework, the amount varying from member to member and from inquiry to inquiry. Chairmen and members were assisted by briefs written by the clerks (in consultation with specialist advisers in the few cases, early on, where they were employed). Once a subject had been agreed, the responsibility for planning the pattern of the investigation fell upon the clerk and the chairman, working in collaboration. The Committee sometimes met privately at the outset of an inquiry to discuss objectives and strategy: the value of proceeding in this way was increasingly recognized as the Committee gained experience.

The main Committee held fifty-five formal evidence sessions (some with more than one witness or group of witnesses) and fifty-three deliberative sessions during the Parliament; the Sub-Committee held sixty-five evidence sessions and forty-five deliberative sessions.[35] On just one occasion oral evidence was heard in camera, with sidelining in the published transcript.[36] There were also a few private informal sessions, such as the meeting with Lord Scarman mentioned earlier, and informal visits by the Sub-Committee to Brixton (Racial Disadvantage), St Mary's Hospital (NHS Charges), Home Office Outstations at Croydon (Nationality Fees), the Office of Population Censuses and Surveys at St Catherine's House (Ethnic and Racial Questions), and the London offices of the Commission for Racial Equality (CRE).

Although the main Committee did not venture away further from Westminster than Brixton Prison, the Sub-Committee was quite mobile. Apart from the excursions just mentioned and the four day-long visits to provincial cities in connection with the Racial Disadvantage inquiry, it went to Lewisham, Haringey, and Birmingham in connection with the Ethnic and Racial Questions inquiry. Several members of the Sub-Committee agreed that such visits can be useful in bringing Parliament closer to the public, as well as yielding worthwhile evidence; but one also observed that there might be a danger, in the sensitive field of race relations, if local groups were to misunderstand the status and function of the exercise or took an over-optimistic view of the Committee's capacity to exercise a benign influence upon events.

Three inquiries took the Sub-Committee overseas: to the USA and Jamaica (Racial Disadvantage), Bangladesh and India (Immigration from the Indian Subcontinent), and USA and Canada (Ethnic and Racial Questions). A visit to Hong Kong was planned in connection with the inquiry into the Chinese community, still in its early stages at the dissolution, though the necessity of such a visit was strongly disputed by one Conservative member of the main Committee. Extensive use was made of such overseas evidence and experience in preparing the relevant reports, and the Immigration inquiry, in particular, would hardly have been feasible without visiting the countries involved.

The main body of evidence was obtained in oral sessions. Selective reference has already been made to some of the sources of such evidence: the accompanying table gives the overall picture, emphasizing the variety of sources called upon and the relatively small proportion of the evidence that came from the Home Office itself. Before witnesses from other departments were invited before the Committee, the clerk or the chairman always wrote to his opposite numbers on other relevant departmental committees. Apart from one instance, early on, when the Attorney-General declined to appear before the Committee,[37] ministers showed no discernible reluctance to give evidence: indeed the Home Secretary was indignant at not having been invited to defend his department's position in the Home Office Reports inquiry. This exercise—an investigation into why so little progress had been made towards implementing various reports on matters like data protection (Lindop) and privacy (Younger)—was the only clear instance where the Committee embarked on a head-on confrontation with the Department. None of the sixteen sessions involving ministers gave rise to any noticeable friction between witnesses and Committee; nor were there any overt instances of official witnesses invoking the Memorandum of Guidance as a basis for declining to co-operate with the Committee. Most oral (and *a fortiori* written) evidence came from non-departmental sources. This was particularly true of the Sub-Committee, much of whose work entailed monitoring the experiences and perceptions of minority groups and those who have immediate dealings with such groups.

Most reports were drafted by the clerks. Members interviewed had found the latter to be sensitive to nuances of opinion and skilful in achieving balanced drafts, though it was seldom possible to please everyone. Unlike most of the committees the HAC made very little use of specialist advisers, though there was some enthusiasm for them at the outset. Sean McConville, a lecturer in social administration, who had assisted the Expenditure Committee in its earlier inquiry into prisons, played a large part in drafting the reports on public order and on prisons; in the former case he had support from David Williams of the University of Cambridge. We have already noted the contribution of David Smith to the Sub-Committee's work on Racial Disadvantage but he played little part in drafting the report. Members became generally sceptical of the value of employing advisers, and wary of the possibility that they might, consciously or unconsciously, smuggle in well-honed academic prejudices; there

Table 10.2. *Home Affairs Committee: sources of oral evidence*

	Main Committee		Sub-Committee	
	Whole Sessions	*Part or Shared Sessions*	*Whole Sessions*	*Part or Shared Sessions*
Home Office Ministers	4	–	7	1
Other Ministers[a]	2	–	2	2
Home Office Officials	10	4	3	3
Other Officials[b]	1	3	6	6
Civil Service Unions/Staff Associations	4	–	–	2
Public Corporations	–	1	–	–
Professional Bodies	1	5	–	3
Other Unions/Staff Assocs.	–	1	1	4
Local Authorities/Health Authorities	2	1	1	2
Local Communities (i.e. UK Visits by the Committee)	–	–	7	–
Police	4	10	–	4
Magistrates	1	–	–	1
Lawyers/Judges	–	–	–	5
Other Groups & Assocs.	9	8	7	11
Other Individuals	1	1	–	3
Commission for Racial Equality	1	–	6	1
Other Public Bodies	2	1	1	–
TOTAL	42	35	41	48

Notes: (s = part or shared session of evidence).

a 'Other Ministers' appearing before the main Committee were Lord Hailsham (Lord Chancellor) and Nicholas Fairburn (Solicitor General for Scotland), Norman Fowler and Tony Newton (DHSS); Sir Keith Joseph (DES)(s) and Sir George Young (Environment)(s) gave evidence to the Sub-Committee.

b Other departmental civil servants submitting oral evidence to the main Committee were: (FCO(s), DPP (2s), and Scottish Home and Health (1), and to the Sub-Committee: OPCS (1), Environment (1+s), Employment and MSC (1+s), Education (1+s), FCO (1+s), DHSS (1+s), and Civil Service Department(s). The DPP also appeared before the main Committee as a member of the Home Office working party on prosecutions, categorized here as an 'other public body'. Two appearances by FCO officials accompanying a Home Office minister, Timothy Raison, in giving to the Sub-Committee are not counted separately.

was an implicit view that the committee should generally stick to subjects within the compass of members' own expertise, though it was recognized that advisers might be necessary in particularly technical fields.

POLITICAL CHEMISTRY

The HAC contained a fairly wide spread of political opinion. George Gardiner, a right-wing member of the Sub-Committee, often found an ally in Jill Knight on the main Committee. They were balanced by the presence of more left-wing Conservatives, like John Hunt and John Wheeler. The Labour group was made up of an interesting mixture of well-informed individualists with strong, but often divergent, views on most issues.

Despite the political sensitivity of some of the subjects investigated and the opinionated temperaments of several Committee members, consensus and compromise were very much in evidence from the outset. Most of the sixty-three divisions were on more or less insignificant matters of detail and emphasis and only twenty-eight (44.4 per cent) of them were strictly on party lines. The Public Order and NHS Charges reports provided the two clear instances of straightforward party disputes.

Chairmanship is a key ingredient in the political chemistry of a committee. Some Labour members had been unhappy about the lack of consultation preceding Sir John Eden's appointment, but felt that he, like his predecessor, had been a fair and competent chairman. One suggested that the Opposition had benefited from serving under Conservative chairmen who did not have axes to grind and who fell over backwards to be fair to all shades of opinion. No one seems to have suspected these Conservative ex-ministers (Heath-men, rather than Thatcherites) of having a dangerously cosy relationship with the executive. A rough count of the distribution of questions, and limited observation of the chairmen in action, suggests that they orchestrated but did not attempt to dominate proceedings. The cohesiveness of the Sub-Committee was undoubtedly helped by its small size: an *esprit de corps* quickly developed, any potential dissentient found himself in a minority of one, and enthusiasts could get things off their chests without feeling the inhibition of having to share limited time with ten colleagues. Credit is also due to the chairmanship of John Wheeler, particularly in view of his lack of previous parliamentary experience.

A SUCCESSUL COMMITTEE?

The HAC exhibited various characteristics that might be considered indicative of 'success': consistently high attendance (81 per cent for the main Committee, 89 per cent for the Sub-Committee),[38] absence of 'passengers' among the members (particularly on the Sub-Committee), moderately low turnover of membership, and a high level of cross-party consensus. The subject areas covered by the HAC and its Sub-Committee guaranteed high political appeal and extensive media coverage, something which most members interviewed regarded as the hallmark of a successful committee. To those who may complain that select committees pursue media attention at the expense of less newsworthy but necessary tasks, such as financial monitoring (a role which the HAC did not undertake), the retort must be that the 'success' or otherwise of any committee is largely a matter of harnessing the enthusiasms of MPs. Members of the HAC tended to dismiss low-profile, technical exercises as simply not being what committee work is about. One member said that he had been offered membership of the prestigious Public Accounts Committee, but had asked instead to join the better publicized HAC. Members of the Committee regarded it as having enriched their own parliamentary lives, both by providing them with useful information in a specialist field and, in some cases, constituting a useful medium through which prior expertise and opinion could be consolidated and translated into political pressure. However, there were doubts whether many Members outside the Committee were more than superficially and intermittently aware of its work.[39] And no HAC report was ever formally debated in government time on the floor of the House.

What of the impact upon government? Indirect consequences of a committee's work are every bit as important as direct ones but are, of course, much harder to measure. It is difficult, and will become more difficult as time passes, to be sure whether and to what extent moves to combat racial disadvantage—an amorphous and by definition controversial social problem-area—are a response, conscious or unconscious, to the Committee's catalogue of findings and recommendations on the subject. And we must take account of the inertial resistance of the door against which the Committee is pushing. Its report on the Representation of the People Acts was in harmony with Home Office evidence and could therefore expect a favourable government response. The report on Miscarriages of Justice endorsed the submissions of Justice in preference to those of the Department, and the Government turned down the recommendations; but the report clearly prompted concern in official and judicial circles, and perhaps, in the long run, the quantum of influence exercised in this instance will prove to be greater than in the former case.

The causal connection between a particular report and action taken (or avoided) by government is further obscured by the fact that reports themselves are not discrete entities but the products of cumulative committee activity. Some inquiries—such as the sequels to the Racial Disadvantage inquiry are in follow-up to previous exercises. The need for improved government co-ordination in the field of race relations was stressed in the Racial Disadvantage report, re-emphasized in the follow-up sessions with ministers, and raised again in the report on Racial Attacks. The desirability of instituting independent prosecution machinery was canvassed both in the report on Miscarriages of Justice and that on Police Complaints Procedure. Keeping an issue alive by follow-up exercises and by repetition in a variety of contexts is (as the history of the Public Accounts Committee demonstrates) a valuable by-product of a committee's permanency and continuity—something which the HAC seemed increasingly to realize as it developed experience and self-confidence. Patterns will become clearer over a longer time-span.

The HAC seldom sought confrontation with departments. In the one clear instance where it did so—Home Office Reports—the reply was predictably tart and defensive.[40] A style that ministers and officials tended to regard as non-partisan and constructive rather than confrontational maintained the working relationship between the Committee and the Home Office on a cordial footing, and there is no evidence that cordiality ever lapsed into unhealthy over-intimacy. Most reports that called for a reply (the several evidence-only 'reports' clearly did not) were given one, promptly—within an average of seventy days, much faster than was the case with most of the committees—and in the form of a White Paper. Occasionally other forms of reply were used, for example a private letter to the chairman in the case of the NHS Charges. Most replies were fairly substantial and sympathetic in tone, even where, as was often the case, most of the specific recommendations were being politely turned down. However, the reply to the CRE report provided at least one instance where the Committee felt aggrieved by the negative and unhelpful nature of the Government's response.

Outside groups tend to evaluate a committee by its capacity to deliver the goods that the group wants. Inevitably there were many disappointments, if only because select committees are not in the delivery business: CHAR (notwithstanding the support of Robert Kilroy-Silk) got no joy at all from the Vagrancy Offences inquiry; the Liberal party, not represented on the HAC, found itself bracketed with the National Front in being denied the opportunity to give oral evidence to the Public Order inquiry, and later complained both about the narrow terms of reference and the conclusions of the Representation of the People Acts inquiry. Pressure groups which gave evidence sometimes complained that the Committee, in pursuit of consensus, was offering only half a loaf.

The Sub-Committee's capacity to gain and retain the confidence of minority groups was crucial to its role. It worked hard at this and canvassed a wide range of opinion in the course of its many inquiries: its widely publicized fact-finding journeys within the UK and overseas evidenced its anxiety to broaden its experience as well as serving a public relations function. The CRE episode was probably at least temporarily damaging. Some self-proclaimed spokesmen for minority group opinion had dubious credentials as representative witnesses.[41] But one's impression is that the Sub-Committee's work in persistently waving unsavoury problems under the noses of ministers served a valuable purpose, building upon the work done by the former Race Relations Committee. The Sub-Committee carved out a distinctive identity of its own: indeed its media profile was probably much sharper than that of the main Committee. Whether it should remain as the mere offshoot of a larger Committee whose role is really quite different seems debatable.

One case which is consistently cited as a success story in select committee folklore is the Sub-Committee's investigation into the 'sus' law, which high-lighted the harm done to race relations by the perceived discriminatory use of s. 4 of the Vagrancy Act 1824 to arrest suspected persons allegedly loitering with criminal intent. The HAC, following evidence from various sources, including the Bar Council, denounced sus as a fundamentally unsatisfactory law in principle. When the report was debated in the Commons, in Opposition time,[42] the Home Secretary declined to take immediate action, pending a forthcoming report by the Law Commission on the law of criminal attempts. But the Conservative chairman of the HAC, Sir Graham Page, forcefully argued his Committee's case for reform and voted with the Opposition; the Committee then took the very unusual step of publishing a supplementary report, threatening to introduce a private Member's Bill if the Government refused to legislate.

The sequel was the Government's Criminal Attempts Bill, introduced early in the following session, which *inter alia* repealed sus and created a new summary offence of vehicle interference. At second reading,[43] Mr Whitelaw acknowledged that 'the inclusion in the Bill of a provision to repeal the offence obviously owes a great deal to the Committee's report'; and John Wheeler called the Bill 'the wholly welcome fulfilment of a select committee investigation'. Some civil servants have since privately asserted that the HAC merely anticipated something that would have happened anyway—a claim which is not very convincing but is, by its nature, hard to refute.

There was a further sequel when the Bill was referred to a 'special' standing committee (an experimental innovation stemming from the 1978 Procedure Committee Report),[44] the first three sessions of which, under the chairmanship of Sir Graham Page, were devoted to the taking of evidence, following which the committee reverted to the adversarial format of an ordinary standing committee, with a neutral chairman. The Government, confronted by a procession of critical witnesses (including representatives of the Law Commission, a senior judge, and two eminent law professors) felt obliged to rewrite some crucial clauses. The use at a special standing committee in this instance was, as the Procedure Committee had envisaged,[45] a constructive way of linking departmental committees to the legislative process via overlapping membership.

Sus was a success story in the sense that a Conservative-chaired committee stuck to its guns in the face of government obduracy, having put together an overwhelming case for reform on the basis of authoritative evidence. But the ultimate test must surely be whether the new provisions in the Criminal Attempts Act 1981 are more satisfactory than those they replaced, and several observers have voiced serious doubts about this. The Scarman Report, for instance, noted at least one potential anomaly in the 1981 Act, and called for a close watch to be kept on how the law in this area develops[46]—a future task, perhaps, for the HAC?

The scope of this multi-departmental committee is, as we have noted, very wide indeed. In a report to the Liaison Committee, Sir John Eden noted that in practice 'the crossing of departmental barriers presented few practical problems'.[47] But there remained at the end of the 1979–83 Parliament at least one serious lacuna in the exclusion from the Committee's remit of the Lord Chancellor's Department and the Law Officers' Department, noted earlier. The Liaison Committee agreed with Sir John's view that this was 'quite unjustifiable', and called for the terms of reference of the HAC to be extended.[48] In practice the restriction melted away as it became apparent that in many contexts legal administration and policy simply cannot be partitioned off as a 'no-go area' in the territory of 'home affairs': after the Attorney-General's refusal to appear early on (a special case, given his position as confidential legal adviser), the Director of Public Prosecutions (three times), the Solicitor General for Scotland, and even the Lord Chancellor appeared before the Committee, and the skies did not fall on the shrine of judicial independence. The Home Affairs Committee has more than enough ground to cover, but this is one omission from its jurisdiction that should never have been countenanced.

NOTES

1. See Sir Edward Troup, *The Home Office*, Putman's 1925, pp. 18–19.
2. A. Lawrence Lowell, *The Government of England*, vol. i. Macmillan, 1908, p. 105.
3. Roy Jenkins, 'On Being a Minister', in V. Herman and J. Alt (eds.), *Cabinet Studies: A Reader*, Macmillan, 1975, pp. 215–16.
4. Ibid. p. 212.
5. Cf. Philip Norton, *The Commons in Perspective*, Martin Robertson, 1981, p. 187.

6. HC 321–I, 1979–80, q. 3.
7. HC 388–II, 1977–78, q. 754.
8. HC 388–I, 1977–78, para. 5.44.
9. Ibid., para. 4.24.
10. HC Debs., 25 June 1979, col. 38.
11. See the speeches by Peter Archer, Merlyn Rees, and Michael English.
12. HC 434, 1979–80, p. ix.
13. Ibid., p. xv.
14. HC 46–I, 1981–82, p. xlix.
15. HC Debs., 15 December 1982, cols. 355–439.
16. HC 321–ii, 1979–80, q. 37.
17. HC 405–i–iv, q. 124.
18. HC 631, 1979–80, q. 416 *et seq.*
19. The Committee had already resolved, in setting up the Sub-Committee, 'to adopt the practice of the former Select Committee on Race Relations and Immigration in not attempting to investigate individual cases': HC 434, 1979–80, p. ix.
20. HC 756–I, p. xxxix; Mr Lyon's draft report, which appears in the Minutes, was subsequently refused a second reading, by 5 votes to 3, ibid., p. iv.
21. HC 622, 1977–78.
22. *Report of Committee of Inquiry into the United Kingdom Prison Service,* Cmnd. 7676, 1979.
23. HC 412–ii, 1980–81, p. 238 *et seq.*
24. *The Brixton Disturbances 10–12 April 1981,* Cmnd. 8427, 1981, para. 7.28.
25. HC 32–I, 1982–83, p. xlii.
26. HC 46–I. 1981–82, para. 1.
27. The *Guardian,* 16 December 1981.
28. See Cmnd. 8547, 1981, in particular the revealing comment (para. 4) that 'The Government has considered the Report in close consultation with the CRE'.
29. Cmnd. 8427, 1981.
30. Ibid., para. 6.3.
31. Cmnd. 8476, 1981, para. 2.
32. HC Debs., 22 February 1982, cols. 593 *et seq.*
33. The *Guardian,* 29 July 1983. The formal departmental reply did not appear until March 1984.
34. HC 158, 1980–81, p. x.
35. HC Debs., 29 July 1983, cols. 465–6 (written answers).
36. HC 89–II, qq. 885 *et seq.* Evidence of Sir Peter Mathews concerning the 'Countryman' inquiry into alleged police corruption. Strangers were also excluded from an exploratory evidence session of the Sub-Committee on 25 April 1983 in connection with the inquiry (uncompleted at the dissolution) into the Chinese community in Britain.
37. See HC 434, 1979–80, para. 6. The Attorney's role as the Government's principal and confidential legal adviser makes this rather a special case: though a member of the Government, he is not a minister.
38. HC Debs., 29 July 1983, col. 633 (written answer).
39. However an interview-based survey of the attitudes of MPs towards the departmentally-related committees gave the HAC second place (behind only the Treasury and Civil Service Committee) in a league table of 'effectiveness'. See Michael O'Higgins, *House of Commons: A Study of the Views of MPs,* summary in *The Times,* 10 January 1984.
40. Cmnd. 8214, 1981.

41. The Caribbean Chamber of Commerce claimed to have just sixty active members (see HC 424-III, 1980-81, q. 1944). The Honorary General Secretary of the Association of Jamaicans (UK) Trust gave evidence in the Ethnic and Racial Questions inquiry in such negative terms that the chairman concluded by saying that 'there is no point in continuing with this, a most depressing Select Committee morning'.
42. HC Debs., 5 June 1980, cols. 1963 *et seq.*
43. HC Debs., 19 January 1981, cols. 21 *et seq.*
44. HC 588-I, 1977-78, paras. 2.19 and 2.20.
45. Ibid., para 2.17.
46. Loc. cit. paras. 7.4 to 7.6.
47. HC 92, 1982-83, p. 85, para. 11.
48. Ibid, p. 12, para 24.

Annex 10.1 Home Affairs Committee

Report (*denotes inquiry by sub-c'tee)	Date of first oral evidence/(no. of evidence sessions)	Date of publication of report	Date and form of govt. reply	Length of report (pages)	No. of oral qq./no. of written submissions	No. of divisions
Session 1979–80						
1st *Proposed New Immigration Rules & the European Convention on Human Rights*, HC434.*	20.12.79 (2)	11.2.80	n/a	4	149/8	5
2nd *Race Relations & the 'Sus' Law*, HC559.*	7.2.80 (7)	21.4.80	14.7.80 HC Debs Cols. 359–60W	12	407/16	1
3rd *Deaths in Police Custody*, HC631.	4.2.80 (6)	16.6.80	11.11.80 HC Debs Cols. 150–2W	12	539/18	3
4th *Race Relations and the 'Sus' Law, No. 2.* HC744.*	n/a	5.8.80	n/a	2	n/a	0
5th *The Law Relating to Public Order*, HC576-I	28.1.80 (9)	7.8.80	not yet published	30	681/25	6
Session 1980–81						
1st *Home Office Reports*, HC23 (Evidence, 1979–80, HC755).	30.7.80 (1)	24.11.80	31.3.81 Cmnd. 8214	6	150/1	0
2nd *Numbers and Legal Status of Future British Overseas Citizens without other Citizenship*, HC158.*	12.2.81 (2)	16.3.81	n/a	6	193/4	2[a]
3rd *Vagrancy Offences*, HC271.	6.4.81 (2)	19.5.81	21.7.81 Cmnd. 8311	8	137/12	12
4th *The Prison Service*, HC412-I	3.11.80 (11)	20.7.81	8.12.81 Cmnd. 8446)	44	1,038/22	2
5th *Racial Disadvantage*, HC424-I*	22.5.80 (20)	20.7.81	26.1.82 Cmnd. 8476	91	2,415/108	6
Session 1981–82						
1st *Commission for Racial Equality*, HC46-I*	30.3.81 (7)	23.11.81	27.4.82 Cmnd. 8547	44	687/15	1
2nd *Racial Attacks**	14.12.81 (2)	27.1.82	n/a	1[b]	79/2	0

Annex 10.1 *Home Affairs Committee (cont.)*

Report (*denotes inquiry by sub-c'tee)	Date of first oral evidence/no. of evidence sessions	Date of publication of report	Date and form of govt. reply	Length of report (pages)	No. of oral qq./no. of written submissions	No. of divisions
3rd NHS Charges for Overseas Visitors, HC 121*	21.12.81 (2)	18.5.82	2.7.82 (private letter)	9	153/17	3
4th Police Complaints Procedure HC98-I.	4.12.81 (11)	9.6.82	19.10.82 Cmnd. 8681	23	1,186/26	6
5th Immigration from the Indian Sub-Continent, HC 90-I*	7.12.81 (5)	23.7.82	25.11.82	42	513/30	5
6th Miscarriages of Justice, HC 421	23.6.82 (3)	20.10.82	13.4.83 Cmnd. 8856	11	257/5	
7th Revised Immigration Rules, HC 526.*	25.10.82	27.10.82	n/a	1[b]	93/1	0
Session 1982–83						
1st Representation of the People Acts, HC 32-I.	10.11.82 (10)	21.4.83	31.1.84 Cmnd. 9140	28	1,001/56	7
2nd Ethnic and Racial Questions in the Census, HC 33-I*	15.11.82 (10)	11.5.83	29.11.84 Cmnd. 9238	36	1,515/124	0
3rd British Nationality Fees, HC 248.*	7.3.83 (2)	4.5.83	7.3.84 Cmnd 9183	12	147/45	1

Notes:

[a] Includes a division on whether the sub-committee be permitted to undertake the inquiry.

[b] Not a report as such—evidence only.

Other Proceedings

1. 10.12.79 and 17.12.79 (1979–80. HC 321-i and ii). Exploratory meeting (97. qq.) with Home Secretary and Home Office Officials.
2. 8.12.80 (1979–80, HC 89) Sub-committee evidence session (193 qq. and one written submission) on 'Immigration Topics'.
3. 4.6.82 to 19.7.82 (1981–82. HC 405 (i–iv)). Four sub-committee evidence sessions (282. qq.) with Home Office and other ministers on Progress in implementing the Report on Racial Disadvantage.
4. 27.10.82 (1981–82, HC 527). Evidence session (68. qq.) with members of the Government Working Party on Prosecution Arrangements.

CHAPTER 11

The Industry and Trade Committee

J.M. Lee and Donald Shell

'The bland leading the bland.' That description by one inside observer, in the context of the inquiry into Rolls Royce Ltd. in 1982, was considered by several of those involved to be an appropriate comment both upon the Government *and* upon the Committee. The latter had simply underlined the importance of collaboration in expensive and high-risk projects and of being as efficient and competitive as the company's American rivals. Yet at the same time the testimony of the Chairman of Rolls Royce before the Committee on 28 April 1982 had been a notable advance on the earlier sessions held in February.[1] A normally phlegmatic company chairman, responsible for spending large amounts of public money, had shown his sense of accountability and had even betrayed his view that it would not be practical to 'privatize' his organization. The Committee felt satisfied that it had seen behind the veil of confidence which necessarily surrounds the company's operations, even if the published evidence available to Parliament and the general public did not quite convey that sense of success. The blandness of the Committee was not a disarming and ingratiating manner—*suaviter in modo*—but a remedial and alleviative dose of good sense—hopefully *fortiter in re*.

Its acknowledgement that industry and trade cannot be examined with total frankness, and its insistence that gestures can be made to improve accountability to the public, made the style of the Committee difficult to describe. Yet such a combination was characteristic of committee members acting collectively when their individual interests were so diverse. Each member brought to its work his own direct experience in industry or trade. Although the main outlines of each inquiry were agreed in committee and the questions to be put were drawn up in a common set of documents, the practice of questioning in public sessions often reflected private sources of information or the personal involvement of individual members. The latter frequently spoke from briefs acquired from groups outside the Committee or from experience on their own companies. Each inquiry not only provided a hearing at Westminster on a subject of public concern but also gave opportunities by virtue of its very existence to elicit information useful to particular companies or trade unions.

The Committee quickly established its own distinctive style. Its remit was larger than that of the former Trade and Industry Sub-Committee of the Expenditure Committee, and included almost half the scope of the former Select Committee on Nationalised Industries. These wide terms of reference,[2] which also covered the responsibilities of the Secretary of State for Northern Ireland in these fields, led the Committee to see itself in the role of an auditor who undertakes spot checks into state-owned concerns, and whose very existence with the power to investigate in a random manner will instil discipline into both ministers and Civil Servants. The Departments of Industry and Trade, with their associated bodies, learnt to expect that the Committee might enter any area giving rise to substantial public expenditure.

PERSONNEL

Because the Committee retained the same chairman and the three changes of membership which occurred during the life-time of the Parliament made no significant impact on the proceedings, it enjoyed a strong sense of continuity. Sir Donald Kaberry as chairman conducted the Committee's business with the even-handedness of the provincial solicitor which he had been. The whips had determined that the Conservative Party should provide the candidate for this particular chairmanship, and the Labour members of the Committee preferred him to the other Conservative nominated for election, Peter Emery, who had been Under-Secretary for Trade and Industry in Edward Heath's administration. Kaberry, who had not held office since 1955—when for six months he had been Parliamentary Secretary at the Board of Trade—was acceptable, in spite of his advancing years (he was 75 in 1982). He did not stand at the 1983 general election, so his chairmanship had the air of a parliamentary swansong, his last contribution to back-bench life.

Five or six of the eleven members of the Committee were more active than the others, in the sense that the role of committee members was an important element in their parliamentary lives. The official attendance figures were not always a reliable guide to the assiduity of members. At least from the evidence of public sessions it is clear that some members arrived late, left early, and gave little attention to the business in hand. The figures do, however, indicate that three members attended 90 per cent or more of the sittings, while two members attended less than 60 per cent.[3] Though to begin with, committee members did not sit separately according to their parties, this became the usual practice by midway through the Parliament, with the five Labour members and one Conservative sitting on the right of the chair, and the other four Conservatives sitting on the left in the company of the clerk. The chairman, who tended to allow questioning from each side alternately, had to rely on the same regular attenders.

On the Conservative side, Eric Cockeram, Peter Emery (knighted in 1982), and Robin Maxwell-Hyslop were the most assiduous, having, as they did, the closest contacts with commerce. Cockeram, who was chairman of a family menswear business (Watson Prickard) and the Member for Ludlow, had represented Bebington in the 1970–74 Parliament and was closely associated with the business life of Liverpool. Emery, the Member for Honiton since 1967, who had previously sat for Reading (1959–66), had a wide range of business interests, particularly in insurance and petroleum, and had been director-general of the European Federation of Purchasing. Maxwell-Hyslop, the Member for Tiverton since 1960, had worked before his election in the aero–engine division of Rolls Royce, and through contacts developed by that company had become familiar with Brazil and with Latin American trade. He attended virtually every session of the committee, and was particularly assiduous in pressing witnesses on procedural or quasi-legal points, as well as any area where he believed he could detect an inconsistency. Apart from the chairman, the other two Conservative places were held by members brought in after the Committee's work had begun. James Hill, the Member for Southampton Test, who had also held that seat in 1970–74, was appointed to the Committee in January 1981 after Donald Thompson, the Member for Sowerby, had accepted office as a Conservative whip. Hill's main interests were in European transport. While serving as a member of the European Parliament before 1975 he had been chairman of its committee for regional policy and transport. Martin Stevens, the Member for Hammersmith Fulham, elected for the first time in 1979, was appointed to the Committee in December 1981 after Kenneth Carlisle, the Member for Lincoln (also first elected in 1979) had been invited to become a PPS to Hamish Gray, the Minister of State at the Department of Energy. Neither Hill nor Stevens exercised a major influence on the Committee's work.

On the Labour side, Stan Crowther and Ian Mikardo made their presence felt. Crowther, the Member for Rotherham since 1976, had been a journalist and member of Rotherham Borough Council, a position which gave him regular contact with the iron and steel industry in his constituency. Mikardo, sponsored by the Association of Scientific, Technical and Managerial Staffs (ASTMS) and a Member of the House for most of the period since 1945, was a management consultant with a wide experience of different industries. The other Labour members—Derek Foster, Russell Kerr, and Tom McNally— carried less weight in the Committee's proceedings. Kerr, also sponsored by ASTMS and a Member since 1974, was an air charter executive. After 1981 his contribution to the Committee became very slight owing to ill health. He was defeated in the 1983 election, and died later in the year. Foster, the Member for Bishop Auckland, who had been Assistant Director of Education in Sunderland, entered the House in 1979, and had previous experience as chairman of the North of England Development Council; McNally, the Member for Stockport South, was also a 1979 entrant, having been political adviser to the Prime Minister, James Callaghan, in the previous Parliament. McNally joined the SDP in October 1981, but remained a member of the Committee; he became SDP spokesman on trade.

Michael Martin, the Member for Glasgow Springburn, was appointed to the Committee at a very late stage in its activities— February 1983—after Derek Foster had accepted appointment as Opposition spokesman on social security. Martin, a trades union officer, could hardly have been expected to make an impact on the Committee's work.

The previous select committee experience of the more active members was occasionally significant in this committee's proceedings. Kaberry, Kerr, and Mikardo had all three served on the former Select Committee on Nationalised Industries. That experience stood them in good stead because among the bodies within the remit of the Committee were British Airways, British Aerospace (subsequently privatized), the British Airports Authority, British Shipbuilders, British Steel Corporation, British Telecom, and the Post Office, as well as bodies not within the remit of the previous committee, such as British Leyland, Rolls Royce, the Export Credits Guarantee Department, the National Enterprise Board, and the National Research Development Corporation (NRDC).

Maxwell-Hyslop had previously served on the Trade and Industry Sub-Committee of the Expenditure Committee; he thought that that Sub-Committee had been more effective. From time to time, recollections of the Expenditure Committee's work impinged on discussions of subjects to be examined. The appointment of an adviser who had previously worked for the Sub-Committee enhanced the link. Also in its first session (1979–80), the Committee took evidence on subjects which directly followed earlier inquiries by the previous Sub-Committee, namely measures to prevent collisions or strandings of noxious cargoes in UK waters, and responsibility for civil hydrography.

There appear to have been no significant connections between the work of this Select Committee and that of the functional committees of the political parties. Crowther, Kerr, and Mikardo did not link it with the industry group of the Parliamentary Labour Party. Maxwell-Hyslop was secretary of the Conservative Aviation Committee. Before his appointment, Hill had for a time been Joint Secretary of the Conservative Industry Committee.

The officials contributed to the Committee's style and sense of continuity. George Cubie, who had previously served the Select Committee on Nationalized Industries and the Expenditure Committee, remained clerk throughout the life of this committee. The only major change in staffing was the transfer of Roger Lloyd Thomas, who had been the Committee's assistant clerk, to become clerk to the Select Committee on Welsh Affairs in November 1982. He was succeeded by Sally de Ste Croix, previously a clerk to the Select Committee on Science and Technology.

The Committee also acquired a degree of unity from its retention of two principal advisers who had both served select committees in the previous Parliament. Garel Rhys, senior lecturer in economics at University College Cardiff, had advised the Trade and Industry Sub-Committee of the Expenditure Committee and played a prominent part in that body's investigation into Chrysler. Although originally hired by the Expenditure Committee as an expert in the motor-car industry, he became a general adviser on a broad range of subjects to the Expenditure Sub-Committee. Several members of the new Select Committee thought that he interviewed well on his appointment; they liked him and did not wish to look further afield for other advisers with greater expertise in special fields. The Committee also engaged Tony Cockerill, senior lecturer at the University of Manchester Institute of Science and Technology, who had previously advised the Select Committee on Nationalised Industries. At that time Cockerill had been approached because of his knowledge of the British Steel Corporation. He continued to help the new Select Committee with its inquiries into iron and steel, the Post Office, and British Shipbuilders. (Rhys was used to advise on twice as many inquiries as Cockerill.) Gordon Firth, who as it happened had been a former colleague of Maxwell-Hyslop in Rolls Royce, was appointed as adviser when the Committee turned its attention to Rolls Royce, and he would have returned if the general election had not prevented a further investigation of that company in 1983. Two accountants from Price Waterhouse assisted with the inquiry into the costs of Concorde. But the great bulk of the advisory work was undertaken by Rhys and Cockerill.

CHOICE OF SUBJECT

The Committee's first major inquiry was a formative experience. It lasted twelve months, with evidence being taken from more than 100 bodies, and led to others submitting requests to be heard. The subject of investigation was Britain's import and export trade.[4] The Committee learnt two major lessons from this wide coverage. First, it saw advantages in confining itself to short inquiries which would be spot checks rather than complete surveys. Secondly, it wished to avoid issues which might cause a deep division of opinion among its members, such as the question of free trade versus protectionism that emerged during this inquiry. The chairman claimed that he saw virtue in stumbling across topics and then following them up immediately, rather than working to a more systematic long-term plan for choosing subjects.

Two inquiries involved directly following up themes dealt with in the report on imports and exports. The first of these concerned European air fares,[5] with the Committee bemoaning the degree of protectionism which existed in European trade, and more generally within the European service sector, where Britain probably had competitive advantages. In arguing for free and fair competition, the Committee seemed really to be adding its voice to others in attempting to persuade European Community governments to ensure liberalization; the UK Government's reply[6] indicated a full agreement with the Committee, though in its report an associated body of the Department of Trade—the Civil Aviation Authority (CAA)—was criticized for its lack of commitment to the virtues of fair competition. The second was an inquiry into UK trade with the Association of South East Asian Nations (ASEAN) countries,[7] undertaken in 1982-3 because the Committee thought such an inquiry 'would make a useful case study of current export performance'. In some respects this report contained encouraging news about British export performance in the quick overview it sought to give of trade with this rapidly expanding market. Some of its recommendations related to quite specific matters about which it had found out while visiting Indonesia, Malaysia, Singapore, and Hong Kong: the trade section of the British Embassy in Jakarta was closed three afternoons a week; the office of the British High Commission in Kuala Lumpur was inadequate and unimpressive; the service attaché in Indonesia should perhaps be accorded a high rank, and so on. In more general terms, the Committee concluded that commercial staff should on the whole serve longer in particular posts, describing the FCO's negative response to this view as 'bland and predictable'.[8]

Perhaps the Committee's most characteristic work can be seen in its inquiries into some of the associated bodies of the Department of Industry. These tended to be short, but were deliberately designed to enable those responsible to put on the record some explanation of their activities; the Committee conceived its task as 'monitoring', a term which frequently recurred in its reports. The troubled giants of the public sector were thus invited to explain themselves; three reports on British Steel[9] were issued which variously criticized the Department of Industry for its minimal appraisal of the Corporation's plans, urged the Government to take action against the USA for limiting European steel imports, and criticized the BSC for its failure to consult trade unions more fully about its plans. In January 1983, the Committee investigated the decision to keep the Ravenscraig site open (a government decision overriding the BSC board), and declared, in contradiction of government claims, that 'We take the view that [this decision] was essentially a political rather than an economic decision'.[10]

Likewise with British Leyland, which the Committee touched upon in three successive sessions. In February 1981, following the Department of Industry's announcement that a further £990m. would be made available to BL, the Committee took evidence from Sir Keith Joseph, Secretary of State for Industry, and Sir Michael Edwardes, then BL Chairman.[11] The Committee published this evidence as a report, expressing itself 'greatly concerned at the amount of taxpayers' money being committed to BL, but [believing] ... at this stage HMG was right to provide the funds'.[12] The evidence was published in the belief that 'We have elicited information which will be of interest to the House, and perhaps of use also'.[13] The most lucid analysis of the circumstances surrounding the Government's decision was contained in a ten-page memorandum written by the adviser to the Committee—Garel Rhys—and published with the report.[14] To facilitate the use of the evidence thus elicited, the report on this occasion included an index to the minutes of evidence, indicating questions at which subjects such as commercial vehicles, hiving-off, Japan, etc., were covered. In the following session, the Committee again issued a brief report,[15] having on this occasion taken evidence only from BL itself on the subject of the 1982 corporate plan; the Committee believed this provided the 'most comprehensive public explanation of BL's current situation'.[16]

The report on Rolls Royce made in 1982[17] was again very much an account of the current state of the company, though it did stress the need for commercial viability (necessitating perhaps increased public spending) prior to any likely success in privatization—an important problem not widely discussed and rich in political paradox. During the inquiry the Committee Chairman reassuringly and characteristically opened the discussion with the Minister of State, Norman Lamont, by saying 'We do not intend to be a terrifying or ogre-like collection of individuals, but rather a collection of pleasant colleagues seeking to achieve the truth ...'.[18] The Committee were pleased that, as a result of its inquiry, a brief one-page memorandum of understanding between the Department and Rolls Royce was published for the first time.[19] In 1982, the Post Office came in for similar treatment, the Committee declaring that it believed the time to be ripe for a short review following the split between British Telecom and the Post Office.[20] Its main comments concerned the constitution of the Post Office Users National Council, and the thorny question of Post Office profits being appropriated by the Treasury rather than being more freely available for reinvestment.

When the Committee investigated British Shipbuilders in 1981–82, the legacy of bitterness from the nationalization of this industry was very apparent in its proceedings.[21] In particular, the question was raised of whether or not British Shipbuilders was deliberately under-tendering for ship-repairing work in an effort to put private ship-repairing companies out of business (which had so narrowly escaped the net of nationalization in 1976). To the fore here was Maxwell-Hyslop, whose assiduity on procedural matters in 1976 had been a means of rescue for the private ship-repairers. The Committee allowed its report to become the vehicle through which the two sides in this dispute—the private ship repairers and BS—could attack and counter-attack one another. The Committee concluded that it wished to see 'the clearest evidence within the next year that BS have started to carry out their Chairman's intention of "closing, selling or getting rid of" any company which continues to show no sign of viability'. Meanwhile 'tendering at below cost should cease'.[22]

Prior to the dissolution of Parliament in May 1983, the Committee had announced its intention to inquire into British Airways. It investigated the Concorde programme twice, concentrating on the public expenditure implications of future support for aircraft in service. Its first report took the Government to task for making 'no real attempt ... to appraise all the costs and benefits of continuing or cancelling [the Project]'.[23] It probed the assumptions on which the evidence was based, and quickly came to believe that it had found inconsistencies.

Its second report—made in 1982—indicated continuing dissatisfaction, and claimed some credit for prompting the discontinuance of costly fatigue-testing.[24]

The Committee also investigated government support for trade and industry in Northern Ireland (1981–82).[25] It visited the Province and offered brief comment on numerous issues; the main purpose and the achievement of this inquiry was simply to give some encouragement to those attempting to assist industry there.

This Committee (unlike some others) decided not to investigate where legislation was pending, as in the case of British Telecom. Another important associated body not investigated was the Monopolies and Mergers Commission, although John Biffen as Secretary of State for Trade had hinted that he would welcome such an investigation.

From time to time, the Committee chose a topic largely at the request of one of its members. For example, its last principal inquiry before the general election was undertaken in order to satisfy Ian Mikardo's interest in machine tools and robotics. The Committee had originally been persuaded to invite written evidence on this subject in 1980, but did not proceed with a full inquiry until February–April 1983.[26]

METHODS OF WORK

The Committee developed a routine of meeting thirty-odd times a year on Wednesday mornings while Parliament was in session. The procedures of each week revolved round this point. There was no power to appoint a Sub-Committee, and the device of an informal Sub-Committee was not used.

The Clerk's office was the focal point of weekly exercises in briefing and co-ordination. For example, in those inquiries for which Garel Rhys was the Committee's adviser, he sent to the clerk on Thursday evenings the questions he recommended members to ask. The clerk, on receiving these questions on Fridays, would consider them, along with any ideas of his own, consult his colleagues, and then circulate a list of questions to members of the Committee on Mondays, first putting them in a reasonable order and editing them in accordance with members' known interests. The two clerks usually met the chairman on Tuesdays to consider any problems they anticipated for the Wednesday meeting.

The clerk briefed the chairman, but the latter rarely engaged directly with the advisers as the chairman of the Expenditure Sub-Committee had done. Advisers and the clerk worked much more closely together. For some inquiries, the adviser suggested written questions to be sent to interested parties who might give evidence. The results were analysed along with other written evidence. One of the advisers felt he could begin to draft a report at this stage, that is, before any oral evidence was taken. But members in general valued oral evidence for the way it placed 'on record' fact or opinion otherwise known only privately.

Before the public sessions began on Wednesdays, the chairman allocated questions to each member, taking account of his known interests. The adviser concerned was normally present. He might, as might the clerk, from time to time pass notes or whisper to members as the evidence was being taken in order to ensure that effective supplementary questions were asked.

The visit to Northern Ireland in June 1982, in order to gather information on government support for trade and industry in that Province, was the Committee's only meeting in the United Kingdom outside Westminster, though Committee members did accept a few invitations to make visits connected with the work of the Committee, for example, to the Maestro production line at Cowley while investigating machine tools. Apart from three brief visits to Brussels—once in May 1980 to talk to officials of the EEC about trade questions, once in July 1981 to discuss European air fares and steel, and in July 1982 to discuss trade with Japan, steel, and shipbuilding—the overseas travel undertaken by the Committee consisted of two journeys to the Far East. On the first occasion in October 1980, as part of the imports and exports inquiry, the Committee wished to see the activities of British representatives and British firms in the export trade. Some members visited Japan, South Korea, Taiwan, and Hong Kong, and spoke with ministers and business men. On the second occasion in November 1982, the Committee wished to return to the record of British export performance in the area covered by the ASEAN treaty (Indonesia, Malaysia, Philippines, Singapore, and Thailand). The Committee travelled to Malaysia, Singapore, and Indonesia, via Hong Kong.

There was rarely a difference of opinion between members on the drafting of each report. The tone of each inquiry was designed to achieve a ready consensus. The clerk normally took charge of presenting a first draft to the chairman, although the advisers were involved. Garel Rhys, for example, drafted much of the major report of 1981 on imports and exports.

The value of each inquiry was frequently seen by members to lie outside the formal report itself. Not only did each inquiry attract unsolicited evidence which was sometimes extremely useful, but also those who were called to testify were prepared to make evidence available on a confidential basis. It is difficult on the basis of the published reports alone to assess the extent to which any particular set of inquiries provided material which was valuable both to members of the Committee and to those involved in its deliberations, such as pressure groups or even the departments themselves.

The clerk of the Committee acted as the major liaison-point between the different interests. He would regularly give advance warning to those called to give evidence in public sessions of the kind of questions which they were likely to be asked. For example, during the inquiry into the prospects of the British Steel Corporation in 1982–83 he regularly telephoned not only the management of that company but also the research department of the Iron and Steel Trades Confederation, and the TUC Secretariat. The clerk was also the major point of contact for the liaison officers of government departments.

IMPACT

Members of the Committee had a sense of achievement at a number of different levels; they tended to judge their record not by the measurement of any direct impact upon government policy-making but by evidence of the respect which their activities had engendered. The advisers also tended to think of the Committee in terms as much of its by-products as of its public influence. Indeed, the two principal advisers who had direct experience of select committees in the previous Parliament were not convinced that the departmental select committees were an advance on what had gone before.

There was general agreement that the Committee's major influence on government policy was in changing opinion on the costs of maintaining the Concorde programme. This achievement was recorded in the report of the Liaison Committee of December 1982.[27] When the Committee took evidence in January 1981, witnesses maintained that fatigue-testing of the Concorde airframe would be necessary until at least 1986–87; the Committee in its report suggested that such testing could be terminated earlier because utilization of the aircraft was decreasing.

The Government's reply issued in July indicated that some curtailment would be possible,[28] and by December the Government announced the virtual cessation of the fatigue-testing programme (saving £36m. over a five-year period). The Committee believed its own probing on this point had established the possibility of such a saving and prompted the Government's decision.[29]

In its final special report of the Parliament, the Committee itself gave two further examples of 'changed Government policy subsequent to Reports we have made'.[30] In both cases, the change is by no means obvious from the published reports and government replies, perhaps because of the general nature of the recommendations made. One concerned the need for greater flexibility on the part of public sector purchasing bodies to facilitate the placement of orders with British companies. The government reply to this report[31] agreed on this need, and included a memorandum on the subject drawn up by the Secretary of State for Trade and endorsed by the National Economic Development Council (NEDC). The whole case arose out of the placement of an order for radar equipment by the CAA with a Dutch firm. The second example concerned policy on the use of standards as a technical barrier to trade, where the Committee appeared to encourage the Government to adopt a more robust retaliatory attitude, though it is hard to infer from the Government reply that it agreed with this as a matter of policy (whatever might have happened in relation to a specific example).[32] But perhaps actions speak louder than words. The subsequent rejection of ultra heat tested (UHT) milk on the grounds that it failed to reach a proper standard, and the introduction of type approval for commercial vehicle imports, could be interpreted as signs of a changed government attitude.

There was little regret that none of the Committee's reports were debated in the House. Provided that comment was made in the 'quality press' or that the evidence was summarized in the 'trade press' of the industry under scrutiny, the Committee was fairly satisfied with the publicity which its activities received. The chairman made a habit of inviting journalists to a press conference on the publication of each report. Although press reaction to reports was monitored by the clerk, no comprehensive record of press cuttings concerning the Committee was maintained.

CONCLUSION

The Committee very firmly rebutted the suggestion that separate committees be established to cover the two departments of trade and industry, deploring the fact that its own views had not even been sought by the Liaison Committee before the latter made this recommendation.[33] In point of fact, after the general election Mrs Thatcher rendered such debate otiose by again merging the two departments. More significant was the question of sub-committees. Though the original motion establishing the departmental select committees had included provision for a sub-committee (constituted from the relevant departmental committees) to cover the nationalized industries, no such sub-committee had been established. The Liaison Committee commented on the reasons for this, which included the fact that six departmental select committees would have an interest in such a sub-committee, and questions about to whom the sub-committee would report, who its chairman would be, and so on, had proved too difficult to resolve to the agreement of all concerned.[34] The case for such a committee rested on the view that in relation to some matters—financing and pricing policy for example—a committee looking at all the nationalized industries together would be advantageous: such a committee would operate in addition to the scrutiny provided by the departmentally-based committees. The Trade and Industry Committee along with the Energy Committee was most directly affected by this question. Neither seemed willing to forgo any of its rights of scrutiny to a sub-committee which might report to a different main committee, though privately some members of the Industry and Trade Committee acknowledged that the absence of such a sub-committee represented a deficiency in the system of scrutiny.

The Liaison Committee also recommended that select committees be given a general right to appoint sub-committees.[35] This provoked the Industry and Trade Committee into a formal division, when in its final report it agreed by a majority of four to two to welcome this proposal. The whole committee agreed that if such a right were given 'it would not consider it desirable to appoint sub-committees on anything other than an *ad hoc* basis for specific inquiries'.[36] This rubric reflected the Committee's sensitivity to the Government's view that sub-committees would absorb proportionately more time for ministers and civil servants, as well as the members' own concern not to increase their committee obligations.

Sensitivity characterized the work of the committee. As the chairman emphasized, industry and trade are activities which rely on discretion and trust. The Committee made no attempt to rock the boat. Its ethos was pragmatic and realistic rather than dogmatic or ideological. Its members shared some fundamental perceptions which enabled the Committee to work within an agreed framework. One constant point of reference was that the taxpayer should have value for money; another was the need to restore public sector companies to a sound commercial basis while at the same time minimizing adjustment costs in employment terms. Finally, there was a consensus within the Committee that trade should as far as possible be both free and fair. Within a broad acceptance of these notions, the Committee embarked upon its particular inquiries. On the whole it deliberately avoided investigating the central policy questions of its associated departments such as those surrounding government industrial strategy, competition policy, protectionism, and so on. Rather than attempting theoretically-based analysis in such areas, the Committee believed it could be more effective by examining particular industries or practical policy concerns. Given the nature of this Committee and the wider environment within which it operated, this was almost certainly a correct assessment.

NOTES

1. Sixth Report from the Industry and Trade Committee, 1981–82, HC 389.
2. The terms of reference were 'to examine the expenditure, administration and policy of the Departments of Industry and Trade and associated public bodies, and similar matters within the responsibilities of the Secretary of State for Northern Ireland'.
3. Calculated from Select Committee Returns for 1979–80, 1980–81, 1981–82.
4. First Report from the Industry and Trade Committee, 1980–81, HC 109.
5. Fifth Report from the Industry and Trade Committee, 1980–81, HC 431.
6. Fourth Special Report from the Industry and Trade Committee, 1980–81, HC 472.
7. First Report from the Industry and Trade Committee, 1982–83, HC 195; (HC 456-i and ii; HC 196-i).
8. Ibid., para. 43. Also Memorandum of Evidence, pp. 88–9.
9. Fourth Report from the Industry and Trade Committee, 1980–81. HC 336-i-ii; Fourth Report, 1981–82, HC 308; Second Report, 1982–83, HC 212.
10. Second Report from the Industry and Trade Committee, 1982–83, HC 212, para. 12.
11. Third Report from the Industry and Trade Committee, 1980–81, HC 294.
12. Ibid., para. 4.
13. Ibid., para. 3.
14. Ibid., pp. 64–74.
15. Third Report from the Industry and Trade Committee 1981–82, HC 194.
16. Ibid., para. 2.
17. Sixth Report from the Industry and Trade Committee, 1981–82, HC 389.
18. Ibid., q. 187.
19. Ibid., Para. 19; see also Annex N, p. 34.
20. Fifth Report from the Industry and Trade Committee, 1981–82, HC 343.
21. First Report from the Industry and Trade Committee, 1981–82, HC 192.
22. Ibid., para. 11.
23. Second Report from the Industry and Trade Committee, 1980–81, HC 265, Conclusion 58 (iii).
24. Second Report from the Industry and Trade Committee, 1981–82, HC 193 (101-i), para. 11(i). See also 1982–83 Liaison Committee Report, para. 13.
25. Seventh Report from the Industry and Trade Committee, 1981–82, HC 500 (398-i-ii).
26. Third Report from the Industry and Trade Committee, 1982–83, HC 346.
27. 1982–83 Liaison Committee Report, para. 12, footnote 24.
28. Second Report from the Industry and Trade Committee, 1980–81, HC 265, para. 28; and government reply Cmnd. 8308, July 1981.
29. Second Report from the Industry and Trade Committee, 1981–2, HC 193, para. 11.

30. Third Special Report from the Industry and Trade Committee, 1982–83, HC 388, para. 2, footnote 4.
31. First Special Report from the Industry and Trade Committee, 1979–80, HC 33. Second Report from the Industry and Trade Committee, 1979–80, HC 700.
32. First Report from the Industry and Trade Committee, 1980–81, HC 109, para. 10. Also Cmnd. 8247, para. 40.
33. Third Special Report from the Industry and Trade Committee, 1982–83, HC 388, para. 5.
34. Liaison Committee Report, 1982–83, paras. 40–4.
35. Liaison Committee Report, 1982–83, paras. 36 and 39.
36. Third Special Report from the Industry and Trade Committee, 1982–83, HC 388, para. 6.

Annex 11.1 *Industry and Trade Committee*

Report	Date of first oral evidence/(no. of evidence sessions)	Date of publication of report	Date and form of govt. reply	Length of report (pages)	No. of oral qq./no. of written submissions	No. of divisions
Session 1979–80						
1st *The Post Office* HC 476; 367–iii	30.1.80(1)	25.3.80	—	1	119(3)	—
2nd *CAA Radar Replacement Programme* (a) HC 700; 442–X	4.6.80(1)	17.7.80	5.12.80 HC 33	6	139(7)	—
3rd *Measures to prevent collisions and standings of noxious cargo carriers in waters around the U.K.* (b) HC 757 (521–i and ii)	26.3.80(2)	26.8.80	18.12.80 HC 72	3	189(13)	—
4th *Nationalised Industries Finances* (c) HC 758	None	26.8.80	—	1	—(5)	—

Other Proceedings

Evidence from Department of Trade (16.1.1980) from Secretary of State (Nott) and Permanent Secretary (Clucas) plus Memo Published 11.4.80 HC 367–i (91 questions).

Evidence from Department of Industry (23.1.80) from Secretary of State (Joseph, Minister of State (Butler) and Permanent Secretary (Carey) Plus Memo. Published 15.4.80 HC 367–ii (94 questions).

Evidence from British Shipbuilders (27.2.80), plus Memo (d). Published 23.5.80 HC 367–iv (172 questions).

(a) Part of inquiry into imports and exports but published separately in advance of main report.

(b) Follow up report to inquiry by Trade and Industry Sub-committee of Expenditure Committee (HC 105, 1978–79) and Govt. reply (Cmnd 7525).

(c) Publication of evidence from various Nationalised Industries in response to an earlier report from the Treasury and Civil Service Committee (HC 584, 1979–80) which questioned assumptions in Public Expenditure White Paper (Cmnd 7841) (Entitled a Report, but really evidence only).

(d) Follows earlier Report of the Select Committee on Nationalised Industries.

(e) Excluding days during visits on which evidence was taken.

Session 1980–81						
1st *Imports and Exports* HC 109 I and II	13.2.80(20)	Vol. 1 12.2.81 Vol. 2 16.3.81	26.5.81 Cmnd 8247	79	2363(85)	0
2nd *Concorde* HC 265	28.1.81(2)	14.4.81	15.7.81 Cmnd 8308	16	289(23)	0
3rd *Finance for BL* HC 294	18.1.81(2)	8.5.81	—	1	239(6)	0
4th *Effects of BSC Corporate Plan* HC 336	11.8.81(7)	Vol. 1 10.6.81 Vol. 2 2.7.81	3.8.81 HC 444	24	1077(33)	0
5th *European Air Fares* HC 431, 431–I	10.6.81(3)	28.7.81 431–I 12.8.81	21.10.81 HC 472	6	354(18)	0

Other Proceedings Session of evidence from C. Parkinson (Minister of State, Department of Trade) on negotiations for a new Multi-Fibre Arrangement, 22.7.81 HC 445–i. Published 21.9.81. (Follow up to HC 109 Imports and Exports Inquiry.)

Session 1981–82						
1st *British Shipbuilders* HC 192	2.12.81(3)	5.3.82	28.5.82 HC 381	11	386(19)	0
2nd *Concorde* HC 193	9.12.81(1)	25.2.82	Letter to the Committee	5	62(5)	0
3rd *BL Limited* HC 194	21.11.81(1)	1.3.82	—	1	118(3)	0
4th *British Steel Corporation* HC 308	25.11.81(2)	19.4.82	3.8.82 HC 491	1	229(5)	0
5th *The Post Office* HC 343	3.3.82(4)	20.5.82	15.11.82 (HC 554) (8th Report)	15	456(17)	0

Annex 11.1 *Industry and Trade Committee* (*cont.*)

Report	Date of first oral evidence/(no. of evidence sessions)	Date of publication of report	Date and form of govt. reply	Length of report (pages)	No. of oral qq./no. of written submissions	No. of divisions
6th *Rolls Royce Limited* HC 389	17.2.82(3)	22.6.82	28.10.82 HC 523	8	380(10)	0
7th *Govt. support for Trade and Industry in Northern Ireland* HC 500	9.6.82(2)	15.9.82	14.12.82 (HC 85 1982–83)	7	222(19)	0

Other Proceedings Session of Evidence from P. Rees (Minister of State, Department of Trade) on Negotiations for a new Multi-Fibre Arrangement. 11.11.81. HC 23–i. Published 28.1,82. (Follow up to earlier inquiry.)

Session 1982–83

Report	Date of first oral evidence/(no. of evidence sessions)	Date of publication of report	Date and form of govt. reply	Length of report (pages)	No. of oral qq./no. of written submissions	No. of divisions
1st *The UK's Trade with ASEAN countries*	7.7.82(3)	13.3.83	24.5.83 (HC 387)	19	314(16)	0
2nd *The British Steel Corporation's Prospects* HC 212	27.10.82(4)	10.3.83	19.1.84 (HC 181)	11	464(12)	0
3rd *Machine Tools and Robotics* HC 346	23.2.83(5)	19.5.83	9.2.84 (HC 222)	19	566(24)	0

Other proceedings

Session of evidence from BL taken on 24.4.83. HC 353–i, published 7.6.83 (i Memo, 138 Oral Q).
Session of evidence from Post Office taken on 4-5.83. HC 366–i, published 7.6.83 (2 Memos, 132 Oral Q).
Third Special Report. HC 388. The work of the Industry and Trade Committee. Published 25.5.83.[a]

Note:

[a] There was a division on 11 May 1983 on a proposal from Sir P. Emery to insert the words 'We welcome this' in relation to a Liaison Committee recommendation that departmental select committees should have a general power to appoint sub-committees. Emery's motion was carried by four votes to two; the paragraph as amended appeared in this Third Special Report.

CHAPTER 12

The Scottish Affairs Committee

H. M. Drucker and J. G. Kellas

In 1979 Scotland was a major concern of British politicians. After a stormy passage in the House of Commons, the devolution legislation to set up an assembly and executive in Edinburgh was put to a referendum of the Scottish people in March. While a small majority of those voting endorsed the Scotland Act, the requirement that 40 per cent of the electorate should vote 'Yes' was not met. The Conservative Government elected in May went ahead with the repeal of the Act in July, although the pro-devolution parties had won 68 per cent of the Scottish vote in the election. The electoral threat from the Scottish National Party receded (only two MPs remained), but the Labour Party won forty-four seats to the Conservatives' twenty-two. This had a double effect on the position of Scotland in Parliament: it confirmed Labour as the majority party, and it kept alive the devolution issue, for not only was Labour still committed to a Scottish assembly, but it could also argue that it had a mandate, not possessed by the Conservative Government, to speak for Scotland in the House of Commons. The effect of the Scottish mandate was felt on the Labour MPs as much as on their party collectively: many had been chastened by the recent popularity of the SNP and determined not to allow themselves to be cast as unionists again. Also, they had caught a bit of the excitement of Scotland during the recent Parliament and had been converted by it: they had come to want to play a role in Scottish affairs as well as in parliamentary business. Such a mandate would be particularly relevant in the purely Scottish committees of the House.

These committees represent a long-established method of dealing with Scottish business in Parliament, and they include the Scottish Grand Committee and the Scottish Standing Committees. From 1969 to 1972 there was also a Select Committee on Scottish Affairs, the precursor of the Committee on Scottish Affairs established in 1979. This Select Committee was one of a number established in the late 1960s. Its remit was general: 'to consider Scottish Affairs'. It considered only two topics before it was wound up in 1972: Economic Planning in Scotland and Land Resource Use in Scotland.[1]

The Scottish committees of the House of Commons face two ways. In one aspect they appear as the equivalent of any other parliamentary committees. They expedite the business of the House, subject to the will of the whole Chamber, which means in effect the Government. Also, their membership is expected to reflect the balance of parties in the House as a whole. To achieve this end, the Scottish Grand Committee had members added to it from outside the ranks of the Scottish MPs, usually when the Conservatives were in office. Only fifteen extra members could be added for this purpose, however, and after 1979 even this addition did not produce a Conservative majority on the Committee.

This points to the other aspect of the Scottish committees. They are also there because Scotland is a distinctive part of the British political system, and they must face Scotland as well as London. Scotland has its own legal system, which requires the passage of Scottish legislation. It has its own Secretary of State, who is accountable primarily to the Scottish Members of Parliament, through Scottish question-time and the proceedings of the Scottish committees. These MPs form a self-conscious group within the House because of such activities, and they relate to each other politically to an extent unmatched by the other territorial groups in the House. They also relate to Scotland through the numerous political and social institutions and organizations which exist within the Scottish political system. These include the Scottish party organizations, the separate local government system, and the newspapers and television channels which report Scottish politics in Westminster in considerable detail. One consequence of the recent difficulties over nationalism has been to strengthen Scottish MPs' awareness of this aspect of their role.

This background makes it easier to understand the peculiar features in the history of the Committee on Scottish Affairs. The 'parliamentary' aspect is the same as that for the other Select Committees described in this book. But the 'Scottish' aspect of the Committee on Scottish Affairs has also been important—indeed, at first, it was more important than the 'parliamentary' aspect. When the Scotland Act was repealed in July 1979, the Conservative Government announced that 'all-party talks' would be held to consider what could be done about Scottish government, and attention switched to the Scottish Committees of the House of Commons. Could these not be reformed in a way which would satisfy the aspirations of the Scottish people for greater control over their own affairs? At least, such reforms would show that the Conservatives were not closing the door to all changes in the government of Scotland.

With this in mind, the Government delayed the setting-up of any committee on Scottish Affairs. It pointed to the fact that the 1977–78 Procedure Committee had not included Scottish and Welsh Committees in its recommendations.[2] This was, of course, because at that time the devolution legislation for Scotland and Wales had just passed through Parliament, and it was not considered necessary, with devolution implemented, to strengthen the Westminster activities of the Scottish (or Welsh) MPs. Now, in June 1979, the absence of devolution and the need for something in its place put these committees back on the agenda. But under pressure from the Scottish MPs, the Government could not delay the establishment of the Scottish committee until the all-party talks had taken place, and a separate motion to set up the Committee was introduced on 31 October 1979. (The Welsh Committee had been initiated in a motion of 26 June 1979.)

The all-party talks did not even begin until 1980 and they led to only minor changes in the operation of the Scottish Grand Committee. The House decided that the Committee could now sit in Edinburgh; could be divested of its added non-Scottish Members; and could have more days to debate Scottish 'matters'. These changes, which did not satisfy devolutionists, emphasized the distinctiveness of Scottish institutions, and helped to keep alive the demand for a Scottish Assembly (the Grand Committee was to meet in the buildings previously set aside for the Assembly).

ESTABLISHMENT OF THE COMMITTEE: CHAIRMAN AND MEMBERS

The Select Committee on Scottish Affairs was finally nominated on 26 November 1979. It was the largest of the Select Committees, with thirteen members. While it seems that this size was originally demanded by Labour Members, in order to make a place for an SNP Member on the opposition side (the offer was not taken up), Labour members came to see the Committee as too large for effective business. Almost from the first, successive chairmen of the Committee were asking for a reduction in committee numbers or for sub-committees; most recently the Committee's third Chairman, David Lambie, reported to the Liaison Committee[3] that he believed that the membership should be reduced to the same as the other committees or that sub-committees should be instituted (these have not been granted).

The Chairmanship also gave rise to some discussion. The Government included the Scottish Affairs Committee among those committees which were to have a Labour (that is Opposition) chairman. This served to underline the Labour majority amongst Scottish MPs, and hence led to some sensitivity among Conservative backbenchers. Conservative members of the committee, one of whose number would otherwise have been the chairman, were not happy about this arrangement, which was the result of an agreement between the whips of the two parties. Their unease was to intensify the diplomatic problems which confronted the first chairman (Donald Dewar). In the event, the Conservative members appointed one of their number, Iain Sproat, as unofficial 'majority leader' and insisted that the chairmanship should be decided on a sessional, not a Parliament-long, basis.

Labour members, for their part, also sought to assert independence from their whips. Nominations to the Select Committees are made by the Committee of Selection, but the whips, particularly on the Labour side, retain an important advisory role. The Scottish Labour MPs decided to hold a ballot among themselves for membership, without consulting their whips. Twenty-two of the forty-four MPs put their names forward. Of these, six were selected. Donald Dewar, who had received one more vote than Norman Buchan, was then proposed as chairman. Buchan's friends were unprepared for the ballot for membership to be used in this way but did not object. The Conservatives held the remaining seven seats on the Committee, and their members were selected along the lines suggested by the Conservative whips. With only twenty-two Scottish Conservative MPs in the House, and nine of these in Government posts, the problem for the Tories was not competition for places on the committee but shortage of available manpower. Nevertheless, the Committee started off with a Conservative contingent which included five Members who would achieve Government office during the 1979-83 Parliament (Labour was to lose five of its original members to the Opposition front benches). This has deprived the Committee of continuity.[4] Of particular importance is the fact that the Committee had to work under three successive chairmen during the period. This high turnover tends to confirm the generally-held view—an inevitable consequence of the realities of executive power—that service with the Committee is not valued as much as a government or 'shadow' government post. On the other hand, service with the Committee may be a stepping-stone to such positions.

SUBJECTS OF INQUIRY

With the nomination of the Committee completed, the next task was the choice of topics and the method of organizing the inquiry. Here the problems of the Scottish Affairs Committee resemble those of the other select committees. Topics may raise the parties' sensitivities so that a unanimous report is difficult. The first, and in many ways politically the most important of the new committee's major reports, on *Inward Investment*,[5] raised just this problem. While the chairman, the advisers, and substantial sections of the relevant part of the Scottish Office, were broadly in agreement with what the Labour members of the Committee wanted to say in the report, and the chairman's draft had been laid before the Committee for endorsment, the Conservative majority rebelled at the last minute, produced its own report, and got this accepted as the Committee's report. The party divisions of the Committee were displayed to the press when the Report was published. At the press conference, each member of the Committee felt obliged to say something. The pro-devolution *Scotsman* commented: 'Such artlessness only serves to damage their already limping credibility.'[6]

This episode pointed up several dificulties for the work of the Committee. At first, especially in its work on *Inward Investment*, the Committee was hampered by the intensity of the party fight in Scotland. The memory of the recent divisions over the constitutional question were too strong to be overcome by any committee *esprit de corps*. This might have been less of a difficulty had the committee members been less well known to one another. Largely as a result of the experience over inward investment, and also because it soon lost its first and most dynamic chairman, Donald Dewar, the Committee then began to take on less controversial subjects. Latterly, it tended more commonly to work on topics which were of particular interest to its members because of their constituency or specialist interests: in this respect its investigations became something of a prolonged question time. A precedent was set for this at the very start of the Committee's life, when the members from constituencies with considerable fishing interests got an inquiry into the White Fish Authority general levy[7] (the Government took immediate action on the Committee's modest recommendations). Other special interests of the members were later served by inquiries into BBC cuts;[8] closure of colleges of education;[9] dispersal of Civil Service jobs to Glasgow,[10] rural road passenger transport and ferries;[11] Prestwick Airport;[12] youth unemployment;[13] housing grants;[14] and the steel industry (Ravenscraig).[15] Although the colleges of education inquiry was a matter of controversy within the

Committee (it divided not only on whether to take evidence but also on whether to report—it decided not to), most of these inquiries represented 'log-rolling' activities. Some of these were concerned with particular local interests within Scottish politics, while others reflected a general Scottish interest in relation to the rest of the country (for example, BBC cuts, civil service dispersal and the steel industry).

The Committee's treatment of more important general topics—and its watch-dog role over the Scottish Office—were less happily discharged. In its departmental role the Committee ought to have subjected the Scottish Office to detailed 'scrutiny and control'. In fact, the inquiries into the public expenditure programme in Scotland,[16] the rate support grant,[17] the housing capital allocation,[18] and youth unemployment and training in Scotland,[19] showed the Committee at its weakest and the Scottish Office at its most imperious.

ROLE OF ADVISERS

There seem to be a number of linked problems here. In the first place, the Committee did not make particularly effective use of specialist advisers. The Scottish Committee has two problems which the non-territorial committees can avoid: its work is so diverse that no one person is likely to be expert in much of the Committee's work; secondly, the Committee decided that it would be politically awkward for it to choose advisers from outside Scotland. This decision imposed real limitations in two respects. First, Scotland is a small country with fewer and smaller social science faculties than England. Most of the advisers were university academics in the social sciences, although they also included a retired civil servant, a private sector economic consultant, and a professional engineer. There was thus a fairly small field of expertise to draw upon. Secondly, contact between the advisers and the Committee was inhibited by the geographical separation between them. The advisers worked in Scotland, and the Committee normally worked in London. Meetings between advisers and Committee members were thus short and somewhat perfunctory. Moreover, since the advisers were chosen separately for each investigation (except that one adviser served on two inquiries, and another advised the Committee on three out of the four public expenditure inquiries), they were not able to build up a working relationship with Committee members; they were certainly not in a position to advise the Committee on what subjects might make suitable future investigations.

Both difficulties with advisers were particularly evident in the sessions in which the Secretary of State gave an account of his stewardship (that is, at the annual inquiries into the Government's public expenditure plans). The Committee's recently appointed advisers scurried around the room with information and advice for members with whom they had no experience of working, while the Secretary of State's team coolly advised their master. The Secretary of State, in this case George Younger, a master at the turning-away of anger, was adept at filibustering any difficult questions and certainly could count on more than a few easy questions from members on his own side of the House. This may be a problem on other committees as well, but the likelihood that, with a territorial ministry shadowed by members from the same territory, any preferment would probably be into the Scottish Office team, did not help matters. Discontent with the annual public expenditure inquiry led to reform in 1983. It was decided to hold three separate sessions in turn with the Convention of Scottish Local Authorities, Scottish Office officials, and the Secretary of State for Scotland. In this way it was hoped to avoid the 'question-time' nature of the inquiry. Unfortunately, only the first meeting was held (9 May 1983) before Parliament was dissolved.

PROBLEMS OF THE COMMITTEE'S REMIT

Many of the subjects which have exercised the Committee have straddled the responsibilities of several government departments. Thus the remit of the Committee 'to examine the expenditure, administration and policy of the Scottish Office and associated public bodies' is an inadequate one when dealing with public expenditure in Scotland, unemployment, the steel industry, Civil Service deployment, and airports (all subjects taken up by the Committee). These may be among the most important subjects in Scottish politics, but they are not entirely (or even mainly) within the functions of the Scottish Office. The same applies to agriculture. Although the Scottish Office administers agriculture in Scotland, the Committee has not investigated any agricultural topic, presumably because the main responsibility for agricultural policy lies with the Ministry of Agriculture, Fisheries and Food, which relates to the Select Committee on Agriculture. Some topics in agriculture such as crofting are distinctively Scottish, but the Select Committee on Agriculture has pre-empted these topics as well. It is perhaps significant that a member of the Scottish Committee especially interested in these topics, Mr Albert McQuarrie, decided in 1983 to join the Agriculture Committee.

With regard to its functional remit, the Committee's weakness reflects the weakness of the Scottish Office within British government. The Scottish Affairs Committee does not link up with the other select Committees investigating these matters elsewhere in Britain. Even the

Welsh Affairs Committee has little contact with the Scottish Affairs Committee, but this may not be as odd as might appear at first. The two committees represent competing interests in the U.K., as for example in the prospects for steel mills at Ravenscraig and South Wales. It was expected that either Scotland or Wales would have to lose a steel mill, so Wales would not speak up for Scotland, or vice versa. Vigorous lobbying by both Committees resulted in the decision in December 1982 to keep the Scottish and Welsh steel mills open. In March 1983, the Industry and Trade Select Committee attacked the decision on Ravenscraig as a threat to the jobs of other steel workers. The *Scotsman* announced that Scottish MPs were 'furious' at this Report.[20] The Liaison Committee recommended that select committees should on occasion take joint action on an inquiry,[21] and this seems appropriate in some cases for the Scottish Committee.

THE STYLE OF THE COMMITTEE

The working practices of the Committee have been distinctive in a number of ways. The Committee has met frequently in Scotland, not just in Edinburgh, but also in Glasgow, Aberdeen, Arran, Islay, Newtown St Boswells, Shetland, and Ayr. It has made trips abroad to Ireland, West Germany (twice), the European Commission in Brussels, and the United States. This contrasts with the Welsh Committee, which has held nearly all of its meetings in Westminster. The Welsh Committee Chairman, Donald Anderson, reported to the Liaison Committee that 'the reason why the [Welsh] Committee has not met more often in Wales is that the transport infrastructure makes it easier to travel to London than to travel within the Principality'.[22] At the same time, the Scottish Affairs Committee chairman (the third since 1979), David Lambie, in contrast, reported that frequent visits to Scotland were needed 'to enable the Committee to appreciate at first hand the problems which are the subject of inquiry and to discuss them with a far wider range of people than would otherwise be possible'.[23]

Despite these visits, there have been problems which have arisen on account of the Committee's operating for most of the time at a distance from Scotland. The advisers have been located in Scotland, while the Members have been mainly in Westminster. Separation has inhibited continuous contact, and this had not been redressed at the short briefing sessions before meetings, nor at the report-writing stage.

ROLE OF CHAIRMAN

The relationship between the members and the chairman has altered with the changes in personnel. There have been three very different chairmen: Donald Dewar, Robert Hughes, and David Lambie. Dewar was a dominant chairman, leading the questioning and pointing the Committee in the direction he wanted to travel. Hughes, in contrast, played a more neutral role, seeking consensus and an equal time for all members. His practice was to alternate questions between the parties, counting the chair as Labour. It was difficult to follow up a line of inquiry or to lead the Committee under these conditions. Party differences were exposed when a decision of 23 September 1981 to investigate the rating system (taken when the Conservatives were in a temporary minority) was overturned on December.[24] Lambie (elected Chairman on 27 January 1982) faced a Committee which at first operated under less party pressure; it was choosing uncontroversial topics, and the political climate in Scotland had cooled. Since the subjects chosen under his Chairmanship were uncontroversial, he enjoyed good relations with the Conservative members. (This situation was to change after 1983.)

IMPACT OF THE COMMITTEE

Any assessment of the impact of the Committee needs to take account not only of the nature of the select committee system, but also of the peculiarities of Scottish politics. The Committee's structural problems have been noted: it has a high turnover of members and chairmen; a poor adviser-member relationship; excessive size and lack of sub-committees; and its subject-matter has lacked cohesion. Some changes in public policy have been forwarded by the Committee: the White Fish Authority general levy; the site of the new Ministry of Defence building in Glasgow; some aspects of rural transport; some aspects of grants to local authorities for the eradication of dampness in housing; the decision to save the BBC Scottish Symphony Orchestra and the Ravenscraig steel mill; and the consideration of Prestwick Airport as a freeport, can all be mentioned here. But no straightforward list of influences is ever possible in a political world. The record of the Committee's report on *Inward Investment* is an example of why this is so. The minority (Labour) report was more acceptable to the Conservative Government than was the majority (Conservative) report. As a result, the Scottish Development Agency (a quango whose power some ideological Tories wanted to curb) was allowed to keep its inward investment functions, under the close supervision of the Scottish Office.

Other examples of possible influence on the Scottish Office can be quoted. When the Secretary of State for Scotland gave evidence to the Committee on 10 November 1982 in relation to the inquiry into the steel industry, he took the line that, as no firm proposals for the closure of Ravenscraig had yet been received, it would be premature to do any contingency planning within the department.[25] However, a few days later it was revealed in the press that a special task force was to be set up in the Scottish Office to prepare a case for the defence of the steel mill.

The Committee's report on Prestwick Airport contained a substantial section on the topic of the establishment of freeports in the UK. Shortly afterwards, the Government set up its own working party on the topic. The working party's report did not contain any reference to the Scottish Affairs Committee's report, but nevertheless there were many similarities between the two documents, and the overall argument was identical. On 2 February 1984, the Government announced that Prestwick was to be one of the six freeports established in Britain, and the only one in Scotland. This was claimed as a success for the Committee by the then Chairman, David Lambie.[26]

During the inquiry into dampness in housing, two points arose continually in the evidence. One was the lack of firm information about the condition of the housing stock in Scotland, and the other was the difficulty that local authorities were encountering in providing adequate funds for remedying dampness. Before the Committee could report, the Scottish Office announced that a centrally-funded sample survey of private sector housing stock built between the wars would be undertaken, and an additional capital allocation (derived from the sale of council houses) was to be given to those local authorities which had identifiable provision in their housing plans for the eradication of dampness. It is difficult to believe that these decisions were purely coincidental with the Committtee's inquiry.

In other cases, the Committee would appear to have been acting— sometimes consciously, at other times not—as a part of the Scottish public relations industry. Some of its work has been no more, arguably less, influential than a local planning authority might expect to be (over the siting of a government building for example); all too often it has acted on *sotto voce* suggestions from Scottish Office Ministers and Civil Servants (for example, with regard to Prestwick Airport).

The record shows that the Scottish Office took what it wished from the Committee's recommendations. It rejected the proposal to speed up the move to a 'road equivalent tariff' in ferries, but accepted other parts of the report. It has not been deeply moved by the Committee's annual inquiries into the Secretary of State's public expenditure pro-

gramme. It is difficult to trace any effect from the Committee's inquiries on the rate support grant, colleges of education, housing
capital allocation, or youth unemployment and training. The first two
of these inquiries did not lead to a report, and the same procedure
was adopted with regard to the inquiry into the BBC cuts in Scotland,
and for all four of the inquiries into Scottish public expenditure. It
may well be that without a report there is less impact in the Committee's deliberations. There is certainly nothing for the Government
to reply to. The absence of a report in the case of the annual public
expenditure inquiry is to some extent made up for by the unusual
practice of publishing the specialist adviser's memorandum along with
the rest of the evidence. While this certainly has something of the
opinion of the Committee about it, it is plainly not a report endorsed
by the majority of the members. For example, the public expenditure
adviser in 1983 gave much more criticism of the Secretary of State
than the Conservative majority would have supported.

Some of the Committee's most interesting reports, for example that
on *Youth Unemployment and Training* (which took nine months to prepare) and that on the steel industry in Scotland, were both effectively
pre-empted by decisions taken elsewhere. Government may dislike it
when a committee comes up with good ideas on a politically important area and may 'gazump' its report at the last minute: something
of the sort seems to have happened over Youth Unemployment and
Training. Or decisions may be well under way while the Committee
is deliberating. Something of this kind clearly happened in the steel
case: the Committee reported on 6 December 1982 and, the Government's decision was announced on 20 December 1982. But even these
cases cannot be unambiguously written off: the work of the Committee
may well have helped the Secretary of State in his battles in the
Cabinet.

Here we see the Committee in its Scottish aspect. It can be seen as
another weapon for Scotland in its fight for a bigger share of public
expenditure. But, as we have seen, the members of the Committee are
by no means united in their appreciation of the Scottish interest, and
each party may be jealous of the attempts the others make to use
the Committee. The decision of the SNP not to sit on the Committee is indicative. They did not want to get trapped into responsibility for decisions they did not accept, nor to give legitimacy to
Westminster-based ways of handling Scottish problems. Their absence
from the Committee might have hurt it had the National Party made
a big impact in the country during the 1979–83 Parliament. In the
event, the threat (as the other parties see it) of nationalism receded
further as the Parliament grew older. Paradoxically, this too weak-

ened the Committee, in so far as it made it easier for Members to take it less seriously. Without the spur of a vital National Party yelping at their heels, Scottish MPs began to forget the lessons of the previous Parliament, and to take their Westminster role more and their Scottish role less seriously. The decision of several Labour members to take minor shadow posts in British departments in place of their Scottish Affairs Committee places would have been much more difficult against a background of resurgent nationalism.

The precise nature of the Committee's effect on British departments is less clear but the general position is obvious enough. Since the Committee speaks largely to the Scottish Office, and to Scottish public opinion, it is not often heard in the Cabinet or in the House of Commons. Yet the subjects which the Scottish Affairs Committee take up, and which are of crucial importance to Scotland, include some over which Great Britain departments have the primary responsibility. In the Commons too, the Committee's reports are debated only in the Scottish Grand Committee. While this is better than no debate at all (the fate of most other committee's reports), it confirms the Scots in their ghetto.

Joint reports of the Scottish Affairs and other committees on matters of mutual concern, as suggested by the Liaison Committee,[22] would be a help. Many aspects of public expenditure, industry, and employment could be included here. A strengthening of the Committee's use of advisers would be helpful and would go some way to counteracting the advantage the Scottish Office has from its Civil Servants. But as the 1979–83 Parliament ended, the Committee was not in a strong position. This related to overwhelming political problems far outside the Committee's control. In 1983, Scotland was no longer a major concern even of many Scottish politicians. But the Committee could have done more to maximize its influence in its reduced circumstances.

REACTIONS TO THE COMMITTEE IN SCOTLAND

The reaction of the Scottish press to the work of the Committee changed during the Parliament. Initially the Committee was fully reported. The Government's delay in appointing the Committee placed it in the context of the then recent devolution debate, and the political energy of that argument warmed and cast a strong light on the new Committee. While this reflection lasted, the Committee was taken seriously: Scottish newspapers like the *Scotsman* and the *Glasgow Herald* assigned their senior political staff, Chris Baur and William Russell, to report the Committee's activities. The early report on the

White Fish Authority (February 1980) was welcomed and the report on Inward Investment (August 1980) was the climacteric. The division between Committee members on that later occasion and the all too obvious determination of most to grab a bit of publicity at the launch Press conference convinced many senior Scottish journalists that, whatever good the Committee might do, it was not going to rekindle the constitutional debate. Thereafter, Press interest waned: reports and some meetings were noticed by the more serious papers and broadcasters, but less senior journalists were assigned to the stories. Each report was covered separately, often in complimentary tones—as when the Committee condemned Whitehall sloth in dispersing public sector jobs to Scotland—but the Committee itself was rarely covered as a story in its own right. Noticing the drift of Press disenchantment even before it hardened, the chairman, Donald Dewar, complained in 1980[28] that the Press were being unfair to the Committee in asking it to be an ersatz Scottish assembly; the Committee labours under real problems (it is too big, its remit is too large) but it must not be asked to do the impossible.

In general, the Committee has retained a degree of credibility in Scotland. It has been seen by Scottish MPs and interests as a means to extract information from the Scottish Office and public bodies such as nationalized industries, and then to influence government decisions in favour of Scotland. A series of industrial crises have hit Scotland since 1979, and the Committee has been involved in investigating several of these (notably Ravenscraig in 1982 and Scott-Lithgow in 1984). Other subjects of this nature, such as the closure of the Linwood car plant in 1981, inspired the Scottish Trades Union Congress to ask the Select Committee to 'take emergency action'.[29] The threatened closure (later realized) of the Invergordon aluminium works was also suggested as a topic for the Committee by the STUC. While these two last-named topics were not taken up, the Committee was seen in Scotland as a potential weapon in the fight for Scottish economic interests, and many requests for inquiries have been made to the Committee by organizations and individuals.

As part of the 'Scottish Lobby', then, the Committee seems to have an assured place in Scottish politics. It can transcend party divides on many of these issues, as there are also strong constituency interests involved, and 'log-rolling' is practised. There is also a natural alliance between the Committee and its department, the Scottish Office, in such inquiries. Whether these practices are consistent with the purposes of the select committee system is another matter. The Scottish Affairs Committee (like the Welsh) is speaking for a nation in the context of a system of committees which was designed to speak for Parliament.

NOTES

1. 1969–70, HC 267; and 1971–72, HC 511.
2. 1977–78, HC 588.
3. 1982–83, HC 92 p. 110.
4. The turnover in membership over the whole 1979–83 Parliament was 77 per cent (only three members served throughout). In addition, two replacement members were themselves replaced during the Parliament.
5. Second Report, 1979–80, HC 769.
6. The *Scotsman*, 29 August 1980.
7. First Report, 1979–80, HC 400.
8. Inquiry, no report, 1979–80, HC 539.
9. Inquiry, no report, 1980–81, HC 204.
10. First Report, 1980–81, HC 88.
11. Second Report, 1981–82, HC 178.
12. First Report, 1982–83, HC 62.
13. First Report, 1981–82, HC 96.
14. Second Report, 1980–81, HC 112.
15. Second Report, 1982–83, HC 22.
16. Inquiries but no reports, 1979–80, HC 689; 1980–81, HC 364; 1981–82, HC 413; and 1982–83, HC 354.
17. Inquiry, no report, 1979–80, HC 345.
18. Second Report, 1980–81, HC 112.
19. First Report, 1981–82, HC 96.
20. The *Scotsman*, 11 March 1983.
21. 1982–83 Liaison Committee Report, pp. 24–5.
22. Ibid., p. 29.
23. Ibid., p. 107.
24. Minutes of Proceedings, Session 1981–82, HC 539, 3 December 1981.
25. 1982–83, HC 22, q. 9.
26. The *Scotsman*, 3 February 1984.
27. 1982–83 Liaison Committee Report, pp. 24–5.
28. Donald Dewar MP, 'The Select Committee on Scottish Affairs' in H. M. Drucker and N. L. Drucker (eds.), *The Scottish Government Yearbook 1981*, Edinburgh: Paul Harris Publishing, 1980, pp. 9–23.
29. The *Scotsman*, 9 March 1981.

Annex 12.1. *Scottish Affairs Committee*

Report	Date of first oral evidence/(no. of evidence sessions)	Date of publication of report	Date and form of govt. reply	Length of report (pages)	No. of oral qq./no. of written submissions	No. of divisions
Session 1979–80						
The proposed increase in the White Fish Authority general levy (HC 400)	4.2.80 (1)	21.3.80	(1)	6	356/9	3
Inward Investment (HC 769–I)	5.3.80 (2)	28.8.80	6.3.81 HC 205, 1980–81	34	1091/28[2]	4
Special report requesting sub-cttees (HC 415)	—	15.2.80	—	2	—	0
Session 1980–81						
1st Dispersal of Civil Service jobs in Scotland (HC 88–I)	29.10.80 (4)	8.1.81	17.6.81 HC 347, 1980–81	17	501/17[3]	0
2nd Housing Capital Allocation (HC 112–I)	28.1.81 (1)	2.4.81	Letter from the Minister to the Committee	7	132/8	0
Special report on the work of the committee Dec '79–Feb '81 (HC 280)	—	28.4.81	—	5	—	0
Session 1981–82						
1st Youth Unemployment and Training[4] (HC 96–I)	16.3.81 (14)	14.12.81 (Typescript) 23.12.81 (Print)	10.2.82 HC 184, 1981–82	43	1096/45[5]	5
2nd Rural Road Passenger Transport & Ferries[9] (HC 178)	3.2.82 (8)	14.6.82	4.10.82 HC 510, 1981–82	40	766/35[6]	2
1st Prestwick Airport (HC 62–I, 1982–83)	23.6.82 (6)	8.12.82	2.3.83 HC 225, 1982–83	26	501/31[7]	2

Annex 12.1. *Scottish Affairs Committee—cont.*

Report	Date of first oral evidence/(no. of evidence sessions)	Date of publication of report	Date and form of govt. reply	Length of report (pages)	No. of oral qq./no. of written submissions	No. of divisions
Session 1982–83						
2nd *The Steel Industry in Scotland* (HC 22)	10.10.82 (3)	6.12.82 (Typescript) 12.1.83 (Print)	Letter[8] from the Minister to the Committee	13	351/9	0
Dampness in Housing (HC 206, 1983–84)	14.2.83 (11)	22.2.84	9.5.84 HC 419, 1983–84[10]	53	1015/69[9]	0

Notes:

(1) No formal Govt. reply but cttee. believes recommendation acted upon in White Fish Authority (General Levy) (Amendment) Regulation 1979, Confirmatory Order 1980 (SI 1980 No. 527), the Sea Fish Industry Act 1980 and in the amalgamation of the WFA and Herring Industry Board. (See debate of 20.2.1980 in the Sixth Standing Committee on Statutory Instruments.)

(2) Includes 7 unpublished written submissions.

(3) Includes 4 unpublished written submissions.

(4) Report discussed by Scottish Grand Committee.

(5) Includes 2 unpublished written submissions.

(6) Includes 14 unpublished written submissions.

(7) Includes 12 unpublished written submissions.

(8) Report believed to have influenced Govt. decision to retain all five integrated steel plants.

(9) Includes 48 unpublished written submissions.

(10) An evidence session was held on this on 6 June 1984, *Minutes of Evidence*, HC 477, 1983–84 (19 pp.).

Other proceedings
Inquiries (no Report):
Session 1979–80

HC 345   Rate Support Grant: Principles and Assumptions (26 pp.)
HC 539   The BBC Cuts in Scotland (66 pp.)
HC 689   Scottish Aspects of the 1980–84 Public Expenditure White Paper (117 pp.)

Session 1980–81

HC 204   Financial Consequences of the closure of Colleges of Education (72 pp.)
HC 364   Scottish Aspects of 1981–84 Public Expenditure White Paper (81 pp.)

Session 1981–82

HC 413   Scottish Aspects of the 1982–85 Public Expenditure White Paper (98 pp.)

Session 1982–83

HC 354   Scottish Aspects of the Government's Public Expenditure Plans, 1983–84 to 1985–86, (82 pp.).

CHAPTER 13

The Social Services Committee[1]

Michael Rush

Most of the departmental committees established in 1979 can be regarded as the linear successors of the specialized sub-committees of
the former Expenditure Committee, although the links are sometimes
fairly tenuous. The Social Services Committee, however, could claim
at least three specific links with the former sub-committee of Social
Services and Employment: first, and most important, both had the
same chairman—Mrs Renee Short (Lab.); second, Nicholas Winterton (Cons.), one of the most active members of the new committee,
and Ron Lewis (Lab.) had also served on the Expenditure Sub-Committee; and third, as its first inquiry the newly-created Social Services
Committee chose to complete the last inquiry of its predecessor—
perinatal and neonatal mortality.

The new committee had, of course, the important advantage of
having a narrower remit than its predecessor, since a separate committee now dealt with the Department of Employment. None the less,
although primarily concerned with a single department—the Department of Health and Social Security and 'its associated public bodies'—the remit of the Social Services Committee remained formidable.
Not only did the Department deal with two major areas of public
policy—health, on the one hand, and social security on the other,
with social services acting rather like a bridge between the two—but
the associated public bodies included the regional and the former area
health authorities and the Committee's concerns brought it into frequent contact with local government authorities. Perhaps, therefore,
it is not surprising that in her report to the Liaison Committee in
1982 Mrs Short should have pleaded that the Committee would benefit from an increase in its membership from nine to eleven members.
Even in the absence of the formal power to appoint a sub-committee,

a larger membership would have helped the Committee to operate an informal sub-committee and facilitated a division of labour between the health and social security aspects of its remit through the ability to conduct major inquiries simultaneously.[2]

The Social Services Committee was one of the four departmental select committees with nine members, of whom five were Conservative and four Labour. At the dissolution of Parliament in May 1983, five of the original nine were still serving on the Committee—a turnover of 44.4 per cent. However, this turnover is reduced to 33.3 per cent if Ron Lewis (Lab.), who replaced William Whitlock (Lab.) in February 1980 after the Committee had held only eight meetings, is counted as one of the original members. Whitlock, in fact, had attended only the first of those meetings. Two further changes occurred in the 1980–81 session, when Frank Field (Lab.) became an Opposition front-bench spokesman and was replaced by Andrew Bennett (Lab.); and Ralph Howell (Cons.), who apparently was less interested in the health aspects of the Committee's work,[3] was replaced by Tom Benyon (Cons.). In 1981–82, Sir Brandon Rhys Williams was replaced by Mrs Angela Rumbold (Cons.). Finally, at the beginning of the 1982–83 session Benyon was replaced by Tim Smith (Cons.); towards the end of the session, however, Smith resigned when he was appointed a Parliamentary Private Secretary and was himself replaced by David Crouch (Cons.).

As might be expected, a number of those appointed to the Committee, both originally and during its life, had had experience relevant to the Committee's remit. Most notably, David Ennals (Lab.) had been Secretary of State for Social Services from 1976 to 1979, having previously been Minister of State in the Department between 1968 and 1970. In addition, while out of Parliament from 1970 to February 1974 he had been campaign director of the National Association for Mental Health. Renee Short (Lab.) was also an obvious candidate for membership: apart from a good deal of relevant experience in local government, she had been the chairman both of Sub-Committee B of the old Estimates Committee, which had dealt with social services matters, and of the Social Services and Employment Sub-Committee of the Expenditure Committee. However, the only other member of the Committee who had also been a member of the Expenditure Sub-Committee was Nicholas Winterton (Cons.). He had also been a members of the Committee had held office on the Conservative back-bench Health and Social Services Committee—Tom Benyon, Sheila Faith, William Rees-Davies, Sir Brandon Rhys Williams and Tim Smith—while Andrew Bennett was the chairman of the Labour back-bench Health and Social Services Subject Group. Bennett and Rees-Davies had also served on the Select Committee on Violence in the Family in the 1975–76 and 1976–77 sessions. Prior to his election in 1979, Frank Field (Lab.) had been a nationally-known figure as director of the Child Poverty Action Group. David Crouch (Cons.) had served as a member of the South-East Thames Regional Health Authority; Sheila Faith was a dentist; and several other members of the Committee had had relevant experience in local government.

In terms of length of parliamentary service, the original nine members of the Committee were a judicious mixture of the experienced, the less experienced, and the inexperienced: four had been first elected in 1964 or earlier; three were elected between 1970 and 1974; and two were elected in 1979. Of particular interest is the fact that two of the subsequent replacements, Mrs Angela Rumbold (Cons.) and Tim Smith (Cons.), became members shortly after being elected to the Commons at by-elections in 1982. Most members said that they had actively sought membership of the Committee, and only one said that he had first been approached by the whips.

It had been agreed through the 'usual channels' that the chairmanship of the Social Services Committee would be held by a Labour Member, but when the Committee came to choose its chairman, two candidates were nominated—Renee Short and David Ennals, Ennals being the nominee of the Labour whips. Both subsequent divisions were tied, with four votes on each side—two Conservative and two Labour members in each case, with one member of the Committee absent. In the event, at its second meeting the Committee elected Mrs Short as chairman unopposed and she held the post throughout the 1979–83 Parliament.

SUBJECTS OF INQUIRY

From the outset the Social Services Committee adopted a clear pattern in choosing its subjects of inquiry: in each session the Committee conducted one major inquiry, an annual examination of public expenditure on the social services and one or more short inquiries on matters arising during the session. Thus the major inquiries, in chronological order, were on perinatal and neonatal mortality, medical education, the age of retirement, and children in care. The short, topical inquiries were on the government's proposals on the arrangements for paying social security benefits, the payment of maternity benefit, government proposals for income during an initial period of sickness, the implications of UGC cuts for medical services, and the health and social security aspects of the Chancellor of the Exchequer's 1982 Autumn Statement.

The Committee's first major inquiry was, in effect, inherited from the Social Services and Employment Sub-Committee of the Expenditure Committee, which had embarked upon an inquiry into perinatal and neonatal mortality in the last session of the 1974-79 Parliament. That inquiry had not been completed by the time of the dissolution in April 1979, although the sub-committee had held fourteen sittings on the subject, thirteen of which had been evidence-taking sessions. Mrs Short had, of course, been Chairman of the sub-committee, but only Nicholas Winterton and Ron Lewis had also served on it, and there was no obligation on the new committee to continue the inquiry. Nonetheless, a substantial amount of evidence had been gathered and the question of infant mortality had been the subject of some concern both to the public in general and more particularly within the medical profession and amongst some of the relevant pressure groups. The Committee therefore agreed to complete the inquiry begun by its predecessor.

The infant mortality inquiry drew the Committee's attention to shortages in some specialized medical areas, and this was a factor in determining the Committee's second inquiry—medical education. Having devoted its first two inquiries to the health aspects of its remit, the Committee turned its attention in the third session of the 1979-83 Parliament to social security topics. The first of these was the age of retirement, which had become increasingly topical as the level of unemployment increased and led to suggestions that retirement earlier than the age 65 would create job vacancies. A further factor was the demand for equality between the sexes, an equality, it was argued by some of its proponents, to be met by lowering the age of male retirement—a proposal which, of course, fitted in with the job vacancy argument. The Committee felt that it could provide a useful basis for discussion of a topic which had been much talked about but little investigated.

The last major topic undertaken by the Committee was on children in care. This too was a question that had received a fair amount of attention in recent years, partly as a result of cases—often tragic— which had received much media attention, and partly because cutbacks in social services had from time to time focused attention on the problem. This inquiry, however, had not been completed by the time of the dissolution of Parliament.

In general, the Committee achieved a good balance between the health and social security aspects of its remit, but did not allow its major inquiries to prevent it from dealing with other matters that arose during those inquiries nor from giving some attention to the important area of public expenditure.

The subjects of inquiry were determined by discussion and, although informal votes were sometimes taken, on no occasion did the Committee formally divide on its choice of topics. Some suitable topics were suggested by members of the Committee, and others by the DHSS.

STAFFING

The Social Services Committee had a staff of a clerk, an assistant clerk, a temporary committee assitant and a secretary. Members of the Committee were generally agreed that this level of staffing was adequate, although in her report to the Liaison Committee Mrs Short warned that 'should fresh tasks be laid on Committees ... further staffing support would be essential'.[4]

The Committee made fairly extensive use of its power to appoint specialist advisers. Rudolf Klein, Professor of Social Policy at the University of Bath, and Michael O'Higgins, an economist (also from the University of Bath), were appointed to advise the Committee generally and came to be used particularly for the annual expenditure inquiry. In addition, specialist advisers were appointed for each of the Committee's inquiries. Thus the three advisers appointed to advise the Social Services and Employment Sub-Committee of the Expenditure Committee in its investigation into perinatal and neonatal mortality were reappointed to assist the Social Services Committee in completing that inquiry; one adviser was appointed to advise on the inquiries into payment of social security benefits, four to advise on medical education, two on the age of retirement, and three on children in care—a total of thirteen.

The advisers assisted in the general planning of inquiries, prepared briefs for each of the Committee's evidence-taking sessions, during which they were normally present, and advised the Committee during its deliberative sessions. As with administrative staff, members of the Committee generally felt that the provision of specialist advisers was adequate, and the contribution made by both administrative staff and specialist advisers to the work of the Committee was regarded as invaluable.

THE COMMITTEE AT WORK

When Parliament was sitting the Social Services Committee met weekly on Wednesdays, with additional meetings on other days as necessary, though these did not usually amount to more than two meetings a week unless the Committee was hearing evidence in some other part of the United Kingdom. Most additional meetings occurred when the Committee was dealing with public expenditure, following the publication of the annual White Paper, or when the Committee decided to conduct a short inquiry into a matter of topical interest or urgency.

The number of sittings[5] varied from fifty-one in the 1980-81 session to twenty-nine in the 1982-83 session, with thirty-nine in each of the other two sessions. The 1982-83 figure was, of course, affected by the dissolution. In three of the four sessions, there were significantly more evidence-taking than solely deliberative sittings—ranging from three-fifths in 1981-82 to four-fifths in 1982-83, a figure again affected by the dissolution. Rather more than half the sittings in 1979-80, however, were wholly deliberative, and this reflected the use of several sessions to discuss the evidence received in the infant mortality inquiry and a number of discussions of what major inquiry to pursue in the 1980-81 session.

The Committee made extensive use of its power to hold sessions away from Westminster. It heard evidence for its perinatal and neonatal inquiry in Manchester, Rochdale and Littleborough, involving seven of the thirteen evidence-taking sessions held in the inquiry. This was, of course, in addition to evidence heard in the 1978-79 session by the Committee's predecessor. The Committee travelled more extensively for its medical education inquiry, hearing evidence in Birmingham, Walsall, Liverpool, Edinburgh, and Aberdeen—a total of eleven out of thirty-one evidence-taking sessions. The children in care inquiry heard such evidence at six out of twenty-one sittings, meeting in Warwick, Stafford, Bradford Huddersfield, Edinburgh, and Glasgow. All the oral evidence on the age of retirement inquiry was heard at Westminster, but the Committee did visit France and Belgium to gather information for the inquiry; it also visited Sweden in connection with the medical education inquiry, and Denmark and the Netherlands on children in care.

Apart from the convenience of those giving oral evidence, the Committee felt strongly that hearing evidence in different parts of the country was a useful way of bringing its work to the attention of a wider audience. More importantly, perhaps, Mrs Short stressed that it enabled the Committee to spend two or three days in a particular part of the country studying the problem at close hand and offered valuable opportunities for informal meetings with people concerned about and interested in the Committee's subject of inquiry, quite apart from the formal meetings the Committee held.[6]

The mean attendance by members at sittings of the Committee was 67.7 per cent, ranging from 78.1 per cent in 1979–80 to 61.1 per cent in 1980–81.[7] Not surprisingly, Renee Short, as chairman, had the highest attendance, missing only five out of a possible 158 sittings, an attendance rate of 96.8 per cent. The next highest level of attendance was that of another Labour member, Ron Lewis (83.3 per cent), closely followed by two Conservatives, Sheila Faith (81.6 per cent) and Ralph Howell (81.1 per cent). The lowest attendance records were those of Tom Benyon (36.4 per cent), Sir Brandon Rhys Williams (43.5 per cent), and Frank Field (46.0 per cent). Excluding the chairman, the mean attendance of Conservative and Labour members of the Committee was basically similar—66.0 and 64.4 per cent respectively.

On average, Committee members estimated that, including committee meetings, they spent five hours per week during the parliamentary session on the work of the Committee. The lowest estimate was four hours and the highest eight. As chairman, Mrs Short spent a much higher proportion of her time on the Committee's business. During the session, this entailed the whole of the Committee's regular meeting day of Wednesday and daily contact with the committee staff on other days, with further time spent reading memoranda and preparing for Committee meetings.

Levels of participation amongst the members of the Social Services Committee, as measured by the questioning of witnesses, varied considerably (see Table 13.1). As chairman, Mrs Short was clearly the most active participant. Bearing in mind that some members of the Committee were not members for the whole of a particular session, several patterns of participation emerge. The major role of the chairman has already been noted, although her level of participation was noticeably higher in the first two sessions of the Parliament. This may have been the result of Mrs Short's desire to give a strong lead to the Committee and a reflection of how other members of the Committee were settling to their task, but it is also a reflection of greater participation by Mrs Short in health compared to social service matters. This was especially true of the infant mortality inquiry, in which Mrs Short asked nearly half the questions. Of course, as the chairman of the former Social Services and Employment Sub-Committee, Mrs Short had been closely involved in that committee's inquiry into the same subject, but her contributions to the inquiries into medical

Table 13.1 *The questioning of witnesses in evidence-taking sessions of the Social Services Committee, 1979–83*

Member	Session and percentage of questions asked			
	1979–80	1980–81	1981–82	1982–83
Renee Short (Lab.) (Chairman)	43.6	44.3	26.1^c	30.3
Andrew Bennett (Lab.)	Nm	0.4^b	10.7	9.6
Tom Benyon (Con.)	Nm	0.6^b	2.3	—
David Crouch (Con.)	Nm	Nm	Nm	0.4^b
David Ennals (Lab.)	13.0	12.2	11.2	11.6
Sheila Faith (Con.)	4.5	6.4	5.6	5.8
Frank Field (Lab.)	5.8	0.0^b	Nm	Nm
Ralph Howell (Con.)	4.6	0.0^b	Nm	Nm
Ron Lewis (Lab.)	1.5^b	3.8	4.0	5.2
William Rees-Davies (Con.)	4.3	13.6	14.7^d	9.1
Sir Brandon Rhys Williams (Con.)	2.1	0.4	10.1	Nm
Angela Rumbold (Con.)	Nm	Nm	—^{e}	5.1
Tim Smith (Con.)	Nm	Nm	Nm	2.9^b
William Whitlock (Lab.)	0.0^b	Nm	Nm	Nm
Nicholas Winterton (Con.)	20.5	18.2	15.3	20.0
Totals	99.0	99.9	100.0	100.0

Notes:
Nm—not a member of the Committee.
[a] The figures shown in the table *exclude* incidental remarks made by the chairman (and other members of the Committee), such as those welcoming witnesses or minor clarifications of questions asked or asides which have no bearing on the evidence being heard. However, they *include* substantive statements made by members of the Committee during the hearing of evidence.
[b] Not a member of the Committee for the whole session.
[c] *Including* two sittings chaired by William Rees-Davies in the absence of Mrs Short.
[d] *Excluding* two sittings when he was chairman.
[e] Not a member of the Committee during any of its evidence-taking sittings that session.

education and the impact of UGC cuts on medical services were also very high.

A second pattern that emerges is that in each of the four sessions a very high proportion—between two-thirds and nearly nine-tenths—of the questioning came from four members of the Committee: Mrs Short, David Ennals, William Rees-Davies and Nicholas Winterton. They were, of course, four of the most experienced members of the Committee, and their dominance, though still considerable, fell markedly in the third and fourth sessions, possibly as other members of the Committee became more experienced and more involved in the Committee's work. It should also be noted that, as might be expected, there is some correlation between high attendance and a high level of participation, in that all four of the members mentioned above had a record of attendance which was well above average; two other members of the Committee, on the other hand, had very high levels of attendance, but considerably lower levels of participation.

Further analysis shows that, excluding the chairman, the division of questioning between Conservative and Labour members of the Committee was generally very close to the expected norms, as calculated by party representation on the Committee. Thus Conservative representation was 62.5 per cent and Labour representation 37.5 per cent. In only one session was there a significant deviation from the expected norms: this was in the 1980–81 session, when 70.5 per cent of questions were asked by Conservative and 29.5 per cent by Labour members. It might also be hypothesized that, as the main opposition party, Labour participation might be greater when ministers and civil servants were being questioned. However, no clear pattern emerged: ministers were questioned on eleven occasions, at which the level of Labour questioning was above the norm in six cases; and officials were questioned on eighteen occasions, but in only five cases was the norm exceeded.

The Social Services Committtee took oral evidence from nearly 700 individuals, of whom some eighty were academics or professional individuals, while the rest represented various organizations, varying from government departments to local government and health authorities, and from various professional bodies and trade unions to straightforward pressure groups.

Ministers appeared before the Committee on eleven occasions and, except when Sir Keith Joseph, Secretary of State for Education, gave evidence on the UGC cuts and medical services and the Chief Secretary of the Treasury on the social services aspects of the Chancellor's 1982 Autumn Statement, all came from the DHSS. The appearance of the Chief Secretary was the first occasion on which he had given evidence to a departmental committee other than the Treasury Committee. The Secretary of State himself gave evidence on seven occasions, Ministers of State on four and Parliamentary Under-Secretaries twice. Over the four sessions, the Committee heard evidence from seven government departments—the DHSS, the Scottish Home and Health Department, the DES, the Department of Employment, the Treasury, the Management and Personnel Office, and the Government Actuary's Department. Only in the first two instances, however, was evidence heard from any department more than twice. Officials from the DHSS appeared before the Committee twenty-nine times and from the Scottish Home and Health Department four times.

Over a hundred organizations, other than government departments, gave oral evidence to the Committee. Most of them were professional bodies or trade unions, but pressure groups such as the

Child Poverty Action Group, the Spastics Society, Age Concern, the National Federation of the Self-Employed and Small Businesses, Help the Aged, the National Society for the Prevention of Cruelty to Children, the National Council for One-Parent Families, and the Family Rights Groups were prominent in presenting oral evidence. Similarly, the various local authority associations and health authorities were also major sources of evidence. This range of sources also applied to written evidence submitted to the Committee, which amounted to more than 400 documents.

The Committee produced eleven reports during the 1979–83 Parliament, of which three—perinatal and neonatal mortality, medical education, and the age of retirement—were major reports; had the 1982–83 session completed its normal duration, a fourth major report—on children in care—would have been produced. The eight remaining reports were responses to current issues or dealt with the social services aspects of public expenditure. Reports were drafted mainly by the clerks, and these drafts were used for informal discussions amongst the Committee members and specialist advisers.

In producing its reports the Committee was remarkably free from party divisions, in spite of the fact that some of the matters were controversial and that major reductions in public expenditure on the social services were a prominent feature of government policy. Only five divisions occurred in the Committee over the four parliamentary sessions, two of which were at the very first meeting over the election of a chairman, and both these were cross-party divisions. Of the remaining three divisions, two were straight party divisions and one was a cross-party vote. In fact, the majority of the Committee's draft reports were approved without amendments and in only one case were more than a few paragraphs of the draft report amended. This was the draft report on the age of retirement in which thirty-eight out of 213 paragraphs were amended, though none involved a division. In the case of this report, however, Andrew Bennett (Lab.) did table an alternative report, but it was rejected on a division. The only other significant clash was over the Committee's report on the 1982 Chancellor's Autumn Statement, in which seven new paragraphs recommending improved social security benefits were proposed by Andrew Bennett and rejected in a single division on straight party lines. It should be noted, however, that the Committee normally avoided major clashes and extensive formal amendments by a process of informal discussion beforehand.

Most members of the Committee felt that party conflicts were not generally important. One newly-elected Labour member remarked that they 'were not as great as I thought they would be', and a

Conservative said that they tended to be limited to a small number of matters, such as the privatization of some health service functions. Only one member of the Committee, a Conservative, thought party divisions were 'quite important'.

THE IMPACT OF THE COMMITTEE

It is no easy task to assess the impact of the Social Services Committee, and indeed members of the Committee were themselves divided on the matter. Half felt that the Committee had had a significant impact on government policy and half did not. They were even less confident about the impact on their back-bench colleagues: a majority felt that the Committee had had little or no impact on the backbenches. On the other hand, a majority did feel that the Committee's impact outside Parliament had been significant, one member remarking: 'Our reports were widely reported and discussed in the professional press'.

Table 13.2 *Government Responses to Recommendations made in Reports from the Social Services Committee, 1979–83*

Response	n	%
Accepted	66	35.1
Keep under review	85	45.2
Rejected	37	19.7
Totals	188	100.0

The Government's responses to recommendations made by the Committee provide one means of assessing the Committee's impact. An analysis on this basis shows that relatively few of its recommendations were rejected outright, but more than half were to be kept under review (see Table 13.2). Of course, not all recommendations can appropriately be the subject of a simple acceptance or rejection and keeping them under review is often a suitable response. As a quantitative measure, this analysis provides some indication of the Committee's impact on the government, but it is a simplistic and limited picture.[8] However, that picture can be clarified a little further, if particular subjects of inquiry are examined.

It can be argued, for example, that the Social Services Committee did have an impact on government policy concerning the payment of social security benefits—in that one proposal made by the Government was dropped and another modified—and also on the Government's proposed pensions 'clawback'; but it is difficult to establish direct and specific influence on the part of the Committee. Did the

Government act the way it did (at least in part) *because* of what the Committee said or would it have acted that way regardless? Even if instances of specific causal links between the Committee's recommendations and government policy could be established, the picture would remain incomplete. It is more realistic to see the work of the Committee as part of a wider process of policy discussion and impact. For instance, the Committee's reports on infant mortality and children in care received a considerable amount of publicity in the professional press; its report on medical education was discussed at a number of professional conferences, including the annual conference of the BMA. These two reports, moreover, were also the subject of full-day debates in the House of Commons (a distinction not achieved by any other departmental committee). Furthermore, in giving evidence to the Committee on its medical education inquiry, Patrick Jenkin, then Secretary of State for Health and Social Services said: 'We were delighted that this Committee decided to take this subject by the horns and with appropriate recommendations my hand will be greatly strengthened'.[9]

In addition, it should be noted that Table 13.2 excludes a significant proportion of the Committee's recommendations because they are not the direct responsibility of the Government. In most cases, these recommendations concern bodies like regional and former area health authorities or local government authorities, but some concern non-governmental bodies, such as universities or professional associations.[10] The Government does quite often reply that it will draw the attention of health authorities or the like to specific recommendations, but this may be the limit of the Government's ability to act on the recommendation concerned. Understandably, this was the Government's response to many of the recommendations contained in the Committee's report on infant mortality.

Whatever specific impact the Social Services Committee may have had, it undoubtedly provided a useful forum for the discussion of problems and as a means of gathering—and subsequently publishing—information on important issues in a way which is not possible on the floor of the House. Evidence was heard from a wide range of sources and those with an interest in or concern about the problems under investigation were able to make their views known. Pressure groups in particular made use of such opportunities. By the very nature of some of its subjects of inquiry, interest in some of the Committee's reports has been largely confined to those professionally involved in or those socially concerned about the particular problem, but a report like that on the age of retirement has been of much wider interest and concern. Each of the Committee's major reports focused attention on a particular problem and, at the very least, made a contribution to the development of policy.

Nonetheless, the experience of the Social Services Committee also demonstrates the limitations of the new departmental committees— indeed of specialized select committees generally. There is inevitably a limit, a severe limit, on the number of topics that can be thoroughly investigated each session. Even if a sub-committee were formally or informally used to increase the number of topics covered, it would not fundamentally alter the situation. Another problem is the following up of reports. Here the Social Services Committee had taken the initial steps to following up some of its reports—notably those on infant mortality, medical education, and the impact of the UGC cuts on medical services—but these were brought to a halt by the disso- lution, and further action was inevitably left to the Committee's suc- cessor in the new Parliament.

Similarly, the Committee's annual sessions on public expenditure produced a great deal of information and members sensed that they not infrequently touched a departmental nerve, but it can hardly be said that this amounted to a systematic scrutiny of expenditure— perhaps inevitably because the distinction between expenditure and policy remains blurred.

One reason for this, of course, is that the Committee has not so far been directly involved in the process by which Parliament approves proposals for public expenditure, but nor is the Committee involved in the passage of legislation. It is true that when the Government set up a Special Standing Committee on the Mental Health Amendment Bill in 1982, Mrs Short chaired the three evidence-taking sessions of the standing committee and two other members of the Social Services Committee were also members of the standing committee. Mrs Short welcomed this development,[11] but in reality the involvement of the Social Services Committee was at best peripheral. Although these problems affected the departmental committees generally, the experi- ence of the Social Services Committee shows how important they are.

CONCLUSION

The Social Services Committee has worked quietly rather than spec- tacularly, seeking publicity for its work rather than the limelight for itself. Party divisions have not been of any great importance and, although this is in part a reflection of the Committee's choice of subjects, it also reflects the attitudes of the members of the Committee towards its role. The way in which the Committee operated owed a great deal to Renee Short, as its very active chairman: she had a long-standing interest in the matters within the Committee's remit and made every effort to make the Committee operate effectively. There was widespread agreement amongst the Committee's members that its main task should be to monitor government policy, but there was also a widespread desire for the Committee to become more involved in the evolution and development of policy. Views were more divided on whether the Committee should be seen as a means of keeping Parliament and members of the public informed, or whether the Committee should act as a channel for the views of pressure or interest groups. To summarize, members of the Committee felt that, on the one hand, the Committee should play a significant role in rendering the Government accountable and, on the other, that it should be more closely involved in the policy process.

NOTES

1. A useful interim study of the Committee can be found in Jaqi Nixon and Nigel Nixon, 'The Social Services Committee: a forum for policy review and policy reform', *Journal of Social Policy*, vol. xii, 1983, pp. 331–55.
2. *1982–83 Liaison Committee Report*, p. 113.
3. Ralph Howell became a member of the Treasury and Civil Service Committee in November 1981 and was active in that Committee's inquiry into the Standing of Personal Income Taxation and Income Support in 1982–83 (see chapter 15).
4. *1982–83 Liaison Committee Report*, p. 114.
5. *The Select Committee's Return for the 1978–80 Session* (HC 217, 1980–81, reports that the Social Services Committee held thirty-four *meetings* in 1979–80, but the total number of *sittings* was thirty-nine, since several meetings consisted of more than one sitting. *The Select Committee's Return for the 1980–81 Session*, HC 245, 1981–82, reports that the Social Services Committee held *fifty-two* meetings, but the Committee's *Minutes of Proceedings for the 1980–81 Session*, HC 489, 1980–81, records *fifty-one sittings*. The figures in this paragraph are based on the relevant Minutes of Proceedings and refer to sittings, *not* meetings, of the Committee.
6. Paper presented by Renee Short, MP to a Royal Institute of Public Administration Conference, 'Public Influence and Public Policy', 10–11 April 1981, p. 5.
7. The median figures are somewhat higher, being 75.3 per cent overall, and ranging from 82.1 per cent in 1979–80 to 71.3 per cent in 1982–83.
8. This is further illustrated by the Government's response to the Committee's report on the age of retirement. The report recommended a scheme for introducing a common age of retirement of sixty-three for men and women. The Government welcomed the report as 'a valuable contribution to the future consideration of pensions policy' (Cmnd. 9085, November 1983, para. 6), but rejected the basic proposal and did not therefore reply to the Committee's detailed recommendations. However, to include the rejection of each of these recommendations in Table 13.2 would distort the figures and they have therefore been excluded.
9. *Social Services Committee, Minutes of Evidence*, HC 31, 1980–81, 29 April 1981, p. 1041, response to Q. 4871.
10. Approximately a third of all the Committee's recommendations fell into this category. These are *excluded* from the figures in Table 13.2.
11. *1982–83 Liaison Committee Report*, p. 113.

Annex 13.1 *Social Services Committee*

Report	Date of first oral evidence/(no. of evidence sessions)	Date of publication of report	Date and form of govt. reply	Length of report (pages)	No. of oral qq./no. of written submissions (not printed)	No. of divisions
Session 1979–80						
1st The arrangements for paying social security benefits (HC 590)	16.1.80(2)	June 1980	Cmnd. 8106, Dec. 1980	16	243/9	0
2nd Perinatal and neonatal mortality (HC 663)	12.3.80(8)[a]	July 1980	Cmnd. 8084, Dec. 1980	173	1,415/78	1
3rd Public expenditure on the social services (HC 702)	23.4.80(3)	August 1980	Cmnd. 8096, Dec. 1980	20	295/5	0
Session 1980–81						
1st Payment of maternity benefits (HC 85)	No oral evidence.	December 1980	1st Spec. Report, (HC 172), Feb. 1981	9	–/1	0
2nd Payment of sickness benefits (HC 113)	No oral evidence.	January 1981	Press release 81-2/7, 23.2.82	13	–/2	0
3rd Public expenditure on the social services (HC 324)	12.5.81(2)	July 1981	Cmnd. 8464, Dec. 1981	22	241/5	0
4th Medical education (HC 31)	26.11.82(32)	October 1981	Cmnd. 8479, Feb. 1982	131	5,006/76(50)	0
Session 1981–82						
1st UGC cuts and medical services (HC 191)	11.2.82(3)	May 1982	Cmnd. 8744, Nov. 1982	29	373/4(44)	0
2nd Public expenditure on the social services (HC 306)	31.3.82(5)	July 1982	Cmnd. 8775, Dec. 1982	53	598/6(9)	0
3rd Age of retirement (HC 26)	11.11.81	November 1982	Cmnd. 9095, Nov. 1983	85	1,613/32(45)	1
Session 1982–83						
1st DHSS aspects of the Chancellor's Autumn Statement (HC 123)	15.12.82(1)	January 1983	1st Spec. Report, (HC 320), April 1983	16	123/2	1
Incomplete inquiries, 1982–83						
Children in Care (HC 26)	24.11.82(21)	—	—	—	2,739/38	—
Public expenditure on the social services (HC 321)	13.4.83(2)	—	—	—	260/1[b]	—

Notes:

[a] Continuation of the inquiry undertaken by the Social Services and Employment Sub-Committee of the Expenditure Committee, which first heard evidence on the 6 December 1978 and held thirteen evidence-taking sessions in the 1978–79 session. See HC 97, 1978–79.

[b] Comprising 111 pages.

CHAPTER 14

The Transport Committee

Gabriele Ganz

The Transport Committee was not a headline-hunting Committee but rather shunned the limelight. It worked hard to produce agreed reports in an area which is highly politically controversial but without stirring up political controversy. It broke new ground and can be called influential, in that in important instances what it recommended has come about, though whether this is cause and effect is impossible to prove.

MEMBERSHIP

The auguries for the Committee when it was set up cannot have been very happy. Its chairman, Mr Tom Bradley, joined the SDP in March 1981; and of its eleven members, the five Opposition members were sponsored by trade unions and declared their interests accordingly (four were ex-railwaymen), whilst three of the Government members declared their interests as consultants or director of a firm.[1] There were only two changes in membership of the Committee and its attendance rate averaged 70 per cent.[2] Though some members were more active than others, none dominated the questioning of witnesses. It was a Committee consisting mainly of present and past back-benchers, only two of its members having held ministerial office.[3]

STAFF

The Committee had a staff of four including the clerk (who changed in 1982) and a temporary full-time assistant, who was a transport economist. It also appointed a number of specialist advisers *ad hoc* for each inquiry, who were paid on a per diem basis. They were academics specializing in transport or economics, engineers and transport consultants. They gave technical advice and checked whether schemes proposed to or by the Committee were sound, advised on the content of the inquiry, suggested expert witnesses to be called, and prepared questions for members to ask witnesses; but did not normally participate extensively in the drafting of reports. This was shared between the clerk and the temporary assistant, though the Chairman had the last word and he made his views clear in advance, as did the rest of the Committee in meetings discussing the issues before and during the drafting process. From the hearings, the clerk also knew how the Committee was thinking. There were informal meetings to discuss the report before it was voted on paragraph by paragraph in private session. The clerk and temporary assistant also briefed the Committee, suggesting lines of inquiry, and which witnesses to call, and in conjunction with the Chairman also put forward subjects for inquiry. But the decision to undertake a particular inquiry came from the Committee, though there might previously have been an initiative from a member or a suggestion from a pressure group. Occasionally an inquiry proposal was even welcomed by the Minister,[4] though the Department did not suggest inquiries.

HEARINGS AND EVIDENCE

The Committee issued a general invitation to submit written evidence in its press releases, but oral evidence was sought by invitation from selected bodies and these were usually the recognized sources of evidence such as the Minister and Department, local authorities, transport operators, and consumer interests. Evidence was normally heard in public, though while the GLC 'Fares Fair' case was *sub judice* some of the hearings in the Transport in London inquiry had to be held in private. This also happened during the main line railway electrification inquiry when the trade unions were giving evidence, because of an industrial dispute with British Rail, and for commercial reasons in the case of contractors with British Rail.

It was in this inquiry that the Committee had its only real clash with the Government over a refusal to produce evidence, namely a report by the Central Policy Review Staff. This issue was taken up in the 1982–83 Liaison Committee Report[5] but in its reply to this report,[6] the Government reiterated that such reports were of a confidential nature and that it would be contrary to convention to make these available to committees.

But the Committee did not only meet in formal session to hear evidence. There were also informal meetings with local authority and nationalized industry representatives, and other interest groups. There were also private meetings of the Committee members before the formal evidence sessions, but there were no novel developments for gathering information such as seminars or round-table discussions. Informal meetings often took place on visits by the Committee both at home and abroad. Expenditure was nominal, except where the Committee travelled abroad. Almost all evidence sessions took place at Westminster.

THE SUB-COMMITTEE ISSUE

The Committee was not one of those which was allowed to appoint a sub-committee and it formally asked for the power to do so.[7] This request was rejected by the Government, mainly on grounds of cost, as it would have required more clerks to service sub-committees. The Committee made its request because it found eleven members too unwieldy a unit for questioning and because a sub-committee would have enabled it to undertake two inquiries simultaneously. The Committee in fact circumvented the ban by forming informal sub-committees under the chairmanship of a senior member of the Committee[8] with a core of members who committed themselves to attend, the quorum for the Committee being three. This in effect enabled the Committee to split itself into two with overlapping membership and to conduct two inquiries at the same time, for example, the inquiries into the roads White Paper and the Channel link and road safety and bus subsidy policy. Hearings might be held consecutively on the same day, on consecutive days, or in alternate weeks. The reports were voted on by the full Committee. The inquiries of the full Committee under the chairman also often overlapped, so that there were two investigations proceeding at the same time either in alternate weeks or on alternate days in the same week. Thus the real advantage of an informal sub-committee was that it eased the pressure on the chairman and some of the members. The chairman pointed out that if more work were expected of committees in the future, the membership would need to be increased so as to enable the work to be spread more, and the power to appoint a sub-committee, even if only used occasionally, would then become essential.[9]

SUBJECTS OF INQUIRY

This brings us to the subject-matter of inquiries. The chairman categorized the Committee's inquiries into three types: 'first, long-running inquiries into major areas of policy of particular interest to Members; second, inquiries into aspects of the current work of the

Department of Transport; and third, inquiries into new government policy proposals in the transport field'.[10] He added to that a report on the nationalized transport industries which fell within the Committee's terms of reference as associated public bodies, and reports following up earlier inquiries.

Under the first heading fall the major inquiries into the *Channel Link*, *Transport in London*, and *Road Maintenance*; the inquiries into *Road Safety* and *Bus Subsidy Policy*, which were cut short by the general election in 1983, would also fit into this category. The Channel link investigation broke new ground in that the Committee investigated the various proposals and recommended a preferred option before the Government had put forward its preferred scheme. It was thus able to insert itself into the policy-making process, in marked contrast to the previous occasion when a Channel tunnel was under discussion, when it was not considered by a Select Committee.[11] No decision was reached by the Government by the end of the Parliament, but the report concentrated the Government's attention on a rail-only tunnel.

The inquiry into transport in London, like the one into road maintenance, arose out of the current inquiries into the Roads and Public Expenditure White Papers. The London transport inquiry ran into the storm of controversy over the GLC's 'Fares Fair' policy, which shifted the focus of the inquiry to institutional problems. Its major recommendation was the creation of a Metropolitan Transport Authority with wide responsibilities which subsequently found favour, in a much watered-down form,[12] with a Conservative Government intent on abolishing the GLC. The inquiry into bus subsidy policy which had to be abandoned, would have investigated the controversial area of cheap fares policy which had been touched on in the London transport inquiry, but from a technical and analytical rather than a political point of view. It would have examined the extent to which the economic and social benefits of fare subsidy policies can be identified and evaluated, how subsidies have been used, and the extent of cross-subsidization. This is a very good illustration of how a 'royal commission' type of inquiry by a select committee can investigate a highly political subject without becoming involved in party political controversy. This could almost be said to be the hall-mark of the Transport Committee.

The inquiries into the Public Expenditure White Papers which were undertaken each year, and in particular the two inquiries into the White Paper on Roads (which was on one occasion combined with the public expenditure inquiry) also broke new ground. This was the first time a White Paper on roads had been examined by a select committee and this was very much welcomed by witnesses, who used it as an outlet for their pent-up frustration over road inquiries and the formation of roads policy. The Committee regarded it as its function to examine the broad strategy of the White Paper and to point out the shortcomings of present procedures, but not to become involved itself in detailed investigations of individual roads. Nevertheless it did comment on certain strategic routes which led to one of the rare votes along party lines in the Committee.

The Public Expenditure White Paper inquiries were the only occasions when the Committee examined public expenditure directly. It did not conduct inquiries into the estimates of the Department. The Committee made a sustained plea for more capital investment in transport infrastructure. In this way it typified the tendency of select committees to act as pressure groups for more public expenditure. This was also the burden of its report on *Main Line Railway Electrification*, though its recommendations were sufficiently qualified to enable the Government to agree with them.[13] However, no decisions were reached by the end of the Parliament.

The Committee reiterated its plea for more investment in railway infrastructure in its brief inquiry into the Serpell Committee's report, the *Review of Railway Finances*. In view of the controversy engendered by that report, the aim of the Committee was to give the members of the Serpell Committee the opportunity to respond to criticisms of the report and to hear the reaction of the British Railways Board and the Secretary of State to it. The Committee was highly critical of the methodology and some of the findings of the Serpell Committee, but it also absolved it from some of the criticisms that had been levelled against its report and commended some of the recommendations made. But the main thrust of the Transport Committee's report was to urge the Secretary of State to make long-term policy decisions about the future of the railways and embody these decisions in a White Paper. The type of policy the Committee would have liked to see was implicit in its concluding remarks that, 'A clear statement of the Government's continued commitment to the railways would do much to recreate a climate of confidence among British Rail's staff, customers and suppliers'. Again the pressure-group approach is evident.

This report could be classified in the same way as the report on *Main Line Railway Electrification*, which was categorized by the chairman under the third heading of inquiries into new policy proposals— as was the report on the European Commission's Green Paper on transport infrastructure, which was the only specific inquiry into a Community topic. This inquiry could also be classified as pre-legislative. The Committee also reported in a pre-legislative capacity on the more controversial topic of heavy lorries. After concern had been expressed in a debate[14] arranged at short notice about the proposals for forty-four tonne lorries recommended in the Armitage Report,[15] the Committee decided to provide an opportunity for the Armitage Committee to be questioned directly on the report and to report the evidence to the House. The Committee was here performing the classic function of select committees, to provide information to the House, but in a direct and immediate way which the House itself cannot achieve. The Committee did not make any recommendations on the substantive issue which, as a result of strong pressure from Government back-benchers, resulted in a compromise of a thirty-eight tonne maximum.[16]

The Committee did, however, bring its influence to bear with a considerable measure of success on another highly controversial pre-legislative issue, the proposed transfer of heavy goods and public service vehicle testing to the private sector. The Committee under the chairmanship of Sir David Price undertook this inquiry because of widespread fears in the industry, which led to the proposal being excluded from the Transport Bill 1980. In spite of the party-political nature of the issue, the Committee reached unanimous conclusions against the proposed transfer with only three divisions on questions of wording. When the proposal was included in the Transport Bill 1981–82, Sir David Price and Mr Peter Fry abstained in the division on the second reading.[17] Sir David stated that parliamentary honour demanded that declared judgements of select committees should be followed by subsequent votes on the floor of the House,[18] whilst Mr Fry, who had changed his mind as a result of the Committee's hearings, asked, 'What are we supposed to be there for?' and then stated the classic case for select committees in reply to his own question, 'Is it not to try to look objectively at serious problems of our time and to reach conclusions that are not biased by political views but are in the best interests of the country as a whole?'[19]

But the story does not end there. The Secretary of State in his reply[20] had rejected the report and said that he and the Committee would have 'to agree to differ', and the junior minister suggested in the debate on the second reading that the transport operators who had given evidence to the Committee had changed their minds.[21] In view of this, the Committee decided to take further evidence from the same witnesses before the standing committee began consideration of the Bill.[22] In doing so, it was consciously trying to perform the functions of a special standing committee which could have heard evidence but which was not used for this Bill. The Committee found that the witnesses had not changed their minds, and reiterated its opposition to the proposals in the Bill. The Committee also put forward a compromise solution of transferring testing to a single organization and recommended an amendment to the Bill making any transfer subject to affirmative resolution. The Government accepted such an amendment at the committee stage,[23] and carried out the former recommendation by negotiating for the transfer of vehicle-testing to Lloyd's Register of Shipping. The Government finally abandoned its proposals for the transfer when these negotiations broke down because of the costs involved.[24] The Committee here acted both in a pre-legislative and later in a legislative capacity, and must be credited with having influenced the Government's change of policy, though it was ultimately frustrated for practical reasons.

NATIONALIZED INDUSTRIES

The Committee did not make an in-depth study of the nationalized industries left within its remit after the National Freight Corporation and the British Transport Docks Board were privatized. It did, however, investigate aspects of British Rail in its reports on *Main Line Railway Electrification*, the Serpell Committee report and the public expenditure White Papers. Its unfinished inquiry into bus subsidy policy was concerned with the National Bus Company, the other nationalized industry left within its remit. But it did not make the sort of investigation formerly carried out by the Nationalised Industries Committee. It came nearest to filling the gap left by the abolition of that Committee in its report on *The Form of the Nationalised Industries Reports and Accounts* which consisted of a paper from its specialist adviser on the intelligibility and meaningfulness of the reports and accounts of British Rail, the National Bus Company, and the British Transport Docks Board. He recommended that the Committee should follow in the footsteps of the former Nationalised Industries Committee in holding an annual meeting with each industry after publication of its report and accounts. The Committee agreed with this advice, though it did not commit itself to accepting it and in its turn recommended that other committees should study the specialist adviser's paper as it was relevant to all nationalized industries. If these recommendations were to be implemented, the Committees would go some way towards performing the functions of the former Nationalised Industries Committee. The 1982–83 Liaison Committee Report[25] recognized that the provision for a sub-committee drawn from several departmental committees to consider the nationalized industries was impracticable and should be repealed, and proposed that Committees be given power to make joint inquiries. The latter proposal has now been implemented.[26]

Follow-up reports

The Committee followed up the work of the former Science and Technology Committee on advanced ground transport by asking the Department to prepare a memorandum on the present position relating to research and development in this area. The Committee deplored the fifteen months' delay in producing the paper whose publication was the main purpose of the report. The initiative for this follow-up exercise came partly from McAlpine and Sons Ltd., who complained to the Committee about the Government's opposition to their search for European Community funds. This was an interesting example of the Committee's responding to a request from private industry for an inquiry.

The Committee also followed up its report on the Channel link in 1981 by taking further evidence from the Secretary of State on the progress that had been made, and at the same time published the Cairncross report which the Secretary of State agreed to submit to the Committee. The most effective follow-up report was that on the transfer of heavy goods vehicle testing. The Committee, like some of the other select committees, had also asked the Department to report its response to each of the Committee's recommendations, but any possible action was overtaken by the general election.

GOVERNMENT RESPONSE

The replies of the Government, which seem to have taken on average five months,[27] rather than the two months recommended in the 1977–78 Procedure Committee Report, were rather bland political statements from which it is difficult to judge the impact of the Committee on the Department. Even where the Committee's recommendations were successful, as in the case of the transfer of heavy goods vehicle testing, it is impossible to measure the impact of the Committee against other pressures. A great deal depends on the timing of the reports and their subject-matter. If they are post-mortems they cannot by definition alter the decision, but may offer a platform for others as well as for the Committee to make their point. But even post-mortems are part of a continuing policy-making process, and the Committee is part of the input into this. The influence of the Committee here will depend on a variety of factors including the degree to which the subject is politically controversial and the depth of its investigation as well as the timing of its reports. It may achieve success because the Government is thinking along the same lines. This happened with respect to the reorganization of London Transport by the formation of London Regional Transport.[28] It has also happened with the reorganization of the Department of Transport to include civil aviation and shipping following the merger of the Departments of Trade and Industry. This met the criticism of the chairman that the responsibilities of the Department were too narrow, thus preventing the Committee from looking at inland transport policy as a whole.[29] It may in future enable the Committee to press more effectively for an integrated transport policy.[30]

RELATIONSHIP WITH PARLIAMENT

It would be quite mistaken to measure the Committee's impact on Parliament by the number of times its reports have been debated. None of the Committee's reports was debated as such but, as we have seen, there was a close correlation between some of the reports and the work of the House. The inquiry into the Armitage Committee Report arose out of a debate in the House,[31] and contributed information to a later debate in which three members of the Committee participated.[32] The reports on the Public Expenditure White Paper performed a similar function but they were not completed in time for the debates on the White Paper, though one member of the Committee referred to the evidence heard by the Committee in one of the debates.[33] The Committee's inquiry into the Serpell Committee Report also post-dated the debates on the report in both Houses.[34] Because of the controversy surrounding the report, the pressure for debates to be held soon after publication was very strong. The Committee recommended that its reports on the White Paper on roads should be the prelude to a debate in the House[35] but they were in fact substitutes, as no debate took place. The Committee was here performing the very function which the House had hitherto failed to perform adequately, namely to examine the Government's Roads Programme.

The Committee also complemented the House when it acted in a pre-legislative capacity, examining proposals before they came to the House, as it did in the case of the Channel link and the EEC Green Paper. In the case of the report on *The Transfer of Heavy Goods Vehicle Testing* it performed not only a pre-legislative but a legislative function, when it consciously assumed the role of a special standing committee. The new Estimates days might have provided a further opportunity to link the reports of the Committee with the work of the House if the dissolution of Parliament had not intervened.

In spite of this dovetailing of the Committee's work with that of the House, the Chairman regretted the lack of a formal link between the work of the Committee and that of the House. He called for a 'formal process of reference and reporting' and placing the results of the Committee's work before the House for consideration and approval.[36] This is in line with the recommendations of the Select Committee on Procedure (Supply),[37] which led to the creation of Estimates days, but left each committee to undertake such scrutiny of the Estimates as it thought fit. A formal link such as envisaged by the chairman, between the Committee and the House in respect of delegated and EEC legislation and the Estimates might take away the freedom of members of the Committee to choose whatever topic interested them. It would also require more committee members and staff.

EVALUATION

The Committee followed the consensus model of select committees. It did not choose topics where no agreement could be reached, and was therefore very successful in reaching agreed reports. Only four of its reports gave rise to any divisions. In two of them— *Transfer of Heavy Goods Vehicle Testing* and *Main Line Railway Electrification*—these were purely on matters of emphasis. This was also so in the case of the Roads White Paper inquiry, but there was in addition one division of substance on the paragraph commenting on individual schemes. Only in the *Transport in London* inquiry did a number of divisions occur and most of these cut across party lines. It was only in respect of 'ride-sharing' and subsidies that the Committee split along party lines, the chairman giving his casting vote to the Opposition in the latter instance. The Committee was almost a text-book illustration of the consensus model of select committees.[38]

One could go further and say that the Committee was the epitome of a select committee, performing all the classic functions of such a committee, though with more expertise and greater resources at its disposal than were previously available. It gathered and published information—some of it technical—which would never have been published otherwise. It thus furthered open government, though it could not break through the barrier of confidentiality surrounding reports of the Central Policy Review Staff. It also provided another useful platform for pressure groups, though the Committee heard oral evidence only from the standard recognized bodies. Its reports received some press coverage, even though they were not in general front-page news; but perhaps more importantly the Committee received regular attention in a number of trade papers and specialist journals.[39]

Its impact on the Department cannot be measured purely in terms of the number of successful recommendations. The questioning of ministers, civil servants (not only those in the top echelons of the Department), and members of the nationalized industries keeps them on their toes, aware that their decisions may be questioned, and makes them think and justify themselves. The effects may be felt in the long term. Though the Committee has been critical of the Department, the latter felt it had been primarily supportive. It acted as a pressure group, asking for more public expenditure, untrammelled by the responsibilities of government to suggest cuts elsewhere. The relationship with the Department was the classic one of a critical but not hostile watch-dog. In keeping with this role, the Committee acted mainly in response to Government initiatives, but it did not hesitate to put forward alternative policies, for example, in relation to the reorganization of London Transport. Such consensus politics are abhorred by the opponents of select committees,[40] but they are the hallmark of such committees; and their acceptance by the Government, as in the case of the transfer of heavy goods vehicle testing, is regarded as the highest degree of success.

In this case, the Committee was performing the function—envisaged by the 1977-78 Procedure Committee Report—of acting as the 'eyes and ears' of the House in relation to Government departments by responding speedily to current problems and new policy proposals.[41] Much of its work was devoted to this task, but it was not always linked directly with the work of the House. The Chairman's proposal[42] for a 'formal process of reference and reporting' would provide this link between the House and the Committee if its reports were placed before the House for consideration and approval. If this involved giving the Committee powers, for example to reduce Estimates,[43] even though subject to approval by the House, it would endanger the consensus of the Committee as party loyalties would assert themselves. If consensus is to hold in the Committee, it must eschew power for influence. But the influence of the Committee will not be increased by a more systematic and comprehensive scrutiny of government proposals in time for their consideration by the House, unless the House is prepared to accept its recommendations even where they cut across party lines. The consensus of the Committee can only be transferred to the floor of the House if, in the last resort, more MPs follow the example of the two Conservative MPs, who on the second reading of the Transport Bill in 1981-82, put loyalty to their select committee above party loyalty.

NOTES

1. Minutes of Proceedings of Transport Committee, 1979–80, HC 838.
2. HC Debs., 29 July 1983, col. 633 (written answer).
3. Mr Neil (now Lord) Carmichael and Sir David Price.
4. Minutes of Evidence, Department of Transport, 1979–80, HC 381, Q. 25.
5. 1982–83, HC 92, para. 50.
6. HC Debs., 12 May 1983, cols. 444–7 (written answer).
7. First Special Report, 1979–80, HC 544.
8. Sir David Price, Mr Neil Carmichael and Mr Peter Fry.
9. 1982–83 Liaison Committee Report, p. 120, paras. 7–8.
10. Ibid, p. 119, para. 3.
11. G. Ganz, *Government and Industry*, 1977, p. 13 seq.
12. White Paper, *Public Transport in London*, Cmnd. 9004, and the London Regional Transport Bill in the 1983–84 session.
13. First Special Report, 1982–83, HC 253, Annex A.
14. HC Debs., 27 January 1981, cols. 824 seq.
15. *Report of the Inquiry into Lorries, People and the Environment*, HMSO 1980.
16. HC Debs., 4 November 1982, col. 4 (written answer).
17. HC Debs., 9 February 1982, cols. 865 seq.
18. Ibid., col. 882.
19. Ibid, col. 894.
20. First Special Report, 1981–82, HC 152, Annex B.
21. HC Debs., 9 February 1982, col. 938.
22. First Report 1981–82, HC 203.
23. Standing Committee F, 25 March 1982, col. 552. One member of the Committee was on the Standing Committee.
24. HC Debs., 28 July 1983, col. 553 (written answer).
25. Para. 40 seq.
26. HC Debs., 14 December 1983, col. 1121.
27. HC Debs., 29 July 1983, col. 633 (written answer).
28. *Public Transport in London, op. cit.*, and the London Regional Transport Bill in the 1983–84 session.
29. 1982–83 Liaison Committee Report, p. 121, para. 11.
30. For criticism of the White Paper on roads as myopic, see First Report, 1980–81, HC 27, para. 68.
31. HC Debs., 27 January 1981, cols. 824 seq.
32. HC Debs., 17 June 1981, cols. 1076 seq.
33. HC Debs., 7 May 1980, col. 387.
34. HL Debs., 3 March 1983 and HC Debs., 3 February 1983.
35. First Report, 1980–81, HC 27, para. 66.
36. 1982–83 Liaison Committee Report, p. 121, para. 10.
37. First Report, 1980–81, HC 118.
38. For a rare example of political controversy between two members in a public session, see Second Report, 1982–83, HC 240, Q. 173.
39. E.g. *The Surveyor*, 19 May 1983 and *Transport Policy and Decision Making*, 1982, p. 3.
40. HC Debs., 25 June 1979, cols. 172 seq., Gerald Kaufman.
41. 1977–78 Procedure Committee Report, para. 5.47.
42. 1982–83 Liaison Committee Report, p. 121, para. 10.
43. As suggested by Mr du Cann in evidence to the Procedure (Supply) Committee, 1980–81, HC 118, p. 136 seq.

Annex 14.1 *Transport Committee*

Report	Date of first oral evidence (no. of evidence sessions)	Date of publication of report	Date and form of govt. reply	Length of report (pages)	No. of oral qq./no. of written submissions*	No. of divisions
Session 1979–80						
1st *Special Report: Sub-Committees* (HC 544)	—	22.4.80	—	2	—	—
1st *The European Commission's Green Paper on Transport Infrastructure* (HC 466-v)	27.2.80 (4)	12.6.80	9.12.80 (HC 35 (1980–81))	19	166/27	—
2nd *The Transport Aspects of the Public Expenditure White Paper* (HC 573)	23.4.80 (2)	3.7.80	9.12.80 (HC 35 (1980–81))	8	88/4	—
Session 1980–81						
1st *The Roads Programme* (HC 27)	25.6.80 (7)	17.12.80	18.5.81 (HC 307 (1980–81))	19	402/32	3
2nd *The Channel Link* (HC 155)	13.5.80 (16)	6.3.81	—	49	1032/102 (14)	—
2nd *Special Report: The Inquiry into Lorries, People & the Environment* (HC 192)	25.2.81 (1)	18.3.81	See HC Debs. 17.6.81 Col. 1083	3	42/–	—
3rd *Advanced Ground Transport* (HC 330)	—	2.6.81	11.2.82 (HC 152 (1981–82))	3	–/–	—
4th *The Proposed Transfer of HGV & PSV testing to the private sector* (HC 344)	3.6.81 (4)	31.7.81	11.2.82 (HC 152 (1981–82))	22	246/25	3
5th *The Transport Aspects of the 1981 Public Expenditure White Paper* (HC 299)	15.4.81 (1)	31.7.81	11.2.82 (HC 152 (1981–82))	11	75/9	—

Session 1981–82					
1st *The Proposed Transfer of HGV & PSV Testing to the Private Sector: Supplementary Report* (HC 203)	16.2.82 (1)	22.2.82	—	5	75/—
2nd *Main Line Railway Electrification* (HC 317–1)	24.11.81 (5)	12.5.82	21.3.83 (HC 253 (1982–83))	38	249/33
3rd *The Form of the Nationalised Industries' Reports & Accounts* (HC 390)	—	22.6.82	—	2	—/4
4th *The Roads Programme & the Transport Aspects of the 1982 Public Expenditure White Paper* (HC 334)	21.4.82 (2)	22.6.82	21.3.83 (HC 253 (1982–83))	15	94/3
5th *Transport in London* (HC 127–1)	18.2.81 (21)	28.7.82	21.3.83 (HC 253 (1982–83))	81	1136/56 (67)
Session 1982–83					
1st *Road Maintenance* (HC 28–1)	27.10.82 (9)	23.3.83	Typescript 24.10.83	63	560/54 (20)
2nd *Serpell Committee Report on the Review of Railway Finances* (HC 240)	1.3.83 (4)	18.5.83	11.5.84 (HC 274 (1983–4))	14	297/2
3rd *Transport Aspects of the 1983 Public Expenditure White Paper* (HC 301)	29.3.83 (1)	18.5.83	11.5.84 (HC 274 (1983–4))	6	43/2

* The figures of further memoranda reported to the House but not published are given in brackets. These figures are additional to the unbracketed figures.

Other proceedings
Minutes of Evidence, Department of Transport, 23.1.80, HC 381 (1979–80) (41 questions).
The Channel Link, further evidence from the Secretary of State for Transport, 17.2.82 and Report on the Channel Link by Sir Alec Cairncross, HC 207 (1981–2) (47 questions).

Inquiries not completed
Road Safety, HC 275 (1982–3)
Bus Subsidy Policy, HC 285 (1982–3).

CHAPTER 15

The Treasury and Civil Service Committee 1979–83

Ann Robinson

The Treasury and Civil Service Committee (TCSC) established in 1979 was not an entirely new piece of parliamentary machinery. It inherited some of the members (and ex-members) and specialist advisers of its immediate predecessor, the General Sub-committee of the Expenditure Committee and made full use of these continuities to follow and develop many of the themes that the General Sub-committee had opened. Thus the history of the two committees can be read as a continuous narrative chronicling the establishment and development of machinery for parliamentary scrutiny of the Government's public spending plans and of its handling of economic affairs.[1]

MEMBERSHIP AND PARTICIPATION

The membership of the TCSC is shown in Table 15.1. The chairman, Edward du Cann, remained in office throughout the 1979–83 Parliament. He was not an 'activist' chairman in the sense of one who dominates the questioning during the taking of evidence or dictates the style and content of the inquiries; rather he guided their direction while allowing the interests of the Committee's members to come fully into play. His willingness to permit members to make their own distinctive marks contributed to the Committee's popularity. The turnover in membership was caused primarily by the elevation of members to government office or to positions as opposition front-bench spokesmen. Several of the Committee's most active key members were retained throughout the Parliament including Dr Bray, Terence Higgins, and Michael English. Attendance was generally high, and most members regarded the TCSC as a significant part of their parliamentary duties. Some devoted a high proportion of their working

Table 15.1 *Members of the Treasury and Civil Service Committee and their expertise together with membership of relevant 'financial' select committees*

CONSERVATIVE	
Edward du Cann (Chairman)	City interests. Economic Secretary Treasury 1962–63. Chairman, Expenditure Committee 1971. Chairman, Public Accounts Committee 1974–79.
Kenneth Baker (to Jan. 1981)	Parliamentary Secretary Civil Service Department 1972–74. Member, Procedure Committee 1975–79.
Anthony Beaumont-Dark*	Chairman of Finance Committee, City of Birmingham, 1970–73. Director, investment companies.
Jock Bruce-Gardyne (from Jan. 1981 to Nov. 1981)	Economic leader writer, *Daily Telegraph*. Member, Executive Committee 1972–74. Vice-chairman, Conservative Parliamentary Finance Committee, 1972–74.
Timothy Eggar (to July 1982)	Merchant banker.
Terence Higgins	Economic specialist, Unilever 1958–64. Conservative opposition front-bench spokesman on Treasury and Economic Affairs 1967–70. Financial Secretary, Treasury 1972–74. Opposition spokesman on Treasury and Economic Affairs 1974, on Trade 1974–76. Chairman, Procedure Committee (Finance) 1982–83.
Richard Shepherd	Lloyds Underwriter. Member, South East Economic Planning Council from 1971.
Ralph Howell (from Nov. 1981)	Farmer.
John Browne (from July 1982)	Banker, specialist in gold, Euro-currency.
LABOUR	
Dr Jeremy Bray	Parliamentary Secretary, Ministry of Power 1966–67, Ministry of Technology, 1967–69. Chairman, Estimates Committee sub-committee 1964–65. Member, Select Committee on Wealth Tax 1975.
Michael English	Member, Procedure Committee 1976–79 and 1982–3. Member, Expenditure Committee General sub-committee 1970–79, Chairman 1974–79.
Robert Sheldon (to March 1981)	Opposition front-bench spokesman, Civil Service Treasury and Machinery of Government 1970–72. Chairman, General Sub-committee of Expenditure Committee 1972–74. Member, Fulton Committee on Civil Service 1966–68. Member, Public Accounts Committee 1965–70 and 1974–79. Minister of State, Civil Service Department 1974. Minister of State, Treasury 1974–75. Financial Secretary, Treasury 1975–79. Opposition front-bench spokesman, Treasury from 1980. Chairman, Public Accounts Committee from 1983.
Michael Meacher (from March 1981)	Ex-lecturer in social administration. Parliamentary Under Secretary, Industry 1974–75, DHSS 1975–76, Trade 1976–79.
Ken Woolmer* (to Feb. 1982)	Parliamentary adviser, Inland Revenue Staff Federation.

Table 15.1 (*cont.*)
LABOUR
Austin Mitchell   Journalist. Lecturer in history and politics.
(from Feb. 1982)

LIBERAL
Richard Wainwright   Economic affairs spokesman 1966–70. Trade and Industry
                         spokesman 1974–79. Member, Expenditure Committee
                         1974–79.

* First elected May 1979.

week to its inquiries, participating to the extent of writing either draft reports of their own (for example Ralph Howell, on The Structure of Personal Income Tax and Income Support)[2] or substantial draft chapters (Dr Bray on Monetary Policy and International Monetary Arrangements)[3]. However, towards the end of the Parliament, there were some signs of flagging enthusiasm. One young member (Tim Eggar) left once he felt that he had made as much contribution as he could, and his replacement (John Browne) did not participate very much in the closing stages of the inquiry into *The Structure of Personal Income Tax.* He became a member of the sub-committee for that inquiry, having already indicated that he would have little time for its work. Thus the early enthusiasm for a committee which afforded a variety of attractions to members declined somewhat in the closing months of the Parliament.

At the start of the Parliament, the TCSC had a general attraction for members of all parties. It monitored the central departments of state: the Treasury, the Civil Service Department (until it was largely merged with the Treasury in 1982), and the Revenue Departments. And when it began its work in 1979, a newly elected Government had brought to those departments novel ideas about economic management and about the role and scope of the Civil Service. By 1983, however, some of those ideas had become softened and modified. The TCSC also had, at the outset, several attractions for particular members. It was a vehicle for the exercise of general parliamentary power; it provided an avenue for influence over the government's economic policy and it offered an opportunity to some of its members with special interests to ride their own particular hobby-horses.

One significant feature of the membership of the TCSC that needs to be stressed in view of recent developments in House of Commons financial procedures, is the extent of overlapping memberships with other 'financial' select committees. Some of these are particularly significant. Terence Higgins was active in the TCSC inquiry into Budgetary Reform in 1982 while at the same time being chairman of the Procedure (Finance) Committee from January of that year. Both

Anthony Beaumont-Dark and Michael English were also members of the same committee. Other such overlaps can be traced in Table 15.1. As a result of this feature of committee membership, there has been a cross-fertilization of ideas between the TCSC, the Public Accounts Committee (PAC), and the Procedure Committee. During the 1979–83 Parliament, the Procedure Committee was exclusively concerned with various aspects of the House's financial procedures. References to the reports of the PAC and the Procedure Committee are frequently to be found in the reports of the TCSC, and the compliment is equally often returned.[4] On the subjects of the role of the Comptroller and Auditor-General, Budget structure and information, the Estimates, and the House's financial procedures, the committees have worked in concert.

The members of the TCSD also brought to their work a wealth of economic, financial, and ministerial experience of working with or in the Treasury. The combination of experience on other financial select committees, especially the General Sub-committee of the Expenditure Committee and the PAC, and the expertise of the members, together with the clear stance of the Government on economic policy, ensured that the TCSC was a 'mature' select committee from the start. It did not have to waste any time in its first session by feeling its way towards a role but could plunge straight into substantive work as soon as it was set up.

SUBJECTS OF INQUIRY

Some division of labour was possible because the TCSC was empowered to establish a sub-committee. In the early years the sub-committee dealt mainly with civil service matters. Under the chairmanship of Robert Sheldon (who had been a member of the Fulton Committee), it considered *The Future of the Civil Service Department* in the session 1980–81, and under Dr Jeremy Bray (who had been chairman of the sub-committee of the Estimates Committee which recommended the establishment of the Fulton Committee) it examined *Efficiency and Effectiveness in the Civil Service* in 1981–82. But from 1982, the sub-committee turned away from the Civil Service and took another direction, with an inquiry into *The Structure of Personal Income Tax and Income Support* under the chairmanship of Michael Meacher.

Over the four sessions of the Parliament, the Committee as a whole operated on a number of fronts. According to the chairman's report to the Liaison Committee,[5] the reports of the TCSC may be grouped as follows:

1. Budget and Autumn Reviews
2. Supply and Budgetary Matters
3. Management of the Economy
4. The Civil Service.

There is, however, a certain amount of overlap between these categories because reports often contain references to other reports or deal with more than one subject area. In particular, there is material in the reports on the Budget and the Autumn Review which is directly related to 'Management of the Economy'. And it is difficult to know where to place the draft report on *The Structure of Personal Income Tax* in the Liaison Committee's scheme. An alternative grouping of the reports is as follows:

1. *Monitoring the economy*. This category includes the Liaison Committee's categories (1) and (2). The TCSC reported as a matter of routine on each Budget, public expenditure White Paper, and Autumn Statement. To begin with it examined the Budget and White Paper together, but it later took them separately. Through this series of reports which were re-active, generally short, and in which specialist analysis rather than evidence predominated, the TCSC provided its comments on the Government's regular economic decisions. These routine reports enabled the TCSC to discern trends and patterns that occur in economic policy-making, and thus to uncover themes that it could then examine separately in more detail. Larger-scale inquiries that probed the foundations of economic decision-making, such as that on *Monetary Policy*, were thus closely related to the Committee's regular work.

2. *Oversight of public expenditure*. The comments on the White Paper that were directly related to spending plans, the reports on the Supply Estimates, and the report on *budgetary reform* come into this category.

3. *Taxation*. While there were some comments on taxation in some of the regular annual reports on the Budget the only substantial work in this field was the draft report on *The Structure of Personal Income Tax and Income Support*.

4. *The Civil Service*. The committee examined some aspect of the Civil Service in each session.

Analysis of the amount of time that the TCSC devoted to each type of subject and the volume of evidence heard and read in each group reveals that the TCSC concentrated its efforts on monitoring the economy and to a lesser extent on the oversight of public spending. Most of its time was occupied with examining the public expenditure White Paper, the Budget, and the form of the financial information presented to Parliament, and with delving into the theoretical foundations of government economic policy-making. In addition to all the regular tasks that flowed naturally from its function as monitor of the Treasury, the Civil Service Department, and the Revenue Departments, it undertook a number of large-scale policy-type inquiries (see Annex for a full list of its reports), starting in 1980 with *Monetary Policy*, moving on to *Financing the Nationalised Industries* in 1981 and *International Monetary Arrangements* in 1982. The report on the nationalized industries partially filled the gap in parliamentary scrutiny which had been left when the Nationalised Industries Committee was abolished in 1979. Curiously, however, the TCSC largely eschewed detailed and searching examination of the financing of public expenditure. In this respect, it has not fulfilled all the requirements of a select committee on economic affairs which those who first proposed such a body expected of it.[6] It did not, for example, mount a specific inquiry into any of the three Green Papers on taxation matters issued by the Government between 1979 and 1983.[7] Only one of these three Green Papers was even tangentially considered (*The Taxation of Husband and Wife*). The sub-committee's inquiry into the relationship between income tax and social security benefits, started in 1982, was the only substantial piece of work that the Committee undertook into the subject of financing public expenditure.

Continuity has proved a valuable feature of the work of the TCSC. Through the need to carry out regular routine examinations of the Government's economic policy decisions, the members of the TCSC were able to build up a degree of knowledge and expertise over and above that which they brought to the Committee in the first place. They could refer back to previous inquiries in the series, and probe where actions on their recommendations seemed unsatisfactory. There are now ten years of experience in this sort of inquiry (regular reviews were begun by the General Sub-Committee of the Expenditure Committee) and, through continual references back to previous reports and Government replies, a dialogue was established between the Treasury and the House through the TCSC.

The continuity in the Committee's work also had its effect on the choice of subject for the larger-scale inquiries. Both *Monetary Policy* and *Efficiency and Effectiveness in the Civil Service* were children of previous reports by the TCSC and grand-children of reports from the Expenditure Committee. The same was also true of *Budgetary Reform* which, although presented as a response to the Armstrong Report,[8] drew upon previous work by the TCSC, the Expenditure Committee, the PAC and the Procedure Committee. And some of the themes explored in *Financing the Nationalised Industries* (especially the tests of the 'crowding out' hypothesis) were related to the central concerns of *Monetary*

Policy. International Monetary Arrangements was designed as a sequel. There were thus strong themes running through both the regular short re-active reports and through the larger inquiries.

In its choice of subjects, the TCSC stuck closely to monitoring what the Treasury actually does. It did not consider that its function was to act as an irritant to goad the Government to adopt new forms of economic management or to change the basic direction of economic policy-making. Although the evidence received by the Committee clearly revealed deficiencies in the general approach of the Treasury to economic management, in particular that it is overwhelmingly concerned with short-term macro-economic management and with macro-economics, the TCSC drew few conclusions about whether this state of affairs was desirable. When members of the TCSC were asked whether, as a result of their inquiries, they had thought of recommending that the Treasury pay more attention to micro-economics, they indicated that they considered micro-economic questions to fall within the scope of other departments, notably Industry and Trade and Employment, and therefore to fall within the terms of reference of other select committees. Their job, they felt, was to monitor what the Treasury actually does, not to point it in new directions. In this respect, perhaps, they have proved more timid than their earlier counterpart, the Estimates Committee, which in 1958 made recommendations for sweeping changes in the way that the Government controlled public spending.[9] There are some signs since the 1983 election that the new Chancellor of the Exchequer, Nigel Lawson, will be encouraging a new direction towards micro-economics within the Treasury, and this may have, ultimately, an effect on the type of inquiry selected by the TCSC.

EVIDENCE

The TCSC relied for its evidence on a relatively narrow range of sources in comparison with some of the other select committees. The bulk of its evidence was supplied by the departments, notably by the Treasury, much of it in the form of written memoranda. These were often supplied in response to requests from the TCSC for technical explanations of the Government's documents (sections of the White Paper for example). The TCSC was not the object of continuous attention from pressure and interest groups representing the clientele of the departments concerned. Because—as a rule—it dealt with general and technical aspects of public spending and rarely considered specific items of either spending or taxing, it avoided the attentions of the pressure groups which have begun to cluster round the tax policy-making process. We find that such groups appeared before the TCSC only as witnesses for the inquiry into *The Structure of Personal Income Tax*, where they perceived some gain from making their case in public (the Child Poverty Action Group and Family Forum for example).

Nor did the TCSC often venture out beyond the confines of Westminster and Whitehall into the wider world to collect evidence from the general public. Unlike some other select committees it did not become addicted to overseas trips. The only one it took during the years 1979–83 was when it went to Washington in 1982 for the inquiry into international monetary arrangements—at a cost of £17,075. It did, however, solicit both written and oral evidence from foreign economists, experts and officials (for example, from central banks). When collecting evidence for the larger inquiries, where it wanted to hear answers from a range of different sources to the same questions, it generally issued a questionnaire (published with the report) to try to obtain some consistency in the replies.

For the regular annual reviews, the TCSC relied primarily on the Treasury and other departments. Since, as indicated above, it concentrated its attention more on economic management and public spending than on taxation, it called disproportionately upon the Treasury (and, until it was merged with the Treasury, the Civil Service Department). The TCSC also made a regular practice of calling ministers to give oral evidence, most notably the Chancellor of the Exchequer. Members of TCSC had differing views as to the utility of questioning the Chancellor himself. Some felt that to have him before them drew the attention of press and public to the Committee's work and showed that Parliament had some teeth. But others thought that questioning the Chancellor was largely a waste of time and that more valuable information could be gained from officials. Most agreed that questioning the Chancellor would be more effective if there was a greater lapse of time between publication of the Budget details and debate in the House. The Committee consistently recommended that a 'Green Budget' be introduced to Parliament early in the session so that the Committee could examine the Chancellor on draft proposals some weeks or months before the Budget is actually presented. This might make his appearances before the TCSC somewhat less of a last-minute ritual. The practice of questioning the Chancellor on his autumn statement does not fulfil this objective, since the autumn statement is an incomplete guide to the contents of a spring Budget.

STAFF AND SPECIALIST ADVISERS

The TCSC had the largest staff of any select committee with three clerks, two temporary assistants, and a committee assistant. It also made extensive use of specialist advisers. Specialist advisers were particularly important to the TCSC because of the highly technical nature of the subject matter covered by the committee. Indeed, without technical advice on financial matters, probably no select committee can adequately examine the White Paper or the departmental Estimates. The advisers to the TCSC worked closely with the clerks in their task of interpreting the Government's financial statements and publications. The clerks assisted in the drafting of reports, but some of the subjects undertaken by TCSC were so technical that this task was largely carried out by the specialist advisers, for example on *Monetary Policy*.

The advisers were also particularly useful to the Committee in enhancing its capacity to interpret the evidence presented to it. It is somewhat difficult to draw a clear distinction between evidence that the Committee obtained from witnesses and material that was prepared for it by its specialist advisers. Very often the material prepared by the advisers formed a substantial proportion of the published minutes of evidence and appendices, especially in the regular reports. The overlap was also apparent when the Committee drew evidence from economists and at the same time had other economists as advisers, as for the inquiry into *Monetary Policy*. During the period 1979–83, the TCSC employed a total of twenty-eight specialist advisers. For the regular inquiries they employed a panel of four or five drawn from different institutions and reflecting different political viewpoints. Others

Table 15.2   *The Specialist Advisers*

Name • .	Institutional Affiliation	Reports			
		1979–80	1980–81	1981–82	1982–83
Dr P. G. Neild	Phillips and Drew	HC 584	HC 79 HC 163 HC 232 HC 325	HC 28 HC 270	HC 49 HC 204 HC 286
Mr T. S. Ward	Cambridge, Department of Applied Economics	HC 584	HC 79 HC 163 HC 232	HC 28 HC 137 HC 270 HC 316	HC 39 HC 204 HC 286
Mr P. A. Ormerod	National Institute of Economic and Social Research (NIESR), Henley Centre		HC 282	HC 28 HC 270	HC 49 HC 204 HC 286

Table 15.2 *The Specialist Advisers (cont.)*

Name	Institutional Affiliation	Reports			
		1979–80	1980–81	1981–82	1982–83
Mr D. Savage	NIESR				HC 49 HC 204 HC 286
Dr P.W. Robinson	London Business School (LBS)			HC 28 HC 270	HC 49 HC 204 HC 286
Mr J.A. Likierman	LBS		HC 325	HC 137 HC 236	
Professor B. Tew	Loughborough University of Technology				HC 21 HC 385
Professor J. Williamson	Institute for International Economics, Washington				HC 21 HC 385
Dr D.K.H. Begg	LBS				HC 21 HC 385
Professor W.H. Buiter	London School of Economics (LSE)		HC 163 HC 325		HC 21 HC 385
Mr J.A. Kay	Institute for Fiscal Studies			HC 137	HC 386
Professor A.B. Atkinson	LSE				HC 386
Mrs H. Parker	—				HC 386
Dr A. Budd	LBS	HC 584	HC 79 HC 163		
Professor H. Rose	Barclays Bank	HC 713	HC 163		
Professor D. Hendry	LSE		HC 163		
Professor M. Miller	Warwick University		HC 163		
Mr P.J. Butler	Peat, Marwick & Mitchell		HC 325	HC 236	
Mr M. Stonefrost	Greater London Council		HC 325	HC 236	
Mr B. Henry	NIESR		HC 232		
Mr C. Johnson	Lloyds Bank		HC 348		
Professor M. Beesley	LBS		HC 348		

Table 15.2   *The Specialist Advisers (cont.)*

Name	Institutional Affiliation	Reports			
		1979–80	1980–81	1981–82	1982–83
Mr D. Heald	Glasgow University		HC 348		
Mr M. Marks	Granada Group		HC 348		
Mr J. Redwood	Rothschilds		HC 348		
Mr W. Plowden	Royal Institute of Public Administration			HC 236	
Mr R. Matthews	Ex-Civil Servant			HC 236	
Mr N. Hepworth	Chartered Institute of Public Finance and Accountancy			HC 236	

were recruited for particular inquiries to which they could make an expert contribution. For example, Hepworth and Plowden were called in for the Civil Service, Tew and Williamson for Monetary Arrangements, and Atkinson for personal income tax. Table 15.2 shows the specialist advisers, their institutional affiliation, and inquiries on which they worked.

The Committee was eclectic in its choice of economic advice. They did not rely, as had the Expenditure Committee in its earliest years, on a single source to provide an 'alternative view'. The TCSC took advice from economists known to have left-wing views (for example, Terry Ward of the Cambridge Department of Applied Economics) and from others known to have views of a more right-wing hue (for example, J. Redwood of Rothschilds, and various people from the London Business School). Most advisers were macro-economists and many were notable for their skill as econometricians. The committee did not use theoreticians (although it took evidence from several) nor did it use economic historians, micro-economists (except for the inquiry on nationalized industries), or 'structuralists'. Its choice of expert advisers matched closely the type of expertise found in the Treasury that is, macro-economics but not micro-economics. If the Treasury were in the future to venture out into the world of micro-economics, in an attempt to manipulate the economy sector by sector, then this might affect the sort of specialist adviser chosen by the TCSC. In this, as in many other respects, the TCSC acts as a mirror of the departments that it monitors.

CONSENSUS AND DIVISION IN THE TCSC

By taking a highly technical approach, the Committee was generally able to maintain what Mr David Blake of *The Times* described as 'a fragile unity'.[10] The subject of public expenditure and taxation could easily become a matter of partisan division, if a committee were asked to decide on levels of spending. The TCSC generally avoided such conflictual issues, and as a result there was no clear overall pattern of party voting.

Divisions were relatively rare (see Annex). The TCSC only really confronted the divisive issue of how much public spending and how much taxing is desired when it conducted its regular reviews, of the Budget and the Expenditure White Paper. There was generally a number of divisions on these reports, and the publicly expressed differences of opinion hid even deeper splits of view. These were revealed at a press conference in 1981, when members of the TCSC disassociated themselves from the agreed report on the Budget and public spending.[11] But criticisms in this case came from both Labour and Conservative members. There were also reported splits in the sub-committee that finally produced an agreed report on *The Future of the Civil Service Department*.[12] The longer reports on more technical issues such as budgetary reform, or where a potentially political topic was treated as an intellectual puzzle, such as *Monetary Policy*, caused disproportionately fewer divisions. But divisions are a poor guide to the degree of dispute generated within the Committee by a report. Very often the Committee considered a number of different drafts before it finally agreed on the general approach that the report as a whole should take. Again, a report may contain many qualifications or may lay out options, rather than making any firm recommendations for action. Many of the reports of the TCSC were couched in the form of comments, few contained concrete recommendations. In this respect, the TCSC acted like a long-running academic seminar or permanent commission on government economic policy-making rather than as a sharp political critic.

Only one report was the subject of many divisions and thus brought dissension out into the open. And even this draft report from the sub-committee on *The Structure of Personal Income Tax*, which was the subject of sixty-seven divisions when considered by the full Committee, contained a series of options rather than hard and fast recommendations. When we examine the sixty-seven divisions in detail, there is little evidence of voting on straight party lines. Of the divisions, only twenty-eight contained no cross-party votes: ten of them were Mr Howell (Cons.) alone against four Labour members. He received no support in the full Committee from his party, so these must be discounted as genuine party votes. Only five (some 8 per cent) of the divisions were on clear party lines, with Conservatives ranged against Labour members. These were on the section of the report that dealt with tax allowances and the tax base. The full Committee was interrupted in its consideration of the report by the general election, and so it is not possible to estimate the full extent of likely divisions on this report. However, it is clear that the Conservative members of the sub-committee—Mr Howell apart—had played a limited part in its proceedings and that, when the report came to the full Committee, the Conservative members felt that they had to act to redress the balance. Hence the long and acrimonious debates in the full Committee.

With the exception of the report on *Personal Income Tax* the 'fragile unity' of the TCSC was maintained by a combination of skilful chairmanship, the mutual interests of the members, and the technical approach to much of the Committee's work. The acrimonious debates in full Committee on the report from the sub-committee on *Personal Income Tax*, however, indicated that an element of dissension and disenchantment had taken root. This disenchantment, such as it was, was not due entirely to the effects of a very divisive subject. It can be traced back to other more general factors affecting the Committee before 1983. The TCSC began very well. It was a 'mature' Committee, as was pointed out above, and it began its work when the question of the Government's economic policy was a particularly visible political issue. But this topic lost some of its edge as the Government softened its position. The TCSC reached a peak early, and some decline from this during the course of the Parliament may have been inevitable. Some very active Government members left the Committee, and others appeared to be less passionately interested in its work as the Parliament advanced.

IMPACT: (1) PUBLICITY

In the early days of the Parliament, the TCSC attracted considerable attention from the media. It was frequently referred to as 'the influential all-party Treasury committee'. But as time passed, members of the TCSC were not always happy about the amount and type of publicity that they received. The TCSC got most obvious press attention when there were open quarrels among its members or when its reports could be interpreted as criticism of the Government's economic policy. Reports that comment, make general broad proposals, or sit on the fence, are less obviously 'news'. While there was widespread interest in the arguments at the 1981 press conference for the Budget report, the long report on *Monetary Policy* attracted much less immediate attention. Members of the TCSC felt constrained to write to the newspapers to draw attention to the report on *Monetary Policy*. Dr Bray, for example, wrote to *The Times* saying: 'You have recently used space to comment encouragingly on relatively minor reports ... But you have not so far found space to analyse or comment for your readers on what by any standards is the most substantial review that has been made of the central economic strategy of the Government', and in the same issue, Michael Meacher said in a letter: 'It is unfortunate that as a paper of record *The Times* has not yet carried an analysis of such a major report by its own staff, nor commented on it in a leader'.[13] Often members of the TCSC took matters into their own hands and used evidence which had already been collected as the basis of newspaper articles which they themselves wrote to draw attention to the importance of their inquiry. For example, Michael Meacher wrote an article based on evidence to the sub-committee, entitled: 'Why the poor are getting poorer, faster' in the *Guardian* of 8 February 1982; and Ralph Howell used the pages of the *Daily Telegraph* to put his views on the issue.

While the TCSC got most publicity of an obvious nature when it was in dispute or when it appeared to confront the Government, there is no doubt that it got an even greater volume of publicity of a more diffuse and less obvious type through the use of its evidence by specialist journalists writing feature articles and by academics writing in economics and politics journals. This sort of attention from specialists, however, was less immediately encouraging to members of a select committee than the dramatic stories that showed Parliament as strong against the executive, and displayed to members' constituents that they were actively working on their behalf.

IMPACT: (2) THE HOUSE OF COMMONS

There have been some disappointments, too, on the reception of their work by Parliament. Members of TCSC have not had the satisfaction of seeing their reports as the main focal point of any special debates in the House. But MPs did make use of the reports when the Budget and the White Paper were being debated and frequently quoted from them. This type of impact could be greatly enhanced if there was more time between publication of Government statements and the debate in the House. The present parliamentary timetable still means that the Committee has to do a rushed job and makes its views known rather late in the day: 'Their role in debate is after the horse has bolted and the door shut behind it', said Chris Patten (Cons.) in an article in *The Times* on Budget reform of 11 June 1980. And the tight timetable ensures that the extent of TCSC comment is limited. A book review in *Public Money* (1983) contrasts unfavourably what is available as alternative analysis for United States Congressmen and what the TCSC makes available for MPs.

IMPACT: (3) THE GOVERNMENT AND THE CIVIL SERVICE

The Government's responses to the TCSC's regular reports on the economy and on public spending often came in the form of general statements to the House or as letters from the Chancellor of the Exchequer to the chairman of the Committee. There was a continuous flow of correspondence and telephone calls between the departments and the Committee. Frequently such communications led to the production of further evidence. Some responses came in the form of 'Treasury replies' while replies to the longer reports on policy came in the form of Command Papers or as 'observations' by the department concerned, which the committee then issued itself as a Special Report (see Annex). The capacity of the TCSC to obtain some concrete results for its efforts was related to its ability to refer back to previous reports and to the Government's responses to them. For example, in the report on *The Government's Autumn Statement*,[14] the Committee referred back to its second and fifth reports of the previous session in which it had commented on the Government's ineffective use of cash limits for the control of public sector pay. Cash limits, said the Committee, could be evaded by staging or delaying payment and by double counting (attributing reductions in numbers of Civil Servants to a connected pay rise when the numbers would have been reduced anyway). The report commented: 'The Treasury's observations seemed to show that the Committee had failed to convince the Treasury on these important points. We were therefore all the more pleased to learn from the Chancellor's letter ...'. The TCSC may eventually get the Government to change its financial practices and procedures by continually chipping away at the same points. It had less impact on the Government when it made broad comments or recommendations or when, as in the case of the report, *Monetary Policy*, it simply passed judgement on a policy direction. And it is difficult to see just whom the Committee thought it would influence when it published its draft report on *International Monetary Arrangements* in time for the Williamsburg Summit in 1983. It is doubtful whether any of the British officials or ministers who rushed over to Williamsburg during the general election campaign had read the TCSC report, let alone those from other nations.

The fact that the TCSC could inquire into almost any aspect of the Government's economic work had, however, an impact on the Civil Service. The inquiries themselves had an educative value for Civil Servants because, in order to justify the Government's actions in a public arena, they had to marshal the facts and list the alternatives. Left to themselves it it unlikely that Civil Servants would have indulged in such self-examination. But the TCSC forced them to ask themselves, 'What are we doing and why are we doing it?' There can be no doubt that the existence of the TCSC brought the civil servants who frame economic policy into the public eye. Whereas, before the creation of the Expenditure Committee, and its descendant the TCSC, all was shrouded in secrecy; now only some aspects of economic policy-making remain behind closed doors.

Over the period of the 1979–83 Parliament, the ministers and Civil Servants got better at handling the Committee and at answering its questions. The Chancellor of the Exchequer, Sir Geoffrey Howe, put on a poor performance before the Committee at the start but gained greater self-confidence by the end of the Parliament, although he never attained the skills of his predecessors, especially Joel Barnett, who frequently out-manœuvred the Expenditure Committee.

CONCLUSION

In general the impact of the TCSC on the Government came about because the Committee provided a link between it (especially the Treasury) and the House of Commons. The Government did not always respond immediately or positively to the reports of the TCSC but, by its continued efforts on specific points, the TCSC was able at least to improve the flow and quality of financial information coming before the House.

Select committees can be a remarkably cost-effective means of producing information about how the government works, and the reports of the TCSC are certainly the primary source of what we now know about economic policy-making. In this respect it operated rather like a sort of permanent Commission on economic matters and its costs can be compared favourably with those of any extra-parliamentary body. And it had one inestimable advantage over any research unit in a university or an institute. Much of the information that it unearthed would just not be available at all were it not for the capacity of the House of Commons to extract it. The range and quality of the information contained in the minutes of evidence published by

TCSC is remarkable. The Committee laid out in its reports many highly sophisticated academic views on monetary policy on the one hand and details of the structure and organization of the Civil Service on the other. Even if there were some limits on the capacity of the TCSC to extract information from the Government, it had a greater capacity than any outside body.

Any attempt to assess the impact of the TCSC by a simple measure of the recommendations that the Government accepted would be deficient. Its value lay more in its ability to extract information from the Government and to inject independent analysis into the diffuse processes of government economic policy-making. The Treasury's announcements in 1983 that an extended public discussion would take place on future public spending plans, the changes in Parliament's financial procedures, the establishment of a National Audit Office, and the gradual developments towards more open Budget construction were the results of pressures from many MPs, academics, and commentators who have urged such changes for years. The role of the TCSC in this process of change was not that of the one single authoritative body that compelled the Government to act. Its role was to provide the major public forum in which all of those interested in improving the quality of economic policy-making could state their case. To paraphrase J.S. Mill, the TCSC threw the light of publicity on the Government's acts. It helped to lift the veil from the hidden processes of economic policy-making, and one effect of its existence has been to reassure the Treasury that there is less to fear from public exposure than ministers and civil servants believed in the 1960s.

NOTES

1. For the history of the Expenditure Committee, see Ann Robinson, *Parliament and Public Spending*, Heinemann, 1978 and 'The Experience of the Expenditure Committee 1971–79', in Cedric Sandford ed., *Control of Public Expenditure*, Bath University Centre for Fiscal Studies, Occasional Paper No. 14, 1979, pp. 69–87. For a summary of the arguments for a select committee on economic affairs, see Ann Robinson, 'Monitoring the Economy—the Treasury and Civil Service Committee', in Dilys Hill ed., *Parliamentary Select Committees in Action*, Strathclyde Papers on Government and Politics, No. 24, 1984, pp. 272–301.
2. See also Ralph Howell, *Why Work? A Radical Solution*, Conservative Political Centre, 1981.
3. *Monetary Policy*, HC 163 (1980–81), section on optimal policy-making. See also Jeremy Bray, *Decision in Government*, Gollancz, 1970.
4. See for example, the references to the work of the TCSC in *First Report from the Select Committee on Procedure (Finance)* HC 24 1982–83.
5. 1982–83 Liaison Committee Report, p. 124.
6. Professors Peacock and Wiseman proposed that the House should establish a select committee to consider both public spending and the financing of expendi-

ture in their evidence to *First Report from the Selcect Committee on Procedure: Scrutiny of Public Expenditure and Administration*, HC 410, 1968-69, pp. 249-58. The idea was further developed by Peter Jay and Samuel Brittan in *Second Special Report from the Procedure Committee*, HC 302, 1969-70, pp. 40-56.

7. *The Taxation of Husband and Wife*, Cmnd. 8093, 1980, *Alternatives to Domestic Rates*, Cmnd. 8449, 1981; *Corporation Tax*, Cmnd. 8456, 1982. The Committee commented upon the substance of *The Taxation of Husband and Wife* in its inquiry into the structure of personal income tax.

8. *Budgetary Reform in the UK*, Oxford University Press for the Institute of Fiscal Studies, 1980.

9. *Sixth Report from the Select Committee on Estimates: Treasury Control of Expenditure*, HC 254, 1957-58.

10. *The Times*, 4 August 1983.

11. 'Mr du Cann walks into a storm on Budget report', *The Times*, 9 April 1981.

12. *The Times*, 6 August 1980.

13. *The Times*, 16 April 1981.

14. HC 79, 1980-81.

Annex 15.1 *Treasury and Civil Service Committee*

Report (*denotes inquiry by sub-committee)	Date of first oral evidence/(no. of evidence sessions)	Date of publication of report	Date and form of govt. reply	Length of report (pages)	No. of oral qq./no. of written submissions	No. of divisions
Session 1979–80						
1st *Provision for Civil Service Pay Increases in the 1980–81 Estimates*, HC 371	17.12.79/(1)	6.2.80	16.4.80 Cmnd 7883	3	82/1	Nil
2nd *The Budget and the Government's Expenditure Plans (1980–81 to 1983–84)*, HC 584	2.4.80/(5)	8.7.80	—	8	551/10	2
3rd *Monetary Control*, HC 713	Nil	5.8.80	—	3	Nil/4	Nil
4th *Civil Service Manpower Reductions*, HC 712	28.1.80/(7)	5.8.80	—	5	498/21	Nil
5th *Provision for Civil Service Pay Increases in 1980–81 Estimates*, HC 730	Nil	14.8.80	18.11.80 Third Special Report HC 819[a]	4	Nil	Nil
1st Special Report: *Consideration of Spring Supplementary Estimates*, HC 503	Nil	1.4.80	12.6.80 Second Special Report HC 642	3	Nil/4	Nil
Session 1980–81						
1st *The Future of the Civil Service Department*, HC 54	18.6.80/(7)	22.1.81	12.2.81 Cmnd 8170	14	1152/8	1
2nd *The Government's Economic Policy: Autumn Review*, HC 79	1.12.80/(1)	18.12.80 vol. I 21.1.81 vol. II	—	9	126/10	Nil
3rd *Monetary Policy*, HC 163	30.6.80/(11)	5.3.81	—	113	1132/23	Nil

Report		Date	interim reply received, not published		(b)	Nil
4th *Acceptance of Outside Appointments by Crown Servants*, HC 216	Nil	2.4.81		5	(b)	Nil
5th *Budget and the Government's Expenditure Plans, 1981–82 to 1983–84*, HC 232	18.3.81/(3)	9.4.81 vol. I 6.5.81 vol. II	—	15	392/12	7
6th *The Form of the Estimates*, HC 325	13.5.81/(2)		12.11.81 First Special Report HC 495	8	91/7	Nil
7th *Civil Service Manpower Reductions*, HC 423	Nil	30.7.81	—	1	—/1	—
8th *Financing the Nationalised Industries*, HC 348	8.6.81/(6)	12.8.81 vols. I & III 3.9.81 vol. II	12.11.81 Second Special Report HC 496	20	809/41	7
Session 1981–82						
1st *The Government's Economic Policy: Autumn Review*, HC 28	16.11.81/(3)	16.12.81	—	10	319/9(c)	Nil
2nd *Spring Supplementary Estimates*, HC 226	1.3.81/(1)	16.3.82	—	4	96/4	Nil
3rd *Efficiency and Effectiveness in the Civil Service*, HC 236*	11.6.81/(15)	1.4.82	28.9.83 Cmnd 8616	34	1450/40	5
4th *The 1982 Budget*, HC 270	17.3.81/(3)	23.4.82	—	12	374/8	5
5th *The Government's Expenditure Plans 1982–83 to 1984–85*, HC 316	17.3.82/(2)	19.4.82	—	3	61(d)/6	3
6th *Budgetary Reform* HC 137	18.1.82/(6)	17.6.82	19.10.82 HC 521	23	499/31	5
1st Special Report, *Summer Supplementary Estimates*, HC 448	—	16.7.82	—	1	—	

Annex 15.1 *Treasury and Civil Service Committee (cont.)*

Report (*denotes inquiry by sub-committee)	Date of first oral evidence /(no. of evidence sessions)	Date of publication of report	Date and form of govt. reply	Length of report (pages)	No. of oral qq./no. of written submissions	No. of divisions
Session 1982–83						
1st *The Government's Economic Policy: Autumn Statement*, HC 49	16.11.82/(2)	17.1.83	—	17	270/12	Nil
2nd *Spring Supplementary Estimates*, HC 228	23.2.83/(1)	14.3.83	—	5	132/nil	Nil
3rd *The Government's Expenditure Plans 1983–84 to 1985–86*, HC 204	14.2.83/(1)	3.3.83	—	14	118/5	1
4th *International Monetary Arrangements: International lending by Banks*, HC 21	14.6.82/(16)	31.3.83 vols. I & III; 13.4.83 vol. II	—	34	1528/39	1
5th *The 1983 Budget*, HC 286	23.3.83/(3)	4.5.83	—	14	356/9 (e)	3
1st Special Report, *Civil Service Manpower Reductions*, HC 46	—	7.12.82	—	1		
2nd *International Monetary Arrangements*, HC 385 (Minutes of Evidence as HC 21—Fourth Report)	(f)	24.5.83	—	1	(f)	Nil
3rd Special Report, *The Structure of Personal Income Taxation and Income Support*, HC 386 (Minutes of Evidence as HC 20)*	21.4.82/(12)	16.6.83	—	1	1127/45	67 (g)

Notes:

a See also HM Treasury Press Notice 136/80 14.8.80.
b Reprints oral evidence from the General sub-committee of the Expenditure Committee HC 576 (1977–78) and from TCSC HC 333 (1979–80).
c Three of these published as HC 28 (1981–82) i, ii.
d Plus 31.3.82 which shows qq. 375–481 total = 167.
e Simply reports progress. Should be regarded as Government observations as it contains a report from the Treasury on progress 1981–82. See report on same topic 1980–81.
f For evidence, *see* 4th Report of 1982–83.
g Divisions on report from sub-committee on consideration by main committee. Work uncompleted.

CHAPTER 16

The Welsh Affairs Committee

J. Barry Jones

The Welsh Affairs Committee (WAC), unlike most of the new select committees, did not arise simply from a concern to redress the balance between the House of Commons and the executive. Devolution, or to be more precise its failure in the March 1979 referendum, was the more compelling reason. The Welsh devolution debate, in contrast to that in Scotland, was centred on the principle of public account-ability, and while deep divisions in Welsh society were highlighted by the devolution issue, there gradually emerged a conviction that the growth since 1964 of a specifically Welsh administrative machine had not been matched by effective scrutiny and control procedures.[1] How-ever, Labour's prescription of an elected assembly was rejected by the Welsh electorate in the devolution referendum, an event which appeared to vindicate the Conservative Party's belief that an appro-priate degree of public accountability was possible *within* the frame-work of the Westminster Parliament by using the select committee device. The tendency to associate the WAC with the demise of devolution and to regard it as an alternative to the assembly was also encouraged by the Conservative Government's decision to debate both the repeal of the Wales Act and the motion setting up the Committee on Welsh Affairs at the same time. It led one Labour back-bencher to express the view: 'Clearly the Assembly is dead—rejected decisively on St David's Day. Now long live the Select Com-mittee.'[2] The aspiration was shared by several Welsh anti-devolution-ists and particularly by the three members of the 'Gang of Six' Labour MPs who, having campaigned to such great effect against the Labour Government's proposed assembly, now found themselves on the Com-mittee. They hoped to eliminate devolution from the political agenda by demonstrating the effectiveness of the new Committee. To a degree, this depended on engaging the interest of Welsh public opinion, a

tactic that ran the risk of raising political expectations which a parliamentary select committee might find difficult—if not impossible—
to satisfy. The WAC thus found its devolution antecedents a mixed
blessing.

MEMBERSHIP, CHAIRMANSHIP AND STYLE

The Committee's eleven members, originally nominated on 26 November 1979, consisted of six Conservatives, four Labour, and one
Liberal—to reflect the balance of political forces in the House of
Commons. It was not a typical select committee; an unspoken understanding on both sides of the House that its membership should be
drawn exclusively from Wales created what was in effect a 'territorial'
committee within the framework of a 'unitary' Parliament. This constitutional paradox had implications for the Committee's representative character, operational effectiveness, and political role. Labour's
electoral dominance in Wales (it held twenty-one of the thirty-six
seats in the 1979 election) was not reflected in the Committee's membership. With five of the eleven Conservative Welsh MPs in the
Government, there was an absolute constraint on the selection of six
Conservative back-benchers to the WAC, the remaining seat was occupied by the only Welsh Liberal MP, to the total exclusion of Plaid
Cymru who, despite setbacks, were still a force in Welsh politics and
held two parliamentary seats. The limited pool of back-benchers—
from which the two major parties were obliged to select their nominees
for the Committee—posed additional problems. Parties had little or
no choice. The new Committee was deficient in parliamentary experience; four of its original members were newly elected MPs and
only one of the senior members had experience of the Expenditure
Committee. Some back-benchers were 'pressed' into service on the
Committee whether or not they had an interest in the 'Welsh political
dimension', a factor reflected in the WAC's attendance record.
Whereas the figure overall was 78 per cent; the Conservatives were
notably less enthusiastic; their attendance record of 70 per cent compared with 88 per cent for Labour members.

The question of the Committee's chairman also presented difficulties.
After some party political manoeuvring, the WAC was designated a
'Labour' committee. Alan Williams—Labour's nominee for the chairmanship—had been a member of the previous government and
appeared to possess the kind of qualities necessary to a relatively
inexperienced committee. However, he was Labour's front-bench
spokesman on industry, and Conservative members were adamant
that he should not occupy both positions. Obliged to make the choice,

he opted for the front bench and resigned from the Committee on 15 January 1980. On 25 January, Leo Abse agreed to be drafted as 'chairman designate', but only on the understanding that he would serve for no more than two years, as he was reluctant to be permanently side-tracked on Welsh issues. The WAC was the last of the new select committees to come into operation, and its first public session was held on 10 March, almost exactly twelve months after the devolution referendum.

The WAC's operational style was strongly influenced by two considerations: the breadth of its remit and the nature of its membership. Standing Order No. 86B made on 26 June 1979 required the Committee to examine the expenditure, administration, and policy of the Welsh Office and associated public bodies. The Welsh Office had assumed a wide range of responsibilities since its creation in 1964; as a result of promptings from Labour back-benchers, it became clear that the term 'associated public bodies' would not be interpreted in the limited fashion specified by Norman St John-Stevas in respect of the other departmental committees,[3] but in such a manner as to cover the whole range of public administration in Wales. The Committee's wide responsibilities thus encouraged the assumption of broad-gauge characteristics and wide-ranging inquiries which would attract public interest.

The second consideration to influence the WAC's style was the relative inexperience of the members, although this weakness was progressively overcome as they developed procedures and acquired expertise. Continuity of committee membership, a product of scarce back-bencher resources, also helped. While the Labour Party had

Nominated in November 1979	*Date of Leaving Committee and replacement(s)*	*Members of Committee in May 1983*
Keith Best (Cons.)	Nov. 1981	Ian Grist (Cons.)
Ioan Evans (Lab.)	Jan. 1983	Gareth Wardell (Lab.)
Roy Hughes (Lab.)	Dec. 1979	Donald Anderson* (Lab.)
Alan Williams (Lab.)	Jan. 1980 Leo Abse* (Lab.) Nov. 1981	Ray Powell (Lab.)
Sir Raymond Gower (Cons.)	Member of the Committee for duration of Parliament	Sir Raymond Gower (Cons.)
Tom Hooson (Cons.)	,,	Tom Hooson (Cons.)
Geraint Howells (Lib.)	,,	Geraint Howells (Lib.)
Sir Anthony Meyer (Cons.)	,,	Sir Anthony Meyer (Cons.)
Geraint Morgan (Cons.)	,,	Geraint Morgan (Cons.)
Dr Roger Thomas (Lab.)	,,	Dr Roger Thomas (Lab.)
Delwyn Williams (Cons.)	,,	Delwyn Williams (Cons.)

* Denotes Chairman.

greater choice than the Conservatives, it was obliged to turn for its replacements to parliamentary newcomers.

The lack of experience was most evident in the Committee's early operations which displayed a weak inquisitorial technique and a tendency on the part of several members towards special pleading for constituency interests. In subsequent inquiries, as its members became more conversant with their role, this behaviour was less evident but it was never completely eradicated. Members' questions sometimes developed a momentum of their own and extended into political speeches which, while good copy for the local press, failed to put witnesses under serious pressure. Making a virtue out of necessity, the Committee progressively adopted the approach of concerned laymen trawling for information (sometimes in an indiscriminate fashion) and seeking advice from interested parties and expert witnesses. The net effect was the accumulation of an impressive volume of documentary information on Welsh affairs, which in the opinion of the Committee's second chairman, constituted 'fairly comprehensive works for opinion formers in the Principality'.[4] It could thus be argued that both devolution antecedents and operational style inclined the WAC to identify public opinion in Wales as its primary audience.

The chairmanship of the Committee changed hands once during the lifetime of the Parliament. The first chairman, Leo Abse, brought considerable parliamentary experience and oratorical skills. A House of Commons man, he was deeply committed to the parliamentary process and at a stage in his career when he no longer nourished ambitions for ministerial office. As one of the chief architects of the defeat of Labour's devolution proposals, he was intent on proving Parliament's ability to meet the needs and aspirations of the political community in Wales. Given the relative inexperience of many Committee members, Leo Abse assumed a dominant role and one which, with his developed forensic skills, he filled with some ease and distinction. He had the lawyer's instinct for the jugular of a witness, and was not averse to taking over a member's line of questioning whenever he felt it was being pursued with insufficient zeal. His successor, Donald Anderson, another anti-devolutionist, was motivated by similar considerations but ran the WAC on more democratic lines, granting members greater latitude to develop sometimes idiosyncratic lines of questioning. However, as members became more conversant with the Committee's operations they assumed a more positive role. An increasingly experienced Committee, allied to a less forceful chairman, produced a more consensual procedure. During the two inquiries chaired by Leo Abse in which oral evidence was taken, the chairman asked 50 per cent and 47 per cent of the questions respectively; in the two inquiries under Donald Anderson, the corresponding percentages were 26 per cent and 47 per cent.

THE SECRETARIAT

For many members the WAC imposed additional burdens and obligations. The flow of paper generated by the Committee's activities made demands which some members were unable fully to meet. In these circumstances, considerable responsibility was placed on the clerk to the Committee who established effective procedures for its deliberations. His duties included drawing up lists of potential witnesses, liaising with them, preparing questions, advising on the strategy to be followed during the evidence sessions, and drafting the reports. All functions, other than routine administration, were exercised in close consultation with the chairman and, though more rarely, the whole Committee. Inevitably much of the WAC's dynamic, and most of its operational efficiency, was dependent upon the close working relationship built up between chairman and clerk; their involvement and commitment to the Committee in terms of time and effort dwarfed that of ordinary Committee members. Most of the WAC's organizational and policy initiatives were exercised by the chairman and clerk acting in concert, and subsequently endorsed by the Committee. While the chairman/clerk axis was the efficient secret of the Committee's operation, its very importance disconcerted some members, who regarded it as somewhat exclusive. However, members did readily admit the central role played by the clerk in the Committee's operations.

No similar consensus existed concerning the role played by specialist advisers. The Committee as a whole was reluctant to provide them with the opportunity to take the lead in policy formulation. There was little direct contact between members and advisers; either by chance or design, the clerk played the role of an intermediary. Some members were also reluctant to grant the advisers too important a role lest they disrupt the dynamic relationship between the Committee and witnesses giving evidence. They were also apprehensive that questions which were too structured and technical would undermine the generalist style which the WAC had assumed for itself. The attitude may have been the rationalization of an insecure committee anxious to preserve its authority and status, but it did reflect the prevailing view in the Committee that it was primarily a political body. With this in mind, the Committee was careful whenever possible to appoint advisers with Welsh connections. Of the eight appointed at various times, five were either Welsh or had a Welsh background. Two of the exceptions to this rule were the regional economists from Cambridge appointed by the WAC for its first inquiry. Their anti-monetarist attitudes fortuitously coincided with the political inclinations of the Committee's Labour members, and did much to encourage the Conservative majority to adopt a more circumspect view of the role advisers should play.

ESTABLISHING A ROLE

The Committee's first meeting, held on 10 March 1980 in the 'people's castle in the heart of the capital city of Wales',[5] was an historic occasion which attracted extensive coverage in the Welsh media. The precedent this created of holding public sessions in Wales, was followed on only one further occasion when the Committee took evidence in Gwynedd county hall. The expectation that improved public accountability would also be more visible in Wales was not therefore realized. There are obvious difficulties in holding regular meetings in Wales. The singular character of the transport infra-structure—which 'makes it easier to travel to London than to travel within the Principality'[6]—is a major deterrent. But the scrutiny of Welsh Office departments could have been held in Cardiff. Doubtless some difficulties would have remained—for example, pairing and finding a suitable and available meeting place; but the WAC members apparently decided that the resulting personal inconvenience would not be matched by any appreciable gain. While a minority favoured regular evidence sessions in Wales, there was another consideration: too high a political profile in the Principality might have stimulated nationalist sentiments which would have run counter to the political rationale behind the establishment of the Committee.

The Committee's essential conservatism in the location of its formal sessions was matched by a radical assertion of its rights in the parliamentary arena. From the outset, its supporters were anxious that it should be able to inquire into the whole range of government activities in Wales including nationalized industries,[7] and in practice the WAC adopted the broadest possible interpretation of its remit. It moved into areas which overlapped the boundaries of other departmental committees, any demarcation 'problems' being resolved on a bilateral basis, and the Committee took evidence from a wide range of politicians and public bodies outside Wales; including the Secretary of State for Industry and the Home Secretary; the BBC, the IBA, the National Coal Board, and the British Steel Corporation (BSC).

The Committee's first chairman aimed to exert pressure on the Government by exploiting public opinion. The Committee's decision to exercise its parliamentary privilege and publish a BSC confidential document may be interpreted as part of this strategy. 'Return to Financial Viability: Presentation of South Wales Option', prepared by BSC's Chief Executive for a board meeting on 17 January 1980, detailed the manpower and social implications of a substantial rundown of the Port Talbot and Llanwern steel plants in South Wales. The publication of BSC's probable intentions, and the resulting publicity, consolidated the political campaign in Wales opposed to the steel cutbacks. The circumstantial evidence suggests that the Committee's ability to focus Welsh public opinion on the issue was instrumental in preventing the total closure of one or other of the two threatened steel plants.

The relationship between a committee and its department is inevitably variable, given the nature of the political process. Of the two polarities, that of an adversary and that of a client, the WAC tended towards the former. In the Committee's first formal session Leo Abse declared his intention to wage war on the mandarins, an aspiration which the Welsh Office scrutiny sessions revealed to be as much a form of rhetoric as a statement of intent. However, the Committee did not lack the will to stand up to the Welsh Office. In the course of its inquiry into water in Wales, the Committee took evidence from Arthur Andersen & Co., a firm of accountants retained by the Welsh Office to investigate the Welsh Water Authority's finances. The Committee was unable to make progress because of a Welsh Office instruction to the witness 'not to reveal to the committee anything that was disclosed to you in confidence in the course of your enquiry ... into the Welsh Water Authority in February 1981'.[8] The WAC took exception to what it construed to be an infringement of its constitutional rights. Proceedings were adjourned while the chairman of the WAC held discussions with the chairman of the Liaison Committee and, later, with the Welsh Secretary of State. As a result of these deliberations the Welsh Office settled on a formula which, while conceding much of the substance, preserved the principle. A qualified concession was made to allow Arthur Andersen & Co. to disclose previously restricted factual information,[9] and another precedent was established in the evolving relationship between the Committee and its department.

A review of the role played by the WAC would be incomplete without reference to the Committee's dual mandate; the one formal, constitutional, and parliamentary, and the other imprecise, but potent and Welsh. A sensitivity to this second mandate was evinced by the Committee's attitude towards the vexed question of the constitutional status of the Welsh language. In its first deliberative session the Committee decided on bilingual stationery; the Committee's letterhead carries the legend 'Committee on Welsh Affairs' and 'Pwyllgor Materion Cymreig', while press notices are flanked by a parliamentary portcullis on the left and by a Welsh dragon on the right. Later that year, the Committee decided to investigate broadcasting in Wales and, while considering the possibility of receiving evidence in the Welsh language, inquired of the Lord Chancellor about the practice of the courts in Wales. His reply appeared to anticipate the Committee's intent. He was reluctant to set a precedent which might be exploited by other minority language groups in the United Kingdom, nor was he prepared 'to countenance any action that would undermine the position of the English language in parliamentary proceedings in Westminster'.[10] However, as the Welsh Language Act 1967 gave equal status to the language in Wales, the WAC's sessions held in Wales could take evidence and ask questions in Welsh, provided that there were simultaneous translation facilities and a complete record of proceedings was kept in English. On 16 February 1981, the Committee conducted part of its proceedings in Welsh. For the first time since the demise of Norman-French, a language other than English had legitimately been used in the formal proceedings of a parliamentary body.

MAJOR INQUIRIES

In the course of four parliamentary sessions, the WAC evolved a flexible programme of operations involving major inquiries into policy, periodic reviews of public administration in Wales, and the financial scrutiny of the Welsh Office Estimates. The greatest effort by far was invested in lengthy inquiries and in producing substantial reports. As the Committee became established, there was a tendency for its inquiries to be spread over longer periods. Whether measured in terms of sessions held or questions asked, the Committee's work effort was concentrated in the area of inquiries, and this clearly reflected its priority.

The first report, *Developing Employment Opportunities in Wales*, made specific recommendations but its underlying analysis and prevailing tone were unequivocally hostile to the Government's monetarist policies. The language of the report was deliberately political, and some of its statements were highly tendentious. Reference was made, for example, to the 'continued emasculation of steel capacity in Wales'; the Committee accepted that 'there were very real possibilities of disorder'; and Leo Abse warned that 'if condemned to suffer the worklessness of the 'thirties, Wales was unlikely to respond with apathy and despair'.[11] The report attracted detailed and comprehensive coverage in the Welsh media but antagonized the Government; only two of the thirty-eight recommendations were accepted.

However, the fact that this report gained the unanimous support of all committee members embarrassed the Government, as did the attendant publicity. The attack on the central thrust of the Government's economic policy may also have contributed to its reluctance to concede too much to the Committee, but it is doubtful whether a less hostile report would have attracted a more favourable government response. There are indications that the Committee's influence in certain limited policy areas was by no means insignificant. For example, the Government rejected the WAC's recommendation that the Development Corporation for Wales should be wound up. However, the Corporation's fairly disastrous evidence session must have raised doubts about its future role beyond the ranks of the Committee. Some two years later, the Government announced that the Corporation's functions would be transferred to the Welsh Development Agency and the Welsh Office, but—reluctant to give credit to the Committee— insisted that the switch in policy was the product of new circumstances. A similar delay accompanied the Government's decision to take up the Committee's suggestions to fund the Wales Worker Co-operative Centre.

In the second report, *Broadcasting in the Welsh Language*, the Committee refrained from taking issue with government policy, which had, after an initial U-turn, confirmed support for a Welsh language fourth television channel. The report presented a comprehensive, detailed, and highly technical review of the broadcasting system in Wales. It highlighted the problems of transmission posed by the terrain, and the political, financial, and technical difficulties which confronted attempts to cater for two linguistic groups. It was a unique compendium of facts and attitudes, more concerned with influencing forward planning than with eliciting immediate decisions, and reflected a more realistic assessment of a committee's political influence and constitutional role. However, the policy significance of the inquiry lay not in its report but in the evidence presented to it. The Government's policy for the Welsh television channel (S4C) was being formulated while the Committee was taking evidence, and witnesses were able to use the Committee as a platform from which to present views, in the expectation that they might well influence a government whose mind was not yet made up. It appears that the most significant contribution came from representatives of the Association of Welsh Broadcasters who demonstrated that a 'wrap-around' programme schedule would enable most English Channel Four programmes to be viewed in

Wales, thus removing a central apprehension of the English-speaking community. The WAC, anxious to obtain a fair deal for both English and Welsh viewers, made much of this evidence and the wrap-around technique was subsequently employed by S4C.

The Committee returned to a more politically contentious issue with its inquiry into water in Wales. The high level of Welsh water rates and the huge volume of water 'exported' to England had pro-jected the issue into the forefront of Welsh politics. In this respect, it had much in common with the subject matter of the first report, but the WAC now displayed little of the political single-mindedness which had characterized that inquiry. Instead, the progress of the water inquiry demonstrated a lack of certainty as to the Committee's objec-tive; whether it should directly confront government policy and call for the equalization of water charges across Britain or whether it should make a series of limited administrative recommendations which the Government would be more likely to accept. The Com-mittee attempted to do both. An interim report on consumer repre-sentation was published in May 1982 and won praise for the clarity of its analysis and its proposals for the membership, organization and powers of consumer advisory councils in the Welsh Water Authority. They were implemented virtually intact by the Government. But twelve months elapsed before the major report was published. The 'Arthur Andersen affair'—as we have noted—caused some delay, but the root cause of the hold-up was the political predicament in which the Committee found itself. The latter stages of the inquiry ran parallel with the committee stage of the Water Bill, which reconsti-tuted the water authorities and was the subject of a continuous flow of government amendments. The WAC was therefore dealing with a moving target. Furthermore, what was already a contentious issue in Wales became embroiled in the tactics and confrontations of the West-minster party-political battle.

This variable and hostile environment had much to do with the deterioration of personal relationships within the Committee in the last few weeks before Christmas 1982. On 16 December, the Cardiff *Western Mail* published a confidential letter which had come into its possession, written by Tom Hooson to his fellow Conservatives on the WAC. It asserted that the draft report was full of 'astonishing attacks on Nick and the Welsh Office' and suggested that the Conservatives should use their majority on the Committee to 'delete or compress' many of the 'contentious and opinionated sections'. The Committee's Labour chairman accused the Welsh Office of putting pressure on Tory members, and threatened to resign rather than allow it to be turned into 'a poodle of the Welsh Office'.[12] The following day, Ray

Powell (Lab.)—whose membership of both the WAC and the Water Bill's standing committee epitomized the complexity of the situation—made two demands: that the WAC's draft report be immediately published; and that the Committee should take evidence from the Welsh Water Authority's new chairman. Both would have provided valuable ammunition for opposition members on the standing committee, but in the context of the WAC the demands were incompatible. Another evidence session would further delay publication and play into the hands of Conservatives, who were quite happy to spin out discussions on what was known to be a critical report.

But Labour members failed to hold the line, the Chairman's authority was called into question, the cohesion of the Committee was seriously impaired, and the eventual publication of the report was delayed four months. It eventually emerged comparatively unscathed. Although the WAC divided thirty-three times, it rarely did so on straight party lines, and the Chairman was able to use his casting vote on no fewer than twenty-six occasions. The report as a whole was eventually agreed unanimously, despite Tom Hooson's misgivings, and was yet another embarrassment to the Government. It accused the Secretary of State of gagging witnesses; it claimed that Welsh Office civil servants were inept in financial and accounting matters; and it called for the equalization of water charges. However, by May 1983, the attention of the Welsh public and politicians was occupied by the impending general election. Its immediate public impact was slight and hence a disappointment to a committee which placed great store by publicity. The dip into Welsh water provided the clearest possible illustration of the dangers of the over-long inquiry, in particular, its susceptibility to shifts in policy and to changes in the political environment.

ADMINISTRATIVE REVIEW AND FINANCIAL SCRUTINY

Increased accountability of Welsh public administration was an important element in the rationale which led to setting up the Committee. In practice, however, the process of administrative review occupied a secondary role in the Committee's activities, taking up less than a quarter of its time. Nevertheless, all ten departments in the Welsh Office and three Welsh quangos were examined by the Committee. There is some dispute as to the value of these exercises. The sessions took the form of preliminary inquiries designed to familiarize the WAC with the operation and personnel of the Welsh Office. This had an educative function both for the Committee members and for Welsh Office civil servants, for most of whom the experience was completely novel. The sessions also afforded a basis for future inquiries,[13] and provided an opportunity, taken up by Abse and Anderson, to give all members the experience of chairing the Committee.

Whatever the long-term or ancillary benefits, the efficacy of the exercise was not proven. Welsh Office Civil Servants were not subjected to the rigorous interrogation which many had anticipated and prepared for and not all the Committee's members were enthusiastic. Some tended to regard the Welsh Office sessions as 'fillers' designed to keep them occupied while the Chairman wrote up the report of a major inquiry. Welsh Office civil servants gave evidence on six additional occasions in the course of the WAC's major inquiries into policy issues. The evidence suggests that when members of the Committee had a policy focus for their questions, they operated in a more convincing fashion. In the first major inquiry, the Committee detected what it believed to be a defect in the Government's administrative arrangements which rendered the Welsh Office vulnerable to advertent or inadvertent exclusions from consideration of national policy matters.[14] The deficiency was denied by the Welsh Office, but one might reasonable assume that steps were taken to ensure that no similar misapprehension recurred.

The Committee had a limited role in the field of financial scrutiny; it looked in a routine fashion at the Supplementary Estimates, but in practice the major responsibility devolved upon the clerk. He examined half-year expenditure profiles against estimated profiles for significant variations and produced memoranda for the Committee explaining the Estimates. Points of clarification were raised with the Welsh Office and reported to the Committee; on one occasion it followed up the issue in a Welsh Office scrutiny session. Normally, however, the Committee adopted the procedure of 'taking note' of the Estimates, an exercise usually fitted into the private business meetings which preceded the formal examination of witnesses.

EVALUATING PERFORMANCE

An overall assessment of the WAC is hampered by a lack of appropriate points of reference. It had no equivalent predecessor against which its performance might be judged and, whereas other select committees are associated with functionally-oriented departments, the WAC's department—the Welsh Office—has territorial, multi-functional responsibilities. Furthermore, the devolution origins of the Committee ensured that it was activated by two aspirations. One, shared by the other committees, was concerned with establishing and maintaining an appropriate balance between the executive and the legislature; the other could be interpreted as preserving national unity. For these reasons, the WAC's existence—as much as its activities—broke new constitutional ground.

There was a strong and widely held view in the Committee that a cross-party consensus offered the most effective mode of operation and that reports reflecting the consensus would have more popular impact and would be taken more seriously by the Government. Thus, despite some misgivings, Conservative members agreed to endorse the Committee's first report although it was highly critical of the Government's economic policies. The decision could be interpreted as an example of territorial interests gaining preference over partisan loyalties. For the anti-devolutionists, however, it was more a reflection of the Committee's determination in the immediate aftermath of the devolution referendum to project and protect the Welsh interest. A commitment to a consensual approach weakened with the passage of time. In its second inquiry, the WAC divided not on the basis of party, but along linguistic lines. Throughout the later stages of the third inquiry, as we have seen, dissent became a persistent feature. Clearly the topic—water is a politically inflammable issue in Wales—and the approaching general election were both factors. While national partisan differences were bound to manifest themselves in the Committee's operations, consensus remained an aspiration, and the Wales and Europe inquiry may be interpreted as an attempt to re-establish the bi-partisan approach.

The Committee aspired to be topical—to investigate those subjects which had an immediate and direct relevance to Welsh politics. No one endorsed this approach more enthusiastically than the Committee's first chairman, Leo Abse, who considered that the Committee's first task was to establish itself on the political map of Wales. But the strategy was vulnerable on two points. A topical political issue is likely to be a sensitive political issue, which can embarrass and antagonize a government and make it less amenable to committee recommendations. On the other hand, topical issues may be transient; an issue of public concern at the start of an inquiry may either be resolved or irrelevant before the committee can make its report. The WAC suffered both experiences but continued to respond to the attraction of current events. For example, the Committee added its voice to the clamour of public criticisms following the publication of the proposals of the Boundary Commission for Wales.[15] The apprehension expressed by trade unions and employers' associations in South Wales that the Severn Bridge was structurally unsound encouraged the WAC to launch a short, sharp, and—because of the general election—abortive investigation into the need for a second Severn Bridge.[16]

The Committee's inclination to opt for topical subjects was allied with a keen instinct for publicity. Part of the explanation for this preference lay with the members themselves. The majority were anti-devolutionists who had campaigned energetically and successfully against the Labour Government's devolution proposals. Their collective experiences during the referendum campaign provided convincing evidence of the efficacy of bypassing traditional institutions and making a direct appeal to the general public. But the Committee also had an attribute which, with the exception of the Scottish Affairs Committee, was denied to the other new committees. In Wales, it possessed a natural political constituency; the Welsh media concentrated their resources on the Committee and its activities. If the Committee were tempted to indulge in 'showmanship', it was because there was a ready and willing audience. Nor was its success in attracting publicity confined to the Welsh media. Its report on *Employment Opportunities in Wales* was the lead story in both *The Times* and the *Guardian*. But it failed to hold a central position on the Welsh political stage. Doubtless the loss of Abse's flamboyant style of chairmanship, the Committee's infrequent visits to the Principality, the lack of a sub-committee system which would enable it to operate more flexibly and respond more rapidly to political events, and the fact that it became bogged down in the issue of Welsh water are all partial explanations. It might also be that the Committee was anxious not to become another parochial Welsh institution.

Like most of the new committees, the WAC sought to acquire a policy-relevant role. The evidence provided by its three major reports indicates that its potential to influence policy resided not so much in its specific recommendations, as in its ability to stimulate and activate public opinion in Wales. This informal and indirect influence on policy is difficult to identify, given the confidential style of British government. However, the Government's intermittent and delayed policy responses to some of the Committee's recommendations suggest that it was not totally immune to this pressure.

Despite its limitations, the Welsh Affairs Committee did evolve a viable role, but not as an alternative to the assembly. The obvious disparity between the Committee's party composition and the balance of political forces in Wales precluded that possibility. Its broad-gauge remit limited the effectiveness of its scrutiny of the Welsh Office and associated bodies, although, as the report on Welsh water revealed, the WAC was quite capable of making telling criticisms of the Welsh Office, if witnesses provided it with the appropriate ammunition.

However, the Committee acquired its most significant role in another context. It became a remarkably efficient means of gathering information on Wales and, in the process, came to occupy a pivotal position at the centre of a network of Welsh social and economic interests. By its very existence, it stimulated the creation of new interest groups and forced existing organizations to clarify their positions. Through its encouragement of written submissions, the publication of memoranda, the publicity of formal evidence sessions, and the juxtaposition of fact and comment in its reports, the Committee helped to create a political dialogue in Wales. Constitutionally, the Committee on Welsh Affairs had a clear obligation to report formally to the House of Commons and, on a more informal basis, to ensure that MPs and the Government were aware of the particular needs and requirements of Wales, but the role it developed in the extra-parliamentary arena was of equal importance.

NOTES

1. Quoted in 'The Welsh Assembly: Questions and Answers'. Labour Party, Wales, October 1975, p. 12.
2. D. Anderson, HC Debs., 26 June 1979, col. 326.
3. HC Debs., 25 June 1979, col. 44.
4. Liaison Committee Report, HC 92 (1982–83), p. 129.
5. L. Abse, *The Role of the Welsh Office and Associated Bodies in developing Employment Opportunities in Wales*, vol. ii, HC 731, 1979–80, p. 9.
6. HC 92, 1982–83, p. 129.
7. Ibid., p. 131.
8. Quoted in *Water in Wales*, HC 299, 1981–82, p. 336.
9. Ibid., p. 340.
10. Quoted in HC 494, 1980–81, 26 November 1980.
11. *The Times*, 1 August 1980.
12. The *Western Mail*, 17 December 1982.
13. HC 92, 1982–83, p. 130.
14. HC 731–1, 1979–80, col. 78–80.
15. HC 494, 1980–81, Resolution of 21 July 1981.
16. Press Notice No. 69, New Inquiry—The Need for a Second Severn Bridge, WAC, 25 November 1983.

Annex 16.1 *Welsh Affairs*

Report	Date of first oral evidence/(no. of evidence sessions)	Date of publication of report	Date and form of govt. reply	Length of report (pages)	No. of oral qq./no. of written submissions	No. of divisions
Session 1979–80						
1st Special Report Sub-Committees, HC 417	—	9.2.80	—	1	—	—
1st The Role of the Welsh Office and Associated Bodies in developing Employment Opportunities in Wales, HC 731	10.3.80 (12)	31.7.80	1.12.80 Cmnd. 8085	39	1772/44	0
Session 1980–81						
1st Supplementary Estimates. Observations by Committee on Welsh Affairs, HC 61	—	18.12.80	28.1.81 HC 122	2	—	—
2nd Broadcasting in the Welsh Language and the implications for Welsh and non-Welsh speaking viewers and listeners, HC 448	22.10.80 (17)	20.8.81	20.1.82 Cmnd. 8469	38	2619/65	1
Session 1981–82						
1st Consumer Representation in the Welsh Water Authority, HC 335	25.11.81	6.5.82	Special Report 27.7.82 HC 499	13	—/3	0
Session 1982–83						
1st Water in Wales, HC 229	25.11.81 (15)	11.5.83	2.2.84 Cmnd. 9138	91	1701/47	33
Other proceedings						
The Impact on Wales of Membership of the European Community, HC 377	16.6.82 (11)	11.5.83 (inquiry not completed)	—	½	1174/32	—
The Need for a Second Severn Bridge.	(Announced 25.3.83)	—	—	—	—/4	—

Part III
Assessment of the 1979 Reforms

CHAPTER 17

The Financial Work of the Select Committees

Ann Robinson

The terms of reference of the new select committees permit them to scrutinize 'the expenditure ... of the principal government departments and associated bodies'. But they have not used their financial powers to undertake regular and systematic inquiries into public spending. Some of the departmental committees, it is true, have made their sections of the annual Public Expenditure White Paper the subject of short reports and some have, from time to time, considered items that appear in their departmental Estimates. (The committees' work on 'financial' reports is tabulated in chapter 18, Table 18.14.) Since 1982–83 the House of Commons has made three days available each session for debates on the Estimates. These debates, based upon reports from the committees, have so far been largely on Supplementary Estimates. The committees have made it clear that they are not prepared to undertake regular and complete scrutiny of the main Estimates each year as a matter of routine.[1] The committees have not shown much enthusiasm for their financial duties. They are unwilling to devote much time to inquiries on the White Paper and the Estimates (generally only one or two evidence sessions, if any) and leave most of this work to their specialist advisers. This is not to say that the new committees have not made a number of recommendations about public expenditure, but these arise as a by-product of the 'policy' inquiries which form the bulk of their work.[2]

There has been no attempt to achieve a co-ordinated approach to the scrutiny of public expenditure by the committees. Each operates as a discrete individual body and its inquiries are not related either to those undertaken by other committees or to the inquiries on overall expenditure and taxation undertaken by the Treasury and Civil

Service Committee (for full details of its work on financial matters see chapter 15). Furthermore, the committees are not invited by their terms of reference to consider the financing of public expenditure through the tax system, and even the TCSC which examines the Budget has rarely made taxation the main focus of its inquiries. Overall, the effect of replacing the Expenditure Committee by the departmental committees has been to retard the development of a systematic critical approach to public expenditure scrutiny which was just starting to evolve towards the end of the 1974–79 Parliament.

The reluctance of British MPs to play the part of scrutineers of the Government's spending plans and their penchant for regarding expenditure as a mere by-product of policy puts them in line with their counterparts in other legislatures. Many commentators have noted that in the era of 'big government', elected representatives are unwilling to take a critical and balanced stance towards the public budget, that they shy away from making allocative choices between public services; and that they prefer instead to act as advocates for special interests who wish to promote higher spending on individual projects and achieve lower taxation for particular groups of tax-payers.[3] The motto: 'redress of grievance before supply' has, apparently, been replaced with a new one: 'supply will redress our grievance'. This phenomenon of modern legislative behaviour is said to arise from the fundamental contradictions which are inherent in the welfare state itself.[4] The expansion of government has created many organized and vocal interests among those who directly benefit from the state's activities, including those who are employed by the Government to deliver its services to the public. Their voices, being better organized and orchestrated, are more clearly heard than are those of the citizen-beneficiaries of the state (its clients) and the taxpayers in general. Any legislature which establishes specialized investigatory committees opens it doors to all these groups by offering them a new public arena in which they can make their claims for resources. But providing a mechanism for the representation of the 'general interest' of the tax-payers and citizens in general proves much more difficult.

How far does this general argument apply to the new departmental select committees? Have they been captured by the producers and suppliers of the welfare state? Are they convenient arenas for making claims for increased public spending? Are the committee members 'lay-critics' or 'advocates'?[5] Can the committees balance the needs of the clients and the general interest of the taxpayers against the claims of special and individual interests? And how far do the committees consider the effectiveness of spending and whether or not the taxpayers get value for money?

When we examine the committees' work on expenditure related topics and their comments on expenditure appended to their 'policy' inquiries, we can classify them under the following heads:

1. Balancing Committees. These balance demands for extra spending against control of costs and value for money.
2. Spending Committees. These appear to be unashamed filters for the demands of special interests.
3. Non-financial Committees. These either concentrate their efforts on subjects which involve little consideration of public expenditure or make no clear judgements either way on the financial implications of their reports.

THE BALANCING COMMITTEES

Defence is the best example of a 'balancing' committee. It began to examine the expenditure of its department from the start, and it was aided in this by being the direct heir to the Defence Sub-Committee of the Expenditure Committee which had established a pattern of work which included regular examinations of Defence spending. Although disrupted by the Falklands War in 1982, the Committee regularly examined the Defence Estimates (the Defence White Paper), and many of its other inquiries were closely concerned with costs. It is significant that the Defence Committee was assisted in its duties by an official from the Exchequer and Audit Department (now the National Audit Office).

The Committee found some difficulties with its terms of reference. When it began its inquiry into strategic nuclear weapons, attempts were made by the Department to exclude considerations of cost from the scope of the inquiry. In fact the Committee missed the boat on this issue, for the Government announced that it was going to buy Trident when the Committee had only just started to collect its evidence. In the event, the report endorsed the basic decision to purchase Trident and confined its criticism to cost. The failure of select committees to make reports on financial matters in good time for debates on the floor of the House is highlighted by this and other experiences of the Defence Committee; similar incidents also affected the Treasury and Civil Service and Environment Committees. The fact that the reports of select committees on financial matters are not specifically tied to debates on the floor of the House means that the Government has never been required to provide information early enough to ensure that a committee can undertake a thorough inquiry and produce a reasoned report to lay before the House in time for the debate. Committees can only exhort the government to produce timely information and the government does not have to respond positively. The 1980 report on the Defence White Paper had to be a rushed job so that material from the Committee could be available to members of the House before the Commons debate. On this occasion the Committee expressed the hope that in future there would be more time between publication of the White Paper and the debate on it. But the Committee's hopes were not realized. Similarly the 1981 White Paper report had to be produced very hurriedly.

Almost all of the Defence Committee's reports have some financial implications. Its work is naturally concerned with costs. It tries to avoid the broad question of the overall cost of defence, for this is an issue that inflames party passions. But the Committee is deeply concerned with the costs of particular policies and items. In this respect the Defence Committee is in an advantageous position, for it deals with an area of government where costs can be measured and set against physical resources (numbers of planes, soldiers etc.). It has fewer intangibles to deal with than does the Education or Social Services Committee. Real effectiveness of defence is, however, rarely put to the test, for it requires real military operations to test a weapons system properly, as the Falklands War displayed. It can be said of the Defence Committee that as a whole it has sought 'better value for the tax-payers' money' (p. 81).

It is also possible to include much of the work of the Industry and Trade Committee in the 'balancing' category. The Committee considered the financing of nationalized industries on several occasions and it does not emerge as an unremitting 'spender'. Indeed, its reports have frequently been critical of the Government's past and present open-handedness towards nationalized industries and have castigated decisions made on political rather than financial grounds. The claimants for funding in industry and trade often have powerful voices but the Committee viewed the Government's funding of some projects with considerable scepticism. It is worth comparing the attitudes taken by the Industry and Trade Committee with those expressed by some other committees on similar topics (for example, the Transport Committee and the Scottish Affairs Committee, pp. 260 and 223). The Committee criticized the Government's decision to keep the Ravens-craig steel site (in Scotland) open. Their report said 'We take the view that [this] was emphatically a political rather than an economic decision' (p. 211). In February 1981, following the Department of Industry's announcement that a further £990m would be made available to British Leyland, the Committee expressed itself as 'gravely concerned at the amount of taxpayers' money being committed to BL', but then added 'Believing ... at this stage HMG was right to provide the funds'. In the case of British ship-repairers the Committee argued that 'tendering at below cost should cease'. The Committee twice investigated the Concorde programme, concluding (as had other committees before it), that the project had acquired a life of its own and was out of control.

The Energy Committee, too, must be regarded as a 'balancing' committee. Like Industry and Trade it examined the operation of a number of nationalized industries which were heavily subsidized and like Industry and Trade it had a Conservative chairman. The Energy Committee questioned the Central Electricity Generating Board's costings and its forecast of future electricity demand, considering them in its report on the Government's nuclear power programme to be both partial and over-optimistic. It also criticized the Department of Energy for not having a clear idea of whether investment in a nuclear plant would be as cost-effective as spending a similar amount on the promotion of energy conservation. Generally the committee was critical of expenditure on the supply of energy but advocated higher spending on energy conservation. It concluded that the Department lacked a strategy for expenditure and that there was an 'imbalance between the scale of resources devoted to energy supply and the much smaller commitments to reducing demand'. It was also critical of government support for uneconomic coal pits. It conducted two inquiries into subsidies to the coal industry and in the second of these— on the alleged 'hit-list' of pit closures—it drew attention to the sizeable coal stocks held by the National Coal Board and the cost of these to public funds. It urged the Board to cut its capacity and stocks and called upon the Department to avoid further subsidies to uneconomic pits. This inquiry was the only one conducted by the Committee in which there was a division on party lines. A Labour member, sponsored by the National Union of Mineworkers, was unable to support the report on pit closures. Burch comments: 'a select committee largely depends on others for information, opinion and assistance, and connections which become too close and familiar may effectively undermine its ability to speak out boldly and impartially ... the Energy Committee managed to maintain a clear degree of independence from its Department as well as party and pressure group influence' (p. 134).

There can be no doubt that the attitudes of the chairmen and the specialist advisers to these committees were important in determining the ability of the committees to keep up a critical approach to the financing of nationalized industries. It is perhaps not without significance that all the 'balancing' committees had Conservative chairmen and that, in the case of the Defence and Industry and Trade Committees at least, they held those positions because the government whips had determined when they were first established that both committees should have Conservative chairmen.

THE SPENDING COMMITTEES

To call a select committee a 'spending' committee does not mean that it never engages in 'balancing' activities but that the general thrust of its reports and recommendations is more towards higher spending on particular items than on oversight, scrutiny, and value for money. Transport makes an interesting comparison with Trade and Industry and Energy in this context. Several of its reports had public expenditure implications, for example on the Channel Link, on the Greater London Council's Fares' Fair policy, and on British Rail. The Transport Committee also looked at the transport sections of the White Paper each year and at the White Paper on roads (two inquiries). In her chapter on the Transport Committee, Ganz informs us:

The Public Expenditure White Paper inquiries are the only occasions when the Committee has examined public expenditure directly. It did not conduct inquiries into the estimates of the Department. The Committee made a sustained plea for more capital investment in transport infrastructure ... the pressure group approach is evident ... (p. 258).

Ganz states that the Transport Committee 'acted as a pressure group asking for more public expenditure untrammelled by the responsibilities of government to suggest cuts elsewhere' (p. 264). This is perhaps not surprising in view of her comment that 'oral evidence is by invitation from selected bodies who are the recognised groups, such as the Minister and the Department, local authorities, transport operators and consumer interests'. She also makes the point that the committee had a Labour chairman (who defected to the SDP), and that all five of the opposition members were sponsored by trades unions, four of them being ex-railwaymen.

The fact that most agricultural funding now comes from the EEC has not inhibited the Agriculture Committee from pressing new needs on the Government. In its report on Less Favoured Areas, for example, the Committee requested the re-introduction of the full lime and phosphate subsidy, the increase of capital grants to 70 per cent, and the inclusion of machinery and livestock in eligible categories. In rejecting these recommendations, the Minister pointed out that they implied heavy demands on strictly limited public sector funds. This sort of reply illustrates that the Treasury does not stand alone as a bastion against pressure to increase expenditure. Here we see an example of a department rejecting outside pressures funnelled through a select committee. The committee appears less as the ally of the department than as a convenient mouthpiece for pressure groups to make public and apparently legitimate claims on the public purse.

The Agriculture Committee undertook several expenditure-related inquiries, including two on the Common Agricultural Policy and two on Supply Estimates. In each of the two latter cases, the Committee confined itself to a single evidence session. Giddings comments: 'No one can be under any illusion that these committee inquiries amount to in-depth investigations of this block of public expenditure. In particular, it is disappointing that outside evidence has not been taken either on priorities within the agricultural programme or on the value for money obtained' (pp. 66–7). Apart from the Department itself, all the evidence presented to the Agriculture Committee comes from groups which have a direct interest in maintaining and enhancing the level of state support for agriculture and agribusiness. The subject of agriculture poses a paradox. Conservatives are generally less inclined to promote extra spending than are Labour members, but agriculture—together with defence and law and order—is an exception. Giddings tells us: 'agriculture is to some extent a "Conservative subject"' (p. 58), and most of the Conservative members of the Agriculture Committee had some connections with the land or farming.

Much more to the tastes of Labour members are the subjects of the great spending departments of Health and Social Security, Education, Environment (which includes housing), and Employment. The whips permitted all these committees to have Labour chairmen. Health and Social Security is now the largest spending department. And the Social Service Committee, the direct heir of the Social Services Sub-committee of the Expenditure Committee (with the same chairman and the same chief specialist adviser), has taken seriously its duty of examining public spending plans. Although only a small part of its total work load, the Committee has conducted a yearly examination of the social services element of the Public Expenditure White Paper. But it has left most of this work to its advisers, and Rush points out: 'Although the Committee has held one or more sittings each session on public expenditure on the social services it can hardly be said that this amounts to an adequate scrutiny of expenditure—perhaps inevitably the distinction between expenditure and policy issues remains blurred. One reason for this, of course, is that the Committee is not directly involved in the process by which Parliament approves public expenditure proposals' (p. 313).

Several of the Committee's other inquiries have had expenditure implications, for example the Health and Social Security Aspects of the Chancellor's 1982 Autumn Statement, the implications of the UGC grants for medical services, and the large inquiry into pensions. But it would appear that only when a financial issue has political implications are select committees willing to move in. As far as social security is concerned, questions about the size and nature of social security benefits may be too dangerous for the Committee's fragile consensus, for they are likely to encourage divisions on party lines. This happened in the report on the Chancellor's 1982 statement when Andrew Bennett (Labour) wanted to insert into the report seven new paragraphs recommending improved social security benefits. This proposal was rejected in a single division on straight party lines. When the Treasury and Civil Service Committee considered the question of the relationship between income tax and the social security system (p. 279), it too found that the subject matter discouraged consensus. These examples show that with an issue that requires decisions about 'more' or 'less' public spending, there is likely to be either a division on straight party lines, or difficulty in achieving consensus. Issues of public spending levels, or the principles of spending, can therefore prove a threat to committee consensus. It is safer to consider expenditure bit by bit and topic by topic.

Large numbers of pressure groups are attracted to the Social Services Committee. It received evidence from professional bodies, trades unions, local authority associations and health authorities, and groups that comprise the 'new poverty lobby'. Rush comments: 'By the very nature of some of its subjects of inquiry, interest in some of the Committee's reports has been largely confined to those professionally involved in or those socially concerned about the particular problems' (p. 250).

In some committees we find a conjunction of interests between those who provide a service, those who are 'socially concerned' and the interests of the members themselves. In the case of the Education, Science and Arts Committee, Rush states: 'Oral evidence was presented to the Committee by nearly 700 individuals, most of whom represented government departments or other organisations ... Professional bodies, including a number of quangos, and pressure groups were the most common presenters of evidence by outside organisations' (p. 96). And most of the committee's members were ex-teachers and some were ex-members of local education committees. 'The interest shown in the Committee by professional organisations and pressure groups was considerable and the Committee provided them with an additional means of making their views known' (p. 101).

Some committees outside the social spending fields were also 'spenders'. The Foreign Affairs Committee was one of these. Its reports were generally expansionary in their recommendations on spending. They recommended a 'substantial' increase of funds to ensure that the number of trainees under the aid programme did not fall, and that action 'must' be taken to ensure the future of bodies such as the London School of Hygiene and Tropical Medicine, the School of Oriental and African Studies, the London School of Economics, and the University of Manchester Institute of Science and Technology. They urged that aid to various countries should be continued and that more money should be spent on the BBC external services. On a few occasions the committee was critical of poor cost control, but it cannot really be regarded as a 'balancing' committee for, as Carstairs says of its scrutiny of the Estimates:

It cannot be said that the results were of much moment or impact, the upshot largely being recommendations on such matters as the handling of the Government Hospitality Fund and the departmental responsibility for the Passport Office. The basic reason for this state of affairs probably lies not in any lack of zeal on the part of the FAC but in the form and nature of the Estimates as they come before the House (p. 174).

The last committee that must be regarded as a 'spender' is Scottish Affairs. Both the Scottish and the Welsh Affairs committees face a rather different task from the other committees for they confront multi-functional departments. The Scottish Affairs Committee has paid considerable attention to the level of public spending in Scotland, usually finding it to be insufficient especially on individual items (many examples could be cited, including the reports on the *White Fish Authority Levy*, the *Closure of Colleges of Education, Rural Road Passenger Transport and Ferries*, the *Ravenscraig Steel Plant*). Kellas and Drucker consider, however, that the Committee has failed to perform a real scrutiny task. 'The enquiries into the public expenditure programme in Scotland ... have shown the Committee at its weakest and the Scottish Office at its most imperious'. They ascribe its weakness to the poor use made of specialist advisers and the diversity of the subject matter. As a result the Scottish Office 'has not been deeply moved by the Committee's annual inquiries into the Secretary of State's public expenditure programme' (p. 228). The Committee seems equally to have been unable to restrain its propensity for advocating higher spending on specific items. 'It can be seen', says Kellas and Drucker, 'as another weapon for Scotland in its fight for a bigger share of public expenditure' (p. 233).

THE 'NON-FINANCIAL' COMMITTEES

Perhaps the best example of a Committee which spent most of its time on topics which were 'political' in focus rather than 'financial' is Home Affairs. This Committee displayed little interest in finance but concentrated on issues like immigration and the SUS laws where changes in policy without changes in budgetary allocations could be recommended. Some of its inquiries, such as that on prisons and that on the Commission for Racial Equality, could be construed as having an expenditure dimension, being concerned with the 'value for money' obtained from these institutions. But the Committee dealt with these issues in a very broad, unquantified manner.

Employment was another committee which largely avoided consideration of public expenditure, even though it did consider the operation of bodies such as the Manpower Services Commission which spend a great deal of money. Any 'expansionary' attitude that it displayed to its subject matter was matched by the attitudes of the Government faced with steeply rising levels of unemployment and the political necessity to spend money on alleviating its effects. Apart from its scrutiny of the Manpower Services Commission's Corporate Plans, however, few of its inquiries were particularly related to money, and even when examining the MSC it was not really concerned with value for money.

Although the Environment Committee monitored a department with a large budget and did undertake several inquiries with a definite financial theme (such as several studies of housing policy and methods of financing local government in the context of the Government's Green Paper, Cmnd. 8449), it is hard to classify it as either a balancing or a spending committee because it rarely came to any firm conclusions. Reiners (p. 156) suggests that in all respects, expenditure inquiries included, it was one of the most lacklustre and ineffective of all the new committees. Its recommendations on local government finance were ambiguous. It did, however, exhibit some capacity for scrutiny, aided by the efforts of its specialist advisers who pointed out faults in the Department's reasoning on the effects of planned reductions in capital allocations for housing. Also, in its first report it criticized the Department for not providing essential information on which to assess the Government's Housing policies.

Unlike its Scottish counterpart, the Welsh Affairs Committee largely avoided direct investigations of public expenditure. It made only one comment (without taking evidence) on Supplementary Estimates, and never attempted to examine the budget of the Welsh Office. Had it been led more firmly towards expenditure-related topics, the Welsh Affairs Committee might—like the Scottish Affairs Committee—have emerged as a 'spender' for, as Jones comments: 'In common with most MPs, the Committee's members, and particularly its Opposition members, were more concerned to increase rather than limit government expenditure' (ch. 16). In its reports, however, it avoided making firm judgements about expenditure, being more focused on the 'political' aspects of its work. In this respect it hardly acted as a pressure group for more public spending in Wales.

CONCLUSION

We should not perhaps be too surprised to find that the select committees have largely avoided systematic in-depth studies of the public expenditure in their departments; that when they have approached the subject of finance it has been predominantly within the context of their broad 'policy' inquiries; and that few committees have been able to resist the temptation to become advocates for their particular function of government or parts of it.

Several reasons have been put forward to explain why MPs are reluctant to engage in hard critical appraisals of public spending. Some of these have come from MPs themselves. Members have frequently complained that the lack of timely and manageable information from the Government prevents Parliament from playing a proper role in the examination of finance.[6] It is also said that Parliament lacks the special financial expertise that is required to interpret the Public Expenditure White Paper and the Estimates so that policy developments can be deduced from the figures.[7] There have been complaints that since Select Committee reports do not have to be—and rarely are—debated on the floor of the House, the committees' financial work is completely divorced from the financial procedures of the House as a whole.[8] All these factors, taken together, have been put forward to explain why any work that the select committees do undertake on finance merely forms part of the general political background against which the Government makes its budgetary decisions. The committees may have a limited capacity to influence the Government but they have no real powers over money.

But even if the financial information provided to Parliament by the Government were to be transformed, if more specialist advice were made available to the House, and if committee reports were invariably to be made the foundation of debates in the House, it is by no means certain that MPs would want to devote large amounts of their time to close critical analysis of the details of public spending or that they would be encouraged to see the revenue implications of their spending proposals. Their natural inclinations, flowing from their concept of the role of a representative, would seem to lead them away from the model of the 'lay-critic' which is essential if Parliament is to scrutinize the Government. They include much more towards the 'advocate' model. What MPs want to do is to display to their constituents and to the groups whose interests they represent that they are working hard on their behalf. The experience of the new select committees in the 1979–83 Parliament indicates that MPs have used them as an arena for this type of representation, and that many find it difficult to stand back in a more critical or balanced stance. Parliamentary procedure is a living entity, shaped by those who use it. If MPs are not, at heart, interested in the control and scrutiny of public expenditure, then all the procedural changes in the world will hardly encourage them to change their attitudes.

NOTES

1. *First Report from the Select Committee on Procedure (Supply)*, HC 118, 1980–81, p. xvii, para. 46.
2. *First Report from the Liaison Committee*, HC 92, 1982–83, p. 22, para. 16. 'In many cases, a "policy" inquiry raises questions about the expenditure involved, so that the distinction between the examination of policy and the examination of expenditure is not always easy to make.'
3. Allen Schick, *Congress and Money: Budgeting, Spending and Taxing*, Urban Institute, 1980. David Coombes (ed.), *The Power of the Purse: The Role of European Parliaments in Budgetary Decisions*, Allen and Unwin/PEP, 1976.
4. Claus Offe, *Contradictions of the Welfare State*, Hutchinson, 1984. See also Rudolf Klein, *The Politics of the National Health Service*, Longman, 1983. Rudolf Klein is a specialist adviser to the Social Services Committee.
5. The 'lay-critic' model is developed by Nevil Johnson, *Parliament and Administration: The Estimates Committee 1945–65*, Allen and Unwin, 1966.
6. Sixth Report from the Treasury and Civil Service Committee, *Budgetary Reform*, HC 137, 1981–82.
7. This point has been made by several members. See, for example, John Garrett, MP Memorandum of Evidence to the Select Committee on Procedure, HC 588, 1977–78, vol. iii, p. 142. Since 1979 some Committees have used specialist advisers to interpret the White Paper and the Estimates for them, and the Defence Committee has employed a member of the Audit Office. But the House of Commons still has no permanent full-time financial specialists like those in the Congressional Budget Office in the USA.
8. *First Report from the Select Committee on Procedure (Supply)*, HC 118, 1980–81. The House has rejected the idea that Select Committees should review the Estimates as a regular part of their duties and that they should be able to recommend changes to the Estimates which would then be debated by the House as a whole.

CHAPTER 18

Resources and Operations of Select Committees: A Survey of the Statistics

Geoffrey Lock

INTRODUCTION

This chapter presents statistics on the 'departmentally-related' select committees which were first set up in 1979. Like the rest of this book, it leaves out of account those committees, such as the Public Accounts Committee, which were unaffected by the 1979 changes. As sources of the statistics, it draws on answers to parliamentary questions, on various printed sources such as the Select Committee Returns and the 1982–83 Liaison Committee Report, and on the annexes to the chapters of this book on individual committees. (The original versions of these annexes were used as a basis for some of the tables; subsequent revisions may have resulted in a few discrepancies between the annexes and the tables in this chapter, but these are unlikely to be substantial.) The juxtaposition of the figures for the separate committees brings out the diversity of their approaches to their task, and the aggregates for the committees taken as a whole indicate the scale of operation of the whole system. Many of the figures in the tables speak for themselves, so there is no attempt at an exhaustive commentary. It may however be useful to draw out some salient points and to discuss both the interpretation and the limitations of the data. In general, figures are given for each committee separately, and, where available, for each of the three officially constituted sub-committees. Totals are also given for the system of departmental committees taken together. On some subjects data are given for the whole period of the 1979–83 Parliament, and on others for the separate sessions or financial years also (if developments over time seem to be of interest).

Information on the following aspects of committees has been assembled in the tables:

The system — the structure of the system and its relation to the previous arrangements, the composition of committees, use of informal sub-committees, attendance, and turnover:

Input into the system and its operation — witnesses, questions, written submissions, Civil Service time, the use of specialist advisers and other staff, meetings for taking evidence and for deliberation, visits, costs, divisions;

Output — reports, financial work, time taken by the Government to respond to reports, debates. (No figures were collected on the number of recommendations or the proportion which were accepted.)

Except where it is otherwise stated, the data refer to substantive reports of committees and exclude 'Special Reports'. The latter are mostly concerned with the administration of the committees or with government replies to subject reports, but special reports issued just before the General Election relate to uncompleted inquiries.

THE STRUCTURE OF THE SYSTEM

Table 18.1 shows a comparison between the arrangements towards the end of the 1974–79 Parliament and the new arrangements instituted in November 1979. The table shows that there were seventeen 'investigatory units' after the election and sixteen before it; half of the latter figure consisted of sub-committees of the Committees on the Nationalised Industries and on Science and Technology. The numbers of MPs involved rose by over 50 per cent and attendance on the whole was higher, though certain committees (Race Relations, Nationalised Industries, Expenditure General Sub-Committee) had recorded quite high attendance figures under the old system. As a result of the enlargement of the pool of MPs participating in committee work, the average size of unit is larger in the new system—8.7 members compared with 6.1 members. The main committees (that is, excluding the 3 sub-committees) are with one exception nine- or eleven-strong, whereas the Expenditure Sub-Committees were in practice eight-strong, if the Chairman of the main committee—who theoretically belonged to each sub-committee, but did not in practice attend—is omitted.

The Table shows that twelve of the seventeen new committees and sub-committees correspond in their subject field to eight old

The Select Committee systems in the 1974–79 and 1979–83 Parliaments

Committees in existence at March 1979	Members	Attendance[a] %	'Departmental' Committees from November 1979 onwards	Members	Attendance[b] %
Sub-committees of the Expenditure Committee			*Committees with previously covered subjects*		
General	9	73	Treasury	11	85
			Sub-Committee	(7)	71
Environment	9	64	Environment	11	68
Social Services & Employment	9	65	Social Services	9	71
			Employment	9	70
Trade and Industry	9	65	Industry and Trade	11	67
Education, Arts and Home Office	9	61	Education, Science and Arts	9	63
			Home Affairs	11	73
Defence and External Affairs	9	63	Defence	11	73
			Foreign Affairs	11	78
Other committees—subjects continued post-1979					
Overseas Development	9	66	Overseas Development Sub-Committee of Foreign Affairs Committee	(10)[f]	83
Race Relations and Immigration	10	75	Race Relations and Immigration Sub-Committee of Home Affairs Committee	(5)	92
Other Committees—subjects as such discontinued post-1979					
Nationalized Industries (and 5 sub-committees)[c]	15	73			
Science and Technology (and 3 sub-Committees)[d]	14	57			
			'New' committees		
			Agriculture	9	71
			Energy	11	63
			Transport	11	65
			Scottish Affairs	13	71
			Welsh Affairs	11	79
Total Members	97[e]			148	

Notes:

[a] 1977–78, actual attendance as a percentage of possible. For the purpose of reckoning attendance at the Expenditure Sub-Committees, the Chairman of the main Committee was ignored.

[b] 1982–83.

[c] Two of 6 members, two of 7 and one of 10.

[d] Two of 7 members, one of 8.

[e] The Chairman of the Expenditure Committee was ex-officio a member of each sub-committee, but is counted once only. Hence this total is less than the sum of the figures shown.   [f] Subsequently declining to 5.

Sources:

Select Committee Returns 1977–78 and 1979–80; HC Debs. 29 July 1983, cols. 632–3 (written answers).

committees. There is a one-to-one correspondence in four cases, and the remaining eight committees in the upper part of the right-hand side of the table correspond to four former committees. Thus over this group of government departments one could say that the investigative machine had been increased, on a simple-minded measurement, by 50 per cent. This increase is offset by the disappearance of the two committees shown at the bottom of the left hand side of the table: the Select Committee on Science and Technology, which—it will be noted—recorded the lowest attendance figure of any committee shown in the table, and the field of which has now been taken over by a Lords Committee, and the Nationalised Industries Committee. This committee had sometimes undertaken 'across the board' inquiries into such matters as consumer representation and ministerial powers, and after its abolition, if alternative arrangements had not been made, there would have been no machinery for such inquiries. The Standing Orders therefore made provision for co-operation between the relevant departmental committees for this purpose; but as no use was made of it, the Liaison Committee recommended its repeal in its 1982–83 Report.[1]

There remains the group of five new committees shown in the Table as having no obviously corresponding predecessors under the earlier arrangements, though large parts of both Energy and Transport were covered by the late Nationalised Industries Committee, and some aspects of the new committees would have been included within the remit of the Sub-Committees of the Expenditure Committee. Agriculture is the reincarnation of a 'Crossman' Committee, wound up after an existence of only two years. (During most of the 1970s, the subject came within the scope of the Trade and Industry Sub-Committee of the Expenditure Committee.) The Scottish and Welsh Committees did not form part of the Procedure Committee's suggested plan, but were incorporated into the system as partial substitutes for aborted assemblies after the abandonment of schemes for devolution. If these two Committees are left out of account, the growth in the number of Members participating comes down to 28 per cent.

The Procedure Committee had thought that there would be a need for some diversity in size of the new committees, depending on their range of responsibilities;[2] and in the event they varied between a membership of nine and thirteen, the Scottish Affairs Committee being the one committee with thirteen members. Of the committees with eleven members, three were to be permitted to appoint sub-committees and four others were among the committees envisaged as contributing to the proposed Sub-Committee on the Nationalised

Table 18.2 *Composition by Party, Turnover, and Use of Informal Sub-committees*

	Composition by party of members at inception			Party of chairman at inception	Turnover[b] 1979–83 overall %	Use of informal sub-committees
	Conservative	*Labour*	*Others*			
Agriculture	5	4		Cons.	44	
Defence	6	5		Cons.	36	Yes
Education, Science and Arts	5	3	1 (PC)	Lab.	11	Yes
Employment	5	4		Lab.	66	
Energy	6	5		Cons.	36	Yes
Environment	6	5		Lab.	73[c]	
Foreign Affairs	6	5		Cons.	64	
Sub-Committee	(5)	(5)		Lab.	67	
Home Affairs	6	5		Cons.	55	
Sub-Committee	(3)	(2)		Cons.	60	
Industry and Trade	6	5		Cons.	27	
Scottish Affairs	7	6		Lab.	77[c]	
Social Services	5	4		Lab.	44	
Transport	6	5		Lab.	18	Yes
Treasury and Civil Service	6	4	1 (Lib.)	Cons.	36	
Sub-Committee	(4)	(2)	(1) (Lib.)	Lab.	86	
Welsh Affairs	6	4	1 (Lib.)	Lab.	27	
Totals	81	64	3	7C, 7 Lab[a]		

Notes:

[a] Exluding the sub-committees.

[b] The percentage change in membership based on those who were members of the committee at the beginning of its existence and who remained members at the dissolution.

[c] As corrected in Chapters 8 and 12.

Sources:

Chapters 3 to 16.

HC Debs. 29 July 1983, col. 633 (written answers).

Industries. The size of sub-committees was determined by their parent committees; the Foreign Affairs Sub-Committee started life as the whole of the main Committee except the chairman, but subsequently contracted.

Table 18.2 shows the party composition of the committees at their inception, with government supporters having 55 per cent of the places, Labour 43 per cent and the smaller parties 2 per cent or three places. The Liberals had two and Plaid Cymru one (not on the Welsh Committee); but as chapter 12 records, the Scottish National Party declined to participate in the Scottish Committee. Chairmanships of the 14 main committees (that is, excluding the sub-committees) were shared equally between the two major parties. It will be recalled that differences of opinion over the allocation of chairmanships delayed the start of the new committee system in 1979 for a considerable time.

SUB-COMMITTEES

The question of sub-committees has been a cause of difficulty between select committees and the Government, as is shown on p. 15 of the Liaison Committee's Report. Only three of the fourteen committees were given the power to appoint a sub-committee, but six of the remaining eleven have expressed their wish to do so (five in special reports to the House and one in correspondence with the Leader of the House), but the Government has refused to budge from its policy of restricting the number of sub-committees. Four committees have evaded this prohibition by the use of informal sub-committees, chaired by a member other than the official chariman. (These Committees are Defence, Energy, Education and Transport.) The committees which are officially permitted to have sub-committees all consist of eleven members, but six committees of the same size do not have this power; nor does the largest committee of all—that on Scottish Affairs, which is thirteen-strong. This committee was not envisaged when the original scheme was drawn up.

On this matter, Mr George Cunningham said:

As a member of the old Procedure Committee, I still hold the view ... that the new Select Committees should be prevented from setting up Sub-Committees, except in the cases which we identified. It is necessary, however, for the Leader of the House to recall that there are two of the new Committees which we had nothing to do with, namely the Select Committees on Scottish and on Welsh Affairs ... The case which we mounted against allowing the other subject Committees to have Sub-Committees freely does not apply to the freedom of those two Committees to have Sub-Committees.[3]

Two of the official sub-committees have pre-determined subjects inherited from earlier autonomous committees—Overseas Development and Race Relations; one—the Treasury and Civil Service Committee—has more latitude in its choice of subject, but has in fact largely occupied itself with Civil Service matters, turning to a taxation subject for the final, but uncompleted, inquiry of the Parliament. Sub-committees are not free agents to the same extent as the main committees: parent committees can decisively influence both the choice of subject and the form of the final report. (Technically, the report to the House is the report of the parent committee.) As the proceedings of sub-committees are not published, the traditional way of showing dissent from a report, or of putting a minority report on the record, is not available in the sub-committee: procedures have to be followed in the main committee if dissent is to be made public.

TURNOVER

The percentage rates of turnover shown in Table 18.2 must be interpreted with some care. For one thing they take no account of the replacement of replacements, so that several changes in the same 'slot' in the course of a period count only once. For this reason, the total number of Members serving on a particular committee during, say, a Parliament might be a better indicator than the turnover percentages shown. Even this may not reflect the attachment that Members have to Select Committee work, since vacancies in committees may result from deaths and promotions to ministerial rank or to the front bench, rather than from resignations stemming from disenchantment. The figures in Table 18.2 show the extent to which committees preserved or failed to preserve continuity of membership (a low figure shows a high degree of continuity), but cast no light on the reasons for the outcome in the case of individual committees.

Over the course of the Parliament, a total of eighty-seven of the Members who had been originally appointed ceased to serve on the committees. Of these, one died, and fifty-three were promoted to ministerial posts or the opposition front bench. Various reasons applied to the remaining thirty-three discharges from the committees— change of party, resignation from Parliament, ill health—and disenchantment with the work is mentioned by monitors in only a few cases. The Scottish and Environment Committees were most affected by changes in membership—with nineteen and twelve changes respectively—and the Education Committee least affected, with only one change during the period.

ATTENDANCE

A point that should be borne in mind on the attendance figures (in Table 18.3) is the practice adopted by four committees of operating at least partly through informal sub-committees (as mentioned in the section on sub-committees above). Under this system, members would be expected to attend certain meetings but not others, and this factor would necessarily affect total attendances both for individual members and for the committee as a whole. Thus three of the four committees at the bottom of the ranking order for attendance over the Parliament were committees operating informal sub-committees. Secondly, the

Table 18.3   *Attendance (Per cent)*

	1970–80	*1980–81*	*1981–82*	*1982–3*	*1979–83 overall*
Agriculture	84	77	80	71	78
Defence	72	72	75	73	73
Education, Science and Arts	71	68	72	63	69
Employment	74	69	70	70	71
Energy	71	66	54	63	64
Environment	69	67	71	68	69
Foreign Affairs	81	69	84	78	78
Sub-Committee	45	75	84	83	72
Home Affairs	92	84	75	73	81
Sub-Committee	89	89	87	92	89
Industry and Trade	84	81	71	67	76
Scottish Affairs	86	78	74	71	78
Social Services	73	66	70	71	71
Transport	73	69	74	65	70
Treasury and Civil Service	92	88	85	85	88
Sub-Committee	75	73	61	71	69
Welsh Affairs	81	75	76	79	78

Source:
HC Debs. 17 November 1982, cols. 176–7 (written answers) and 29 July 1983, cols. 632–3 (written answers).

limitation of the figures pointed out by Lee and Shell in Chapter 11 must also be remembered, namely that 'attendance' is defined as the presence of a member for some part, however brief, of a meeting.

Nevertheless, the statistics present an encouraging picture. It was only to be expected that attendance at some committees would decline over the Parliament—Home Affairs showed the biggest decline, but it started from a high initial percentage. However, mostly rates of attendance held up well, and Table 1 and the Liaison Committee's Report show that the new committees were better attended than their predecessors. Paragraph 5 of that Report shows, for example, that whereas average attendance in 1980–81 was 75 per cent, the figure for 1972–73 for corresponding committees was only 65 per cent.

EVIDENCE

Tables 18.4 and 18.5 include figures on the oral and written evidence received by select committees: Table 18.4 relates just to government departments (strictly defined and excluding quangos)—a major source of evidence for most committees, whereas Table 18.5 covers evidence received from all quarters. The statistics of oral evidence in Table 18.4 are of appearances by witnesses, rather than the number of witnesses appearing: the published figures on the latter subject seem to involve double-counting. (In statistics for the Parliament, the same Minister appearing in four sessions is counted as four witnesses, not one.) However, the aggregation of *appearances* over the course of the Parliament gives rise to no conceptual difficulties, so these were the figures chosen to illustrate this aspect of committee activity. The

Table 18.4   *Witnesses and Memoranda from Government Departments*

| | Totals for the 1979–83 Parliament | | | |
| | Appearances by Witnesses before Select Committees: | | | Memoranda |
	Cabinet Ministers	Other Ministers	Officials	
Agriculture	2	—	73	51
Defence	7	2	397	92
Education, Science and Arts	19	21	140	101
Employment	12	11	41	14
Energy	6	3	73	52
Environment	3	4	45	47
Foreign Affairs Sub-Committee }	9	18	201	{ 202 121
Home Affairs Sub-Committee }	7	16	158	{ 36 61
Industry and Trade	9	11	57	172
Scottish Affairs	6	10	80	67
Social Services	8	8	96	62
Transport	6	3	82	53
Treasury and Civil Service and Sub-Committee	17	4	238	173[a]
Welsh Affairs	6	2	98	24
Total Departmental Committees	117	113	1,779	1,328

Notes:
[a] Separate figures are not available for the main committee and the sub-committee.
Source:
HC Debs. 29 July 1983, cols. 637–43 (written answers).
Figures for each session are also given.

Table 18.5 *Select Committees 1979/80 to 1982/83: Questions, Written Submissions, Visits* *(Numbers)*

	Questions asked[a]	Written submissions received[ac]	Visits	
			Abroad	In the UK
Agriculture	4,365	220	9	11
Defence	10,094	192	10	16
Education, Science and Arts	7,157	595[b]	7	41
Employment	4,011	150	7	16
Energy	5,024	339[b]	5	11
Environment	3,288	632	1	6
Foreign Affairs	3,335	204 ⎱	15	4
Sub-Committee	3,610	263 ⎰		
Home Affairs	5,043	165 ⎱	3	12
Sub-Committee	6,351	370 ⎰		
Industry and Trade	7,966	323	5	4
Scottish Affairs	4,794	182	5	41
Social Services	9,907	368	3	9
Transport	4,463	454	6	7
Treasury and Civil Service	7,540	253 ⎱	1	—
Sub-Committee	2,602	48 ⎰		
Welsh Affairs	7,266	191	3	4
Total—Departmental Committees	96,816	4,949	80	182

Notes:
[a] In connection with completed substantive reports, i.e. excluding uncompleted reports and proceedings such as 'scrutiny sessions'.
[b] In addition, some reports mentioned unpublished submissions without specifying their number.
[c] Including submissions not published. These are deposited in the House of Commons Library. Memoranda from government departments as a category are shown separately in Table 18.4. They are included in the figures of written submissions shown above.
Sources:
Chapters 3–16; HC Debs. 29 July 1983, cols. 633–6 (written answers).

figures show the great variations in practice between committees in the summoning of Ministers, with the Education Committee well to the fore and the Agriculture Committee making the fewest demands. The statistics of appearances by officials reflect not only the number of occasions on which evidence was given, but also departmental variations in practice as to whether one or two officials are sent or a baggage-train in support of the star witnesses.

Some of the chapters on the individual committees have supplementary data on questions—those on the Agriculture, Environment, Social Services, and Education Committees have figures of questions asked by each member, and that on the Welsh Committee gives the percentage of questions in each inquiry asked by the Chairman. The chapters on the Agriculture, Home Affairs, and Treasury Committees have information on the origin of evidence, analysed by types of agency, and the Agriculture chapter also tabulates evidence from lobbies separately.

Where the information is available, the figures of written submissions received include memoranda that the committee did not publish with its papers, but which were simply lodged in the Library. At one time if a pressure group (for example), hoping to give evidence to a committee, was not given the opportunity to give oral evidence, it usually had the consolation prize of seeing its submission published among the committee's papers, and securing some publicity in that way. However, committees are now becoming more conscious of printing costs (see Table 18.12 and paragraphs 77-9 of the Liaison Committee's Report), so the practice of depositing many of their papers rather than publishing them can be expected to develop. In relation to three inquiries of the Transport Committee, 101 were deposited compared with 212 which were published. The Energy Committee, in some of its reports, does not list the bodies or individuals responsible for unpublished memoranda, or indeed say how many papers it received which it decided not to publish. The chapter on the Environment Committee (which recorded the highest figure for written submissions) refers to the high cost to witnesses of the preparation of submissions, and mentions that, in the case of one inquiry—which resulted in an eight-paragraph report—none of the 116 submissions received was published. Memoranda not chosen for publication are not necessarily negligible. In 1959, the Select Committee on Procedure did not publish a paper put in by Professors Hanson and Wiseman, founder members of the Study of Parliament Group, the current members of which have written this book. Hanson and Wiseman were then in some difficulty because, under the rules of the House then in force (they have since been changed), they were not allowed to publish the paper themselves elsewhere.

Some committees believe that the publication of evidence is at least as important as the publication of reports. This matter will be dealt with in the section on reports below.

CIVIL SERVICE STAFF TIME

Table 18.6 includes estimates of the time of civil servants devoted to work connected with the departmental select committees. These are derived from an exercise carried out by the Civil Service Department (as it then was) over a twelve-month period early in the life of the new committee system. Speaking in a debate in January 1981, the then Leader of the House had said that Ministers were 'slightly concerned that the extra cost to Departments was more considerable than had been anticipated',[4] and this inquiry by the CSD provided the

Table 18.6 *Estimates of Civil Servants' time spent on work for Departmental Select Committees, 18 Feb. 1980–15 Feb. 1981*

Grade of officials involved	A Preparation of written memoranda	B Provision of briefing	Man-days Totals Col. A + Col. B
Under Secretary and above	470	715	1,185
Assistant Secretary	927	1,066	1,993
Principal	2,104	2,121	4,225
Senior Executive Officer and below	2,701	1,935	4,636
Total	6,202	5,837	12,039
			Thousand £
Estimated staff costs[a]	673.3	676.7	1,350

Notes:
[a] Including an allowance for accommodation and certain other overheads, as shown in note to Table 18.13.
The figures exclude the time needed for officials' appearances before Select Committees.
Source:
Memorandum by Management and Personnel Office—Review of the Work of the Departmental Select Committees.

facts which made an assessment possible. Two years later, the Liaison Committee commented:

Considerable anxieties were expressed on the subject of increased work-load, though we hear less of the point now that there has been some practical experience of the working of committees ... In any event it is a matter of duty that those who constitute and support the Executive should be publicly answerable for their activities. If an extra work-load derives from a reversal of an old tendency to work too much in private, so be it.

The purpose of the inquiry was to provide a broad-brush assessment of the work-load imposed by the committees. On a rough conversion of the figures of man-days in the table into numbers of officials, the equivalent of about fifty-four officials (in terms of full-time occupation) were engaged on committee work, of whom five were under-secretaries, nine assistant secretaries, nineteen principals and twenty-one senior executive officers or officials of lower rank. These figures refer to the aggregate of all government departments, but the answers to two parliamentary questions indicate the impact of committee work on an individual department—the Foreign and Commonwealth Office, including the Overseas Development Administration. It was stated that in 1983, the equivalent of 1.6 members of staff were engaged full-time on committee work, and that possibly a further ninety devoted some of their time to serving the Foreign Affairs Committee and its Sub-Committee.[5] An earlier answer gave figures of the grades involved, based on the 1980–1 exercise mentioned earlier.[6] This indicated that, in terms of time spent, the equivalent of six officials was involved in committee work—about a quarter of an under-secretary (or higher official), half an assistant secretary, and rather more than two-and-a-half each of principals and SEOs or officials of lower rank. These figures represent about a ninth of the involvement of Whitehall as a whole, and so indicate that the FCO bears an untypically heavy load—reflecting not only the fact that its associated committee has a sub-committee, but also that the department is from time to time called upon to supply memoranda to other committees. The tables of the CSD inquiry show that in the inquiry period, the FCO proper submitted papers to five committees other than the Foreign Affairs Committee, and the Overseas Development Administration to three. Furthermore, Table 18.4 shows that the Foreign Affairs Committee displayed the largest appetite of any Committee for official memoranda, and that, together with its Sub-Committee, it accounted for almost a quarter of the official memoranda submitted to all committees during the 1979–83 Parliament.

On the costs to government departments caused by committees, a 'Rayner' review indicated that a more critical attitude might be adopted:

The restraint imposed by true cost consciousness on both Ministers and officials is unquestionably rigorous ... Select Committees and Royal Commissions may have to obtain their own information, with their own budgets for the purpose, if the information is not available already within the Department, and may have to work without some of the accumulated trend data that has been available hitherto.[7]

On liaison work, the Leader of the House said in 1983 that only four government departments had staff whose time was principally devoted to liaison with departmental select committees—the Ministry of Defence, FCO, and Department of Trade and Industry each having two such officials, and the DES having one.[8]

The cost of Civil Service staff time shown in Table 18.6 is of the same order of magnitude as the cost to the Government of answering parliamentary questions. Based on estimated average costs in January 1981, the latter was put at about £1.4 million a year.[9]

STAFF

Over the years, various committees have commented on the small amount of staff available to them in relation to the government departments which they monitor. For example, the Expenditure Committee said: 'the Committee has not been able to develop its surveillance of Government policies and spending programmes as we would have liked ... The Committee has not had sufficient specialist staff properly to examine, or to call departments to account for policies and programmes.'[10] The Procedure Committee considered requirements for both specialist and generalist staff and recommended increases in both,[11] turning down a suggestion that a solution to the problem lay in an increase in the recruitment of retired civil servants.[12] By early in the new Parliament, these staffing proposals had been implemented and 'when the new committees began to operate ... each did so with a permanent staff of the minimum size recommended by the Procedure Committee.'[13]

The Procedure Committee recommended that the terms of reference of specialist advisers should be widened. This change was made, and the Liaison Committee commended 'the imaginative use which committees have made of their power to appoint Specialist Advisers'. Table 18.7 gives some information on these advisers—the numbers appointed and days worked by them—and Table 18.10 on the costs involved. These advisers are part-time, and they function only in relation to inquiries on which they have expertise; therefore their activity is intermittent. They are remunerated on a daily fee basis in accordance with their academic rank if they are academics (as many of them are), or with their status, otherwise determined, if they are not. The daily fees quoted in 1982 were £50-£70 for professors, £40-£50 for senior lecturers and readers, and £22-£42 for lecturers; expenses were payable in addition.[14]

Thus, the numbers of appointments may give a misleading impression of the use made of advisers, and the expenditure figures are influenced partly by the status of those appointed. The best indicator may therefore be of days worked. The published figures do not cover the short 1982–83 Session, but it may be estimated from expenditure figures that advisers worked about 1,400 days in 1982–83. The amount of use made of advisers differed very widely between committees, with Foreign Affairs making by far the most use and Home Affairs the least. (Indeed in the last two sessions of the period, the Home Affairs Committee made no use of them at all.) From the figures, it does not appear that, for most committees, full-time research staff and part-time advisers were seen as alternatives: four of the six top users of part-timers also had a full-time researcher. These committees were presumably especially keen on research support, and used both the forms that were available. (However, the Foreign Affairs Committee, which was keenest of all on part-timers, did not employ a full-time research worker.)

As shown in Table 18.7, five committees employed full-time research workers—designated 'Select Committee Temporary Assistants'.

Table 18.7   *Specialist advisers and research staff of Select Committees*

	Number of Specialist Advisers appointed in the 1979/83 Parliament ·	Days worked by Specialist Advisers, Sessions 1979/80–1981/82	Number of full-time research staff
Agriculture	5	177	
Defence	9	314	1[c]
Education, Science and Arts	20	745	1
Employment	9	212	
Energy	10	646	
Environment	9	676	1
Foreign Affairs[a]	29	985	
Home Affairs[a]	3	91	
Industry and Trade	6	318	
Scottish Affairs	11	156	
Social Services	15	552	1
Transport	7	235	1
Treasury and Civil Service[a]	28	499	2
Welsh Affairs	10	116	
Total	171	5,722[b]	7

Notes:
[a] including Sub-Committee
[b] of which 1979–80   1,953 days
            1980–81   2,052 days
            1981–82   1,717 days
[c] audit adviser.
Sources:
HC Debs.   7 April 1982 (written answers) col. 371;23 November 1983 (written answers) cols. 479–480; 29 July 1983 (written answers) cols. 644–645.

(The Treasury Committee had two, and four other committees one each. The Defence Committee's audit adviser is in a different category, and will be considered separately.) These members of staff were recruited from candidates in the 28–35 age group with relevant subject knowledge or experience, were graded as either Higher Executive or Senior Executive Officers, and were engaged for two years, extendable to four years. The decision to opt for temporary rather than permanent recruitment might seem to some people to imply a certain scepticism over the permanence of the committee system; but it does enable members themselves to play a part (if they wish) in the selection of committee staff, whereas such participation would not be permissible if Civil Service Commission procedures were to apply, as they do to the recruitment of most of the senior staff of the House. Furthermore, Select Committee Temporary Assistants are employed on terms that for the first time permit the secondment of mainstream civil servants to the service of the House: they can work for a committee for two to four years and then return to their parent department—a possibility that has not previously existed, and of which so far only a limited use has been made. In the past, such a possibility has been frowned on: the earlier Agriculture Committee wrote that they 'consider it of vital importance that their staff should be independent of the Executive— and be seen to be independent'. A system of secondment of a civil servant to the service of the Committee 'would be scarcely fair to the civil servant attached to the Committee, whose future would lie with the Department under scrutiny and whose loyalties would inevitably be divided'.[15] These fears are now presumably regarded as exaggerated.

The third form of support consists of assistance given by the staff of the Exchequer and Audit Department. Two officials from that Department were seconded to the service of the Defence and External Affairs Sub-Committee of the Expenditure Committee from 1973 onwards[16], and the Procedure Committee recommended the development of this practice.[17] Sir Derek Rayner (now Lord Rayner) also advocated the extension of this type of arrangement.[18] However, as Dr Borthwick records in chapter 4, only one official is now seconded; thus the system has not expanded, as had been hoped.

MEETINGS

Table 18.8 shows the variation in the frequency of meetings of committees—from seventy-four meetings during 1979–83 of the Treasury and Civil Service Sub-Committee to 166 of the Education, Science and Arts Committee. Some correlation can be noticed between meetings and the output of reports in terms of pages, as shown in Table 18.14, with the Education Committee at the head of both leagues, and Social Services second for output and third for meetings. It is also possible to see a relationship between a large number of divisions (Table 18.9) and a high proportion of meetings devoted to deliberative sessions rather than to the taking of evidence. The Environment Committee spent almost 60 per cent of its meetings on deliberation (a higher proportion than any other Committee) and recorded the highest number of divisions—indications of a difficult passage for draft reports.

VISITS

Figures of visits made by Select Committees and of their cost are shown in Tables 18.5 and 18.10 respectively. Wide variations in practice between committees are discernible from these tables: the Treasury Committee left Westminster only once during the period, whereas other committees made extensive use of their power to sit elsewhere. Where a resemblance might be expected, for example between the

Table 18.8 *Meetings of Select Committees 1979–80 to 1982–83*

	Evidence Sessions					Deliberative Sessions					Total Sessions				
	1979–80	1980–81	1981–82	1982–83	1979–83	1979–80	1980–81	1981–82	1982–83	1979–83	1979–80	1980–81	1981–82	1982–83	1979–83
Agriculture	16	16	14	13	59	18	8	9	5	40	34	24	23	18	99
Defence	23	21	26	22	92	20	19	14	14	67	43	40	40	36	159
Education, Science and Arts	20	36	30	20	106	25	8	21	6	60	45	44	51	26	166
Employment	21	25	23	15	84	11	8	7	2	28	32	33	30	17	112
Energy	25	19	18	21	83	10	22	22	13	67	35	41	40	34	150
Environment	11	2	13	21	47	26	22	12	9	69	37	24	25	30	116
Foreign Affairs	22	14	20	15	71	12	24	16	12	64	34	38	36	27	135
Sub-Committee	15	12	10	13	50	12	18	24	10	64	27	30	34	23	114
Home Affairs	18	12	15	10	55	14	18	13	8	53	32	30	28	18	108
Sub-Committee	23	17	13	12	65	11	18	9	7	45	34	35	22	19	110
Industry and Trade	24	19	18	11	72	7	19	13	8	47	31	38	31	19	119
Scottish Affairs	18	18	15	16	67	18	15	13	5	51	36	33	28	21	118
Social Services	13	35	23	24	95	21	17	16	5	59	34	52	39	29	154
Transport	30	19	18	22	89	15	15	12	6	48	45	34	30	28	137
Treasury and Civil Service	23	12	22	16	73	22	27	12	18	79	45	39	34	34	152
Sub-Committee	10	7	19	2	38	11	7	6	12	36	21	14	25	14	74
Welsh Affairs	21	28	24	11	84	15	7	5	6	33	36	35	29	17	117
Total Departmental Committees	333	312	321	264	1,230	268	272	224	146	910	601	584	545	410	2,140

Source:
HC Debs., 29 July 1983, cols. 645–6 (written answers).

Table 18.9   *Divisions in Select Committees, 1978/79 to 1982/83*

	Total divisions	Reports giving rise to divisions
Agriculture	19	3
Defence	7	2
Education, Science and Arts	114	6
Employment	—	—
Energy	13	3
Environment	159	5
Foreign Affairs	93[a]	11[a]
Home Affairs	60[a]	14[a]
Industry and Trade	—[b]	—
Scottish Affairs	16	5
Social Services	3	3
Transport	15	4
Treasury and Civil Service	40[ac]	11[a]
Welsh Affairs	32	2
Total—all departmental committees	571	67

Notes:

[a] Of which the following related to inquiries by sub-committees:	Divisions	Reports
Foreign Affairs	16	5
Home Affairs	24	8
Treasury and CS	6	2

[b] One division took place on a special report.
[c] Sixty-seven divisions took place in relation to a special report on an uncompleted inquiry.
Source:
Chapters 3 to 16.

Scottish and Welsh Committees, it may not be found: the Scottish Committee held many sittings in Scotland, whereas the Welsh Committee held few in Wales.

No limit is placed on expenditure on visits within the United Kingdom, but as Table 18.10 shows, these are not particularly expensive. However, committee travel overseas is strictly regulated. The right of committees to travel abroad was finally accepted—after something of a struggle—in 1966[19], and a specific sum was subsequently provided in the Estimates for the House of Commons. In recent years this sum has been £250,000. Responsibility for the House of Commons Vote lies ultimately with the House of Commons Commission, but at their request this matter is administered by the Liaison Committee, who have to approve proposals for overseas visits by each select committee. In the 1979–83 Parliament, expenditure was always well within the prescribed upper limit, the highest figure being £205,000 in the financial year 1982/83.

Table 18.10 *Estimated Costs of Each Select Committee, and Expenditure on Certain Items, 1979/83 Parliament*

	Costs of:			Thousand £
	Overseas visits	Visits in UK	Specialist advisers	Total costs[c]
Agriculture	23	8	18	62
Defence	74	8	30	133
Education, Science and Arts	35	11	57	137
Employment	46	8	14	94
Energy	49	3	45	123
Environment	7	2	32	51
Foreign Affairs[a]	118	b	53	227
Home Affairs[a]	29	2	4	64
Industry and Trade	65	1	27	126
Scottish Affairs	16	19	15	81
Social Services	15	7	50	104
Transport	34	3	16	83
Treasury and Civil Service[a]	17	b	51	111
Welsh Affairs	10	2	13	60
Total—Departmental Committees	539	75	423	1456

Notes:
[a] including sub-committees.
[b] less than £500.
[c] including items not shown.
The figures may not add to the totals shown because of rounding. The table refers to the costs, other than printing costs, shown in the Select Committee Returns.
Sources:
1979–80 to 1982–83 Select Committee Returns; HC Debs., 29 July 1983 cols. 633–6 and 646 (written answers).

COSTS

Figures on the total costs of Committees are not given in any one published table, but have to be brought together from various sources. The sessional *Select Committee Return* shows expenditure by each Select Committee under eight different headings, but it excludes important items of expenditure from its main tables, and its basis changed from parliamentary session to financial year in the course of the period surveyed by this book, thus giving rise to statistical problems. Answers to parliamentary questions can be used to supplement the *Return*. The principal exclusions from the main tables in the *Return* are:

1. Printing and publishing costs, which are shown in the *Return's* concluding table. This table shows the gross costs of HMSO, with no allowance for revenue from sales.
2. The costs of the full-time committee staff employed at the House

Table 18.11 Costs of the Select Committee System by Category 1979–80 to 1982–83

	Sessions		Financial Years			£ Thousand Estimate 1979–83 Parliament[a]
	1979–80	1980–81	1980–81	1981–82	1982–83	
Witnesses' expenses	2.6	6.2	3.0	8.2	6.1	19
Overseas visit undertaken by or on behalf of committees	108.3	144.8	118.7	164.9	204.8	539
Visits within the UK undertaken by or on behalf of committees	24.4	14.5	27.2	11.8	29.7	75
Remuneration of Specialist Advisers	74.2	101.0	95.1	108.7	118.0	423
Expenses of Specialist Advisers	20.4	31.3	26.5	29.8	28.0	
Work commissioned	4.9	0.6	3.5	0.9	2.2	9
Entertainment	0.2	0.7	0.5	0.8	0.3	2
Preparation for publication of the Minutes of Evidence	84.0	90.3	107.4	111.9	127.6	389
Total[b]	319.1	389.3	381.8	437.0	516.8	1,456

Notes:
[a] For basis, see text.
[b] Items may not add exactly to totals because of rounding.

Sources:
1979–80 to 1982–83 Select Committee Returns. HC Debs., 29 July 1983, cols. 633–6 and 646 (written answers).

of Commons, which may be roughly estimated from various sources, as shown in Table 18.13.

3. The cost of civil service staff time, as shown in Table 18.6.

There are other costs of select committees which are not quantifiable from published data, for example costs incurred by the Foreign and Commonwealth Office in looking after committees when they are abroad. The accompanying table brings together the available estimates for 1980–81, as an indication of the broad magnitude of total costs.

Costs of departmental committees, 1980–81

	£000
Costs of items shown in the Select Committee Return	380
Printing and publishing, *gross*	1,540
Civil service time[a]	1,350
House of Commons full-time staff[a]	1,210
Total of items shown above	4,480

Note:
[a] Including some overheads.

This estimate does not include any element for MPs' salaries. It also excludes the substantial costs incurred by organizations other than government departments (and by individuals) in submitting evidence to select committees. Table 18.5 records the total number of memoranda received in the period 1979–83 as 4,949. (This is an understatement, as some committees do not give figures for unpublished memoranda.) Table 18.4 gives the number submitted by government departments as 1,328, so the majority originate elsewhere in the community—in local authorities, quangos, and pressure groups, for example. Thus, over a thousand papers a year, ranging in length from half a page to many pages, are submitted by authors other than government departments, and the compilation of these must be time-consuming. On account of the expense, many of these submissions are not printed (as is mentioned in the section on evidence above), and some are not even listed in reports as having been received.

Too much precision should not be attached to the financial figures in the tables in this chapter. Although costs are shown in the published *Return* to the nearest pound, some items are in fact estimates, as final bills may not have been received by the accounting date; thus there are sometimes discrepancies between the *Return* and later answers to parliamentary questions. More important, however, with regard to my estimates for the 1979–83 Parliament (the last column of Table 18.11), was the change in the period covered by the *Return*. Figures were needed for four parliamentary sessions, but for some items figures were published only for financial years for much of the period. For visits (in the UK and overseas) and specialist advisers (fees and expenses) sessional figures were available in Hansard, but for other items the figures are my own estimates, based on the grossing up of totals for the three financial years 1980/81–1982/83.

The three most important committee costs covered by the *Return* are (as shown in Table 18.11) specialist advisers, the preparation of evidence and overseas travel. All three rose over the financial years 1980/81 to 1982/83, overseas travel the most steeply, though still well within the prescribed ceiling. The Foreign Affairs Committee is shown

Table 18.12   *Printing and Publishing Costs Incurred by Select Committees*

	Sessions		Financial Years		
	1979–80	1980–81	1980–81	1981–82	£ 1982–83
Agriculture	66,240	98,957	50,537	73,590	56,611
Defence	29,520	83,976	26,393	97,958	104,970
Education, Science and Arts	127,440	125,681	148,680	100,697	198,951
Employment	46,800	97,640	61,712	58,170	88,213
Energy	51,840	219,078	184,232	69,078	112,452
Environment	31,440	48,527	31,764	52,759	135,907
Foreign Affairs	98,880	127,334	151,620	62,544	112,288
Sub-Committee	22,080	6,297	18,720	13,118	61,710
Home Affairs	81,120	80,771	71,408	65,594	71,437
Sub-Committee	65,280	49,665	71,130	34,606	55,822
Industry and Trade	62,160	176,471	137,313	78,906	72,147
Scottish Affairs	71,280	76,692	76,049	62,639	79,186
Social Services	158,160	174,666	175,503	128,728	127,260
Transport	51,840	104,145	96,744	49,933	125,622
Treasury and Civil Service	70,560	131,715	108,285	69,652	174,210
Sub-Committee	24,960	22,800	19,440	37,840	50,707
Welsh Affairs	83,520	107,399	106,059	74,759	75,825
Total Departmental Committees	1,143,120	1,731,814	1,535,589	1,130,571	1,703,318

Notes:
The costs of printing and publishing are not borne on the Vote of the House of Commons, but are provided by Her Majesty's Stationery Office on an 'allied service' basis. The figures shown in Table 18.12 are the estimated gross costs, i.e. no allowance has been made for revenue from sales of publications.
From 1980/81, by direction of the House of Commons Commission, costs have been shown for financial years, whereas they were earlier shown for sessions. For 1980/81 costs are shown for both types of period.
Sources:
1979–80, 1980–81, 1981–82, and 1982–83 Select Committee Returns, pp. 42, 48, 48, and 48 respectively.

Table 18.13   *Staffing of Departmental Select Committees*

Posts	Civil Service Grade	Number
Clerk of Committees	Deputy Secretary	1[a]
Principal Clerks[b]	Under Secretary	2
Clerks to Committees	Under Secretary[c]	1
	Assistant Secretary	6
	Principal	7
Assistant Clerks to Committees	Principal	9
	Higher Executive Officer (A)/ Administration Trainee	6
	Higher Executive Officer	5
	Executive Officer	6
Temporary Assistants	Senior Executive Officer/ Higher Executive Officer	6
Audit Adviser	Principal	1
Secretaries	Personal Secretary	17
Other supporting staff:	Clerical Officers	6[d]
	Attendants[e]	3[d]
		76

Notes:

[a] Head of the whole Committee Office, which provides staff for all select committees of the House, not just for the departmental committees. In 1980/1 there were 14 committees other than departmental committees.

[b] Supervising groups of committees, including non-departmental committees.

[c] Acts also as a supervisor of a group of committees, including a non-departmental committee.

[d] Estimated share of the total strength of the Clerk's Department in this grade.

[e] Linked with the paperkeeper grades.

Most of the figures refer to January 1981, but the number of temporary assistants refers to a later date. The table covers full-time staff; figures of part-time specialist advisers are given in Table 18.7.

It is estimated that at salary rates of May 1980, the annual costs of the salaries of this staff was £750,000. Their annual cost was about £1,210,000 on the same basis as the costs of civil servants' time shown in Table 18.6, i.e. with an allowance for the following overheads in addition to basic salaries: superannuation, employer's national insurance contributions, stationery, telephones, postage, small office machines, and accommodation costs.

Sources (inter alia):

The House Magazine, 23 January 1981; *Annual Report of the House of Commons Commission for 1980–81*, HC 385 of 1980–81, p. 31; and *Ready Reckoner for Staff Costs* (HM Treasury).

in Table 18.10 as incurring the most expenditure, but the picture would be changed if printing costs, as shown in Table 18.12, were taken into account. Unfortunately HMSO is unable to estimate revenue from sales of select committee reports, so figures of net printing costs are not available. Nevertheless it is clear that printing costs are substantial, and are probably considerably larger than any of the items covered by the *Return*.

On costs generally, the Liaison Committee, after quoting some average figures for certain items for 1980–81 concluded: 'It is for the House to say if these costs are in any way excessive. It is our view that the benefit has been out of all proportion to the expense, which has been minor and, compared with some overseas legislatures, trivial.'[20]

DIVISIONS

Almost two-thirds of the reports made during the period were approved by committees without any divisions (Tables 18.9 and 18.14). Table 18.9 shows the contrast between committees in this respect—a reflection both of the subject under investigation and of style of operation. One committee (Employment) recorded no divisions at all, and another (Industry and Trade) none on its substantive reports; on the other hand there were five committees in which half or more of the reports involved divisions (Agriculture, Foreign Affairs, Home Affairs, Scottish Affairs and Environment, with Environment having by far the highest absolute number), and another (Treasury and Civil Service) where there were divisions on just under half. As mentioned in chapter 6, the Employment Committee achieved its result, in spite of tackling controversial subjects, by its practice of acknowledging the differences of opinion within the Committee and expressing the views of both sides. (Chapter 11 mentions this practice in connection with the Industry and Trade Committee also.)

REPORTS

The different committees placed varying degrees of emphasis on the reporting aspect of their work, as opposed to the monitoring side. For most of them the reporting side was probably the more important; reports, often substantial, represent the culmination of several months' work and provide a committee with its opportunity to influence policy. As Table 18.14 shows, there was a considerable range in output during the period—from two to twenty-two reports. (Because of the exclusion of 'special reports', mentioned earlier, these figures may in some cases understate the actual amounts of work carried out.) Reports varied also greatly in length: the average for all committees in the period was 22.8 pages, and the average lengths for eight of the committees or sub-committees fall into the twenty to twenty-six page range. At the extremes, average lengths range from less than five pages (Employment) to over fifty pages (Social Services), and this variation obviously reflects a different conception of committee activity.

Eight of the fourteen committees (and one sub-committee) published papers which were not reports as such, but which contained only

Table 18.14 Reports of Select Committees 1979/80 to 1982–83

| | Totals 1979/80–1982/83 | | | | Features of reports | | |
	No. of reports[b]	Aggregate length of reports (pages)	Average response times (days)	Reports debated[c]	Financial scrutiny — Estimates	Financial scrutiny — Public Expenditure White Paper	Evidence-only reports
Agriculture	6	198	110	1	*		*
Defence	13	261	90	(2)	*		*
Education, Science and Arts	19	569	116	—	a	*	*
Employment	11	52	60	1			*
Energy	11	258	86	—	*		
Environment	9	196	95	—	*	*	
Foreign Affairs	12	310	115	(4)			*
Sub-Committee[f]	9	231		(1)			
Home Affairs	8	260	70	1			*
Sub-Committee[f]	12	162		—			
Industry and Trade	19	236	81	—		*	*
Scottish Affairs	8	186	123	e		*	*
Social Services	11	567	125	2	g	*	
Transport	15	355	150	—		*	
Treasury and Civil Service	22	330	87	(7)	*		
Sub-Committee[f]	2	48		—			
Welsh Affairs	6	184	98	1	*		*
Total—Departmental committees	193	4,403	102	6(13)[d]	8	6	9

Number of committees/sub-committees with this feature

Notes:

a Corporate Plans of the Manpower Services Commission.

b Excluding special reports.

c The unbracketed figures refer to reports debated either on specific motions or on the adjournment; the bracketed figures refer to reports mentioned on the Order Paper as relevant to a debate.

d 3% and 7% of reports made, respectively.

e Two reports were discussed in the Scottish Grand Committee.

f Strictly, reports of sub-committees are reports of their parent main committees. These figures refer to inquiries carried out by the sub-committees.

g Aspects of Chancellor's autumn statement.

Sources:

Annexes to Chapters 3–16. HC Debs., 29 July 1983, cols. 633–4 and 643–4 (written answers).

written or oral evidence, or both. The idea was sometimes to give a public airing to a topic on which a committee did not wish to add its own views, for example, the abolition of Industrial Training Boards—a subject considered by the Employment Committee, which several times published evidence unaccompanied by a report. Other papers of this type covered ground on which committees felt that the evidence, perhaps covering a range of topics in one paper, could be left to speak for itself, for example annual scrutiny meetings between ministers and officials and the Education, Science and Arts Committee; and annual financial sessions of that Committee and of the Scottish Committee.

The complementary course—of publishing reports without evidence—was also followed by, for instance, Education, Science and Arts (on two occasions). But the typical committee product remains the report—containing views and recommendations; and evidence—often in supplementary volumes of appendices and memoranda, and sometimes partly in unpublished form.

The Study Group made no systematic attempt to collect figures of recommendations contained in reports, let alone data on the proportions accepted by the Government. In March 1983, the Government declined a request to list committee recommendations that had been accepted, saying that 'this would not be practicable. There have ... been over 130 reports from the Departmental Select Committees since 1979, some containing as many as 100 recommendations.'[21]

However, two chapters contain figures on recommendations, which are of interest because they provide an indication of the final outcome of this aspect of committee work. The figures are:

Government responses to recommendations of:

Response	Social Services Committee	Education, Science and Arts Committee
	(% of total recommendations made 1979-83)	
Accepted	30.3	28.5
To be kept under review	54.5	43.8
Rejected	15.2	27.7
	Number of recommendations	
	132	130

(Recommendations unconnected with the Government's direct responsibilities were excluded.)

Thus, if these two committees are typical, rather under a third of the total of recommendations were formally accepted by the Government.

On speed of response, the official 'Memorandum of Guidance for Officials' recommended that 'departments should do their best to meet the 2 month timetable recommended by the Procedure Committee'. (In para. 6.17 of its report.) 'Where this is not possible, the reply should certainly be provided within 6 months and letters should go to the Committee before the expiry of the 2 month period explaining why the earlier deadline cannot be met.'[22]

Table 18.14 shows that most departments were a long way from meeting the target period of two months for a government reply to committee reports, but the average (of under three and a half months) is reasonably creditable and is an improvement on earlier practice. (In the early 1970s the average time taken was seven and a half months. The longest interval in that period was twenty-two months, but later in the decade the Select Committee on Race Relations and Immigration experienced a delay of more than four years over a reply to one of its reports.[23])

Replies to the Employment Committee were the only ones which were usually given within the target period, but this Committee's reports (under five pages long on average) were very much shorter than those of any other committee. From the figures there seems to be no special reason why the longest response time should apply to the Transport Committee, as its reports were only of average length. The Committee affected by the second-longest response time wrote by far the longest reports (the Social Services Committee).

Only a small minority of reports was debated. As shown in Table 18.14 only nineteen reports, or 10 per cent of the total, were debated directly or indirectly in the House, plus a further pair of Scottish reports debated in the Scottish Grand Committee. The Liaison Committee, writing of a slightly shorter period, puts the proportion of reports debated in one way or another at one in six. 'Many other reports have been substantially covered in debates on government business or on Supply Days. We calculate that 33 reports, or about one in six, have been debated to a greater or lesser extent in this way.'[24] It is not clear from the context if this passage refers to the departmental committees or to *all* committees (including such other committees as the Public Accounts Committee), but whatever measure is adopted, the proportion of reports debated is small, and the Liaison Committee requested an improvement. 'This is a major shortfall in the support which the Government promised (and have generally given) to the select committee system. We request an undertaking from the Government that more days will be made available for these debates in the future, and that they should be regularly spaced out through the year.'[25] In his reply, the Leader of the House said that 'it would, in the Government's view, be inappropriate ... for time on the floor to be allocated in advance of each session to the debate of a fixed number of select committee reports. I would hope, however, that it may be possible in future to provide more time for such debates.'[26]

CONCLUSIONS

One theme that has recurred in many of the sections of this chapter has been the diversity between committees in their approach to their task. The Liaison Committee put the matter thus: 'As committees have come to independent views on how best to carry out their order of reference, they have adopted a wide variety of different styles and this has been reflected in the reports they have made.'[27] Thus committees have varied greatly in the frequency of their meetings and of their summoning ministers; in visits made, both overseas and in the UK; in the number of divisions held; in the length of reports; and in the use of advisers. On these and other matters, uniformity of practice is neither conceivable nor desirable.

Almost 150 MPs are involved in the departmental committees. In the three and a half years surveyed by this book, the committees published almost 200 reports (but only nineteen were debated, directly or indirectly by the House). The reports totalled 4,400 pages and cost about £5 million to print. There were 230 appearances before the committees by ministers and almost 1,800 by civil servants. The committees paid 80 visits overseas and 180 in the United Kingdom. They held over 1,200 evidence sessions, asked almost 100,000 questions, and received about 5,000 memoranda.

The committees had arrived.

NOTES

1. 1982–83 Liaison Committee Report, para. 42.
2. The 1977–78 Procedure Committee Report, paras. 5.53 and 5.54.
3. HC Debs., 16 January 1981, cols. 1704–5.
4. Mr Francis Pym, HC Debs., 16 January 1981, col. 1696.
5. HC Debs., 29 July 1983, cols. 657–8 (written answer).
6. HC Debs., 5 April 1982, col. 246 (written answer).
7. Review of Government Statistical Services—Report of the DHSS Study Team, 1981, p. 26.
8. HC Debs., 29 July 1983, col. 637 (written answer).
9. G.F. Lock in M. Rush (ed.), *The House of Commons: Services and Facilities, 1972–1982*, London, 1983, pp. 18 and 23.
10. Third Report from the Expenditure Committee, 1978–79, HC 163, para. 19.

11. Op. cit., paras. 6.37–6.41.
12. On the employment of retired civil servants, see Lock, op. cit., p. 28.
13. Liaison Committee, op. cit., para. 66.
14. HC Debs., 6 April 1982, col. 332 (written answer).
15. Report of the Select Committee on Agriculture, 1966–67, HC 378–XVII, para. 7.
16. D. Millar in M. Rush (ed.), op. cit., p. 37.
17. Op. cit., para. 6.44.
18. Committee of Public Accounts, 1979–80, *Role of the Comptroller and Auditor General*, Appendices to the Minutes of Evidence, vol. ii, HC 653–vii, p. 74.
19. See M. Rush and M. Shaw (eds.), *The House of Commons—Services and Facilities*, London, 1974, p. 229–31.
20. 1982–83 Liaison Committee Report, para. 76.
21. HC Debs., 9 March 1983, col. 389 (written answer).
22. *Select Committees—Memorandum of Guidance for Officials*, Civil Service Department, May 1980, para. 58.
23. HC Debs., 2 April 1973, col. 25; and the 1977–78 Procedure Committee Report, para. 6.17.
24. 1982–83 Liaison Committee Report, para. 61.
25. Ibid., para. 65.
26. HC Debs., 12 May 1983, col. 446 (written answer).
27. Op. cit., para. 8.

LIST OF STATISTICAL TABLES

1 The select committee systems in the 1974–79 and 1979–83 Parliaments
2 Composition by party, turnover, and use of informal sub-committees
3 Attendance, by session and for the Parliament
4 Witnesses and memoranda from government departments 1979–83
5 Questions, written submissions, and visits 1979–83
6 Civil Service staff time devoted to select committee work, 1980–81
7 Specialist advisers and research staff of select committees
8 Meetings of committees: evidence-taking and deliberative, by session and totals for 1979–83
9 Divisions in select committees 1979–83
10 Costs of each select committee, and expenditure on certain items, 1979–83
11 Costs of the committee system by category 1979–83
12 Printing and publishing costs by committee, annually 1978/80 to 1982/83
13 Staffing of departmental select committees
14 Reports of select committees 1979–83: number, length, response time, debates, and selected features of reports

CHAPTER 19

Scenes from Committee Life—The New Committees In Action

Gavin Drewry

Parliament works for the most part by responding to the actions and perceived inactions of government. It is a mirror in which we can see reflections of aspects of executive activity which would otherwise be hidden. This optical metaphor, like all metaphors, has its short-comings (some might prefer an analogy with the refractive properties of a prism, while others may argue that Parliament itself can, at least on occasions, be a source of light), but it does usefully highlight some of the main limitations of parliamentary action. Mirrors are of limited dimensions and cannot reflect more than a tiny fraction of the universe—any more than Parliament can hope to cover the entire span of governmental responsibilities. They are never perfect and thus they present more or less distorted images of reality: the observer of events through the artificial medium of parliamentary debate must be cautious in interpreting what he sees. And even the best of mirrors can only reflect faithfully, for better or worse, the quality of the objects held before it. If the observer does not like the image that confronts him then he should not blame the mirror. Parliament has its imperfections, but the strengths and weaknesses of parliamentary government are by and large consequent upon the characteristics of the executive machinery to whose actions and products the legislature spends most of its time responding.

Select committees are of course extensions of Parliament. Although designed to sharpen parliamentary scrutiny of the executive, they are, even more than the body of Parliament itself, ultimately reflectors and reactors—striving to influence, scrutinize, and expose, but not to govern. Inevitably they share many of Parliament's own basic weaknesses, or variants of them. Committees have limited angles of vision;

considered collectively, their coverage may leave significant gaps, or give rise to conflict and overlap. They are very small, a feature which may make them more cohesive and manageable (if more vulnerable to disruption by one or two dissentients); but one might ask whether such small bodies can hope to grapple effectively with the diverse parts of a strong governmental machine and claim to speak authoritatively for a legislature of more than six hundred members. There is always a danger that any small group will become introverted and self-important and spend too much time riding its members' hobby-horses. The investigative mode of working of select committees makes them quite different in style from the floor of the House of Commons, which is dominated by an adversarial tradition. The ritualized inter-party bickering that characterizes a lot of proceedings in the Commons chamber has often been criticized. But are not inquisitorial and investigative methods themselves also open to criticism? May it not be, for example, that the choice of subjects for investigation is influenced, and the exercise of scrutiny thereby distorted, by a temptation to choose anodyne topics in the interests of preserving cross-party unity? Do committees have, and deploy effectively, the expertise that is necessary for the sharply focused interrogation of experienced witnesses on their home subject-territories?

Not all these questions can be accorded definite answers. What the preceding chapters provide is a basis for informed discussion. We will begin this overview of patterns of committee activity (one which inevitably overlaps with the statistical survey in the preceding chapter) with one specific problem, not so far mentioned. The committees with which we are concerned reflect the organizational shape of central government—they are departmentally-related. But government departments are, notoriously, diverse entities. They have grown up by 'a continuous process of creation, fusion, fission and transfer';[1] functions are distributed somewhat haphazardly among them; they vary greatly in size and structure; their diversity has even led some commentators to question the definitional status of the term 'department';[2] around them orbits a bewildering array of 'associated public bodies', also the subject of some definitional controversy,[3] which the committees are expected to monitor. Yet these diverse departments are the constituent parts of a monolithic 'government machine'. They are bound together by the constitutional principle of collective responsibility (a shield against parliamentary assault upon any one department); they operate within the financial strait-jacket of Treasury discipline; the Secretaries of State who are the ministerial heads of the main departments are, in strict constitutional terms, joint shareholders of a single office; everything that one department does, and everything that is done to any department, affects—to varying degrees—all the others.

The image of these committees must to a significant degree be a mirror-image of this sprawling and diversified, yet mutually supportive, assortment of departments and departmental satellites. Herein lies at least a partial explanation for the most obvious characteristic of the post-1979 'system' of select committees—the sheer diversity of its component parts.

DEPARTMENTAL LINKAGE

The 1978 Procedure Committee report attributed 'the unsystematic character' of the committee arrangements then in existence largely to the fact that 'the House has at no point taken a clear decision about the form of specialization to be adopted'.[4] Having accepted a widespread view expressed in evidence that committees should scrutinize all government activity, the Procedure Committee plumped for an extension of the organizing principle used in demarcating the boundaries of the sub-committees of the Expenditure Committee: 'The committee structure should in future be based primarily on the subject areas within the responsibility of individual departments or groups of departments'.[5]

The idea of departmentally-related committees goes back at least as far as the Haldane Report on the 'Machinery of Government' in 1918,[6] and probably a lot further. It resurfaced in the procedural debates of the 1960s, when there was much earnest debate about the relative merits of 'departmental' and 'subject' (or 'functional') committees. Although the early experiments with specialist committees in and after the Crossman era attempted to operate the distinction, it was, as the Procedure Committee itself pointed out, largely academic, 'because in practice committees have decided for themselves how to operate and have interpreted their orders of reference with considerable latitude'.[7] One significant, if unsurprising, conclusion to be drawn from the present study is that they still do, and that the new arrangements are still far from being systematic.

The Procedure Committee recognized 'that the boundaries drawn between the responsibilities of the various government departments are to some extent artificial and reflect administrative convenience or expediency as well as natural subject boundaries'. Hence: 'Any system of committees based on the responsibilities of government departments is bound to reflect this sometimes artificial grouping of subjects. We therefore accept that this principle must be tempered by some element of flexibility in the boundaries between committees and by adequate provision for co-operation between them'.[8]

The Committee's recommendation that provision be made for liaison and co-operation between committees was effected at a formal (and largely administrative) level by the setting-up of a Liaison Committee of select committee chairmen and, informally, through the grapevine of chairmen and clerks using 'one of the most vital phenomena of British government, "the chat" '[9] over the telephone or in the tea-room. The necessity for such co-operation is underlined by the fact that most of the departmentally-related committees, at some time or another, took evidence from ministers and officials and representatives of 'associated public bodies' of departments within the primary jurisdiction of another committee. None of the committees was strictly faithful to the 'departmental' principle, though some (for example, Education, Home Affairs, Treasury and Civil Service, and the Scottish and Welsh Affairs Committees) were more promiscuous than others (such as Defence). In some cases, a committee seems consciously to have adopted a relatively narrow focus (for example, Employment and Social Services) while others (for example, Education) deliberately cultivated a wide breadth of coverage; the Industry and Trade Committee spent a lot of time looking at 'associated public bodies', while the Social Services Committee spent relatively very little. House of Lords committees were not designed to be departmentally-related—indeed, part of their purpose has been to plug gaps in the Commons committees' coverage—and have spent a lot of time looking at inter-departmental co-ordination.

Many instances could be cited of overlapping subjects of inquiry by Commons committees. Employment and Home Affairs both looked at aspects of the work of the Commission for Racial Equality and at the law on picketing; the Home Affairs Committee investigated prisons, the Education Committee looked at prison education and the Social Services Committee examined medical education. One does not need to study Clausewitz to recognize the inter-linkage of Foreign Affairs and Defence—as exemplified by the relevance of the Falklands episode to both committees' work.

There were few overt demarcation disputes, nor is there any evidence to suggest that the informal machinery for liaison needs reinforcement, except perhaps in the field of financial scrutiny (see Chapter 17). The Scottish and Welsh Affairs Committees (rather special cases, given their explicitly territorial orientation and their origins in the collapse of devolution policies) are reported to have established only limited links with other committees, and even with each other. Joint inquiries—another integrative device favoured by the Procedure Committee[10]—were not used, and the Liaison Committee has recommended that the express provision for such inquiries in the context of the activities of nationalized industries be repealed.[11] The Commons committees seem to have made no obvious effort to liaise with their House of Lords counterparts (which are organized on 'functional' rather than 'departmental' lines), which seems a pity given that the two sets of committees could probably complement one another by tackling similar subjects from different vantage points (for example, the Commons Employment Committee and the Lords Unemployment Committee).

Several chairmen (notably those of Education, Industry and Trade, Scottish Affairs, and Treasury and Civil Service) noted, in their 1982 submissions to the Liaison Committee, the breadth and/or in some cases (for example, Agriculture) the technicality of their committees' remits, and this has been echoed in many of the chapters in Part II. The apparently narrow remit of the Agriculture Committee, it has been noted, conceals the fact that this subject-area has an extended (and politically divisive) basis in the Common Agricultural Policy of the EEC; the responsibilities of the Environment Committee overlap with those of the Scottish and Welsh Affairs Committees, and include a large local government element; the Social Services Committee is described as having a 'formidable' area of coverage, even though, unlike the Expenditure Committee sub-committee that preceded it, it does not directly deal with employment matters; as for Home Affairs, *res ipsa loquitur*—though the chairman's main complaint to the Liaison Committee was that its terms of reference need *widening*, to encompass the Lord Chancellor's Department and the Law Officers' Department.[12]

The chairman of the Transport Committee complained to the Liaison Committee that the committee's order of reference 'is arbitrarily tied to the responsibilities of the Department of Transport, which are, in my view, themselves too narrow',[13] and he described as 'unfortunate' the linkage between committees and departments given that so many functions—transport being one—cut across Whitehall boundaries.[14] At the same time, however, he noted that his committee's coverage of the Department had been 'selective' and 'neither systematic nor comprehensive', and he argued strongly for a power to appoint sub-committees. This reminds us that the breadth of a committee's remit has not only an *objective* aspect (some departments/subject-areas are manifestly bigger and more complex than others) but also a *subjective* one. Some committees (like Employment) *chose* to adopt a narrow focus while others (like Education) chose to interpret their terms of reference very broadly. And when committees complain about overload, their motives for so doing may sometimes include the wish to secure more resources.

The fact remains, however, that—given their small size, their modest budgets, their part-time membership and, above all, the constitutional realities which constrain all parliamentary activity in an executive-dominated system—the select committees are a small squad of Davids facing an army of departmental Goliaths. The judicious use of specialist advisers may improve the accuracy of their slings; the use of sub-committees, formal or informal, may increase their range and angle of fire; but a shortage of pebbles and the daunting size and proven defensive capability of the target means both that strategy has to be planned with care and that the precise target area of each inquiry must be identified before a shot is fired. Members of the committee must broadly agree that the topic is a good idea—and this necessitates compromises. At the same time, as Ann Robinson noted in her study of the Expenditure Committee, departments themselves impose a constraint upon the range of feasible inquiries given that committees are often dependent upon their co-operation in order to obtain the necessary information.[15] It is to the choice of topics of inquiry that we now turn.

TOPICS OF INQUIRY

And it is here that the diversity of committees is most striking. Geoffrey Lock has suggested in the preceding chapter that the wide variations in the number and length of the reports produced by each committee—not a perfect measure of the overall productivity of a committee—'obviously reflected a different conception of committee activity'. The same can be said of the variety of subjects examined by the committees.

The Procedure Committee, as already noted, recognized the tendency of the pre-1979 committees to interpret their orders of reference 'with considerable latitude'. In recommending that 'the orders of reference of the new committees should ... be widely drawn and should be permissive rather than mandatory in character', the Committee implicitly endorsed this tendency. But it did hint at its own views of the direction in which the pattern of committee scrutiny should develop:

We hope that, as the new committees become established and familiar both with the government departments and agencies with which they deal and the subjects which they are charged to consider, they will develop methods of work which will enable them to respond more speedily to current problems and to new policy proposals in their respective fields. In the long run the departmentally-related committees may well become the 'eyes and ears' of the House in relation to Government departments, drawing the attention of Members to matters which require further political consideration and providing Members with advice and informed comment which can nourish the work of the House in scrutinizing and criticizing the activities and proposals of the Executive. In particular we would expect less time to be devoted in the future to the long and intensive inquiries of the 'Royal Commission' variety which have been favoured by many of the existing select committees, and more to specific analyses of the proposals and Reports of the Government or of other agencies and organizations.[16]

The most that can be said by way of generalization about the subjects chosen for inquiry is that the pattern is both blurred and asymmetrical. Several chairmen in their reports to the Liaison Committee divided their committees' inquiries into neat categories; and some of the authors of chapters in Part II of this book have devised useful typologies of committee exercises. It is probably fair to say, however, that the variety of inquiries militates against any single typology. It should also be said that, while such typologies may be helpful to a retrospective analysis of committee work they do not necessarily reflect any coherent strategic choices consciously made by the committees themselves. Several committees do seem to have arrived fairly quickly at decisions about how best to conduct their work (for example to hold at least one large-scale inquiry in each session and to look each year at relevant parts of the expenditure white paper); but a good deal of activity was necessarily and unpredictably reactive—to departmental policy pronouncements, to legislative proposals, to media stories, and so on.

The committees were in any case, despite some continuity with previous arrangements, forced to feel their way around somewhat experimentally in the early stages. It is evident that they learned some lessons from early experiences, and it is possible that more coherent strategic patterns may be discernible in the continuing work of the post-1983 committees. Meanwhile, however, the observation by the authors of the chapter on the Industry and Trade Committee, that the choice of subjects by that committee was fairly haphazard and not informed by any theoretical analysis, seems to have some general validity—though it would be unfair to criticize select committees for declining to enter into the business of theorizing, a role which they are, manifestly, not designed to undertake.

The chapters in Part II show the variegated pattern of subject choice. The Agriculture Committee, for instance, concentrated upon inquiries 'of the wide-ranging general variety which help to form the background to public policy-making rather than seeking to change its direction'. The Employment Committee eschewed 'Royal Commission' types of inquiry, concentrating upon 'continuing administrative oversight'. Most committees undertook a mixture—though the composition of the mixture varied a good deal—of large-scale inquiries into substantial areas of current or prospective departmental interest, shorter inquiries into continuing aspects of administration and/or finance (there seems in several cases to have been a growing realization of the value of returning repeatedly to the same subject in order to maintain pressure) and responses to sudden crises or outbursts of political and media concern. Rather curious instances of the latter were the interventions by the Education Committee in industrial disputes which threatened the Promenade Concerts and the future of *The Times* Supplements. More orthodox examples of the genre include the Home Affairs Committee's short inquiries into the allegations about deaths in police custody, and into disquieting media stories about miscarriages of justice.

A few 'in-depth' inquiries can consume a disproportionate amount of a committee's limited time and resources: just seven of the Energy Committee's fifteen reports accounted for 95 per cent of published pages. Council house sales dominated the early life of the Environment Committee. The Immigration and Race Relations Sub-Committee of the Home Affairs Committee spent more than a year over its racial disadvantage inquiry, which provided a basis for subsequent investigations. Trends cannot be measured accurately over such a short period. Industry and Trade, after one large (and divisive) 'formative' inquiry into imports and exports at the beginning, moved towards shorter exercises, with an emphasis on the monitoring of 'associated bodies'. Welsh Affairs concentrated from start to finish upon in-depth inquiries, which tended to get larger as time went on. 'Follow-up' inquiries became more important once the committees had done some things to follow up. Although there are indications of an increasing recognition by several committees of the value of such exercises, more of this kind of work might usefully have been attempted.

Several of the committees inherited personnel and areas of inquiry from the pre-1979 select committees. Thus both Defence and Foreign Affairs are characterized in the relevant chapters as immediate successors to the Defence and External Affairs Sub-Committee of the Expenditure Committee. The Defence Committee inherited three members and the clerk and two advisers from the former Sub-Committee, built upon its work, and maintained the 'established liaison system between the Ministry of Defence and a Commons committee'. The Sub-Committee of the Foreign Affairs Committee acquired four former members of the Overseas Development Committee and developed a similar style and approach. The Treasury and Civil Service Committee took over the role of the General Sub-Committee of the Expenditure Committee, and continued the valuable line of communication between the Treasury and the House of Commons that had developed over the previous ten years. The Social Services Committee included both the Labour chairman and one particularly active Conservative member of the Expenditure Committee's Sub-Committee of the same name, and began its work with a follow-up inquiry into perinatal and neonatal mortality. Industry and Trade also inherited members from the corresponding Sub-Committee and followed up some of the work both of the latter and of the Select Committee on Nationalized Industries. The Transport Committee's inquiry into Advanced Ground Transport followed up an earlier exercise by the Science and Technology Committee.

The Home Affairs Committee, on the other hand, displayed little obvious continuity with the former Education, Arts and Home Office Sub-Committee, one exception being its prisons inquiry, which was partly a follow-up to a report by the Expenditure Committee and made use of the same specialist adviser. Its Sub-Committee on Race Relations and Immigration was a direct successor to the select committee of the same title, and continued its work (with five members as compared with the previous committee's ten) though the two former members of the select committee who joined the Home Affairs Committee did not go on to the sub-committee. Agriculture and Scottish Affairs might be seen as descendants of the 'Crossman' committees that came and went in the late 1960s and early 1970s, but the relationship is a remote one.

The marked congruence between the pre- and post-1979 committees may give comfort to those who believe that committees benefit from a continuity that enables them both to build up cumulative wisdom and to follow up work that has been done before. The accumulated products of the work of the old-style committees were not obliterated by the advent of the departmentally-related committees. On the other hand, there can be little comfort in this for anyone who applauded the new committees for being an exciting and radical break with the past.

We have not so far considred *how* subjects were selected for inquiry by these committees, whose terms of reference were deliberately drawn widely to give an almost infinite freedom of choice. Hard evidence is lacking given that the deliberative sessions at which such matters are thrashed out take place in private, and this is true *a fortiori* of any informal exploration and bargaining that occurs beforehand. The interviews used for the chapters in Part II throw some light on the matter and suggest that here, as elsewhere, the keynote is diversity. External factors play a part—the occurrence of events that demand investigation; the willingness of a department (which will be influenced by varying political and other contingencies) to co-operate in supplying necessary evidence. Only very occasionally did inspiration for an inquiry seem to come directly from departments themselves (though they may sometimes have exerted less obvious forms of influence, both negative and positive); ideas came much more often from chairmen and members of the committee and from suggestions from outside. Much depends upon the 'political chemistry' of each committee. And the processes of choosing subjects for inquiry are heavily influenced by the desire of many committees to secure media attention and by the anxiety of most to maintain a continuing consensus. These are matters to which we must return.

MANNING THE COMMITTEES

Select committees are small groups of individual politicians, loosely, artificially and temporarily harnessed together to exercise functions, the precise nature of which is open to a variety of interpretations. The character of a committee, like that of any group, depends very much upon the interactive chemistry of the members who belong to it. The unique political chemistry of each committee, compounded by the diversity of subjects covered by the committee's terms of reference, goes a long way to explaining the patchwork appearance of the 'system' of departmentally-related committees.

Members' backgrounds and extra-parliamentary interests have a considerable bearing upon the orientation and operation of committees, though it is difficult (and no attempt has been made to do it here) to measure systematically the links between such attributes and the behavioural traits of committee members. This calls into question the rationale underlying the proliferation of select committees in a House of Commons which has increasingly recognized the need for division of labour on specialist lines while largely retaining, in the chamber itself, practices based upon a mixture of party discipline and an implicit philosophy of generalism.[17]

The membership of committees—including the backgrounds of members and the inevitable tendency of some members to be much more active and forceful participants in committee work than others—have been discussed at some length in all the chapters in Part II, while various matters such as party composition and the turnover and attendance rates of members have been dealt with in the preceding chapter. We have, in the present chapter, already touched upon the considerable, though uneven, carry-over of personnel from the pre-1979 committees. Chapter 21 includes observations on the role of the Committee of Selection in blunting (though not eliminating) the influence of party whips on membership selection.

As well as noting the incidence and value of previous committee experience, many of the chapters in Part II underline the unsurprising tendency for MPs with 'relevant' background experience to gravitate towards appropriate committees. Thus agricultural interests enjoyed substantial representation on the Agriculture Committee; a lot of ex-teachers found places on the Education Committee; most members of the Environment Committee had had local government experience; several Labour members of the Transport Committee were ex-railwaymen.

Some committee members (including a number of chairmen) had held front-bench office: David Ennals, recently Secretary of State for Health and Social Services, joined the Social Services Committee, while Alex Lyon, a former Home Office minister, was an active member of the Home Affairs Committee; but not all such gamekeepers-turned-poachers (or perhaps it should be *vice versa*) were appointed to committees whose subjects corresponded to their former front-bench portfolios. Some members of select committees were also active on party and all-party back-bench committees, though committee monitors did not note much overt cross-fertilization between these two kinds of specialist activity. Committees also attracted some members who were themselves prominent pressure group activists—Frank Field's membership of the Social Services Committee is one striking example. This may involve the risk of insidious lobbying, but only in a few instances have monitors suggested that outside interests may directly have influenced committee activity. In any case all MPs are, in the nature of their trade, inveterate lobbyists for one thing or another and highly sensitized to axe-grinding by others.

The membership profiles of most of the committees exhibited features that are worth commenting upon. Particular care seems to have been taken in selecting the Labour members of the Defence Committee, which takes a lot of its evidence in confidence and could hardly function at all without the continuing trust of ministers and officials.[18] The Overseas Development Sub-Committee of the Foreign Affairs Committee had some difficulty in retaining a viable quota of Conservative members. The chapters on the Scottish Affairs and Welsh Affairs Committees highlight particular problems arising from the limited numbers of Scottish and Welsh MPs who were available to man the committees, especially as the party balance in Scottish and Welsh constituencies was quite different from that of the House as a whole. Because five of the eleven Welsh Conservatives had government posts several newly-elected MPs had to be pressed into service on the Committee. The need to fill Scottish and Welsh front-bench posts accounts for the high turnover and uneven work-distribution exhibited by both committees. Indeed, appointments to front-bench positions were the main factor underlying the turnover of members on all the committttees and—as the chapter on the Agriculture Committee points out—this erodes the quality of membership since it is often the best members who are promoted.

It is abundantly clear from this study, as from previous work,[19] just how important is the part played by a chairman in setting the individual tone of each committee. Working closely with the clerk, sometimes also with specialist advisers and not infrequently in more or less regular collaboration with one or more senior members of the opposite party, as well as with ones of his own, the chairman takes much of the initiative in key decisions about investigative strategy (for example, whom to call to give evidence), has more influence than most members—though this varies a lot from case to case—in determining the topics of inquiry and normally takes the lead in the conduct of deliberative meetings and evidence sessions, sometimes to the extent of dominating such sessions.

The chairmanships of the departmentally-related select committees and their 'official' sub-committees were shared between the main parties, though as some accounts (for example, those covering Home Affairs, Scottish Affairs, and Social Services) make clear, the election of chairmen, which is a prerogative of the committees themselves, did not always proceed as smoothly as party managers would have wished. Several committees changed chairmen in mid-stream (Defence and Scottish Affairs did so twice). In some instances (Environment, Scottish Affairs, and Welsh Affairs and, *quaere*, Employment) monitors remark upon shifts in the character of committees coincident upon changes of chairman, such as greater consensus and less autocratic chairmanship; but such trends may also be attributable to a committee settling more comfortably into its role as time passes and learning by early mistakes, and to members themselves becoming more self-confident and assertive. The chairman's role may also be affected by (as well as affecting) the subjects of inquiry: on the Social Services Committee the chairman took a markedly dominant role in early inquiries dealing with health matters, but much less so subsequently when the committee moved into other areas. In any case, it is difficult to isolate the chairman's part in the chemistry of a committee from other factors including the turnover of members and

changing perceptions of the committee's role both among those serving on it and those outside (such as departments, pressure-groups and
the media) with whom it interacts.

Notwithstanding considerable variations in styles of chairmanship,
in most committees the chairman played an important part in maintaining consensus among members, making sure that the chemistry
yielded a worthwhile product and that explosions, if they could not
be avoided, were at least muffled. On several committees (for example
Employment, Energy, and Environment) chairmen are said to have
cultivated close working relationships with the senior member of the
opposing party: even where this was not the case, on practically all
the committees consensus-seeking chairmanship was very much in
evidence. We will return later to the issue of committee consensus.

METHODS AND STYLES

Various aspects of the *modus operandi* of committees have been discussed
in the preceding chapter, and some related issues (such as the relationship between committees and departments, media coverage, etc.)
are dealt with in the next chapter, under the heading of 'impact'. A
few specific points are singled out rather arbitrarily for discussion here.

The first is that the requests by many committees to be allowed
sub-committees and the use, to a widely varying extent, of specialist
advisers, both reflect in different ways a desire to compensate for basic
structural weaknesses in the select committee system itself. One weakness, already noted, is the difficulty of covering huge expanses of
governmental activity; another is the problem of getting to grips with
highly technical subjects and of matching the specialist expertise of
the departments and associated bodies under review.

So far as sub-committees are concerned, one can readily sympathize
with the anxiety of committees to broaden their span of coverage. But
sub-committees (both formal and informal) are necessarily very small,
and there may come a point at which such investigatory bodies—
which are, after all, acting on behalf of a large and politically complex
House of Commons—are too diminutive to have either the weight of
authority or the spread of talent to do adequately the job required of
them. The problem of limited available manpower has long been
recognized as a constraint upon expansion of the committee system
and it is arguable that the further proliferation of sub-committees
would undermine rather than enhance the credibility and effectiveness
of the present arrangements. Perhaps lessons could be learned from
the experience of Lords committees in making substantial use of co-
opted members.

Some committees—notably Education, Foreign Affairs, Social Services, and Treasury and Civil Service—made extensive use of specialist advisers. Most of the others were more cautious, having recourse to small, more or less permanent teams of two or three advisers, supplemented on an *ad hoc* basis for particular exercises. The chairman of the Education Committee told the Liaison Committee that he considered specialist advisers to be 'one of the greatest strengths of committees';[20] but the chairman of the Employment Committee felt, according to the committee monitor, that subjects of inquiry 'should be within the grasp of any competent member without the need for elaborate theoretical instruction'. Members of the Home Affairs Committee felt much the same and after making very modest use of advisers in early inquiries the Committee dispensed with them altogether. Both the Scottish Affairs and Welsh Affairs Committees were markedly 'political' in their approach, and this tended to discourage the extensive use of advisers.

The facility undoubtedly has value, though over-indulgent use of advisers (who, in many cases, played a significant part in drafting reports) may distance members themselves from the committee's work. To an outside observer it sometimes appeared as though the Treasury and Civil Service Committee, concerned admittedly with matters of high technical complexity, was working in the shadow of its large team of expert economists. There was a risk that some of its activities would degenerate into a dialogue between the Committee's economists and the Treasury's, with the members acting as observers on the sidelines.

The departmentally-related committees followed the time-honoured methods of oral interrogation, supplemented by written submissions. Nearly all evidence sessions took place in public, though the Defence Committee had sometimes to sit in camera, and the monitors of several other committees (for example, Education, Industry and Trade, Home Affairs, and Transport) report instances of evidence taken in private session. Several committees held informal meetings and visits, and proposed lines and subjects of inquiry were often discussed with departments (the telephone lines between committee clerks and the departmental liaison officers being particularly important channels in this context), though the extent and effectiveness of this obviously depended on the general state of the relationship between committee and department. Excessive 'cosiness' does not seem to have been a by-product of such dialogue. Deliberate sessions of committees, where future topics were discussed and draft reports considered, took place in private, though divisions and amendments are noted in the minutes of proceedings.

Most of the committees took advantage of the facility to travel, both abroad and in the United Kingdom, although, as the last chapter showed, there was wide variation from one committee to another. Apart from travel as such, the Defence and Energy Committees are recorded as having established valued contacts with overseas bodies and international organizations.

Travel has a function in the gathering of evidence, and it helps members to get to know one another, so reinforcing a committee's sense of corporate identity. It also plays a part in taking Parliament, whose home base is hardly situated at the centre of the universe or even of the United Kingdom, to parts that might not otherwise be reached. The Scottish Affairs Committee attached particular importance to its role in promoting political debate in Scotland and held a lot of sittings there; the Welsh Affairs Committee had similar feelings about its role but held far fewer sittings in Wales because of practical problems of travel. The monitor of the Foreign Affairs Committee notes the value of overseas visits by a committee in stimulating diplomatic missions to establish local contacts that might not otherwise be made; he also notes the 'unique' attendance of the local populace at the public hearings on the Falklands inquiry. The Immigration and Race Relations Sub-Committee of the Home Affairs Committee held, and attached great importance to, a number of 'open' evidence sessions outside Westminster—notably those held in several English provincial cities in connection with its racial disadvantage inquiry, and those held in the Indian Sub-Continent in the context of the inquiry into immigration procedures. The importance, both actual and potential, of the 'ambassadorial' role of select committees is considerable, given the vulnerability of the Westminster Parliament to charges of remoteness and insularity.

THE QUEST FOR HARMONY

Many factors contributed to the individualism and diversity of the select committees, but one thing that most of them had in common for most of the time was a clear recognition of the virtues of bipartisan investigation culminating, wherever possible, in an agreed report on the basis of evidence received. In this respect the departmentally-related select committees inherited the established wisdom of their predecessors.[21] The pursuit of consensus does, of course, depend upon a committee's perception of its role as being primarily one of dispassionate and constructive policy analysis and departmental monitoring. The Scottish Affairs and Welsh Affairs Committees, which saw themselves more as forums for political debate

in their respective territories, can be fitted less readily into the consensus model: the Welsh Affairs Committee exhibited increasing
symptoms of partisan tensions as time went on, particularly as the
general election approached; on the other hand, the Scottish Affairs
Committee, after a divisive initial inquiry, eventually settled into a less
tempestuous style under a chairman who actively pursued consensus.

And harmony was by no means the universal rule with the other
committees. Divisions were not uncommon, though—as shown in the
preceding chapter—their incidence varied enormously from inquiry
to inquiry and from committee to committee, and many were not on
party lines. In any case, the number of recorded divisions is at best a
very crude indicator of dissonance: distinctions have to be drawn
between issues of principle and marginal disagreements over grammar
and presentation; several divisions may arise from the antagonism of
one or two members towards one narrow aspect of a wide-ranging
report—as witness, for example, the implacable opposition of George
Gardiner and Jill Knight to proposals for ethnic monitoring in employment in the Home Affairs Committee's massive report on racial
disadvantage. 'Agreed' recommendations may be disputed or even
repudiated outright by committee members at the press conference to
launch a report (examples can be found in the chapters on the Environment, Treasury and Civil Service, and Scottish and Welsh Affairs
Committees). A committee may—as was the case with Employment
and, less markedly, with Industry and Trade—avoid divisions by
producing 'agreed' reports which frankly acknowledge the impossibility of reaching full agreement and set out the opposing arguments
rather than making firm recommendations.

By contrast, however, the Foreign Affairs Committee made no
attempt to accommodate differences through the device of stating on
a divisive issue that (in the words of the committee monitor) 'some
thought this and others that'. Relations between the parties varied
from inquiry to inquiry but although the Committee recorded a large
total of divisions, these were concentrated upon a small proportion of
reports, many were on matters of style and there was a lot of cross-
voting.

With the qualified exceptions of Scottish Affairs and Welsh Affairs,
already cited, the main departures from the consensus rule were on
Education, where party conflict is said to have been of 'intermittent'
importance, and in the early work of the Environment Committee,
which became more consensual after a change of chairman. But even
in these two instances, consensus was the norm, with conflict confined
for the most part to a small number of deeply divisive inquiries. The
Treasury and Civil Service Committee is said to have preserved a

'fragile unity', thanks to a combination of skilful chairmanship, a recognition of mutual interests and the technicality of the subject-matter.

Emollient styles of chairmanship, often manifested in careful cultivation of collaborative relationships with senior members of the opposite party (the emergence of *de facto* posts of deputy chairman or of chairman of an 'informal' sub-committee sometimes helped in this) have been cited by several committee monitors as key factors in the maintenance of harmony. Having reached a consensus about the desirability of consensus, most committees proceeded towards that goal by carefully avoiding topics of inquiry that might be expected to foment discord; this often became translated into an emphasis upon the task of monitoring departmental activities and administrative efficiency rather than straying too far into minefields of substantive policy. These strategies are mentioned as significant in the chapters on Agriculture, Defence, Employment (which, as we have seen, also made a point of avoiding specific recommendations in areas of controversy), Energy, Industry and Trade (after some early controversy), and Social Services. The Transport Committee is depicted as a 'textbook example' of the consensus model, having assiduously avoided contentious topics.

This leaves (apart from some qualified exceptions already mentioned) the Home Affairs Committee which, as its chairman told the Liaison Committee, 'deliberately avoided confining ourselves to "safe" or uncontroversial subjects, despite the risk of producing "split" reports'.[22] And this committee, despite the potentially explosive nature of some of its subject-matter, proved, save in very few instances, to be as harmonious as almost any of the committees—probably a result of a group of members with knowledge of and an interest in the subjects under investigating being willing to work constructively together. And this perhaps—at the risk of begging some questions yet to be discussed in the next chapter—is the best recipe for any successful committee.

But 'successful' in what sense? Consensus is a necessary goal for select committees if they are not to degenerate into arenas for replays in miniature of the inter-party battles that happen every day on the floor of the House. But such consensus can be bought at the high price of excessive blandness and marginality as committees cast around for subjects that will not be too divisive and, at the same time, are not wholly destructive of good relations with the departments from which much of a committee's raw material ultimately derives. This must not be exaggerated. There have been plenty of instances of committees burying their differences in order to pursue large and important subjects which ministers would probably have preferred them to leave alone; but one does have some sympathy with those members who, like Bruce George (cited in the chapter on the Defence Committee), yearn for more opportunities to get their teeth into 'the red meat of policy and expenditure' rather than having to chew their way through repeated helpings of 'the limp lettuce of administration'.

The foregoing comments are extensions of familiar arguments deployed by those parliamentary traditionalists who condemn select committees as cosy, non-partisan cliques, remote from the 'real' world of confrontational politics. Such critics can be silenced only by the production of convincing evidence of the positive achievements of committees and by demonstrations of their effectiveness in furthering the ends for which the House of Commons exists (assuming, perhaps unrealistically, that there is at least a broad consensus about what those ends are). How have committees themselves seen their roles? What has been the impact of committees upon the House itself and upon government? Have their activities made an impression upon informed opinion outside Westminster? These questions are examined in the next chapter.

NOTES

1. A.H. Hanson and Malcolm Walles, *Governing Britain*, 3rd ed., Fontana, 1980, p. 140.
2. C. Hood *et al.*, 'So you think you know what government departments are ...', *Public Administration Bulletin*, 27, 1978, pp. 20-32. D.N. Chester and F.M.G. Willson, *The Organisation of British Central Government 1914-1964*, 2nd edn., Allen and Unwin, 1968, p. 17.
3. See the (Pliatzky) Reports on *Non-Departmental Public Bodies*, Cmnd. 7797, 1980; this is cited at Annex 2 of the submission to the Liaison Committee by the Chairman of the Education, Science and Arts Committee, 1982-83, HC 92, p. 50.
4. 1977-78, HC 588-1, para. 5. 16.
5. Ibid., para. 5. 18.
6. Cd. 9230, 1918, para. 48.
7. Loc cit., para. 5. 16.
8. Ibid., para. 5. 19.
9. Hugh Heclo and Aaron Wildavsky, *The Private Government of Public Money*, Macmillan, 1974, p. 70.
10. Loc cit., para. 5. 20.
11. Loc cit., para. 42. But successive governments have, themselves, tended to treat nationalized industries in an unsystematic way.
12. Ibid., p. 85.
13. Ibid., p. 120. The Department's responsibilities have since been extended as a consequence of a re-merging of the departments of Industry and Trade in 1983; another consequence was that the Industry and Trade Committee was renamed Trade and Industry.
14. Ibid., p. 121.
15. Ann Robinson, *Parliament and Public Spending*, Heinemann, 1978, p. 95.

16. Loc. cit., para. 5. 47.
17. See David Judge, *Backbench Specialisation in the House of Commons*, Heinemann, 1981, especially ch. 7.
18. The same applies to specialist advisers: see *Statement on the Recommendations of the Security Commission*, Cmnd. 8540, 1982, para. 24.
19. Robinson, op. cit., ch. 4.
20. Loc. cit., p. 47.
21. Robinson, op. cit., pp. 127–30.
22. Loc. cit., p. 84.

CHAPTER 20

What Has Been Achieved?

Philip Giddings

Any assessment of an institutional development must begin from an understanding of its purpose. For the new parliamentary committees this is peculiarly difficult to achieve. As has been pointed out in the previous chapter, the committees are but part of the institution of Parliament itself, and while to some extent they obviously share its characteristics, in other ways they are in marked contrast with them. Moreover, since in a system of government which fuses rather than separates the legislative and executive branches the purpose of Parliament itself is a matter of considerable debate, it is hardly to be expected that there would be unanimity about the purpose of its committees. In assessing the impact of departmentally-related select committees, therefore, we have to keep in mind widely differing expectations about their purpose as well as contrasting perceptions of their function amongst the committees themselves.

RATIONALE AND ROLE

The Leader of the House of Commons when the committees were set up spoke boldly and perhaps rhetorically in terms of a radical constitutional innovation.[1] He, and other advocates of the new system, saw it as a shift in the balance of power between government and Parliament, an episode in the Commons' historic struggle to control the executive. But what has actually happened is rather different. It is a marginal, incremental adjustment to one of the features of the complex web of inter-relationships between the House of Commons and Ministers of the Crown in a system of parliamentary government. This does not preclude the possibility that this feature may come to be seen as one small step in a more fundamental shift in constitutional practice. But such a shift was not, in fact, the intention of the authors of this change, has not yet been identified as actually occurring, and if it does occur will be seen to have had its origin somewhat earlier than 1979 in the changing attitudes of back-bench MPs to their role. If perceptions of the role of the back-bench MP are changing, the new committee system is a symptom, not a cause—though as experience of the system affects back-benchers' attitudes, it may also prove to be a catalyst in such a change. Whether a fundamental change in attitude is taking place, we have yet to see—it will certainly need more than one Parliament to provide convincing evidence.

As has been explained in earlier chapters, the rationale of these departmental committees was set out in the 1977–78 Procedure Committee report.[2] It is a rationale of information gathering and informing ('the eyes and ears'), of scrutiny and publicity, of investigation, questioning, calling to account. This the Standing Order makes quite clear with the word 'examine', though the word most frequently used in practice has been 'monitor'. The committees have not been given a role in the process by which the government obtains its legislation (with the rare exception of special standing committees) or its finance or maintains the confidence of the House which is the *sine qua non* of its existence. The committees' operations are thus ancillary to the principal work of the House, for the decisions, whether legislative or executive, are made elsewhere. But it is precisely because the decisions are made elsewhere that the committees are able, albeit indirectly, to exert an influence and to achieve an impact. How extensive is that influence, how significant the impact, we must now consider.

Although we have often referred in this study to the select committee 'system', it has been made abundantly clear, especially in the last chapter, that it is hardly 'systematic'. This is nowhere more apparent than in the committees' own view of their function. Quite simply, they have defined their functions in ways which owe more to their own political chemistry than to any sustained analysis of their given task of examining expenditure, administration, and policy, as the Standing Order puts it. Thus we have found a wide variety of objectives set out by the committees. For example, while the Industry and Trade Committee had no wish to become involved in fundamental and divisive policy,[3] the Scottish and Welsh Affairs Committees saw themselves as part of the 'public relations industry', advocating the claims of their respective countries.[4] While the Defence Committee saw its task mainly as providing information to the House, the Employment Committee was noted as being intent on improving the system of accountability.[5] Similarly, the Energy Committee was intent on establishing the facts and contributing to long-term thinking,[6] while the Treasury and Civil Service Committee was perceived to be a major public forum for discussion of economic policy-making, throwing the light of publicity on what the government was doing.[7] We have noted again and again the stress on the need for consensus within a committee if its work was to achieve anything, and that this imperative has on occasion severely limited a committee's conception of its objective, sometimes becoming the principal objective itself (for example, Industry and Trade, Employment).

Those reports have been amply borne out by the comments of the committee chairmen, which put a great deal of stress on 'influence' as an objective. Thus, the Education, Science and Arts Committee's chairman cites reports designed 'to influence government thinking', 'to influence government policies and spending decisions', and even 'to influence an immediate situation'.[8] More reflectively, the Employment Committee's chairman writes that his 'Committee have considered it to be of first importance to clarify issues and sharpen the detailed exposition of major topical issues of public and parliamentary concern ... I do not consider that we can be a realistic source of coherent alternative policies but we can highlight the issues raised by government policies'.[9] This is significant in a policy field (industrial relations) on which partisan opinion ran very high during the course of the Parliament. In similar vein, the Energy Committee's chairman noted his Committee's belief that it had 'unearthed significant facts and opinions which might not otherwise have emerged'[10] and his Environment Committee colleague referred to 'a closer understanding between Parliament and Ministers' and 'a better informed exchange' at Question Time.[11] Similar observations were made by the chairmen of other committees.[12]

Thus, from the committees themselves and from observers of their work, it is clear that while the form in which objectives have been set may have varied, the committees have in general focused on indirect influence, information, and accountability. No easy measure of their achievements or effectiveness under such heads is possible, given the imprecise nature of such objectives. We shall, therefore, look not at measures of achievement, recommendations accepted or whatever, but rather at the three directions in which such influence is directed— the House, the government, and public opinion—in order to see what effect it has had.

IMPACT UPON THE HOUSE

It will be clear from our account of the committees' rationale that they are not in a position to exert a direct impact upon the principal activities of the House. Assessing their influence must, therefore, involve a subjective judgement about indirect effects. Undoubtedly the committees have produced a mass of material—evidence taken, recommendations made, reports issued—which has ensured a great flow of information, fact, and opinion to the House. No judgement of the quality of that material is attempted here, though the chairmen in the Liaison Committee's report noted varied assessments.[13] Irrespective of their quality, considerable disappointment has been expressed at the failure to have more reports debated.[14] Several have been referred to in debates in which they were not the principal topic, but there is little doubt that that is perceived rather as a consolation prize. Nevertheless, some notable instances of impact upon the House have occurred, such as the reports on the Sus law and on patriation of the Canadian constitution. Such examples show what is possible with an authoritative and well-timed report on an issue on which the government's position is open to change. What has yet to be demonstrated is whether a significant dent can be made in the position of a government which has publicly committed itself on an issue. Subsequent experience with GCHQ suggests not. Timing is thus of the essence—and so often that is not within the committee's control, for it is governments which make decisions and announce them.

In a less dramatic way, there is some evidence of the committees acting in something of a pre-legislative mode and thus being able to affect opinion in government and parliament before it becomes too set. Notable examples here are the Transport Committee's reports on the Channnel Link[15] and HGV/PSV duty,[16] and the Agriculture Committee's report on Animal Welfare.[17] Similarly, the Foreign Affairs Committee's reports on the Moscow Olympics and the BNA Acts could be described as providing 'useful background' to the work of the Chamber as a whole.[18] Whether such reports make any real difference is difficult to say on the evidence. In the HGV/PSV testing case the Government persisted and in the end was frustrated as much by practical obstacles as by political ones. Nevertheless, it is clear that a select committee report can influence opinion in the House, helping to mould that elusive phenomenon—'the mood amongst back-benchers'. That is one reason why governments are concerned to ensure that they are well-managed. If committees had no influence, the whips would not bother with them.

There is also evidence of some impact upon the quality of parliamentary scrutiny at question time, and in adjournment and similar debates. This follows on from the 'ammunition' which the committees provide in their reports, and also from the fact that those putting the questions are better provided with background information and analysis through select committee work—or so the argument runs.

The validity of such arguments is hard to judge. We have not done a content analysis of questions or adjournment debates, nor have we noted evidence of any change in the questioning habits of Members. But it would seem that civil servants have detected a better quality of debate and sharper parliamentary questions. What is beyond issue is that the committees' investigations enable MPs to question ministers at greater length and depth in the committee room than on the floor at question time or in debate, as well as giving them an opportunity to question civil servants and officials of associated bodies which is not available to them in the House. In this respect there has been a marked extension of parliamentary scrutiny. We shall return to this below.

Thus, in terms of impact upon the House of Commons, it would be difficult to argue on the evidence so far that the departmentally-related committees have had a significant direct impact on its major activities, on legislation, debates, questions. The Liaison Committee itself voiced some concern about this in arguing for 'closer ties between the work done by Members in select committees and on the floor of the House',[19] and in seeking an undertaking that the Government would make more days available for debates explicitly on committee reports, spaced regularly through the year.[20]

But to look at debates and questions is to an extent only to look at the surface. For a rounded assessment of the impact of the committees, and one which fits more closely the rationale for their operation, we need to look not so much at what the House does, as at the attitudes, perceptions and expectations Members bring to its work. While we have not done a survey of MPs to test this, there is solid evidence that the committees are having an impact here.

For a decade or more, observers of the parliamentary scene have been suggesting that back-benchers' perceptions of their role might be changing.[21] In part this has reflected the less certain atmosphere of the 1974-79 Parliament in which the Government's majority was at first very small and then non-existent, but in part it also reflected a deeper and longer-standing reaction of increasingly professional politicians to the 'lobby fodder' style of government and the advent of policy issues—like membership of the European Community—which transcended traditional party allegiances. For whatever reason, over the period the ability of governments to rely on the unhesitating support of their back-benchers on every single issue became less secure. Independence, or revolt, is a habit of mind. It is also catching. The enormous emphasis upon party and governmental unity/solidarity has been exposed as a chimera—even defeat of the government did not necessarily produce the cataclysm the whips used to pretend. In consequence, not only do back-benchers know that their front bench is not always right, but it has become very evident that there is no harm in saying so and even occasionally voting accordingly—even in a governing party. The system of adversarial politics does not require monolithic partisan unity in the voting lobbies or in debate: it is, it has become apparent, a system which can well withstand revolt and dissent, even if party leaders find the experience emotionally disturbing.

The significance of that background for the committee enterprise is that inter-party dissent can connect with inter-party consensus. It is evident that most committee members believe that select committees, to be effective, must adopt a consensual style. That can mean avoiding partisan issues, as some have. Or it may mean exploiting the willingness of some back-benchers to dissent from their party's front-bench line. Moreover, just as 'independence' may become a habit, so may cross-party agreement, particularly when it is based on perceptions as constitutionally legitimate as 'control of the executive'. To this extent, the experience of inter-party co-operation and agreement may encourage the habit of dissent from monolithic partisan unity, particularly if it can be dressed up as 'a House of Commons matter'. And there is some evidence that a growing number of MPs perceive their role as much in terms of executive control as in supporting the party programme or the front bench. One must not exaggerate this: party loyalty is still the dominant motive and party solidarity the dominant mode of MPs' behaviour. But signs of the beginnings of a change in perceptions are there, and the development of select committee work—with its emphasis on inter-party consensus and executive accountability—is encouraging that change, not diminishing it. Such changes as these are almost imperceptible except over the period of several parliaments. It remains to be seen whether this one will continue to develop or decline. Experience of the select committees' work will be an important factor in determining which.

IMPACT UPON GOVERNMENT POLICY-MAKING

Turning from the House to the government, we have first to note the imprecise nature of that term: 'the government' may mean in one instance the collectivity which is 'Her Majesty's Government', in another instance a particular minister, in another a part or layer of a department. Parliamentary activity has an impact upon government at each of these levels, but the nature of that impact may not always be the same. At one level it may be principally the increased workload which parliamentary interest engenders; at another level it may be the realization of the political cost of overriding substantial parliamentary opposition in pursuit of a chosen policy objective. Thus for the purposes of this analysis, while constitutionally government is of course indivisible, we shall treat it as a multi-faceted phenomenon—and include associated public bodies as well.

The committees' Standing Order refers to the examination of 'expenditure, administration, and policy'. As expenditure presents special problems, it is being analysed separately,[22] so here we shall focus on policy and administration. More radical advocates of parliamentary reform take as their objective the reversal of governmental policy or administrative decision as a result of parliamentary action. On this view, the need for reform is shown by the absence of governmental defeat or frustration. Such a view of parliamentary reform is not the one which has informed the establishment of departmentally related select committees or the way in which they have operated. It was not to be expected, for it was not sought, that such committees would impose wholesale changes on government policy or administration. The relationship between government and committee was intended to be both more subtle and more complex.

And so it has proved. We have already referred to the varying forms of committee objectives, which are characterized by terms like 'influence', 'constructive dialogue', and 'forum for debate', and thus disavow the cruder forms of policy impact in favour of a monitoring role. Yet, for all that, it is significant that some direct impacts have been achieved. The leading examples, already noted, are the repeal of the Sus law and the patriation of the Canadian constitution, but they do not stand alone. One might also cite the privatizing of HGV/PSV testing or the White Fish Authority levy. In each of these examples there was an impact on the government line. While this is not *characteristic* of the committees' activity, it does show what can be achieved in certain circumstances or, from the whips' perspective, what might happen if one is not careful. Select committee examination and influence is an additional factor which government—ministers, whips, and administrators—have to take into account.

Such an effect is precisely what some of the committees have been seeking to achieve by regular monitoring of departmental activity. The fact of having to give evidence, which is there on the record, concentrates the minds of witnesses. This in itself can result in a reappraisal of current attitudes or policies.[23] And this is not merely a *post hoc* effect. 'Equally important is the deterrent effect on the government of the new arrangements—the knowledge that members are now able, at short notice, to inquire into anything that may arise in the administration of departments.'[24] And if that view from the

Liaison Committee sounds self-congratulatory, it is underpinned by the comments of a senior civil servant on the beneficial effects of the new system on policy-making: 'The knowledge that your department is going to be examined in detail on the background to a policy statement is a great encouragement to be rigorous in formulating your justification for [it] ... one question has become commonplace "how do we explain this particular awkward fact to the select committee?" ' And this is not just a matter of presentation: 'Whenever ministerial decisions are plainly questionable, their weakness is now more likely to be exposed by the committees than was possible when the debate and questioning were largely confined to the floor of the House'.[25]

Several examples can be quoted in support of such opinions, as the committees have sought to contribute their own influence to the complex process of long-term government policy formulation. Thus the Agriculture Committee's report on *Animal Welfare* added to the pressure on MAFF to evolve tougher controls, though it could not be argued that different decisions would have been made without it.[26] Similarly, the Energy Committee was 'pinpointing and publicizing' a bias in departmental policy against conservation and, rather than achieving a change in the broad thrust of policy-making within the Department, the Committee 'did help to concentrate the minds of ministers and officials and to place questions before them about certain apparently neglected areas of energy policy-making'.[27] Or again, the Employment Committee, by establishing itself as an 'interlocutor' rather than seeking to gain major influence on decisions, became 'an accepted point for the exchange of information and arguments between the administration and Parliament' such that the Department was usually willing to make a serious attempt to accommodate the Committee's suggestions, as for example in the reports on the new training initiative in youth unemployment.[28] Or again, the Treasury Committee, anxious to avoid being an irritant to goad the government (not always successfully), concentrated on establishing a dialogue between the Treasury and the House through which the government might be persuaded to change its practices and procedures through the continual chipping away of the Committee at some points—'like a tap dripping away to build up a layer of sediment'.[29] Sir Douglas Wass confirms the effectiveness of this in succeeding in obtaining the release by the Government of estimates of revenue from North Sea Oil tax, forecasts of the likely course of manufacturing output, and details of a number of important assumptions upon which economic policy is founded.[30] This did not change the course of the Government's economic policy, but it did contribute to a better informed debate upon it, and perhaps to a more rigorously prepared defence.

How much weight can be put on such examples? We have noted that public policy-making is a complex process to which select committees are only one of many contributors. Alongside examples of apparently effective influence, we have also seen instances of the direct rebuff—the future of the Civil Service Department,[31] a Minister of State for Rural Affairs,[32] and sales of council houses.[33] Moreover, our assessment of some committees has been one of relative ineffectiveness in policy influence. Of the Employment Committee we have read that there is 'little evidence of its work having a marked impact on either the Department of Employment and its dependencies or on the House of Commons'.[34] Of the Home Affairs Committee, with the exception of the Sus law, the impact on the Government was 'difficult to discern',[35] and the members of the Industry and Trade Committee judged their success not by their impact on government policy but by 'evidence of respect which their activities had engendered',[36] the only explicit example of impact being to contribute to changing opinion on the costs of maintaining the Concorde programme. Of the Scottish Affairs Committee, we read that while it can be said that some changes in public policy were 'forwarded' by its activities, the fact remains that the Scottish Office 'took what it wished from the Committee's recommendations'.[37]

Perhaps the balance of evidence is best illustrated by the Transport Committee. It was able to investigate the Channel Link before the Government made its decision, and so to interpose parliamentary views and comments into the process—a marked contrast with previous decisions on the subject. Its report on heavy lorries, including evidence from the Armitage Committee itself, undoubtedly contributed to the climate of parliamentary opinion which the Government had to 'manage'. And, even more significantly, its investigation of privatizing HGV and PSV testing led to the Government's being forced to back down on the issue. And yet, in spite of those examples, a rounded assessment of the Transport Committee's impact notes that it can at best be part of the input into the continuous process of governmental policy-making. It can gather and publish information; it can provide a platform for pressure groups to comment; it can generate publicity. But, 'if consensus is to hold in Committee, it must eschew power for influence'. Its impact cannot therefore be measured purely in terms of successful recommendations but rather by the longer-term effects of being 'a critical but not hostile watch-dog', keeping decision-makers on their toes, making them think and justify themselves.[38]

It has to be acknowledged, in comment upon that assessment, that while it is indeed undoubtedly true that looking only at the acceptance rate of committee recommendations would be to take too narrow a view, if the position were different and large numbers of recommendations were being accepted in spite of initial departmental opposition, proponents of the committee system would undoubtedly cite this as notable evidence of their powerful impact—and rightly so. It cannot be denied that no such impact has been achieved (nor indeed, as stated above, was it expected). The effect of these committees on ministerial and departmental policy-making has been indirect and marginal, contextual rather than substantive.

IMPACT UPON ADMINISTRATION

Not all government is policy-making. Indeed, it can be argued that the administration of public policy is at least as important as its content. And here there can be no doubt that the departmentally-related select committees have had a considerable impact. There has been a substantial increase in overt accountability. In a governmental system predicated on the doctrine of ministerial responsibility, the mere possibility of parliamentary interest in a decision which might manifest itself in a question or an intervention in a debate is the enduring context of administration. It is the fundamental feature of British administrative culture. The new system of select committees considerably increases the possibility of parliamentary interest and, moreover, does so in a way which could produce a much more probing intervention than an oral question or an adjournment debate. We have already noted the evidence of Sir Douglas Wass on the reality of this. It is supported by the observations of several of our monitors and in the reports of the committee chairmen annexed to the Liaison Committee's report. To quote the chairman of the Employment Committee as an example, 'the Committee has been effective in increasing the accountability of ministers, chairmen of associated public bodies like the MSC, and senior civil servants ... the extension of procedures for enforcing executive accountability is where the Committee sees its principal achievement'.[39] Though it may be accountability rather than control, after rather than before the event, the new system has substantially increased the liability of decision-makers—political and administrative—to answer to Parliament, to explain, justify, defend, and to do so (largely) in public and on the record.

Two elements of that assessment need elaboration. It is a feature of the select committee system that both civil servants and ministers appear before them. As the statistics show,[40] the new committees have made substantial use of their power to examine ministers, civil servants, and the officers of associated public bodies. While the calling of ministers, civil servants and officers of some associated public bodies before select committees was not new, the comprehensive nature of the liability to be called meant that the net of accountability has been cast much wider. The ability of committees which are permanent and control their own agenda to return to topics over several parliamentary sessions is the notable feature—as, for instance, in monitoring the MSC's Corporate Plan.[41] That, coupled with their near comprehensive coverage of departments, has significantly increased the accountability of the administration: the likelihood of individual decision-makers, whether in government departments or associated public bodies, having to explain themselves to Parliament has undoubtedly increased.

The second element of our assessment which needs elaboration is that examination takes place on the record, and (usually) in public. This, together with the opportunity to call witnesses from non-governmental sources, gives the committees power to test the evidence by putting it to other witnesses, particularly expert ones—a power made the more potent when the committees make use of expert specialist advice. What might therefore pass unchallenged on the floor of the House is not so likely to slip through an alert select committee, particularly on an issue which has excited the attention of interest groups. This, of course, works both ways. It is an opportunity for officials and ministers to put on record a reasoned version of the government's view and dispose of comments from critics. And ministers and departments lobbying within Whitehall or Brussels find the committees a useful platform for underlining their case and (they hope) enlisting parliamentary support for it.[42]

If ministers and officials are more extensively held to account, this is bound to be reflected in the Whitehall work-load. Concern about this was one of the major causes of apprehension prior to the setting-up of the committees, and it is still occasionally surfaces (for example, with regard to the number of sub-committees that can be allowed). Various attempts have been made to quantify the effect on the Whitehall work-load: one estimate of £14 million per annum was noted to be broadly equivalent to the cost of parliamentary questions.[43] It seems to be received opinion within Whitehall now that the workload generated has not been as great as many thought, and is not insupportable. The Liaison Committee's robust comment put this issue in its proper perspective. 'It is a matter of duty that those who constitute and support the Executive should be publicly answerable for their activities. If an extra work-load derives from a reversal of an old tendency to work too much in private, so be it.'[44]

On the evidence available to us, the response of the Civil Service to the committees was predictably positive, once it became clear that they are here to stay. There has been virtually no evidence of lack of co-operation, and most have been anxious to exploit the positive opportunities which the committees offer to put the departmental view on record. There is, as already noted, a heightened awareness that decisions might be questioned, and might need to be justified more rigorously. Equally, there has been some disappointment at the perceived failure of the committees to follow up their own work and particularly to exploit expenditure issues—an awareness that the committees' actual performance (for example in the examination of witnesses) has not always been very impressive.[45] On both sides there has been a keen awareness of the dangers of 'cosiness', though, as this study shows, that has not always meant that it has been avoided. The same can be said about the risks of antagonism.

IMPACT OUTSIDE WESTMINSTER

A desire to increase openness in government has been a commonly expressed objective for the committees. It is apparent in the Liaison Committee's report.[46] As we have noted, the taking of evidence has usually offered an opportunity for interested groups to express opinions and make comments upon matters under investigation. Providing a forum for debate on such issues has been a significant achievement for the committees, on issues as diverse as animal welfare, D-notices, and monetary policy. The established interest groups welcomed the opportunity to put their views on record and to offer an appraisal of the evidence of competing groups as well as departmental witnesses. With some exceptions, however, this has not spread much beyond the established interest groups and it is certainly those which have made most impact, no doubt reflecting their greater resources. There has been no significant widening of the policy community as a result of the committees' calls for evidence. What has happened is that more of the debate within that community has been on the public and parliamentary record, rather than in confidential and bilateral exchanges between interest group and department. To quote, for illustration, Ann Robinson on the Treasury Committee: 'Its role is to be the major public forum in which all of those interested in improving the quality of economic policy-making can state their case'—and, one might add, have it answered—'. . . it throws the light of publicity on the Government's acts'.[47]

   Publicity means media attention. The concern of the committees about lack of coverage in the national media has made some observers wonder whether it was because the Government and the House were not paying the committees attention that they were seeking it in the press. The media, of course, like a row and are not much concerned whether it is between members of a committee at a press conference, between a committee and recalcitrant witnesses, or between a committee and the government. This is bound to mean that the froth rather than the substance of committee work is what is generally reported. By contrast, coverage in the specialist press has been considered good and it is this, insofar as it contributes to opinion formation within departments, which can enable committees to influence policy formation. Publicity is one of the few levers the committees have in the process of policy-making and administration. Since they are not an integral part of the decision-making process even within the House itself, their impact upon that process can only come through making themselves, and their doings, known. Given the very limited time made available for committee reports to be debated, they are dependent upon publicity for making themselves known and especially for getting themselves noticed by other MPs and by government. But what attracts the attention of the media (for example, a row) may not be what impresses fellow MPs or ministers and their advisers.[48] The weighty and authoritative report which might impress the latter, while not likely to attract much attention in the national media, may through the specialist press have a significant influence on the thinking of departments, particularly if it stimulates reaction from interest groups.

An alternative response to this is the short, sharp report on a topical issue. But that is a tactic fraught with danger. The exercise of producing an agreed report, or even just taking and publishing evidence, can hardly be quick: the more controversial an item, the less likely it is that agreement can be reached, even on terms of reference for the inquiry. Moreover, with speed there is always the danger of superficiality. But above all there is always the risk that events, or government decisions, will overtake a committee's work, so that what seemed likely to be topical proves to be about yesterday's news. Nevertheless, some committees have overcome these risks and produced reports successful at least in the sense of being well timed. The Treasury Committee has produced, albeit with the aid of a photocopier,[49] a series of reports on the Chancellor's Budget and Autumn Review statements in time for debate in the House. The Education Committee produced reports on the Promenade Concerts and *The Times* Supplements, as well as interim reports on specific issues on funding of the Arts.[50]

AN ASSESSMENT

It will be evident from the foregoing that the committees have not changed the basic patterns and relationships of British parliamentary government. Their creation was an opportunity to improve accountability and increase parliamentary input into the background of public decision-making. While the committees have not worked systematically and their performance on their disparate chosen themes has been uneven, it cannot on the evidence be doubted that increased accountability of government has been the main outcome. Whether that has led to a better quality of decision-making is an open question, as is whether the increase in information and comment available to the House has improved the quality of its debates and legislation. But through small groups of Members, in a variety of ways, on a variety of themes, the ability of the House of Commons to require ministers and public servants to give an account of their activities has been increased. Accordingly, those ministers and public servants have added the select committees to the complex demands and pressures to which they must respond in policy-making and administration. The committees are by no means the most significant part of that complex most of the time. But they are there—'a cloud no bigger than a man's hand'.[51]

NOTES

1. HC Debs., 25 June 1979, col. 35.
2. First Report, HC 588, 1977–78.
3. Chapter 11.
4. Chapter 12, p. 232.
5. Chapter 4, p. 80, Chapter 6, p. 111.
6. Chapter 7, p. 129.
7. Chapter 15, p. 281.
8. Liaison Committee, First Report, *The Select Committee System*, HC 92, 1982–83, (henceforward, Liaison Committee) pp. 47–48.
9. Ibid., p. 56.
10. Ibid., pp. 64–5.
11. Ibid., p. 73.
12. E.g. Home Affairs, ibid., p. 84, para. 7; Industry and Trade, ibid., p. 88; Scottish Affairs, ibid., p. 109; Social Services, ibid., p. 112, para. 6; Welsh Affairs, ibid., p. 129.
13. E.g. ibid., p. 64, para. 4 (Energy); p. 72, para. 5 (Environment); p. 79, para. 2 (Foreign Affairs); p. 88, paras. 6–8 (Industry and Trade).
14. Ibid., p. 20, paras. 63–5.
15. Chapter 14, p. 262.
16. Ibid., pp. 259–60 and 262.
17. Chapter 3, p. 62.
18. Liaison Committee, p. 79, para. 2.
19. Ibid., p. 26, para. 94.
20. Ibid., p. 21, para. 65.
21. See, for example, the writings of Philip Norton and David Judge.
22. Supra, Chapter 17.

23. A point noted by several monitors: see, e.g. p. 215.
24. Liaison Committee, p. 10, para. 14.
25. Sir Douglas Wass, Reith Lecture, no. IV, The *Listener*, 8 December 1983.
26. Chapter 3, p. 63.
27. Chapter 7, pp. 138 and 139.
28. Chapter 6, pp. 120 and 121.
29. Chapter 15
30. The *Listener*, 8 December 1983.
31. HC 54, 1980-81.
32. Chapter 3, p. 64.
33. Chapter 8, pp. 153-4.
34. Chapter 6, p. 120.
35. Chapter 10, p. 197.
36. Chapter 11, p. 215.
37. Chapter 12, p. 232.
38. Chapter 14, pp. 263-4.
39. Liaison Committee, p. 57.
40. Chapter 18, Tables 18.4 and 18.6.
41. Chapter 6, p. 112.
42. E.g. Scottish Affairs (Ravenscraig) and Agriculture (Dairy Policy and Horticulture).
43. Supra, Chapter 18.
44. Liaison Committee, p. 10, para. 15.
45. Sir Douglas Wass, The *Listener*, 8 December 1983.
46. Liaison Committee, pp. 9-10, paras. 10, 14, and 15.
47. Chapter 15, p. 284.
48. Ibid. pp. 281-2.
49. See their footnote, Liaison Committee, p. 127.
50. Liaison Committee, p. 48.
51. 1 Kings 18:14.

CHAPTER 21

The 1979 Reforms—New Labels On Old Bottles?

Gavin Drewry

No procedural reform can be assessed in isolation from its context. The establishment of the new committees in 1979 was, as we have stressed from the outset, an episode in a long evolutionary process. The departmentally-related committees inherited and built upon the work of earlier committees—in particular the Expenditure Committee—just as the latter had, in its time, taken on and expanded the roles of the Estimates Committee and the 'Crossman' specialist committees of the 1960s. It is beyond dispute that the post-1979 arrangements, even if they still fall short of being a comprehensive and coherent committee system, are much tidier than those they replaced; and they have also been given additional resources and a degree of permanency denied to their predecessors. But, given the evolutionary character of the 1979 reforms, it is not at all surprising that some of our conclusions have echoed those reached in previous studies of select committees. Indeed it might be concluded that the Stevas reforms were purely cosmetic—a case of relabelling old bottles whose contents had gone stale.

Is such a dismissive verdict upon the 1979 reforms a fair one? Our own broad conclusion is that it is not, but the task of demonstrating this is far from straightforward. This is partly because of the lack of a consensual basis from which to arrive at clear-cut judgements: views about committees differ according to the observer's standpoint and must vary, in any case, from committee to committee. It is also because the evolution of select committees, as well as the pattern of their current activities and the ways in which those activities are perceived by the House itself, are linked in complex ways to a bewildering and changing array of contingent factors.

It has, for example, often been pointed out that select committees cut across the grain of the adversarial traditions of the House of Commons: proponents of committees see this as a strength, equipping the House to undertake in-depth, specialist scrutiny which could not otherwise even be attempted; opponents see committees as irrelevant in a system where the confidence of ministers and the survival of government depends only upon what happens on the floor of the House. It is apparent, however, that the direction and texture of the 'grain' has itself undergone significant change. The chemistry of the House of Commons has not stayed constant; select committees in the 1980s do not see themselves, and are not seen by others, in the same way as their predecessors in the 1960s and 1970s. And the chemical reaction is still proceeding.

Another area of change is Whitehall. A significant consequence of the expanding investigative work of select committees has been in short-circuiting the direct accountability of ministers by calling extensively upon civil servants to give evidence. One can, indeed, explain the development of committees as being a very belated acknowledgement of the fact that ministers are far too narrow a channel through which the necessary two-way interaction between the legislature and a highly complex and diversified government machine can flow. This is an area of the highest importance; but as we shall see, the exciting prospect of civil servants being held directly accountable through the medium of select committees is partly nullified by the constitutional constraints upon what they are allowed to say.

Civil Servants have indeed, as was observed in Chapter 1, had to learn to live with select committees. But this adaptation has not occurred in isolation from other changes in the pattern of life in Whitehall. The eternal triangle of interrelationships between Parliament, ministers, and civil servants may have altered little in terms of constitutional principle, but it has certainly undergone a substantial reappraisal—markedly so in the years following the advent of the Thatcher Government. And this, too, forms a necessary backcloth to any verdict upon the new select committees, and to any prognosis about the future.

COMMITTEES IN A CHANGING PARLIAMENT

The Chairman of the Energy Committee, Ian Lloyd, in his submission to the Liaison Committee,[1] described as 'ludicrous and quite unrealistic' a ruling by the Inland Revenue that MPs' travel expenses in central London in connection with committee work are not incurred 'wholly, necessarily and exclusively' in discharge of their duties:

the cost of visiting ministries on constituency welfare matters *is* allowable. This apparent fiscal anomaly—small in itself—reminds us of the era, not long past (and a product of the growth of executive government in the second half of the nineteenth century),[2] when select committees were generally seen as marginal if not alien to parliamentary life. Back-benchers were, for better or for worse, and so far as party discipline would allow, individualists and generalists in the Burkean tradition.

The departmentally-related select committees are now an integral and (so far as most back-benchers are concerned) a cherished feature of the parliamentary scene. The attitudes of MPs towards committees have changed, at least to the extent that the burden of proof now rests upon the antagonists. This has been evident in the changing balance of argument in successive procedural debates since the 1960s. After 1979, as Geoffrey Lock observes in Chapter 18, 'the committees had arrived'. And they established themselves in, as well as helping to establish, a parliamentary environment the texture of which has become more amenable to committee activity.

There are various explanations for this environmental change, the most obvious being that the evolution of committees has generated its own momentum and its own climate of rising expectations among MPs. It is one thing for ministers to resist a procedural innovation as a dangerous leap in the dark, very much another to repeal something that is already there and has demonstrated its worth (or at least its harmlessness). Episodes of commmittee reform have been associated with successive influxes of new MPs bringing freshly critical perspectives to bear upon cherished traditions. Thus the Crossman reforms were encouraged by an active Labour Reform Group;[3] and the 1979 reforms have been linked to an influx of new Members, of all parties, with 'more "professional" attitudes towards their parliamentary duties'.[4] There is evidence that, since the early 1970s, MPs have become more full-time, and make greater use of secretaries and research assistants.[5]

Underlying the reforms has been a growing recognition of the need for a sensible division of labour in the House of Commons; of the need to counter the specialist and sectoral skills of administrators and to extend the range of parliamentary scrutiny to cover a vast network of government and quasi-government. New policy making and planning machinery in Whitehall itself (see below) has also helped to underline the antiquated nature of many traditional parliamentary procedures. MPs cannot have been unaware of the tendency for decision-making to move away from the Whitehall–Westminster arena, where they can at least hope to exert intermittent influence, into specialized, sectoral

policy communities   it. Although parliamentarians might stop sho   s tendency as a movement
towards 'post-parli   there is undoubtedly a
good deal of unea   the tendency to by-pass
Parliament. The re   king processes in the European Communities   s (though House of Lords'
committees have done more than the Commons' committees to
provide an antidote to the isolation of Parliament from the European
arena).

The party-political undercurrents of the House of Commons have
also been changing in ways that bear upon our assessment of the new
committees. One obvious aspect of this has been the partial disinte-
gration of the Labour Party after the 1979 general election, and the
emergence of a new Liberal–SDP Alliance. The committees began
their life against a background of political turbulence which still continues and whose medium and long term effects may prove momen-
tous for the parliamentary system. So far as the immediate effect on
the committees is concerned, there was from the outset a problem of
how the minority parties were to be accommodated and this, as we
shall see, became more acute after the 1983 general election. Of the
seven Labour chairmen originally elected by the new committees, two
defected to the SDP: Mr Bruce Douglas-Mann (Environment) resigned his parliamentary seat, but Mr Tom Bradley remained as
chairman of the Transport Committee until the dissolution.

The recent incidence of intra-party dissent in the House of Com-
mons has also been significant. In the late 1970s, when the Procedure
Committee was working out its package of reforms, the minority
Labour Government was many times defeated on the floor of the
House, often through the defection of its own back-benchers;[7] the
Callaghan Government eventually fell on a vote of no confidence.
Although we must not exaggerate the significance of all this—party
loyalty and predictable government majorities are still the norm—it
is certainly necessary when comparing the new committees with their
predecessors to acknowledge the probability of an overall increase in
the independent-mindedness and the self-confidence of back-benchers
(see chapter 20). And select committees badly need members who
display such attributes if they are to flourish. The effectiveness of
committees depends much more on the positive attitudes of their
members than on the proliferation of artificial aids like travel facilities
and specialist advisers. Evidence of such positiveness—keenness to
serve, a low proportion of 'passengers' among members of most committees, willingness of Conservative back-benchers to ask ministers
tough questions, resentment at the more obvious signs of attempted

interference by the whips—is one of the most encouraging findings of the present study.

Once again we must not exaggerate either the interconnection between intra-party dissent on the floor and cross-party consensus on committees, or the extent to which the new committees exhibited independence from party pressures. The whips were never far away, though the Committee of Selection (see below) did act as a buffer and, as Philip Giddings points out (Chapter 20), 'if committees had no influence, the whips would not bother with them'. Predictably, chairmanship of a committee is still not regarded as any real substitute for front-bench office (though Mr Edward du Cann and Mr Christopher Price may be qualified exceptions to this general rule), and most committees lost good members through promotion to the front benches. And although a slight blurring of the hard edges of adversary politics on the floor of the House may provide a climate that is more receptive to the work of select committees, the interconnection between committee activity and proceedings on the floor has been disappointingly patchy.

COMMITTEES AND GOVERNMENT EFFICIENCY

Yet another array of circumstantial factors to be borne in mind in our appraisal of the committees derives from the complicated relationship between parliamentary reform and the continuing quest for improved efficiency, effectiveness, and rationality in the machinery of government itself. Parliament tries (with variable alacrity and enthusiasm) to keep abreast of the latest fads and fancies of Whitehall reform, and select committees are an important means of doing this. And, as noted in chapter 19, the new committees explicitly reflect, for better and for worse, the departmental structure of the governmental machine.

The recent evolution of select committees has occurred against the backcloth of fluctuating preoccupations with ways of improving both the institutional structure of government and the techniques and procedures deployed therein. The Crossman reforms were formulated in the context of a general sense of unease (manifested by a minor rash of commisions and committees of inquiry) about the workings of established institutions such as the Civil Service and local government. The advent of the Expenditure Committee was partly a response to the development in the 1960s of the PESC machinery for medium-term expenditure planning. Its activities must be interpreted in that light, as well as in relation to such matters as Mr Heath's white paper on *The Reorganisation of Central Government*[8] (heralding such innovations as Programme Analysis and Review and the Central Policy Review Staff,

as well as important experiments with 'giant' departments), the introduction of cash limited expenditure in the mid-1970s (an innovation
preceded by the Expenditure Committtee's discrediting of PESC),[9]
and by the continuing debate about the merits or otherwise of more
'open government'.[10]

What of the operational context of the new committees? Mrs
Thatcher's first term of office was characterized by a preoccupation—
unprecedented in degree if not entirely novel in kind—with effectiveness, efficiency, and economy in government. It saw the establishment
of the 'Rayner' efficiency unit, a programme of drastic cuts in Civil
Service manpower, 'privatization' of public services, a concerted
(though not in the result very far-reaching) attack upon quangos, and
the imposition of tighter financial controls upon local authorities. A
new generation of acronyms was born—notably MINIS (Management Information System for Ministers) and FMI (Financial Management Initiative), in both of which developments the new Treasury
and Civil Service Committee played a part.[11] The Committee also
involved itself in the debate which culminated in the abolition of the
Civil Service Department (its qualified support for retaining the CSD
was initially accepted by the Government, but the decision was reversed a few months later).[12] And the work of *all* the new committees,
as reflectors of a changing Whitehall environment, was necessarily
affected—directly and indirectly—by this new zeal for financial re-
trenchment and administrative efficiency.

The Government (especially, it has been said, the Prime Minister
herself) had mixed feelings about the new committees. This is nothing
new. Select committees that fail to make themselves something of a
nuisance to ministers and civil servants—where exactly they should
draw the line is, of course, open to legitimate dispute—are not doing
their job. But it has become increasingly apparent since the Crossman
era that a simplistic conception of committees merely as thorns in the
flesh of government is grossly misleading. As the chapters in Part II
of this book make clear, it is very much a matter of swings and
roundabouts. Departments often welcome, even encourage, committee
investigations; most ministers have come to value opportunities for
committee apppearances as forums for extended policy justification
and explanation. In so far as the expansion of select committees has
been a belated response to the decline of ministers' capacities to control large and complex portfolios (and hence a decline in their ability
to account convincingly to Parliament through traditional procedural
devices such as question time), then such committees are natural allies
of government—even though the confrontational habits of parliamentary life may require that this truth be camouflaged by both sides.

Select committees must adapt to their environment. The new committees, as well as enjoying the advantage of soil that had already been tilled by their predecessors, faced an environment—both in Parliament and in Whitehall—that was broadly supportive. Their consensus-seeking style shifts the emphasis towards means rather than ends. They are natural and comfortable adjuncts to the age of MINIS and Rayner, though they themselves may not take this statement as a compliment given that administrative 'limp lettuce' is the normal Rayner diet.

THE NEW COMMITTEES AND THE CIVIL SERVICE ACCOUNTABILITY[13]

It is a logical extension to this line of argument to hold that select committees may provide a means whereby civil servants can be held directly accountable to Parliament. And it is here that the new committees, building upon the activities of their predecessors, might rest their strongest claims to having effected a significant constitutional change. Can such claims be justified?

Civil servants have always given a high proportion of the evidence, both written and oral, taken by select committees. Most of that evidence then appears, some time later, in printed form. But since the advent of the Crossman committees, most hearings (including, since 1978, those of the Public Accounts Committee, before which permanent secretaries regularly appear in their capacities as departmental accounting officers) are in public, and the utterances of civil servants, like those of other witnesses, can be seized upon by the media. Civil servants, traditionally anonymous and politically detached figures (though these attributes have come in for some critical reappraisal in the era of Mrs Thatcher), can find themselves asked to perform in a political arena, before a critical audience of back-benchers and journalists quick to seize upon the slightest evidence of departmental ambivalence or of division between a minister and his advisers.

However, things seldom happen this way in practice, for reasons that are made clear in the Memorandum of Guidance for officials appearing before committees, revised in 1980.[14] This, paradoxically, is a most revealing document: its real purpose, it has been suggested, is not, as it claims, to preserve ministerial responsibility but to protect civil servants.[15] It begins by exhorting civil servants to 'be as helpful as possible to committees' and by suggesting that information should be withheld only in the interests of 'good government' or of national security. But it then goes on to set out a dispiriting list of 'limitations on the provision of information', beginning with the injunction that 'committees' requests for information should not be met regardless of cost or of diversion of effort from other important matters'.

Collective responsibility must be safeguarded, which means that: 'the advice given to ministers should not be disclosed, nor should information about interdepartmental exchanges on policy issues, about the level at which decisions were taken or the manner in which a Minister has consulted his colleagues. Information should not be given about Cabinet Committees or their discussions.' Thus the notorious 'departmentalism' of Whitehall is carried over into the departmentally-related committees by those giving official evidence.

So far as possible, official witnesses should 'confine their evidence to questions of fact relating to existing Government policies and actions'. They should avoid being drawn into discussion of alternative policy. If pressed by the committee to go further 'they should suggest that the questioning be addressed, or referred, to Ministers'.

The Liaison Committtee describes the Memorandum as 'a fair statement of a not very satisfactory situation',[16] pointing out that the 1978 Procedure Committee Report found an earlier version of the document 'broadly unobjectionable'.[17] The fact that it did so, and that the Liaison Committee seems willing to shrug its shoulders about the restrictions, underlines the minimalism of the 1979 reforms. The Memorandum is indeed a fair and explicit statement of constitutional realities which constrain the ultimate power of select committees and which the 1979 reforms left untouched. Although seldom explicitly invoked, it lurked continuously and ominously in the background of committee activity. Mr Edward du Cann, chairman of the Treasury and Civil Service Committee, went so far in debate to describe it as 'a poor and miserable document' and, to say that 'its whole flavour is wrong'.[18]

On the other hand, the 'open government' implications of extended committee activity cannot lightly be dismissed. A great deal more information from the private world of Whitehall is entering the public domain. Senior civil servants are becoming public figures, not in the sense of being household names to the readers of the tabloid press but certainly being widely read and quoted by those with specialist interests in particular areas: and their performances are open to critical inspection, not just by outside observers but also by their own colleagues. Even given the constraints laid down in the Memorandum, it is significant and useful to have officials' views and interpretations set out in cold print for purposes both of current policy debate and future reference. This small dent in the minister's personal monopoly of departmental answerability is probably the most significant constitutional by-product of committee development over the last two decades, and the new committees have considerably deepened the dent.

Many committee inquiries were cut off in mid-stream by the dissolution of Parliament in May 1983, though committees had taken some account of this possibility and adjusted their plans accordingly. No one seems seriously to have doubted that the committees would be set up again after the election. The ensuing delay seems not to be attributable to government procrastination (though some ministers were rumoured to be not entirely displeased by the turn of events) but to the Labour Party's desire to fill Shadow Cabinet posts first and then to wrangling over membership.

We have noted elsewhere that the 1979 reforms incorporated the innovation that members of select committees, like those of standing committtees, should be nominated by the Committee of Selection rather than by the party whips. The nomination of the original committees in 1979 had proceeded fairly smoothly, though a measure of controversy over alleged interference by Labour whips had led the chairman of the Committee of Selection to explain and defend the Committee's role to the House.[19] We have also noted the continuing presence of whips in the background of the selection processes, perhaps even an occasional hint of the 'nobbling' of a committee's membership (for example, the Treasury and Civil Service Committee, in the later stages of the 1979–83 Parliament), but have observed that this is a back-handed compliment to the efficacy of committees as perceived by party managers.

After the election there was a hiatus in the process of re-establishing the committees because of the need to await the outcome of the Labour Party's elections to Shadow Cabinet posts. It was not until mid-November that the Committee of Selection agreed upon the nomination of ninety-one Conservatives, forty-eight Labour MPs, and nine representatives of the various minor parties. This imbalance reflected the Conservatives' overall majority in the House of 144; the Labour Party had also, in due course, to relinquish one of its former chairmanships—that of the Education, Science and Arts Commmittee.

In the end, however, the formula agreed by the Committee of Selection was forestalled by the resistance of the Ulster Unionists, who sought more than the single seat originally allocated to them. After much wrangling, Mr John Cartwright, an SDP Member, was voted off the Defence Committee to make way for a Unionist; all the committees (except Scottish Affairs, which remained at thirteen) were given a standard membership of eleven to accommodate, as far as possible, the disparate interests in the House.[20] The Industry and Trade Committee became the Trade and Industry Committee, in recognition of the merging under this title of two separate (though formerly married) government departments. The committees resumed work early in 1984. The limitations upon the coercive power of the whips were underlined by the election as chairman of the Liaison Committee of Mr Terence Higgins (new chairman of the Treasury and Civil Service Committee) in preference to the Government's choice, Sir Humphrey Atkins (new chairman of the Defence Committee).

Several former chairmen—notably Mr Edward du Cann (Treasury and Civil Service—resigned chairmanship), Sir John Eden (Home Affairs—did not stand in the general election), and Mr Christopher Price (Education and Science—lost his seat)—had to be replaced. There was a high turnover of members, a factor which is conducive to freshness but not to continuity. Among the newly appointed committee members, on the Foreign Affairs Committee, was Mr Norman St John-Stevas.

THE FINAL VERDICT

British government is founded upon executive initiative tempered by answerability to Parliament. The 'balance of power' (an oft-used, but less than meaningful phrase) is not susceptible to adjustment merely by the setting up of more and better select committees. (We should, in any case, be wary of taking for granted the validity of an assertion that such adjustment, in Parliament's favour, is self-evidently desirable.) Thus, as Nevil Johnson has observed, 'the expanded activity of committees has so far brought little genuine change in the manner in which Parliament operates, nor in the relationship between it and the Executive'.[21]

But the impossibility of effecting constitutional revolution by procedural reform does not mean that the 1979 reforms can be dismissed as mere cosmetic tinkering. It is clear that the new committees, significantly more extensive, better equipped, and more coherently organized than their predecessors, are an important evolutionary step in the modernization of a House of Commons that has been slow to adapt to the realities of a complex and highly diversified polity. Committees cannot fill the yawning gaps in traditional modes of parliamentary accountability, but they go some way towards doing so. The links between the work of committees and what happens on the floor of the House still leave much room for improvement; but most observers agree that the new committees have at least intermittently enriched the quality of parliamentary debate and sharpened the edge of back-bench and Opposition interrogations of ministers. The linkage between select committees and the legislative process via the use of special standing committees is something well worth retaining and expanding.

The new committees offer something to everyone. Back-benchers (148 of them in the 1979–83 Parliament, 156 since the committees were re-established—significantly more when account is taken of turn-over) have a much welcomed chance to specialize; ministers have a chance to explain themselves to a parliamentary audience which is concerned more with discovery than with scoring debating points; pressure groups are given extended opportunities to lay out their case in public and are themselves brought into public scrutiny; civil servants, though they may sometimes grumble about the added burdens, probably recognize the benefits of arguing publicly a departmental case and having their views put on record.

Probably the greatest beneficiaries are those seeking knowledge and information. The minutes of evidence generated by select committee activity are goldmines in this respect and many matters that would otherwise not be discussed in Parliament at all are comprehensively examined and opened to public attention. The 1970 Green Paper (as quoted in chapter 1) observed that 'the House has yet to learn how to make the most of its Committees',[22] and it is apparent that this is still true. Nevertheless, there are encouraging signs that a learning process is occurring. Meanwhile the new committees have not only arrived, they are in our view here to stay—certainly for the foreseeable future.

NOTES

1. 1982–83, HC 92, p. 66.
2. S. A. Walkland, *The Legislative Process in Great Britain*, Allen and Unwin, 1968, pp. 70–1; Bernard Crick, *The Reform of Parliament*, 2nd edition, Weidenfeld and Nicolson, 1968, pp. 99–100.
3. Anthony Barker, 'Parliament and Patience', *Political Quarterly*, 38, 1967, p. 75.
4. David Judge, *Backbench Specialisation in the House of Commons*, Heinemann, 1981, p. 197.
5. Michael Rush (ed.), *The House of Commons: Services and Facilities, 1972–1982*, Policy Studies Institute (PSI), No. 614, 1983, pp. 4 and 119.
6. J. J. Richardson and A. G. Jordan, *Governing Under Pressure: The Policy Process in a Post-Parliamentary Democracy*, Martin Robertson, 1979, *passim*; also, 'The British Policy Style or the Logic of Negotiation?' in J. J. Richardson (ed.), *Policy Styles in Western Europe*, Allen and Unwin, 1982.
7. Philip Norton, *Dissension in the House of Commons 1974–79*, Oxford University Press, 1980.
8. Cmnd. 4506, 1970.
9. 1975–76, HC 69; and see Maurice Wright, 'Public Expenditure in Britain: the Crisis of Control', *Public Administration*, 55, 1977, pp. 143–69.

10. See Rosamund Thomas, 'The Secrecy and Freedom of Information Debates in Britain', *Government and Opposition*, 17, 1982, pp. 293–311.
11. 1981–82, HC 236-I, paras. 64–5; Government Observations, Cmnd. 8616, 1982, paras. 12–16.
12. 1980–81, HC 54; Government Observations, Cmnd. 8170, 1981.
13. Some of the material in this section is adapted from parts of a paper by Gavin Drewry, 'The New Select Committees—a Constitutional Non-Event?', in Dilys M. Hill (ed.), *Parliamentary Select Committees in Action: A Symposium*, Strathclyde Papers on Government and Politics, No. 24, 1984, pp. 30–55.
14. CSD Gen. 80/38, Civil Service Department, 1980. See comment by David Judge, 'Ministerial Responsibility', *The House Magazine*, 26 November 1982; also Geoffrey Marshall, *Constitutional Conventions*, Clarendon Press, 1984, pp. 73–7.
15. Lord Beloff, letter to *The Times*, 24 May 1980.
16. 1982–83, HC 92, para. 46.
17. 1977–78, HC 588-I, para. 7.12.
18. HC Debs., 16 January 1981, col. 1666.
19. HC Debs., 26 November 1979, cols. 1029 *et seq*. See also Anne Davies, *Reformed Select Committees: The First Year*, Outer Circle Policy Unit, 1980, pp. 15–19. For a more recent comment, see letter to *The Times*, 18 February 1984, by Sir Philip Holland and Sir Kenneth Lewis, refuting allegations about the influence of government whips upon selection.
20. HC Debs., 14 December 1983, cols. 1128–47.
21. Nevil Johnson, 'Select Committees as Tools of Parliamentary Reform: Some Further Reflections', in S. A. Walkland and Michael Ryle (eds.), *The Commons Today*, Fontana, 1981, p. 228.
22. *Select Committees of the House of Commons*, Cmnd. 4507, 1970, para. 13.

Appendix: Standing Orders of the House of Commons 1979–83

as numbered and printed in revised edition, March 1983 (HC 307, 1982–83)

99. Select committees related to government departments.—(1) Select committees shall be appointed to examine the expenditure, administration and policy of the principal government departments set out in paragraph (2) of this order and associated public bodies, and similar matters within the responsibilities of the Secretary of State for Northern Ireland.

(2) The committees appointed under paragraph (1) of this order, the principal departments of government with which they are concerned, the maximum numbers of each committee and the quorum in each case shall be as follows:

Name of committee	Principal government departments concerned	Maximum numbers of Members	Quorum
1. Agriculture	Ministry of Agriculture, Fisheries and Food	9	3
2. Defence	Ministry of Defence	11	3
3. Education, Science and Arts	Department of Education and Science	9	3
4. Employment	Department of Employment	9	3
5. Energy	Department of Energy	11	3
6. Environment	Department of the Environment	11	3
7. Foreign Affairs	Foreign and Commonwealth Office	11	3
8. Home Affairs	Home Office	11	3
9. Industry and Trade	Department of Industry, Department of Trade	11	3
10. Scottish Affairs	Scottish Office	13	5
11. Social Services	Department of Health and Social Security	9	3
12. Transport	Department of Transport	11	3
13. Treasury and Civil Service	Treasury, Management and Personnel Office, Board of Inland Revenue, Board of Customs and Excise	11	3
14. Welsh Affairs	Welsh Office	11	3

(3) The Foreign Affairs Committee, the Home Affairs Committee and the Treasury and Civil Service Committee shall each have the power to appoint one sub-committee.

(4) There may be a sub-committee, drawn from the membership of two or more of the Energy, Environment, Industry and Trade, Scottish Affairs, Transport, and

Treasury and Civil Service Committees, set up from time to time to consider any matter affecting two or more nationalised industries.

(5) Select committees appointed under this order shall have power—

(a) to send for persons, papers and records, to sit notwithstanding any adjournment of the House, to adjourn from place to place, and to report from time to time;

(b) to appoint specialist advisers either to supply information which is not readily available or to elucidate matters of complexity within the committee's order of reference; and

(c) to report from time to time the minutes of evidence taken before sub-committees;

and the sub-committees appointed under this order shall have power to send for persons, papers and records, to sit notwithstanding any adjournment of the House, and to adjourn from place to place, and shall have a quorum of three.

(6) Unless the House otherwise orders, all Members nominated to a committee appointed under this order shall continue to be members of that committee for the remainder of the Parliament.

101. Liaison Committee.—(1) A Select committee shall be appointed, to be called the Liaison Committee—

(a) to consider general matters relating to the work of select committees, and

(b) to give such advice relating to the work of select committees as may be sought by the House of Commons Commission.

(2) The committee shall report its recommendations as to the allocation of time for consideration by the House of the estimates on any day allotted for that purpose; and upon a motion being made that the House do agree with any such report the question shall be put forthwith and, if that question is agreed to, the recommendations shall have effect as if they were orders of the House.

Proceedings in pursuance of this paragraph, though opposed, may be decided after the expiration of the time for opposed business.

(3) The committee shall have power to send for persons, papers and records, to sit notwithstanding any adjournment of the House, and to report from time to time.

(4) Unless the House otherwise orders, each Member nominated to the committee shall continue to be a member of it for the remainder of the Parliament.

(5) The quorum of the committee shall be six.

Bibliography of Selected References

The following list combines references to the main sources cited in the text with a select bibliography of the subject.
The list is divided into four sections: (i) General works on parliament and government; (ii) parliamentary papers and government publications; (iii) select committees prior to 1979; and (iv) recent developments of committees.

(i) GENERAL WORKS ON PARLIAMENT AND GOVERNMENT

Barker, Anthony *and* Rush, Michael, *The Member of Parliament and his Information*, London: Allen & Unwin, 1970. pp. 443.

Bradshaw, Kenneth *and* Pring, David, *Parliament and Congress*. 2nd edn., London: Quartet Books, 1982. pp. 512.

Chubb, Basil, *The Control of Public Expenditure: Financial Committees of the House of Commons*, London: Oxford University Press, 1952. pp. 291.

Crick, Bernard, *The Reform of Parliament*, 2nd edn., London: Weidenfeld & Nicolson, 1968. pp. 320.

Erskine, May, *Parliamentary Practice*, 20th edn., edited by *Sir* Charles Gordon, London: Butterworth, 1983.

Hansard Society, *Parliamentary Reform: a Survey of Recent Proposals for the Commons*, 2nd rev. edn., London: Cassell, for the Hansard Society, 1967. pp. x, 208.

Jennings, *Sir* W. Ivor, *Parliament*, 2nd edn., Cambridge: Cambridge University Press, 1957. pp. 574.

Johnson, Nevil, *In Search of the Constitution: Reflections on State and Society in Britain*, Oxford: Pergamon Press, 1977. pp. 239.

Judge, David, *Backbench Specialization in the House of Commons*, London: Heinemann Educational, 1981. pp. viii, 243.

—— *The Politics of Parliamentary Reform*, London: Heinemann Educational, 1983. pp. 212.

Laski, Harold J., *Parliamentary Government in England: a Commentary*, London: Allen & Unwin, 1938 (4th imp. 1950). pp. 454.

Lees, John D. *and* Shaw, Malcolm (*editors*), *Committees in Legislatures: a Comparative Analysis*, Oxford: Martin Robertson, 1980. pp. 449. Chapter 7, pp. 242–87. Walkland, S. A., 'Committees in the British House of Commons'.

Marshall, Geoffrey, *Constitutional Conventions: the Rules and Forms of Political Accountability*, Oxford: Clarendon Press, 1984. pp. 256.

Morrison, Herbert, *Government and Parliament*, 3rd edn., Oxford: Oxford University Press, 1964. pp. 384.

Norton, Philip, *The Commons in Perspective*, Oxford: Martin Robertson, 1981. pp. 265.

—— *Dissension in the House of Commons, 1974–79*, Oxford: Oxford University Press, 1980. pp. 560.

Pollitt, Christopher, *Manipulating the Machine: Changing the Pattern of Ministerial Departments, 1960–83*, London: Allen & Unwin, 1984. pp. x, 243.

Radice, Lisanne, *Reforming the House of Commons*, London: Fabian Society, 1977. pp. 19. (Fabian Tract 448.)

Richards, Peter G., *The Backbenchers*, London: Faber and Faber, 1972. pp. 248.

—— *Parliament and Foreign Affairs*, London: Allen & Unwin, 1967. pp. 191.

Richardson, Jeremy J. (*editor*), *Policy Styles in Western Europe*, London: Allen & Unwin, 1982. pp. x, 213.

Rush, Michael *and* Shaw, Malcolm (*editors*), *The House of Commons: Services and Facilities*, London: Allen & Unwin, 1974. pp. 302. (PEP, Study of Parliament Group.)

Rush, Michael (*editor*), *The House of Commons: Services and Facilities, 1972–82*. London: Policy Studies Institute, 1983. pp. iv, 156.

Taylor, Eric, *The House of Commons at Work*, 9th edn., London: Macmillan, 1979. pp. 190.

Walkland, S. A., *The Legislative Process in Great Britain*, London: Allen & Unwin, 1968. pp. 109.

Walkland, S. A. *and* Ryle, Michael (*editors*), *The Commons in the '70s*, London: Fontana, 1977. pp. 285. Chapter 9, pp. 175–201. Johnson, Nevil 'Select Committees as tools of parliamentary reform: some further reflections'.

—— *The Commons Today*, London: Fontana, 1981. pp. 220.

Walkland, S. A. (*editor*), *The House of Commons in the Twentieth Century: Essays by Members of the Study of Parliament Group*, Oxford: Clarendon Press, 1979. pp. 649. Chapter 8, pp. 426–75, Johnson, Nevil, 'Select Committees and administration'.

Wass, Sir Douglas, *Government and the Governed*, (BBC Reith Lectures 1983), London: Routledge & Kegan Paul, 1984. pp. viii, 120.

Wheare, K. C., *Government by Committee: an Essay on the British Constitution*, Oxford: Clarendon Press, 1955. pp. 264.

(ii) PARLIAMENTARY PAPERS AND GOVERNMENT PUBLICATIONS

Cabinet Office (Machinery of Government Division), *Departmental Select Committees: a List of Reports (and any replies) up to June 1983*, London: Cabinet Office (Machinery of Government Division), 1984. pp. 54.

Civil Service Department, *Select Committees: Memorandum of Guidance for Officials*, London: Civil Service Department, 1980. pp. 24.

Cmnd. 4507, *Select Committees of the House of Commons*, London: HMSO, 1970. pp. 11.

Cmnd. 7982, *The Government's Reply to the First Special Report from the Education, Science and Arts Committee, Session 1979–80, HC 606: the Provision of Information by Government Departments to Select Committee*, London: HMSO, 1980. pp. 2.

Education, Science and Arts Committee (Session 1979–80), *1st Special Report. The Provision of Information by Government Departments to Select Committees*, HC 606, London: HMSO, 1980. pp. 2.

Expenditure Committee (Session 1978–79), *3rd Report. The Work of the Expenditure Committee throughout the first Four Sessions of the Present Parliament*, HC 163, London: HMSO, 1979. pp. xvi, 176.

House of Commons (Public Information Office), *The New Departmental Select Committee Structure*, London: House of Commons (Public Information Office), 1980. pp. 10. (Factsheet No. 6).

Liaison Committee (Session 1982-83), *1st Report. The Select Committee System*, HC 92, London: HMSO, 1982. pp. 133.

Select Committee on the House of Commons (Services) (Session 1976-77), *3rd Report. The Recording of Select Committees*, HC 205, London: HMSO, 1977. pp. 31.

Select Committee on Procedure (Session 1968-69), *1st Report. Scrutiny of Public Expenditure and Administration*, HC 410, London: HMSO, 1969. pp. 280.

Select Committee on Procedure (Session 1977-78), *1st Report. Vol. I. Report and Minutes of Proceedings*, HC 588-i, London: HMSO, 1978. pp. 88.

—— *1st Report. Vol. II. Minutes of Evidence*, HC 588-ii. London: HMSO, 1978. pp. 269.

—— *1st Report. Vol. III. Appendices to the Minutes of Evidence*, London: HMSO, 1978. pp. 161.

Select Committee on Procedure (Supply) (Session 1980-81), *1st Report. Vol. I. Report and Minutes of Proceedings*, HC 118-i, London: HMSO, 1981. pp. 60.

(iii) SELECT COMMITTEES PRIOR TO 1979

Byrne, Paul, 'The Expenditure Committee: a Preliminary Assessment', in *Parliamentary Affairs*, 1974, vol. xxvii, no. 3 (Summer), pp. 273-87.

Clarke, Sir Richard, 'Parliament and the Public Expenditure', in *Political Quarterly*, 1973, vol. xliv, no. 2 (April-June), pp. 137-53.

Coombes, David, *The Member of Parliament and the Administration: the Case of the Select Committee on Nationalised Industries*, London: Allen & Unwin, 1966. pp. 221.

Drewry, Gavin, 'Reform of the Legislative Process: Some Neglected Questions', in *Parliamentary Affairs*, 1972, vol. xxv, no. 3 (Summer), pp. 286-302.

Griffith, J. A. G., *Parliamentary Scrutiny of Government Bills*, London: Allen & Unwin, for Political and Economic Planning and the Study of Parliament Group, 1974. pp. 285.

Hanson, A. H. *and* Wiseman, H. V., 'The Use of Committees by the House of Commons', in *Public Law*, 1959 (Autumn), pp. 277-92.

Hyder, Masood, 'Parliament and Defence Affairs: the Defence Sub-committee of the Expenditure Committee', in *Public Administration*, 1977, vol. lv, (Spring), pp. 59-78.

Johnson, Nevil, *Parliament and Administration: the Estimates Committee 1945-65*, London: Allen & Unwin, 1966. pp. 187.

Lee, J. Michael, 'Select Committees and the Constitution', in *Political Quarterly*, 1970, vol. xli, no. 2 (April-June), pp. 182-94.

Mackintosh, John P., 'Failure of Reform: MPs Special Committees', in *New Society*, 28 November 1968, pp. 791-2.

Morris, Alfred (*editor*), *The Growth of Parliamentary Scrutiny by Committee*, Oxford: Pergamon Press, 1970. pp. 141.

Myers, P., 'The Select Committee on Scottish Affairs', in *Parliamentary Affairs*, 1974, vol. xxvii, no. 4 (Autumn), pp. 359-71.

Norton, Philip, *The House of Commons in the 1970s: Three Views on Reform*, Hull: University of Hull Politics Department, 1978. pp. 14. (Hull Papers in Politics, no. 3.)

Partington, Martin, 'Parliamentary Committees: Recent Developments', in *Parliamentary Affairs*, 1970, vol. xxiii, no. 4 (Autumn), pp. 366-79.

Popham, G. T. *and* Greengrass, D., 'The Role and Functions of the Select Committee on Agriculture', in *Public Administration*, 1970, vol. xlviii (Summer), pp. 137-51.

Robinson, Ann, *Parliament and Public Spending: the Expenditure Committee of the House of Commons, 1970-76*, London: Heinemann, 1978. pp. 184.

Ryle, Michael, 'Committees of the House of Commons', in *Political Quarterly*, 1956, vol. xxxvi, no. 3 (July-Sept), pp. 295-308.

Shell, Donald R., 'Specialist Select Committees', in *Parliamentary Affairs*, 1970, vol. xxiii, no. 4 (Autumn), pp. 380-404.

Silkin, Arthur, 'The Expenditure Committee: a new development?', in *Public Administration*, 1975, vol. liii (Spring), pp. 45-67.

Study of Parliament Group, 'Parliament and Legislation', in *Parliamentary Affairs*, 1969, vol. xxii, no. 3 (Summer), pp. 210-15.

—— *Specialist Committees in the British Parliament: the Experience of a Decade*, London: Political and Economic Planning, 1976. pp. 48.

Walkland, S. A., 'The Politics of Parliamentary Reform', in *Parliamentary Affairs*, 1976, vol. xxix, no. 2 (Spring), pp. 190-201.

—— 'Science and Parliament: the Role of the Select Committees of the House of Commons', in *Parliamentary Affairs*, 1965, vol. xviii, no. 3 (Summer), pp. 266-78.

(iv) RECENT DEVELOPMENT OF COMMITTEES

Atkinson, A. B., 'Taxation and Social Security Reform: Reflections on Advising a House of Commons Select Committee', in *Policy and Politics*, 1984, vol. xii, no. 2, pp. 107-18.

Davies, Anne, 'Reformed Select Committees: the First Year', London: Outer Circle Policy Unit, 1980. pp. 77.

Doig, Alan, 'Self-discipline and the House of Commons', in *Parliamentary Affairs*, 1979, vol. xxxii, no. 3 (Summer), pp. 248-67.

Downs, Stephen J., *Select Committees in the House of Commons: an Ineluctable Development?* Hull: University of Hull Politics Department, 1983. pp. 48. (Hull Papers in Politics, no. 32).

Drewry, Gavin, 'The Outsider and House of Commons Reform: Some Evidence from the Crossman Diaries', in *Parliamentary Affairs*, 1978, vol. xxxi, no. 4 (Autumn), pp. 424-35.

Drucker, H. M., *The Select Committee on Scottish Affairs: a Research Report*, Edinburgh: University of Edinburgh (n.d.) (unpublished paper available from the author or for loan from the RIPA Library).

Du Cann, Edward, 'Parliament, Select Committees and Democracy', in *Public Money*, 1981, vol. i, no. 1, pp. 25-8.

Englefield, Dermot J. T. (*editor*), *The Commons' Select Committees: Catalysts for Progress?*, Harlow: Longman, 1984. pp. xxvi, 288.

Flegman, Vilma, *Called to Account: The Public Accounts Committee of the House of Commons, 1965-66 and 1977-78*, Aldershot: Gower, 1980. pp. 318.

—— 'The Public Accounts Committee: a Successful Select Committee?', in *Parliamentary Affairs*, 1980, vol. xxxiii, no. 2 (Spring), pp. 166-72.

Gregory, Roy, 'The Select Committee on the Parliamentary Commissioner for Administration, 1967-1980', in *Public Law*, 1982 (Spring), pp. 49-88.

Hetherington, Alastair, 'Parliamentary Select Committees: the Pips are Beginning to Squeak in the Treasury', in the *Listener*, 1980, 14 August, pp. 198-9.

Hill, Dilys M. (*editor*), Parliamentary Select Committee in Action: a Symposium. Glasgow: University of Strathclyde *Department of Politics*, 1984. pp. 316. (Strathclyde Papers on Government and Politics, no. 24).

Hills, J., 'A Co-operative and Constructive Relationship? The Treasury Response to its Select Committee, 1979-82', in *Fiscal Studies*, 1983, vol. iv, no. 1 (March), pp. 1-13.

Himelfarb, Sheldon, 'Consensus in Committee: the Case of the Select Committee on

Race Relations and Immigration', in *Parliamentary Affairs*, 1980, vol. xxxiii, no. 1 (Winter), pp. 54–66.

Isaacson, Paul, 'Reforming Parliament: a Footnote to a Saga. A Review of a Report from the Select Committee on Procedure', in *Public Administration Bulletin*, 1979, no. 30 (August), pp. 61–8.

Jones, J. B. *and* Wilford, R. A., 'The Welsh Affairs Committee: its Evolving Role', in *Agenda*, 1982, no. 2 (Summer), pp. 4–15.

Kennon, Andrew, 'Recent Work of the General Sub-committee of the Expenditure Committee', in *Parliamentary Affairs*, 1980, vol. xxxiii, no. 2 (Spring), pp. 159–65.

Lankester, R. S., 'House of Commons Select Committees related to Government Departments', in *The Table*, 1980, xlviii, pp. 29 and 34.

Mackintosh, John P., *Specialist Committees in the House of Commons: have they failed?*, 2nd edn. with appendix by David Christie, Edinburgh: University of Edinburgh, 1980. pp. 100. (Waverley Occasional Paper, no. 11).

Norton, Philip, 'The Changing Face of the British House of Commons in the 1970s', in *Legislative Studies Quarterly*, 1980, vol. iii (August), pp. 333–57.

—— 'The House of Commons and the Constitution: the Challenges of the 1970s', in *Parliamentary Affairs*, 1981, vol. xxxiv, no. 3 (Summer), pp. 253–71.

—— 'Party Committees in the House of Commons', in *Parliamentary Affairs*, 1983, vol. xxxvi, no. 1 (Winter), pp. 7–27.

Palmer, Geoffrey, 'Reforming Parliamentary Select Committees: a Personal View', in *Public Sector*, 1983, vol. 5, nos. 3/4 (May), pp. 17–18.

Poole, K. P., 'The Powers of Select Committees of the House of Commons to send for Persons, Papers and Records', in *Parliamentary Affairs*, 1979, vol. xxxii, no. 3 (Summer), pp. 268–78.

Price, Christopher, 'Making a select committee work', in *Public Money*, 1984, vol. iii, no. 4, pp. 29–33.

Pring, David, 'The New Select Committee System at Westminster', in *The Parliamentarian*, 1983, vol. lxiv, no. 1, pp. 57–63.

Rush, Michael, 'Parliamentary Committees and Parliamentary Government: the British and Canadian Experience', in *Journal of Commonwealth and Comparative Politics*, 1982, vol. xx, no. 2, pp. 138–54.

Schwarz, John, 'Exploring a New Role in Policy Making: the British House of Commons in the 1970s', in *American Political Science Review*, 1980, vol. lxxiv, no. 1 (March), pp. 20–8.

Stancer, John, 'The Public Accounts Committee: a Review Article', in *Public Administration Bulletin*, 1981, no. 37 (December), pp. 55–66.

Starkie, David, 'Reassessing the Impact of Select Committees', in *Public Administration Bulletin*, 1983, no. 41 (April), pp. 2–13.

Taylor, Robert, 'The new Watch Dogs of Parliament', in *New Society*, 1981, 15 January, pp. 96–8.

Whitley Bulletin, 'House of Commons: Select Committees', in *The Whitley Bulletin*, 1979, vol. lxix, no. 9 (Sept.–Oct.), p. 144.

Index

Index of Members of Parliament

The designation of parties and titles is as at the dissolution of the 1979–83 Parliament